Programming Portlets

Second Edition

Programming Portlets

Second Edition

From JSR 168 to IBM® WebSphere® Portal Extensions

Ron Lynn, Joey Bernal, Peter Blinstrubas, Usman Memon,

Cayce Marston, Tim Hanis, Varadarajan Ramamoorthy, Stefan Hepper

IBM Press
MC Press Online, LP
Lewisville, Texas

IBM Press Program Manager: Tara B. Woodman, Ellice Uffer
Cover Design: IBM Corporation
Published by MC Press Online, LP
Publishing as IBM Press

Programming Portlets, 2nd edition
From JSR 168 to IBM® WebSphere® Portal Extensions
Ron Lynn, Joey Bernal, Peter Blinstrubas, Usman Memon, Cayce Marston, Tim Hanis, Varadarajan Ramamoorthy, and Stefan Hepper

IBM Press offers excellent discounts on this book when ordered in quantity for bulk purchases or special sales, which may include electronic versions and/or custom covers and content particular to your business, training goals, marketing focus, and branding interests. For more information, please contact:

MC Press
Corporate Offices:
125 N. Woodland Trail
Lewisville, TX 75077
817.961.0660

MC Press Online, LP
Sales and Customer Service
P.O. Box 4300
Big Sandy, TX 75755-4300
www.mcpressonline.com/ibmpress

ISBN: 1-931182-23-X
Printed in Canada, at WebCom, Toronto, Ontario.
First printing: March, 2007

Acknowledgements

I don't know who said it, but it rings true: "Families are like fudge…mostly sweet, but with a few nuts." All my love goes to my family—Jeannette, Rowan, Claire, and Sophia—for putting up with this nut. I'd like to say a heartfelt thanks to my co-authors, reviewers, editor, publisher, teammates, and colleagues. Your thoughts and insights are and have been a constant source of inspiration. Thank you all for sharing yourselves and your vast knowledge. I'm constantly awed and humbled by you.

—*Ron Lynn*

Thank you first to my family: my wife, Christiane, and my kids—Daniel, Christopher, Julia, and Oliver. Thanks to my manager Ken Polleck for being continually supportive of these efforts and to Alistair Rennie as our executive sponsor. Also many, many thanks to my co-authors, teammates, and colleagues within IBM, for helping me continually grow and learn with endless discussions of new ideas.

—*Joey Bernal*

I would like to thank Ron and Joey for the extraordinary leadership they provided while writing the book. This book would not have been possible without their hard work and dedication. I would like to thank Amber Roy-Chowdhury for his insights and generous help. Finally, I would like to thank my wife, Kate, for her encouragement and support and for helping me understand what truly is important.

—*Peter Blinstrubas*

I would like to thank my wife, Susan, and my family for their encouragement and support. I would also like to thank all the people at IBM who know how to share a smile and a laugh between frequent meetings, crammed schedules, and approaching deadlines. I would like to thank Stefan Hepper for his thorough review of my chapters and Marzi for being my constant companion.

—*Tim Hanis*

I want to thank my wife, Dr. Sayma Memon, and my father, Razak Memon, for their support and guidance while contributing to the book.

—*Usman Memon*

I would like to extend special thanks to my parents, Ben and Alvina Marston, for their support of my career and also to my manager, Adriana Robinson, for her excellent guidance.

—*Cayce Marston*

I would like to thank my wife, Ramya, for supporting me in writing this book and my kids, Ganesh and Keshav, for their forgiveness for not spending the time with them. I also would like to thank my Mom, Dad, and father-in-law for their encouragement.

—*Varadarajan Ramamoorthy*

I would like to thank my managers, Martin Scott Nicklous and Ralf Grohmann, for supporting me in writing parts of this book besides the challenges of my daily job. I would also like to thank Richard Jacob for input on the WSRP part of chapter 4. Most of all, I need to thank my family, who allowed me to spend all these hours on this book instead of with them. Thanks, Tina, Jonas, Thomas, and Sarah.

—*Stefan Hepper*

Contents

Foreword

In a very short time, portal technology has become a critical element in today's IT environments. According to a 2006 IDC market analysis report:

"The portal has become an established piece of the corporate information infrastructure, and over the past decade, the portal has elbowed its way into contention as the primary user interface of enterprise users."[1]

The demand for portals has grown quickly and is forecast to remain strong as their value and use continue to increase. In 2005, the revenue for worldwide enterprise portal software (EPS) was $855.7 million and is expected to reach $1.4 billion in 2010.[2]

I think the driving factors behind this trend have little to do with technology and everything to do with the needs of business. The concept of "portals" has enabled companies to address various internal and external business requirements and needs. These needs often revolve around empowering employees or partners with relevant content, creating direct relationships with customers or suppliers, and aggregating myriad applications into a workplace that is relevant and personalized for each individual. Multiply these needs by the compressed time available to deliver projects and the need to leverage existing investments in software, and the subsequent growth in the portal market is a natural outcome. This growth will accelerate with the increased adoption of service-oriented architectures, which will become visible to end users primarily through the use of portals.

The team of authors who collaborated to write this book represents some of the most experienced portal technologists in the world. I've seen them create solutions that have helped companies provide secure access to information and applications for tens of thousands of portal users working around the globe. Whether individually or teamed together, this group has been instrumental in creating, customizing, deploying, and maintaining portlets on a wide variety of WebSphere Portal projects for customers in all different types of industries. From their work developing the IBM Portal Catalog internally to putting their

[1, 2] *Market Analysis: Worldwide Enterprise Portal Software: 2006-2010 Forecast Update and 2005 Vendor Shares.* IDC, July 2006: #202688.

skills and expertise with Java and Bowstreet portlets to work for our customers, their solutions have put customized information at our fingertips. In doing so, their collective efforts have advanced our understanding of portals and portlet technology and changed the way many people work.

This book is a must-read reference for any professional seeking to understand and implement a portal project. The authors have struck an excellent balance between covering the core concepts and providing in-depth material on how to apply them. The decision to focus on new open standards (JSR 168 and JavaServer Faces) reinforces the importance of standards and their ability to simplify and streamline projects. The additional focus on services unique to WebSphere Portal will help you to unlock the value of the most robust portal product in the market.

On a personal note, I'd like to congratulate the authors. The decision to write a book like this is motivated by a desire to give back to the technical community and help others succeed. Work like this is done on top of the substantial duties in their "day jobs." It is a privilege to lead a team of such exceptional people.

Enjoy the book, and embrace the opportunities it can open up for you and your teams.

Alistair Rennie
Vice President, Software Services
Workplace, Portal and Collaboration
IBM Software

Introduction to Part I

JSR 168 PORTLET PROGRAMMING

Welcome to the second edition of *Programming Portlets*. This edition revises and adds a lot of new material to our original *Programming Portlets* book. Technology is changing at a breakneck pace, and portals are not immune from this trend. In fact, you could make the case that portals themselves are feeding many of the new advances in technology. As specifications change and new ways of delivering value for customers emerge, keeping pace with change is extremely difficult. This book is our attempt to help you keep up with some of these advancing technologies.

Much has changed since our last edition. Portal developers need to understand new APIs and specifications and bone up on some new approaches to building functionality. Regarding IBM WebSphere Portal, there's so much to say that it's difficult to know where to start. This product has evolved so quickly and matured so fully that volumes can be (and have been) written about the topic. In deciding the direction this book would take, the authors looked at where the gaps in public knowledge and WebSphere Portal documentation seemed to be. We also talked about the types of questions that we or, more commonly, people new to the product normally asked.

Most of this book's authors have worked with WebSphere Portal since its initial release and have watched it grow and mature, often feeling, firsthand, the pains of being an "expert" in the product. With this book, as with the previous edition, we decided to take a development focus, centering specifically around portlets and helping beginning portlet developers who may be working on their first portal project. Many of the questions from this audience have a common thread: How do I really build a portlet? What's the best way to approach my design? Where can I get more information or examples for this type of portlet? We've tried to focus the content in this book to stay within the portal container as much as possible to ensure we provide the right level of information to portlet developers. Unfortunately, as technology evolves, so does the level of complexity surrounding what developers need to understand to build robust portal applications. As we studied and wrote sample portlets for the various chapters, we did as much learning as we did teaching, and we're sure there's a lot of information buried within the pages of this book that even advanced portlet programmers will appreciate. (The code for the sample portlets and sample database are available for download at *www.bernal.net* or *www.portalpatterns.org.*)

Before you start writing, however, there are some initial ideas to understand. We can teach you the mechanics of writing portlets, but it's harder to convey the idea of a good design or show you the things you shouldn't do. We mention this point because we've seen many developers make unknowing decisions, mainly because they didn't understand the portal framework. For this reason, we kick off our exploration of portlets in Chapter 1 with an overview of the fundamental concepts, defining portals and portlets and introducing the framework within which you'll create your portlet applications. With a full understanding of the entire portal framework, you can make better-informed decisions about the architecture and design of your portal and how you'll integrate it into your enterprise architecture. The idea isn't to scare you away but rather to temper your enthusiasm with a bit of reality regarding the complexities of building an enterprise portal for your organization. Having laid the foundation in Chapter 1, we move on to create some actual portlets and go deeper into aspects of building WebSphere Portal portlets that can fully take advantage of the environment.

WHY TWO PARTS?

When initially challenged with the purpose of a second edition to this book, we immediately started to focus on JSR 168 and the fact that a major industry change was beginning to move more toward an open-standard approach. The first edition concentrated solely on the IBM WebSphere Portlet API, and although this API is still supported within WebSphere Portal, the general consensus is that at some point in the future it will be deprecated in favor of an industry standard.

As we continued our discussion about the Table of Contents and chapter outlines, we quickly realized that this book was going to be about a lot more than just JSR 168. Building real-world, robust, scalable portlets requires so much more. And the truth is that WebSphere Portal provides that "more" that developers need.

Our vision was, and still is, to provide the book in two sections. Part I provides pretty simple introductions to the Java Portlet API, while Part II provides that "more" that lets the reader become an efficient and reliable portlet programmer.

Along the same lines, we made a choice to include the JavaServer Faces (JSF) chapter in Part I. Because JSF is based on an open-source standards framework, the basic concepts are less specific to WebSphere Portal and geared more toward portlet programming in general. Our examples do tend toward using the IBM implementation of JSF rather than any generic framework; however, this is to gain the benefit of the tools and enable easier deployment and maintenance of the portlets. If you'd like to use another JSF implementation, you'll have to refer to the documentation around that specific framework for guidance.

With these points in mind, realize that it's almost impossible to have a total and complete separation of the two parts, so there will be some overlap within different chapters. But our intent is honest enough that we think you'll forgive any oversight on our part.

We hope you're as excited to be reading this book as we were in writing it. Happy programming! Let's get started.

Chapter One

Portals and Portlets: The Basics

Without a portal to plug into, portlets by themselves are quite useless. Put another way, just as you put letters together to form words and put words together to create sentences, you put portlets together to create one portal page. To understand what portlets are and where they come into play, we must therefore look at what a portal is. To do otherwise would be like trying to explain why letters are such a great thing without mentioning that you can combine them together to create words and sentences.

In this chapter, we briefly consider the different types of portals that exist and how portlets fit into the picture. Then, we take a closer look at the runtime environment of portlets: the portlet container. Just as the servlet container provides the infrastructure for running servlet components in the servlet world, so the portlet container provides the infrastructure for running portlets.

To get started, let's first look at what a portal is and explore the key benefit portals offer to the user — namely, the integration of several independent applications on one screen.

WHAT IS A PORTAL?

Figure 1.1 depicts a typical portal page. This portal consists of several pages, including Welcome, My Workplace, and My Finances. The figure shows the My Finances page of the portal, on which five portlets interact with each other.

Figure 1.1: Sample portal page

At the top of the portal page, a navigation bar lets the user move between portal pages. On the upper-right side, administration links let the user log in or out of the portal, access the user profile, and get help. Immediately below this upper bar, two finance-related portlets appear below:

- The CT Profile portlet displays details about a specific company.
- The CT Chart portlet displays charts and graphs relevant to the company.

These portlets, and the others you see in the figure, are placed on the page and represent applications with which the user can interact. These different applications are now integrated onto one page with one consistent API and are managed centrally. This approach offers advantages for the user, who now can access different applications consistently and in one place, and for the portal administrator, who can manage access to back-end services for a specific user in one place. If we examine this example more closely, you can see what a portal really offers. Portals enable users, even when they're using the Web, to work more as they do on their desktop, with different applications on one screen that can be interconnected and exchange data.

Most readers of this book probably have an understanding of what a portal is, and specifically of what WebSphere Portal Server is and how it generally works, but for completeness we should go over some obligatory information. If you're unfamiliar with WebSphere Portal, the references at the end of this chapter will point you to more information.

Types of Portals

We encounter the concept of portals throughout our daily lives. Newspapers, magazines, company bulletin boards, and car dashboards are all examples of portals we take for granted every day. Newspapers and magazines are general portals into world events, sports scores, stock market prices, and local happenings. Company bulletin boards are tailored, providing a look at the world through the eyes of the company — for example, by displaying the cafeteria's current lunch menu, clippings from the latest CEO memo, and workplace safety information. Each posting on the bulletin board is a view into the company. Automobile dashboards offer us a very specific portal into the inner workings of the different systems of our cars. The speedometer, oil pressure gauge, temperature gauge, and odometer all provide crucial information about the current condition of our vehicle's systems.

Web pages, too, provide a view of some type of information. With the rise of the World Wide Web, sites such as Yahoo and Excite started turning up as some of the first examples of portals on the Internet. These portals give users access to the latest news, weather, and stock reports. Some current Internet portals let you make stock trades or book flights and hotel rooms. They act as a single point of entry into applications and information on the Internet or your intranet. Today's portal combines applications and information into a consistent, single user interface (UI). It also supports user customization, personalization, and single sign-on.

IBM's WebSphere Portal product, shown in Figure 1.2, is essentially a framework for building portals. WebSphere Portal is capable of creating portals that are more general (like magazines and newspapers), tailored (like a company bulletin board), or very specific (like a car dashboard). You can use WebSphere Portal to create portals you can access from a desktop computer, your cell phone display, a PDA, or even your voice telephone. WebSphere Portal enables this functionality by combining portlets on a single Web page to give the end user access to information.

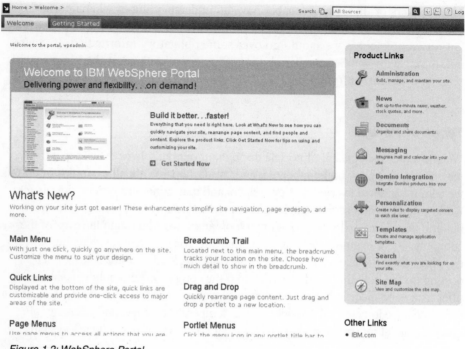

Figure 1.2: WebSphere Portal

Although we tend to imagine a browser interface when we think of WebSphere Portal, the product is really a set of complementary products that all combine to provide a dizzying array of function. These individual products that combine to create the portal include IBM DB2 Universal Database, IBM Tivoli Directory Server, and IBM WebSphere Application Server, as well as development tools, collaboration components, and, of course, IBM WebSphere Portal Server. To learn more about the various options of the product, visit *http://www.ibm.com/software/genservers/portal.*

What Does the Specification Say About Portals?

So how shall we define a portal? Many of the definitions available center on aggregation and integration. We'll take the following definition from the Java Portlet Specification V1.0 (Reference 1):

"A portal is a web based application that — commonly — provides personalization, single sign on, content aggregation from different sources and hosts the presentation layer of Information Systems. Aggregation is the action of integrating content from different sources within a web page. A portal may have sophisticated personalization features to provide customized content to users. Portal pages may have different set of portlets creating content for different users."

In the next sections, we shed some more light on the different parts of the portal definition that all center on the main portal theme: application integration.

PORTAL APPLICATIONS AND PORTLETS

A *portal application* is a group of portlets that form a logically associated group. Portlets in an application are installed as a single package. When programmed appropriately, they're able to communicate with one another by sending and receiving messages.

Because WebSphere portal is the framework, you can think of portlets as the pieces of art we place into the frames created by WebSphere Portal. A portlet could be an article, as in a magazine. It could be column, as in a newspaper. A portlet could be the cafeteria menu or a speedometer. A portlet is one small piece of an overall portal. It is one element of many that could appear on the user's screen. In this book, we cover in detail how to create these portlets, and we look at various facilities WebSphere Portal offers for portlets. In addition, in the second half of the book, we discuss composite applications and some of the approaches for designing and developing them.

PORTAL ARCHITECTURE

Portlets are run by a component, called a *portlet container*, that provides the portlet with the required runtime environment. The portlet container manages the life cycle of all the portlets and provides persistent storage mechanisms for the portlet preferences, letting portlets produce user-dependent markup. The portlet container passes requests from the portal on to the hosted portlets. It doesn't aggregate the content produced by the portlets; that's the portal's job. Figure 1.3 depicts the overall portal architecture.

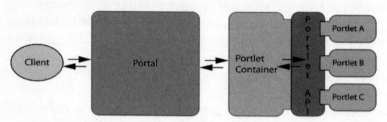

Figure 1.3: Portal architecture, with the portal aggregating the content and the portlet container running the portlets

Here's how it works:

1. A registered user (client) opens the portal, and the portal application receives the client request and retrieves the current user's page data from the portal database.

2. The portal application then issues calls to the portlet container for all portlets on the current page.

3. The portlet container, which holds the user's preferences, calls the portlets via the portlet API, requesting the markup fragment from each portlet and returning the fragment to the portal.

4. The portal aggregates all markup fragments together into one page, which the portal finally returns to the client/user, giving the user the integrated, useful interface he or she is used to on the desktop.

You'll learn more details about the portal architecture in later portions of this book as we explain the components and their subcomponents in more detail. For now, it should be enough to keep in mind that there are the two major components: the portal itself and the portlet container. Now that you know this much about portals, let's take a closer look at what portlets really are and what their role is in the big picture.

And What Is a Portlet?

Now that you know how a portal functions, it's time to take a closer look at portlets and their role in this environment. Let's start with a definition.

A *portlet* is a Java-based Web component that processes requests from a portlet container and generates dynamic content. The content generated by a portlet is called a *fragment*, which is a piece of markup (e.g., HTML, WML, XHTML) adhering to certain rules. A fragment can be aggregated with other fragments to form a complete document, called the *portal page*.

One could ask why portlets were invented and specified in the Java Portlet Specification at all. Why were existing J2EE concepts (namely the servlet) not enough? As you've already seen, that would lead to challenges in creating a consistent user experience. But what else is there that justifies creating a new component? Table 1.1 lists the reasons we think portlets are a separate component.

Table 1.1: Portlets vs. servlets as portal components

Servlets	Portlets
Web clients interact directly.	Web clients interact with portal. Portal acts as mediator, provides infrastructure.
Each servlet assumes it is the only responding component and produces a complete document.	Portlets assume other portlets are responding to the portal's request and produce markup fragments. Portal coordinates response to client, handles character set encoding, content type, and setting of HTTP headers.
Directly bound to a URL.	Addressed only via portal.
Less-refined request handling.	Request handling includes action processing and rendering options.
	Portlets have predefined modes and window states that indicate the function the portlet is performing and the amount of real estate in the portal page available to the portlet.
	Numerous portlets exist on a portal page and therefore require concepts such as the portlet window and portlet entity.

Table 1.1: Portlets vs. servlets as portal components (continued)

Servlets	Portlets
	Portlets need means for accessing and storing persistent configuration and customization data on a per-user basis. Because portlets need to be plugged into an existing portal, these storage functions must be provided by the portal infrastructure for the portlet and thus need to show up in the portlet API.
	Portlets need access to user profile information to generate user-specific output.
	Because portlets are plugged into portal systems, they need URL rewriting functions for creating hyperlinks within their content, letting URL links and actions in page fragments be created independently of the specific portal server implementation.

All these requirements made it a cleaner choice to introduce a new component, portlets, instead of bending the servlet definition to also fulfill these requirements. However, the Java Portlet Specification is closely aligned with J2EE concepts to permit the reuse of as much of the existing J2EE infrastructure as possible. The following points reflect this close alignment:

- Portlet applications are packaged as WAR files, with an additional portlet deployment descriptor (portlet.xml) for the portlet component, and can be deployed using the existing J2EE Web application infrastructure for WAR files.

- Portlet applications reuse the standard HttpSession; thus, portlets can share data via the session with other J2EE artifacts, such as servlets and JavaServer Pages (JSPs).

- Portlets can access the Web application context via the portlet API and share data with other J2EE artifacts on the context level.

- Portlets can access Web application initialization parameters defined in the web.xml file via the portlet context.

- Portlets can include servlets and JSPs via a request dispatcher.

- Portlet J2EE roles defined in the portlet.xml file can reference J2EE roles defined in web.xml, enabling a unified role mapping between portlets and servlets.

To leverage the existing J2EE infrastructure for portlets today, we can wrap them as servlets and deploy them in the Web container with the portlet container running on top of the Web container (see Figure 1.4). The Pluto Java Specification Request (JSR) 168 portlet reference implementation as well as the Jetspeed portal both take this approach.

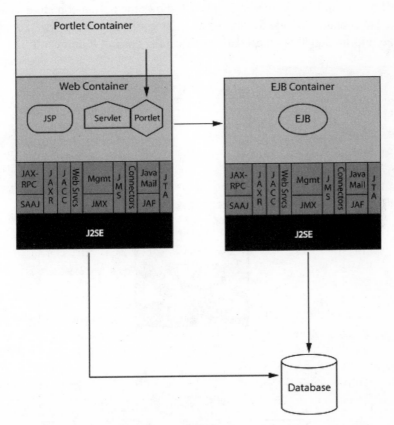

Figure 1.4: How portlets relate to J2EE

Today, while using as many J2EE concepts as possible, portlets aren't an integral part of J2EE. Thus the portlet container is running on top of the servlet container.

The plan is to keep future portlet specification aligned with the next J2EE versions. The goal is to integrate the Portlet Specification into J2EE in the future. This integration would permit treating portlets as first-class J2EE citizens, and the whole J2EE infrastructure, including application management, monitoring, deployment, and authorization, would support them. When this happens, a portlet container will be part of the application server and leverage the server's entire infrastructure, including administration and performance tuning. Portals will then be Web applications running on the application server and leveraging the different containers provided by the application server. Figure 1.5 shows the portlet container as an independent container beside the servlet and Enterprise JavaBeans (EJB) container. For more information about the J2EE specification, consult Reference 2.

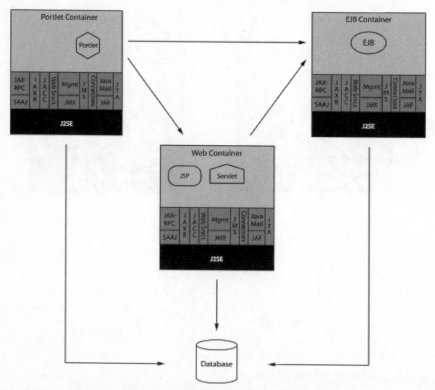

Figure 1.5: Future scenario in which portlets are part of J2EE and the portlet container is another J2EE container, like the servlet and EJB containers

The Java Portlet Specification is also aligned with another upcoming important J2EE technology, JavaServer Faces (JSF), which enables server-side user interfaces for Web components. For more information about JSF and portlets, see Chapter 6.

Portlets in Practice

What does our definition of portlets mean in practice? You've already seen a real-life portal page in Figure 1.1. Figure 1.6 depicts the basic structure of such a portal page.

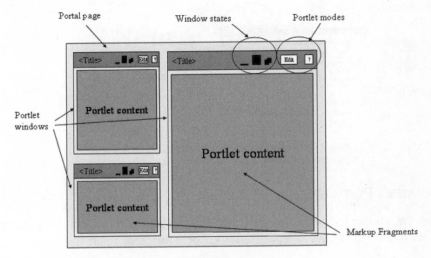

Figure 1.6: Portlet windows on a portal page

The markup fragments produced by portlets are embedded into a *portlet window* as *portlet content*. Portlet windows on a page have several basic elements. In addition to the portlet content, the portlet window has a *decoration area* that can include the portlet title and controls to influence the window state and the mode. The user can control the size of the portlet window via the portlet window controls, from minimized (only the title is displayed) to normal to maximized (only portlet on the page). The *portlet mode* influences the requested function of the portlet. A portlet may offer help in a help mode or allow customizing the behavior in an edit mode.

The portal may aggregate several portlet windows to produce a complete portal page. This means that each portlet produces only the portlet content and the portal produces everything else visible on the portal page, such as the portlet window, the portlet window controls, and the layout of the page.

Until now, all our examples have been HTML-based, but portlets aren't restricted to HTML. Figure 1.7 shows an example of a portlet that can produce different markups for different devices. For desktop browsers, it produces HTML markup; for Wireless Markup Language (WML) devices (e.g., mobile phones), it produces WML markup. This multidevice support offered by portlets lets users access the same applications regardless of the device they use.

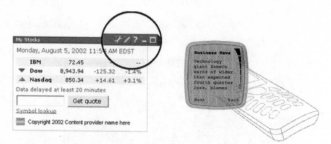

Figure 1.7: Alternative portlet markups (HTML for a desktop browser and WML on a mobile phone)

CREATING PORTLETS

Thus far, you've learned a lot about what portals and portlets are. In this section, we start looking at how to make portlets. There are three main scenarios:

- creating a new portlet-based application project

- migrating a portlet-based application from a proprietary portlet API to the standard portlet API (Java Portlet Specification)

- transforming an existing Web application into a portlet-based application

We'll cover all of these scenarios, beginning with creating new portlet applications from scratch.

Creating Portlet Applications from Scratch

Why would someone write portlet-based applications? That's a good question and one we'll answer in this section.

Previously, we defined a portlet as a Java-based Web component that processes requests and generates dynamic content. Thus our question should have been more precisely: Why would someone write portlet-based Web applications? In the days before portlets appeared, the Web programming model consisted of servlets and JavaServer Pages. We explain this programming model in more detail later, but for now we can concentrate on its major characteristics:

- *Adherence to a request/response paradigm:* Web applications communicate with the Web client by having the client send a request, and the Web application responds back to the client.

- *Self-contained application:* A Web application comes with all needed components and doesn't interact with other applications installed on the server running the Web application. This means you get one monolithic, consistent application that solves a specific problem, such as an Internet store.

While the first bullet also holds true for portlet applications, the second does not. In fact, this monolithic structure of Web applications was the reason portlets were invented. The monolithic structure of a complete application still has its use scenarios in a world of portlets — for example, in a self-contained online shop that doesn't need further customizations. However, more and more Web applications are becoming portal-like to permit users, as we've said, to work more in a desktop manner with different applications on one screen that can be interconnected and exchange data.

As the demand for more portal-like applications grows, the need to manage multiple applications in a single portal becomes critical. In all likelihood, more than one provider or group created the many applications typically included in a portal. Therefore, each Web application must be modular enough to fulfill several new requirements:

- Portlet applications must easily "plug in" to an existing portal to provide the portal with new functionality.

- Portlet applications must adhere to some rules to "play well" together with other portlet applications in the same portal.

- The portal must provide a unified user interface across multiple portlet applications.

The servlet API doesn't provide these kinds of rules and integration points; therefore, the new portlet API was created to support building modular Web applications that can be plugged into portals and produce content that is aggregated with content from other portlet applications into one page.

So the answer to the question at the beginning of this section is: You would write portlet applications if they will be used inside portals or if they need to be modular and integrate with other applications. But what if you've already created portlets using a proprietary portlet API? Let's consider this scenario.

JSR 168, the IBM Portlet API, and Other Tools

The current version of the Java Portlet Specification, JSR 168, was created jointly by several companies, including IBM, BEA Systems, Oracle, and Sun Microsystems, and released near the end of 2003. WebSphere Portal includes support for this standard to allow compatibility with other portals and portlet vendors.

IBM's strategy is to embrace open standards such as JSR 168. For this reason, we've decided to focus on that specification fully in this book. The JSR 168 standard is still evolving; the next version, called JSR 286, should be out toward the middle of 2007. (Appendix A describes the features expected in JSR 286.) Because of this, JSR 168 is still not as complete by itself as many portal teams require to achieve the functionality they need. With this point in mind, we focus the first part of this book on plain JSR 168 portlets, while the second part focuses on extensions and additional APIs for JSR 168 portlets that are WebSphere Portal–specific.

On another note, it's necessary to comment on portlet builder tools that have gained some popularity in the market lately. Over the past few years, several such products have become available. Some of these tools are better than others, and any of them may have a place in your organization or development effort. Having used some of these tools recently on various projects, we can say that it they indeed make it possible to quickly put together a simple portlet. Not every portlet or project is simple, however, and we want to caution you that total abstraction from the portlet API may not be possible or useful, and nearly every portal development effort requires some Java programming skills.

Moving from Proprietary APIs to Standard APIs

Here's another problem. Perhaps you were a portlet early adopter, but no standard existed when you started, or maybe you found the first version of the Java Portlet Specification too restrictive. For these reasons, you programmed your portlets against a proprietary portlet API. Now that the standard is in place, it's a good time to move from proprietary portlet APIs to the standard portlet API. Doing so will make your portlets vendor-independent, broadening their market or letting you move later on from your current portal vendor to a different one without throwing away all your portlet applications.

If you've written a portlet to a proprietary API, your situation looks like the one depicted in Figure 1.8. Here, the portlet is very tightly coupled to the available portal infrastructure because all the portlet APIs available are specific to the portal for which the portlet was developed.

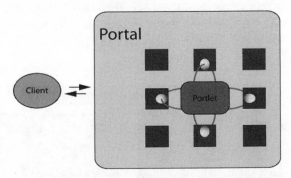

Figure 1.8: Portlets written against a proprietary portlet API

When you move to the standard API, there are two different cases to look at. In the first, the proprietary and standard APIs each support the same feature set; in the second, the proprietary API has a more robust feature set than the standard API.

Migrating Supported Features

The first case is the easy one. Here, the functionality that the portlet uses in the proprietary API is also available in the standard API; you can thus rewrite the portlet against the standard portlet API. This way, you end up with a portlet that's completely vendor-independent, guaranteed to run unchanged for years because new versions of the portlet standard will be backward-compatible and easier to maintain. And even years from now, people will know how to program against V1.0 of the standard portlet API.

Migrating Non-Supported Features

Now for the more complex case. In this situation, your portlet uses some functionality currently unavailable in the standard portlet API, such as sending events between portlets. Even here, it may still be beneficial to move to the standard API and use vendor-specific extensions only for the functions not available in the standard API. You can then program your portlet to query the portal at runtime for supported extensions. If the portal lacks the extension (or extensions) you want, it can still run with degraded functionality.

Figure 1.9 depicts this scenario. As you see, the portlet plugs into two different APIs, the Java Portlet API and the Portal Extension API. Now, the portlet is decoupled from the portal infrastructure and can also run in a standard environment and just offer less functionality.

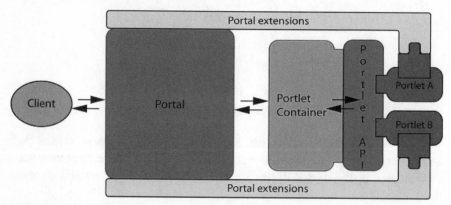

Figure 1.9: Portlet written against the standard portlet API but using vendor extensions when available

Now that we've covered creating portlet applications from scratch and converting portlets written against proprietary portlet APIs, let's take a look at transforming Web applications into portlet applications and thus handle the last use scenario for portlets.

Transforming Web Applications to Portlet Applications

This last scenario deals with another common case. You already have an existing, servlet-based Web application, and now you've read all this exciting stuff about portlets and want to leverage the advantages of portals and portlets. Of course, you'd like to avoid throwing away your existing code and starting again from scratch. It would be rather nice to put your existing Web application into a tool and have the tool transform it into a portal application. Unfortunately, reality isn't so easy, and only limited automated-tool support for transforming Web applications to portal applications is coming in the latest tool versions.

Let's look at the different ways your Web application might be implemented to see how easy or complicated it is to transform it into a portal application.

As with the last scenario, one implementation method is easier to transform than the other. If you were lucky enough to have written your Web application from scratch without using any Model-View-Controller (MVC) framework, such as Struts, just a few considerations apply. The answer largely depends on how modular your Web application is and whether you can easily factor out and remove the parts that don't fit in the portlet programming model we'll discuss in the next few chapters. These parts include

- using HTTP error codes or error JSPs. These parts must now be delegated to the portal.

- mixing of state-changing code and rendering code. Unless you separate these two, you'll have a hard time moving to the portlet programming model (or any MVC-based framework).

- parts of the code that deal with protocol handling and markup selection that aren't not cleanly separated. The portal handles these tasks in the portlet case.

If you stick to the Sun guidelines for J2EE Web applications (Reference 3), which recommend the MVC pattern, or if you've used an MVC-based framework, transforming your Web application into a portlet application should be a doable effort. You've still done only the first step with this, because your transformed portlet application most likely doesn't leverage the full power the portlet programming model provides. Using the complete data model will take some effort, but it will make your portlet application faster and easier to use.

MORE ABOUT TOOLS

Having mentioned tools above, let's take a quick look at the tools we'll be using for most of the portlets in this book. As Java programmers, we've mainly focused on building portlets in the traditional manner — that is, extending the PortletAdaptor or GenericPortlet class and filling in the code for the various methods (e.g., doView) that are provided. Among the different authors we take a few different approaches, but we developed most of the code, concepts, and images for this book using Rational Application Developer (RAD). Like any technology, these tools are rapidly evolving, and keeping up with the latest versions can be painful. For basic portlet programming, RAD is sufficient to create almost any portlet we discuss in this book. You may need some additional tools for some chapters, such as when we cover the Portlet Factory and WorkPlace Forms.

You can learn more about Rational Application Developer at the following location: *http://www.ibm.com/software/awdtools/developer/application/index.html*.

Required Skills

We've kept this first chapter brief so you can get started writing portlets right away! However, before we move on, some prerequisites will prove helpful in your portal development endeavor. Although we focus on using building portlets using available APIs and design and development best practices, you'll need a basic understanding of several topics to fully appreciate the information provided:

- a solid knowledge of Java and an understanding of server-side Java programming, such as servlets and JSPs

- familiarity with Web protocols, such HTTP

- a basic understanding of Extensible Markup Language (XML) to help understand Extensible Stylesheet Language Transformation (XSLT) and read deployment descriptor files

- basic familiarity with WebSphere Portal concepts, such as how to install portlets and set access control lists (ACLs)

- With this solid background and the information you'll learn from this book, you'll be writing portlets in no time.

SUMMARY

In this chapter, we covered the details of portals and portlets. First, we explained what a portal is and showed different applications of portals. The main point here is that portals are an integration point that integrates other applications into one consistent end-user application so users can work more in a desktop manner.

Next, we covered the role portlets play in the portal environment, noting that ssssthey are the central UI components that are rendered by the portal and that allow developers to extend the portal. We covered how portlets currently fit into existing J2EE architectures, why servlets aren't enough to provide portal components, and how portlets may be even more tightly integrated in future versions of J2EE. If portlets become part of J2EE, this will be a major achievement that will put portlets on par with servlets and enable them to leverage the complete J2EE infrastructure seamlessly.

Now that we've laid down some of the groundwork, let's get real in the next chapter by developing a real portlet in Chapter 2.

REFERENCES

1. Abdelnur, A., and S. Hepper. JSR 168: The Java Portlet Specification. *http://jcp.org/en/jsr/detail?id=168.*

2. Java 2 Platform Enterprise Edition 1.4 Specification. *http://www.jcp.org/en/jsr/detail?id=151.*

3. *Designing Enterprise Applications with the J2EE Platform, 2nd Ed.* Sun Developer Network, 2002. *http://java.sun.com/blueprints/guidelines/-designing_enterprise_applications_2e/index.html.*

4. Gamma, E., R. Helm, R. Johnson, and J. Vlissides. *Design Patterns: Elements of Reusable Object-Oriented Software.* Addison-Wesley, 1995.

Chapter Two

Writing Your First Portlet

"How do I write my own portlet?" This is by far the first question new developers ask when they are looking into WebSphere Portal fossssr the first time. We really don't know who will read this book and what type of experience they will have in Java and server-side programming. In this chapter, we therefore build the simplest possible portlet from scratch, writing directly to the JSR 168 Portlet API.

Many programming books use a "hello world" example as a first program, a tradition popularized by the 1978 classic *The C Programming Language* by Brian Kernighan and Dennis Ritchie. Following in the footsteps of our ancestors, we'll start with a hello world portlet.

We'll build the portlet two ways. The first method uses a text editor to compose the code, Web application, and portlet descriptors. Then, we use the command line to build and package the portlet. Last, we deploy the portlet into a stand-alone WebSphere portal for testing.

The second method uses IBM's Rational Application Developer (RAD), a sophisticated integrated development environment (IDE) that helps developers at every step of the way. RAD includes a test environment for WebSphere Portal that we'll use to test the portlet we build using this method.

We suggest you read the entire chapter but concentrate on whichever method best fits your development environment and taste.

ANATOMY OF A PORTLET

Before we actually start building our first portlet, it's important to understand the various components of a portlet and how they fit together. The illustration in Figure 2.1 is kind of a mishmash, mixing together several types of diagrams, but it helps to illustrate all the different components that come together to form a portlet.

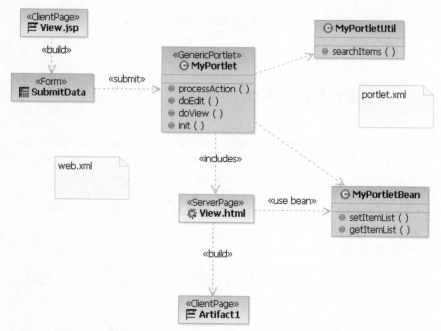

Figure 2.1: Portlet anatomy

In general, when we think of a portlet, we imagine it as a WAR file. WAR stands for Web ARchive. A WAR file is a type of zip file that combines several other files into a format the portal can understand. This file includes a basic directory structure into which files are placed in specific locations. Listing 2.1 shows a sample WAR file directory structure.

The structure in the figure is simply an example, and you can make many changes to the base structure depending on the type of portlet you're creating. For example, you can create additional directories and can move some directories around, such as the jsp, images, and nls directories.

```
+Portlet
  +WEB-INF           - portlet.xml and web.xml files
    +lib             - jar from source dir, or external jar files
    +tld             - JSP tag library description files
    +classes         - individual classes if not put as jar in lib
      +nls           - resource bundles for internationalization
    +jsp             - jsp files for portlet
    +images          - images that may be used in the portlet
    +source
    +com
      +ibm
        +portlets
          +myportlet - portlet controller, util and bean source code
```

Listing 2.1: Sample WAR file directory structure

Now that you know where things go, let's take a look at the specific items a portlet includes and identify what each one does:

- *Portlet controller:* The portlet controller is a class that extends the GenericPortlet class. It is the main controller for your portlet. The portal engine calls the portlet controller to render the portlet. The developer must code all control for a portlet to determine what the portlet does.

- *JSP files:* You use JavaServer Pages (JSPs) to render output for your portlet. Usually, the portlet controller calls the JSPs based on the state and view of the portlet.

- *View beans:* View beans contain data the JSP will use. This structure ensures that the JSP performs no data logic itself. A bean is populated and passed between the controller and the JSP via the session or the request.

- *Deployment descriptors:* For your portlet to be deployed and run correctly within the portal server, you need two deployment descriptors:

  ➢ *web.xml* is a standard J2EE deployment descriptor for WAR files. It determines the controller status and can contain a lot of information about how your package needs to be deployed.

> ➢ *portlet.xml* is a portal-specific deployment descriptor file. The portal server uses this file's data upon installation to determine parameters for your portlet.

- *Graphics and other files:* A portlet can contain additional files or graphics that can be used by the portlet or included within the JSP or resulting HTML. These files can reside in their own directories within the portlet.

STARTING HELLO WORLD

We'll begin by writing some Java code, then compile and package it into a JAR file. Next, we'll look at the deployment descriptors needed to tell the application server and the portal about the portlet. Last, we'll package everything together and deploy the new portlet into the portal.

For this first portlet, we'll need a much simpler structure with fewer components than the example you saw above. The controller does all the work in this example, so no JSPs will be called to display the portlet view. In later examples, we'll add JSPs and images, as well as view beans and helper or utility classes.

Create the Directory Structure

The first step is to create the directory structure in which we'll create the portlet. Listing 2.2 shows the structure we'll use for this simple example. We create these directories to enable us to easily create the JAR and WAR files. As you'll see, there are other directories you can use for your portlets to enable assorted functionalities.

```
+helloWorld
    +JavaSource
       +com
           +ibm
               +portlets
                   +sample  - source code for HelloWorld.class
    +WebContent
       +WEB-INF                   - web.xml and portlet.xml go here
          +lib                     - jar file will go here
```

Listing 2.2: Directory structure

Create the Java

We'll put the Java source file in the "sample" directory. Create a file named HelloWorldPortlet.java in this directory, and open it in your favorite text editor. Listing 2.3 shows the class to type in to the HelloWorldPortlet.java file.

```
package com.ibm.portlets.sample;

import java.io.*;
import javax.portlet.*;

public class HelloWorldPortlet extends GenericPortlet {

  protected void doView(RenderRequest request, RenderResponse response)
          throws PortletException, IOException {
    response.setContentType(request.getResponseContentType());
    response.getWriter().println("Hello, World!");
  }
}
```

Listing 2.3: HelloWorldPortlet.java

Compile the Code

Once we've created the source file, we're ready to compile the Java code. You can use the script shown in Listing 2.4 in a batch file to compile the portlet. (If you're using Linux, use the commands shown in Listing 2.5.)

```
> @setlocal
> @set JAVAC="C:\WebSphere\AppServer\java\bin\javac"
> @set CP="C:\WebSphere\PortalServer\shared\app\wp.pe.api.standard.jar"
> %JAVAC% -classpath %CP%
    JavaSource\com\ibm\portlets\sample\HelloWorldPortlet.java
> @endlocal
```

Listing 2.4: Compilation

```
$ JAVAC=/opt/WebSphere/AppServer/java/bin/javac
$ CP=/opt/WebSphere/PortalServer/shared/app/wp.pe.api.standard.jar
$ $JAVAC -classpath $CP
    JavaSource/com/ibm/portlets/sample/HelloWorldPortlet.java
```

Listing 2.5: Linux compilation

29

The code begins by defining some environment variables, such as where our Java home is. It's usually a good idea to compile the code using the Java Development Kit (JDK) provided with WebSphere Application Server (WAS) because that's the environment under which we'll be running. For this reason, we point directly to the Java compiler installed with WAS. We then invoke the Java compiler and compile our code. (This example assumes we're in the helloWorld directory; adjust your directory paths as appropriate for your installation.)

If for some reason the code doesn't compile, you'll need to fix the errors before moving on. Some common errors are

- Typos: Check for mistyped class names, paths, and variable names.

- File name: The file name and the class name must match. In our case, the file name is HelloWorldPortlet.java, and the class name is HelloWorldPortlet. If you've changed one name, change the other.

- Editor woes: Make sure your editor really saves the file as text. An editor such as WordPad doesn't save as text by default.

Create the JAR File

Once we've compiled the Java source, we need to create a JAR file in the WEB-INF\lib directory. Again, assume we're in the helloWorld directory. Listing 2.6 shows the code to create the JAR file. (If you're using Linux, use the commands shown in Listing 2.7.)

```
> cd JavaSource
> set JAR= C:\WebSphere\AppServer\java\bin\jar
> %JAR% -cvOf ..\WebContent\WEB-INF\lib\HelloWorld.jar
      com\ibm\portlets\sample\*.class
> cd ..
```

Listing 2.6: Creating the JAR file

```
$ cd JavaSource
$ JAR=/opt/WebSphere/AppServer/java/bin/jar
$ $JAR -cvOf ../WebContent/WEB-INF/lib/HelloWorld.jar
      com/ibm/portlets/sample/*.class
$ cd ..
```

Listing 2.7: Creating the JAR file in Linux

Create the Deployment Descriptors

Next, we create two XML files for the deployment descriptors:

- helloWorld/WebContent/WEB-INF/web.xml — the Web deployment descriptor
- helloWorld/WebContent/WEB-INF/portlet.xml — the portlet deployment descriptor

The Web deployment descriptor defines a Web application under which the hello world portlet is installed. Listing 2.8 shows the contents of the Web deployment descriptor file.

```xml
<?xml version="1.0" encoding="UTF-8"?>
<!DOCTYPE web-app PUBLIC "-//Sun Microsystems, Inc.//DTD Web
Application 2.3//EN" "http://java.sun.com/dtd/web-app_2_3.dtd">
<web-app id="WebApp_ID">
        <display-name>HelloWorld</display-name>
</web-app>
```

Listing 2.8: Web deployment descriptor web.xml

The portlet deployment descriptor, shown in Listing 2.9, defines the portlet to the portal. A portlet application must define a unique ID in the id attribute of the portlet-app element. You'll notice that this deployment descriptor contains a bunch of elements. For now, don't worry about what they all are or what they mean. We'll cover them as needed in subsequent chapters.

```xml
<?xml version="1.0" encoding="UTF-8"?>
<portlet-app xmlns="http://java.sun.com/xml/ns/portlet/portlet-app_1_0.xsd"
  version="1.0" xmlns:xsi="http://www.w3.org/2001/XMLSchema-instance"
  xsi:schemaLocation="http://java.sun.com/xml/ns/portlet/portlet-
app_1_0.xsd http://java.sun.com/xml/ns/portlet/portlet-app_1_0.xsd"
  id="com.ibm.portlets.sample.HelloWorldPortlet.2bb9165d90">

<portlet>
    <portlet-name>HelloWorld</portlet-name>
    <display-name>HelloWorld portlet</display-name>
    <display-name xml:lang="en">HelloWorld portlet</display-name>
    <portlet-class>com.ibm.portlets.sample.HelloWorldPortlet</portlet-class>
```

Listing 2.9: Portlet deployment descriptor portlet.xml (part 1 of 2)

```
    <init-param>
        <name>wps.markup</name>
        <value>html</value>
    </init-param>
    <expiration-cache>0</expiration-cache>
    <supports>
        <mime-type>text/html</mime-type>
        <portlet-mode>view</portlet-mode>
    </supports>
    <supported-locale>en</supported-locale>
    <portlet-info>
        <title>HelloWorld portlet</title>
    </portlet-info>
    </portlet>
</portlet-app>
```

Listing 2.9: Portlet deployment descriptor portlet.xml (part 2 of 2)

Many things can go wrong when you create these XML files, and you won't find out about it until you try to deploy the portlet into the portal. Here are a handful of things to double-check:

- Make sure there's no white space in front of the initial <?xml . . .> tag.

- Verify that for every XML element, you have a closing element.

- Check for mistyped class names, especially (for this example) if you named your class something other than HelloWorldPortlet.

- Make sure your editor really saves the file as text.

Create the WAR File

We're now ready to create the WAR file for distribution. We'll use the standard jar command to build this file. To create the file, run the commands shown in Listing 2.10 from the helloWorld directory. (If you're using Linux, use the commands shown in Listing 2.11.)

```
> cd WebContent
> set JAR="C:\Program Files\Portal51UTE\AppServer\java\bin\jar"
> %JAR% -cvf ..\HelloWorld.war WEB-INF
> cd ..
```

Listing 2.10: Creating the WAR file

```
$ cd WebContent
$ JAR=/opt/WebSphere/AppServer/java/bin/jar
$ $JAR -cf ..\HelloWorld.war WEB-INF
$ cd ..
```

Listing 2.11: Creating the WAR file in Linux

Congratulations! You've created your first portlet. The next step is to install and test the portlet. There are several ways to do so. Using a standalone portal server, you can install the portlet and place it on a page. By updating the portlet when changes are made, you can continue to refine and debug the functionality of your code. If you're new to WebSphere Portal and unfamiliar with basic administration features such as installing a portlet, refer to IBM's InfoCenter or *IBM WebSphere Portal Primer* by Ashok Iyengar, Venkata Gadepalli, and Bruce Olson (IBM Press, 2005) for more information about this topic.

Another approach is to use Rational Application Developer and the Portal Toolkit. It's important to understand that multiple approaches to developing portlets exists, and dependency on a tool can limit your understanding of the process. Within this book, our focus on using WebSphere Studio is limited to getting you started with the process of building portlets. Although the tools are available and fairly easy to use, some organizations choose to standardize on their own development IDE or to code on Linux or Unix workstations.

BUILDING HELLO WORLD WITH RATIONAL APPLICATION DEVELOPER

Rational Application Developer currently comes bundled with the Portal Toolkit, so it's an easy fit to incorporate it into your development environment and process. Launching RAD, we can immediately begin to create a simple portlet using this environment. As we walk through the process, keep in mind that we're skipping much of the background on using RAD to its full advantage. Our examples use RAD Version 7, which is in beta as of this writing but contains all the functionality we need for this exercise. At this time, the RAD V7 beta lacks the embedded test environment, but it does include the server attach test environment, which is configured automatically if you've installed WebSphere Portal V6 on the same machine. We'll use this portal instance to test our code.

Rather than build a portlet from scratch, we're going to use one of the predefined sample portlets that come with RAD. Once you have RAD up and running (as shown in Figure 2.2), you can create a new portlet project by selecting **File > New > Project**, as shown in Figure 2.3.

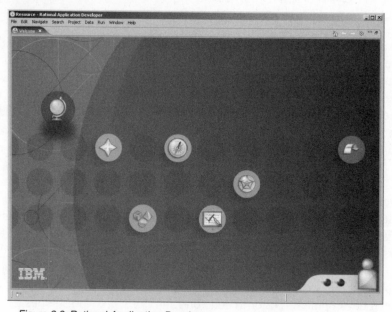

Figure 2.2: Rational Application Developer

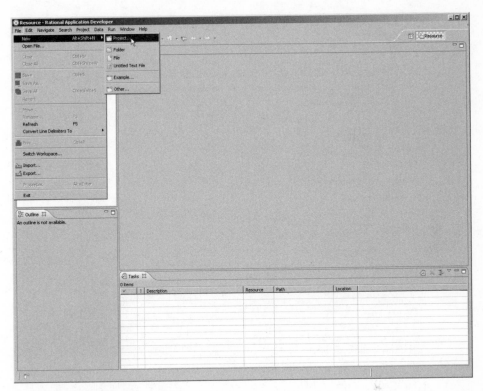

Figure 2.3: Choose a new project

Doing so brings up the **New Project** dialog, shown in Figure 2.4. RAD V7 offers one option for building portlet projects. Select **Portlet Project**, or choose **Portal > Portlet Project**, and then click **Next**.

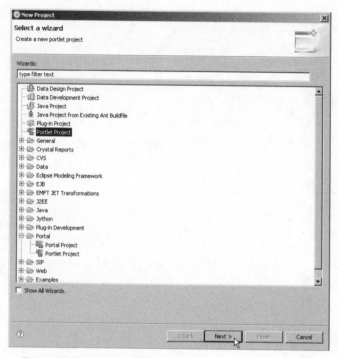

Figure 2.4: Starting the Portlet Project wizard

Next, supply the parameters for the portlet project by specifying the following values in the **Portlet Project** dialog (shown in Figure 2.5).

- For **Project name**, enter **SamplePortlet** (or whatever project name you like).

- For **Target Runtime**, select **WebSphere Portal v6.0**.

- Make sure the EAR membership check-box option is selected, and enter a new EAR project name.

- The **Portlet API** drop-down list lets you choose the JSR 168 API or the IBM API. Leave this option set to the JSR 168 API.

- For **Portlet name**, enter **SamplePortlet**.

- For **Portlet type**, select **Basic Portlet**.

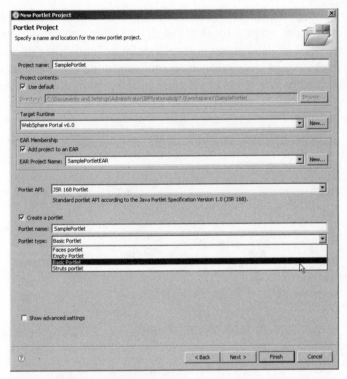

Figure 2.5: Portlet Project dialog

You can see from the figure that RAD provides several built-in templates for creating starter portlets. When you're finished with this screen, click **Next**.

Because we didn't select the preceding screen's option to show advanced settings, we'll skip the features page. For basic portlets, it's best to leave these advanced options at their defaults.

The **Portlet Settings** dialog (Figure 2.6) appears next. Here, you can add different modes to your portlet, change locales, and define other general portlet settings. You can leave most of these settings at their default values. One tip would be to change the package and class prefixes to conform to the development standards of your organization. When you're finished with this dialog, click **Next**.

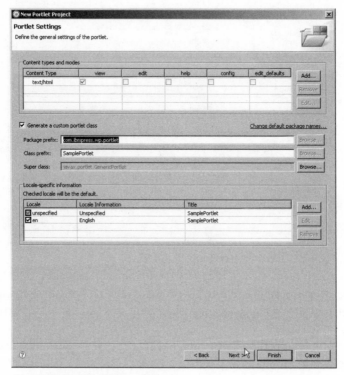

Figure 2.6: Portlet settings dialog

To make sure our sample portlet actually does something, it's important to choose some generic feature during project setup. In the **Action and Preferences** dialog (Figure 2.7), select the option to add an action listener.
Then click **Finish** to create the sample portlet.

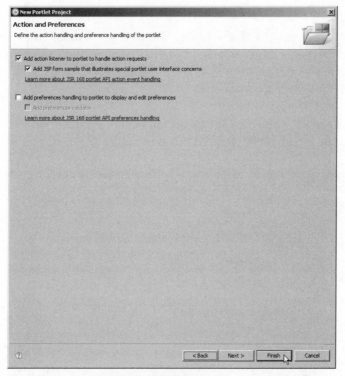

Figure 2.7: Action and Preferences dialog

During the creation of the portlet, you'll probably be prompted to change to the Web perspective. Figure 2.8 shows this prompt.

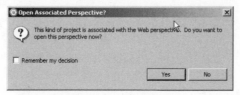

Figure 2.8: Changing perspectives

In general, you want to be in the Web perspective when working on portlets. Later, when you create JSF portlets, you'll see that some tools are available only in this perspective. To continue with the portlet creation, click **Yes** in response to the prompt. The portlet will be compiled and ready to run almost immediately.

Running the Portlet

The pleasure of working and developing within RAD is that RAD provides a single interface in which to develop and test your portlets. With the right configuration, you can perform this develop-and-test cycle repeatedly until you're ready to deliver a portlet.

To run your portlet, right-click the project in RAD's Project Explorer, and choose **Run As > Run on Server**, as shown in Figure 2.9.

Figure 2.9: Running the portlet

If this is your first time running a portlet on your local portal, you'll probably need to define a server to run the portlet. In the **Define a New Server** dialog (Figure 2.10), choose the option to **Manually define a new server**, and select **WebSphere Portal v6.0 Server** as the server type. You may optionally set this server as the default. Click **Next** to continue.

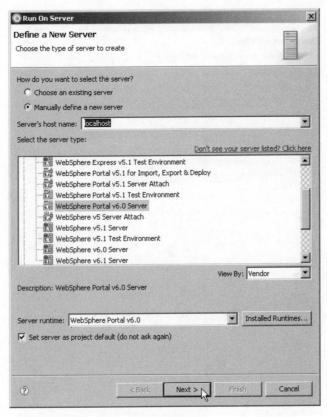

Figure 2.10: Creating a new server

The next screen (Figure 2.11) should already be completed based on the parameters you entered when you installed WebSphere Portal on the local machine. You can accept the defaults for the options shown. Re-enter the WAS user ID and password to be sure, and double-check the Simple Object Access Protocol (SOAP) port. Then click **Next** to continue.

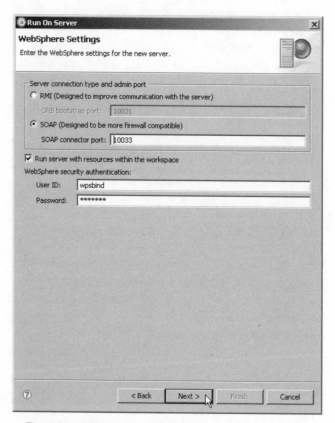

Figure 2.11: WebSphere settings

The portal settings (Figure 2.12) should also be set up to work with your local portal instance. You may need to verify the user ID and password and select the **Enable automatic login** option. Click **Next** when you're finished with this screen.

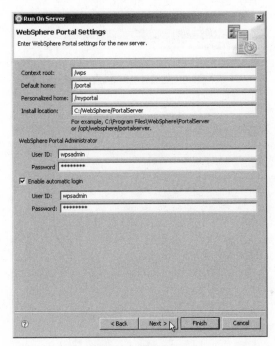

Figure 2.12: WebSphere portal settings

You use the next screen (Figure 2.13) to specify how files will be transferred to the portal server. If the portal server resides on the same machine as RAD, you can choose **Local Copy** as the transfer method; otherwise, you'll need to use FTP. Verify the shared/app location for your local portal, and click **Next** to continue.

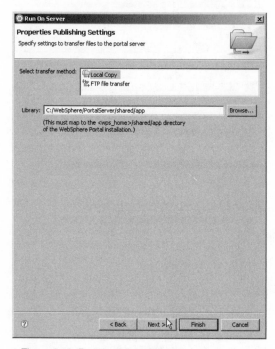

Figure 2.13: Portal publish settings

In the **Add and Remove Projects** dialog (Figure 2.14), make sure your sample project appears on the **Configured projects** side. You'll use this dialog often to add and remove projects from your local portal for testing. Click **Finish**.

At this point, RAD should try to publish the portlet and start the test environment for you. Your **Servers** view (Figure 2.15) shows the progression RAD is going through.

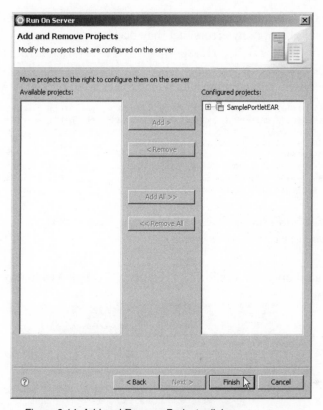

Figure 2.14: Add and Remove Projects dialog

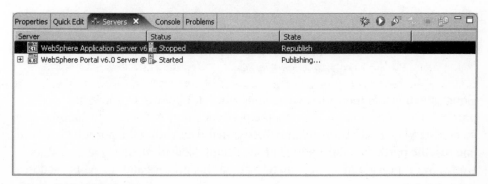

Figure 2.15: Publishing phase

Switching to the **Console** view (Figure 2.16) lets you view the portal's startup progression and observe any errors that may occur.

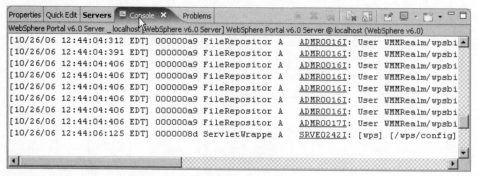

Figure 2.16: Starting the portal test environment

If a security alert appears, as shown in Figure 2.17, click **Yes** to proceed.

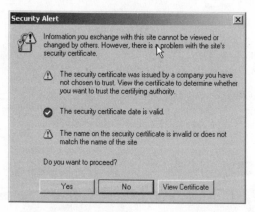

Figure 2.17: Security alert

Congratulations! You now have a running portlet. Figure 2.18 shows the portlet up and functioning. This simple portlet demonstrates how to submit some data via an HTML form and process that data within the portlet. Go ahead and test the portlet and take a look at the sample code to understand how it works. We'll provide more information about this process and the APIs used in later chapters.

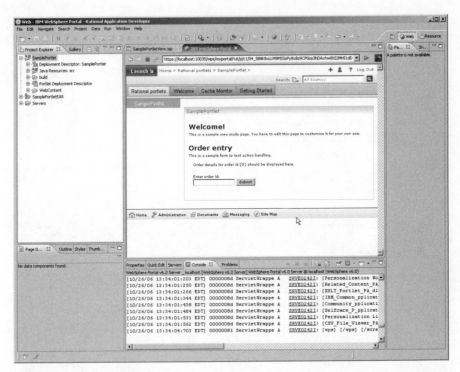

Figure 2.18: Viewing the portlet

A MINOR FIX

At the time of this writing, there was a possible issue with the sample portlet provided here. It may not display the actual value of the data entered into the form. By making one small change to the JSP file associated with the portlet, you can take care of this problem. To make the fix, modify the Order details code in the JSP to include the formText that is returned to the JSP via the session bean. You can see in Figure 2.19 that we entered the code to display the value in the middle of line 23.

```
<%= formText %>
```

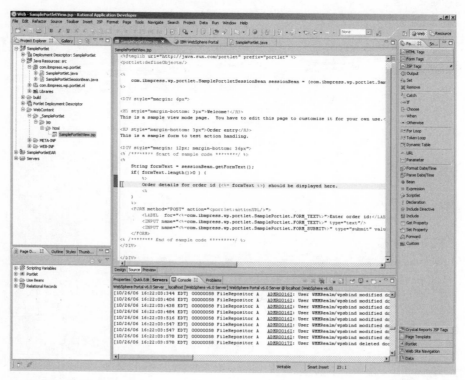

Figure 2.19: Modifying the JSP

If you left the test environment running, the portlet should be republished and initiated after you save your change to the JSP. Go ahead and test the portlet again, making sure the entered value appears on the page, as it does in Figure 2.20.

SUMMARY

In this chapter, we created two sample portlets. In real life, most readers will probably focus on one path or the other depending on their skill and environment choices. There is benefit, however, in looking at how you might accomplish the task in a different environment. If you use only Rational Application Developer for your development, you might not fully understand the process of using commands on the operating system to compile and package your components. On the other hand, seeing how easy it is to accomplish some

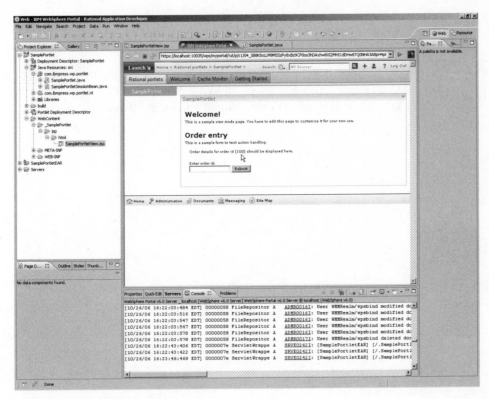

Figure 2.20: Verifying the changes

tasks in an IDE such as RAD might persuade some to switch to this type of environment.

One area we haven't gone into detail on is how to package a portlet you've successfully tested for deployment into another environment. RAD makes this step easy by providing a WAR creation wizard you can use on your project. The following steps can assist in this process.

1. Right-click your project in the navigation window, and choose **Export**.

2. On the **Export** screen, choose **WAR File** and click **Next**.

3. On the **WAR Export** screen, verify the name of the project, and enter the name and folder location to which you want to export the WAR file.

4. Click **Finish**.

The file will be exported to the specified location and ready for deployment into any portlet server.

Now that you understand how to build and package your portlets, the following chapters guide you deeper into aspects of building WebSphere Portal portlets that can fully take advantage of the environment and create successful portals. Have fun!

Chapter Three

Java Portlet API Fundamentals

In the previous chapter, we created our first simple hello world portlet. You may wonder why you need portlets for this task rather than just using a plain servlet to do the job. To answer that question, let's start with the basic requirements for a portlet that aren't present in the servlet Web programming world. The Java Portlet Specification V1.0 defines the following basic capabilities (Reference 1):

- A portlet must support the portlet life cycle, specifying the request/response flow and the life cycle of a portlet by implementing the javax.portlet.Portlet interface.

- A portlet must support modes and window states, defining the function and available real estate for a portlet window.

- A portlet should support several customization levels to permit customizing portlets in different ways.

All these requirements must be met to allow real componentization of the user interface and enable the portal to aggregate different portlets into one page with a consistent behavior, look, and feel. In this chapter, we take a closer look at each of these requirements and then create a portlet application that leverages these different concepts.

PORTLET LIFE CYCLE

Every portlet must implement the portlet interface or extend a class that implements the portlet interface. The portlet interface defines the basic portlet life cycle, which consists of three phases:

1. initializing the portlet and putting it into service (the init method)

2. responding to requests from the portlet container (the processAction and render methods)

3. destruction of the portlet when the portlet needs to be put out of service (the destroy method)

The portlet container manages the portlet life cycle and calls the corresponding methods for each life cycle on the portlet interface. The request handling in the second step of the life cycle consists of two phases:

- *Action handling*: The portlet container calls the portlet's processAction method to notify the portlet that the user has triggered an action on this portlet. Only one action per client request is triggered. During an action, a portlet can issue a redirect, change its portlet mode or window state, or modify its state.

- Rendering: The portlet container calls the portlet's render method to request the markup fragment from the portlet. For each portlet on the current page, the render method is called, and the portlet can produce markup that may depend on the portlet mode, window state, or other state information or back-end data. The portal attaches a list of valid MIME types that must have at least one element the portlet can choose for rendering the markup. The MIME types that the portal sends to the portlet must be a subset of the MIME types that the portlet has declared as supported in the deployment descriptor. The portlet sets the chosen MIME type on the response and generates the markup either by directly writing to the output stream or by including a servlet or JavaServer Page (JSP) that generates the markup.

Figure 3.1 depicts these different request categories and shows the difference between the action call, which is issued only to the portlet with which the user interacts, and the render calls, which are issued to all portlets on the current page.

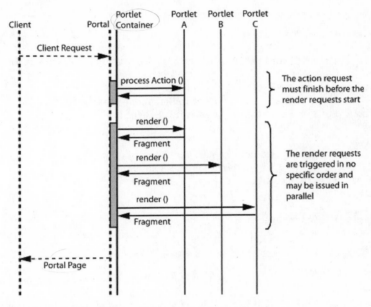

Figure 3.1: Portlet request flow for rendering a page

In the illustration, the user has triggered an action on portlet A, which results in a processAction call for portlet A. The portal page for this user consists of portlets A, B, and C, resulting in render calls for all these portlets to produce the page markup.

The figure also depicts the parts of the request flow that are defined within the Java Portlet Specification — namely, as we mentioned before, the interaction between the portlet container and the portlets. In addition, it shows the parts not defined in the specification (indicated by the dashed lines) — the interaction of the client with the portal and the interaction between the portal and the portlet container.

Listing 3.1 shows the actual portlet interface with all its methods. As you can see, it really is a simple interface and consists of even fewer methods than the servlet interface!

```
public interface Portlet
{
  public void init(PortletConfig config) throws PortletException;

  public void processAction (ActionRequest request,
                                   ActionResponse response)
    throws PortletException, java.io.IOException;


  public void render (RenderRequest request,
                         RenderResponse response)
    throws PortletException, java.io.IOException;


  public void destroy();
}
```

Listing 3.1: Portlet interface

Now that you know the basic life cycle of a portlet, let's take a look at what portlet modes and window states are good for.

PORTLET MODE AND WINDOW STATE

The *portlet mode* advises the portlet what task it should perform for the current request and what content it should generate. As we explained, this additional information is necessary because the portlet doesn't directly interact with the user; the portal exists between the end user and the portlet. Through portlet modes and window states, the portal can enforce a consistent look and feel for all portlets on a page.

Usually, portlets execute different tasks and create different content depending on the functions they're currently performing. When you invoke a portlet, the portlet container provides the current portlet mode to the portlet. Portlets can also programmatically change their mode when processing an action request.

There are three different categories of portlet modes:

- *Required modes* are modes every portal must support. These modes are Edit, Help, and View. A portlet must support the View mode used to render markup for a page. The Edit mode is used to change per-user portlet preferences to customize the portlet markup, and the Help mode displays a help screen.

- *Optional custom modes* are modes listed in the appendix of the portlet specification that a portal may support. However, because these are optional portlet modes, portlets can't count on being called in one of these modes. Therefore, if your portlet supports an optional portlet mode, the portlet should still work even if it is never called in this mode. The optional modes include the About mode, used to display an "about" message; the Config mode, which administrators can use to configure the portlet; the Edit_defaults mode, which lets an administrator preset the Edit mode's values; the Preview mode, which enables a preview of the portlet; and the Print mode, used to render an easily printed view. WebSphere Portal V6.0 supports the optional Config and Edit_defaults mode.

- *Portal vendor-specific modes* are not defined in the portlet specification.

A *window state* indicates the amount of portal page space that the portal will assign to the content generated by the portlet. When invoking a portlet, the portlet container provides the current window state to the portlet. The portlet may use the window state to decide how much information it should render. Portlets can also programmatically change their window state when processing an action request. The following window states are defined:

- *Normal* indicates that a portlet may share the page with other portlets or that the portlet is rendered on a device with a small screen. This is the default window state.

- *Maximized* indicates that a portlet may be the only portlet on the portal page or that the portlet has more space compared with other portlets in the portal page and can therefore produce richer content than in a normal window state.

- *Minimized* indicates that the portlet should render only minimal output or no output at all.

You can call a portlet in any of these three window states, but it is free to produce the same markup for all three states. In addition to these states, the portal may define vendor-specific window states.

CUSTOMIZATION LEVELS: PORTLET DEFINITIONS, PORTLET ENTITIES, AND PORTLET WINDOWS

The beauty of a portlet is that the developer doesn't impose his or her idea about what the user wants on the user. Portlets are designed to be customized. Users normally customize portlets to obtain content for their specific needs. For example, a user might customize a stock quote portlet to show only the desired stock quotes or tailor a news portlet to show just the news topics of interest.

In Java, there are different ways to customize a Java object. The simplest way is to create a copy of the object and customize the new object. For the programmer, this method offers the advantage of being easy to understand, and the object can store data internally in instance variables. However, this method also has a couple disadvantages. Creating a new object is an expensive operation because it requires memory, and you can't inherit settings from the original object. Inheritance of settings plays an important role, as you'll see.

To provide scalable portals for many millions of users, portlets use the *flyweight pattern* (Reference 2) to implement customization. In this pattern, only one very light Java object exists, and the programmer passes the different data sets into the object. There is only one Java portlet instance, even if a million users with different customization settings for this portlet use the portlet, and you can easily implement the inheritance of different levels of customization data. However, as always in life, these advantages come at some cost. Now, the portlet must store the customization data separately and can't store these data in instance variables. To allow the portlet to store these data, the Java Portlet API provides the PortletPreferences interface. You must also program the portlet thread-safe because several threads may call the same portlet code at the same time to generate markup for different users.

You can see that making portlets customizable has dramatic consequences on the portlet programming model. Let's look at the levels at which you can customize portlets.

Figure 3.2 depicts the different levels that influence the data on which a portlet operates. Besides the portlet.xml deployment descriptor, which serves as the initial seed, there are three customization levels: the portlet definition, the portlet entity, and the portlet window.

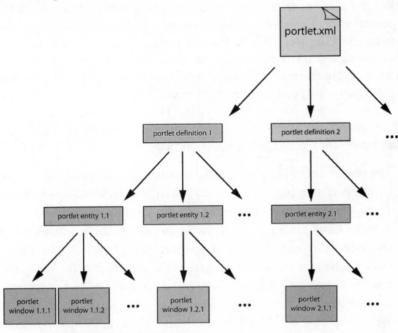

Figure 3.2: Portlet customization levels

It's important that data between these levels are inherited, which means, for instance, that a change in the portlet definition must be visible in all portlet entities created from this definition. Each level (portlet.xml, portlet definition, portlet entity, and portlet window) can define or provide context for the next level down, and each level inherits data from its next level up. As you may remember, this is one advantage the flyweight pattern offers: The data isn't stored in instance variables, but outside the portlet, and it can be merged by the portal infrastructure easily without being visible to the portlet. Several portlet definitions may be created out of one portlet definition in the portlet.xml file, and the administrator can set different configuration settings, thus providing new inheritance trees.

Typically, a new portlet entity is created out of a portlet definition for each user to represent the user-specific preference data. Because these portlet entities may show up on one or more user pages, one or more portlet windows are created pointing to this portlet entity. So, if we have the portlet definition of News, for example, each user can select the sources or types of news, which are then stored in the portlet entity. These news items can appear in different portlet windows on different pages as the user explores the site. Note that in WebSphere Portal V6.0 there is a one-to-one relationship between portlet windows and portlet entities. This means that each time you put a new portlet on your page, a new portlet entity and portlet window are created.

How do these different levels of customization show up in the portlet? Each level has a different representation in the portlet:

- The portlet definition gives the portal administrator the ability to customize portlet settings, such as the stock quote server of a stocks portlet. The administrator can change the settings for the portlet definition in the optional Config mode, and the portlet can access these settings via the read-only preferences. The preferences are called read-only because they can't be changed outside the Config mode and are thus read-only for users who aren't administrators. A typical example of such a setting is the server address of the news portlet from which a portlet retrieves its news. We give more details about the portlet definition in the data model section later in this chapter.

- The portlet entity gives the end user the ability to customize the portlet. New entities are created for each user that puts a portlet on her or his page. The user can then further customize the writable portlet preferences in the Edit mode. An example of a portlet entity setting is the news groups of a news portlet in which a specific user is interested.

- The portlet window is the window that displays the markup fragment the portlet produces. A portlet window is created whenever a user attaches a portlet entity to a specific portal page. This decoupling of the portlet window from the portlet entity lets you have different windows pointing to the same portlet entity. This enables the user to have the same news portlet or calendar portlet on different pages. The portlet window also comes with data (navigational states) attached to it that enable the portlet to render a specific view of the data. Navigational data is represented in the portlet API in the portlet mode, window state, and render parameters. Contrary to the previously mentioned customization levels, this one normally is not stored persistently, which means that if a user logs on again, the portlet may not be in the same portlet mode or window state as the last time the user was logged in.

We've already started to get into the data model and which kind of data the portlet has access to. The data model is an important part of the portlet programming model, so let's take a closer look at it now.

UNDERSTANDING THE PORTLET DATA MODEL

As you've seen, a portlet has access to different data sets that are configured by different user roles: administrator and end user. It's important to understand this data model when you're writing portlets because you can confuse administrators and end users if the portlet doesn't adhere to this data model. For example, if a news portlet provided a section in the View mode where the news server could be changed, an inconsistent user experience would result. The administrator would look for a Config button on the portlet window and wouldn't find one. Thus, she would conclude that she couldn't customize this portlet because the Config button was missing from its usual place in the portlet window.

The portlet data model clearly separates the different roles of administrators and end users and thus lets a portal create different, but consistent, interfaces for each user type. Portlets that don't adhere to this predefined schema, as in the example mentioned, create their own user interface for administrators and thus break the user experience of the whole portal.

In this section, we describe in detail the data model provided by the Java Portlet Specification that the portlet should use for storing and retrieving customization data. All the customization data together defines the state of the portlet. As you may remember from the preceding section, the portlet programming model uses the flyweight pattern, where the Java object itself stores no state but obtains the data for each processing request from outside. We'll cover both the persistent and transient state defined by the portlet specification.

Figure 3.3 summarizes in one picture the different states a portlet can access. The illustration depicts the different types of state information a portlet has access to, including the transient navigational and session states and the persistent portlet preferences. The portlet uses all this information to display a consistent, personalized user interface.

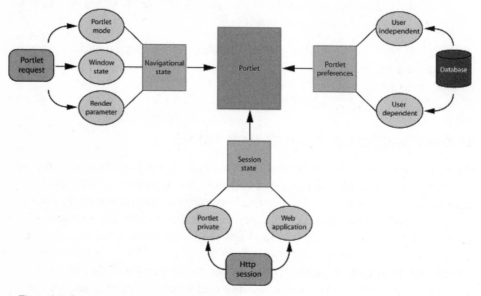

Figure 3.3: Portlet data model state information

Persistent State: Portlet Preferences

The portlet can access two different types of persistent data: the initialization parameters and the portlet preferences. The initialization parameters are read-only data that you can specify in the portlet deployment descriptor; they are the same for all portlet entities created from this portlet definition. Using the initialization parameters, you can set basic portlet parameters, such as the names of the JSPs used to render the output.

The portlet can also access persistent data via the portlet preferences. There are two different categories of portlet preferences:

- *User-independent (administrative) preferences*: You declare these preferences in the portlet deployment descriptor as read-only, and the user cannot change them. Only an administrator can modify these settings (e.g., by using the portlet Config mode or an external tool). Examples of this kind of data include server settings and billing information. All user-independent preferences must be listed in the deployment descriptor as read-only preferences.

- *User-dependent preferences:* Users can set these preferences to customize the portlet, normally using the Edit portlet mode. Examples of this kind of data include the companies whose stock quotes the user wants to see or the news topics in which the user is interested. The portlet can create new user-dependent preferences at runtime.

Both kinds of preferences are merged into one interface that offers this data to the portlet, as you can see on the figure's right side. Keep in mind that preferences can be read and written only in the action phase and are read-only in the render phase. This restriction was introduced to enforce the programming model requirement that changes to the portlet state must take place in the action phase, while the render phase is idempotent (meaning that multiple render calls yield the same result) and replayable. The portlet preferences can be either strings or string array values associated with a key of type String. You can preset the preferences with default values in the deployment descriptor.

To validate that the portlet preferences conform to application-specific restrictions (e.g., the number of news articles per page must be greater than zero), the portlet should specify a preference validator. A preference validator is a class that implements the PreferencesValidator interface and is called automatically by the portlet container each time before any changes are made persistent. Supplying the validator as a separate class permits other tools and generic administration portlets to change the portlet preferences, with the validator being called each time to ensure the preferences are consistent. The portlet must define in the deployment descriptor the class that implements the PreferencesValidator interface under the preference-validator tag.

Transient State: Session and Navigational State

The portlet has access to two different kinds of transient state: session state and navigational state. This distinction reflects the different lifetimes of the data stored in these states. The session state reflects the lifetime of a user session, in which a user logs on to a portal, performs several operations, and finally after some time logs out or is automatically logged out due to a long period of inactivity. The navigational state represents a more short-term store that is bound to the request and may change from one request to the next. Therefore, the portlet accesses these different states through different APIs, as you can see in Figure 3.3 on the left and bottom.

The session state lets the portlet store information in the session using two different kinds of scopes. The session concept is based on the HttpSession defined for Web applications. Portlet applications are Web applications and thus use the same session as servlets.

To permit portlets to store temporary data private to a portlet entity, the default session scope is the portlet scope. In this scope, the portlet can store information needed across user requests that are specific to a portlet entity. Attributes stored with this scope are prefixed in the session by the portlet container to avoid two portlets (or two entities of the same portlet definition) overwriting each other's settings.

The second scope is the Web application session scope. In this scope, every component of the Web application can access the information. The information can be used to share transient state among different components of the same Web application (e.g., between portlets or between a portlet and a servlet).

The navigational state defines how the current view of the portlet is rendered and is specific to the portlet window in which the portlet is rendered. Navigational state can consist of data such as the portlet mode, the window state, a subscreen ID, and so on. Unlike portlet mode and window state, the navigational state is represented in the portlet API via the render parameters. The portlet receives the render parameters for each render call, and they can only be changed by two means:

- in an action where the portlet can explicitly set new render parameters
- via clicking on a render link with new render parameters

The portlet receives these parameters for at least as long as the user interacts with the current page. After executing a bookmark or switching to another portal page and then returning to the old portal page, the portlet may not receive the old render parameters anymore. This behavior depends on the portal implementation, and the Java Portlet Specification does not specify it. Therefore, as portlet programmer, you should expect such behavior in your portlet code and let the portlet act gracefully if all previous render parameters are lost in the next request.

PORTLET URLS

Portlets are components that are aggregated into pages via a portal application. Therefore, they cannot simply create URLs by hand-pointing back to them. For this reason, the Java Portlet API provides a way for the portlets to create such URLs. We'll cover the different URL flavors in this section — first the action and render URLs and then the resource URLs.

Action and Render URLs

Via the RenderResponse interface, the portlet can create two different types of portlet URLs:

- *ActionURLs* trigger the processAction method of the portlet, and the portlet can perform its state changes. These URLs should therefore be issued using the HTTP POST method to indicate that the URLs change the server-side state to the Web infrastructure.

- *Render*URLs let the portlet set a new navigation or view state without going through an explicit action phase. They permit changing the render parameters, the portlet mode, and the window state. Because these URLs don't result in server-side state changes, you should issue them via HTTP GET to indicate that the URLs don't change the server-side state to the Web infrastructure and thus allow caching. The Java Portlet Specification V1.0 leaves it up to the portal/portlet container implementation whether HTTP Form GET submissions with parameters are supported. WebSphere Portal supports this functionality, but other portals may not.

Thus, you should only use the methods on the PortletURL object to add parameters to the URL and not make any assumption otherwise about what the URL returned via toString will look like.

> **Note:** Understand that these URLs aren't "real" URLs. Even if you call the toString method of the PortletURL object, you may not get back a real URL but instead some token or even a JavaScript function that the portal server or Web browser may rewrite into a real URL.

Resource URLs

If the portlet needs to address resources in its WAR file (e.g., include a gif in the markup), it needs to construct the URL and use the encodeURL method of the PortletResponse to encode it. To get to the path of the deployed portlet application, you use the getContextPath. Here's an example of such a URL:

Note: Note that the same restriction as for action and render URLs applies here. The returned URL needn't be a "real" URL but may be a token that is rewritten (e.g., when the portlet is running as a remote portlet). (For more information about remote portlets, see the discussion of Web Services for Remote Portlets in Chapter 4.)

```
String myURL = response.encodeURL(request.getContextPath() +
               "mydir/myGif.gif");
```

Now that we've written our first simple hello world portlet (in Chapter 2) and covered all the portlet-specific concepts, let's get our hands dirtier and create a couple of complete and more function-rich portlets to leverage what you've learned thus far in this chapter.

THE CALENDAR PORTLET APPLICATION EXAMPLE

The calendar portlet application actually consists of two portlets, one showing a calendar and another displaying the day's ToDo's based on the day selected in the calendar. In the Calendar portlet, the user can flip forward and backward between the different months and select a specific date. The ToDo portlet displays all current ToDo's for the selected date in the View mode and lets the user add or remove ToDo's in the Edit mode.

Table 3.1 describes the different tasks we'll cover to create this example.

Table 3.1: Building a calendar portlet

Portlet application task	How to
Enable data sharing between portlets.	• Edit Calendar portlet to store selected date. • Edit ToDo portlet to retrieve selected date.
Create calendar using Java Standard Tag Library (JSTL) tags.	• Add JSTL tags to Calendar portle
Store and retrieve selecteddate using render parameters	• Set render parameters in Calendar portlet. • Set render parameters in viewDate JSP.
Write portlet and JavaBean code	• Write Calendar portlet. • Write ToDo portlet. • Write Calendar bean. • Write ToDo bean.
Write JSP code	• Write viewDate JSP for Calendar portlet. • Write view JSP for ToDo portlet. • Write edit JSP for ToDo portlet.
Package application	• Create deployment descriptor. • Create file structure.
Deploy and run application	• Run application and add new ToDo items.

In this example, you'll learn how to

- share data between portlets to communicate the selected date from the Calendar portlet to the ToDo portlet

- use Java Standard Tag Library (JSTL) tags in the JSPs to remove scriptlet code from the JSPs

- leverage render parameters to page through the different months in the Calendar portlet

- use JSPs to render the markup and the portlet preferences to store the data, implementing the Model-View-Controller (MVC) pattern because we've separated the controller (portlet) from the model (portlet preferences) and from the view (JSPs)

- customize the portlet output, taking into account user-specific data (the ToDo's), which we'll store in the portlet preferences

- handle actions to enable the user to change the ToDo items in the preferences

- use the View mode to display the list of ToDo's and use the Edit mode to manage the ToDo list

Let's start by looking into the sharing of data between portlets.

Sharing Data Between Portlets

To communicate the selected date from the Calendar portlet to the ToDo portlet, we need some means of inter-portlet communication. The first version of the Java Portlet Specification provides only limited support for inter-portlet communication; real eventing between portlets is not yet supported (see Appendix A for information about the event support planned in JSR 286). Thus, we share data via the portlet session.

```
public void processAction(ActionRequest request,
                          ActionResponse actionResponse)
throws PortletException
{
    // get the selected date
    String date = request.getParameter(DATE);
    String month = request.getParameter(MONTH);
    if (date != null)
    {
        request.getPortletSession().setAttribute(DATE, date,
                                PortletSession.APPLICATION_SCOPE);
        actionResponse.setRenderParameter(MONTH, month);
    }
}
```

Listing 3.2: Storing the selected date

Storing the Selected Date

As you've learned, portlets can share data via the session application scope that is accessible for all components in the same Web application. Therefore, the

Calendar portlet will set the currently selected date into the application scope session. Listing 3.2 shows the corresponding code snippet.

We encode the current month as a render parameter using the setRenderParameter call. We'll cover this technique in more detail in the render parameter section below. For now, let's concentrate on the session-sharing part. The portlet retrieves the current date submitted via the DATE parameter to this action and stores it in the application scope session under the key DATE.

Retrieving the Selected Date

Now, the displaying portlet, called ToDoPortlet, needs to retrieve the date from the session again. Listing 3.3 shows the corresponding code lines in the ToDoPortlet for retrieving the date. Because we extend the GenericPortlet, we only override the specific portlet mode method doView instead of implementing the render method, because the render method with the dispatching is already implemented by the GenericPortlet.

```
protected void doView (RenderRequest request,
                       RenderResponse response)
throws PortletException, IOException
{
    response.setContentType("text/html");

    ToDoBean bean = new ToDoBean();
    bean.setDate((String) request.getPortletSession().
            getAttribute("date",PortletSession.APPLICATION_SCOPE));
    request.setAttribute(TODO_BEAN, bean);

    PortletRequestDispatcher rd = getPortletContext().

getRequestDispatcher("/jsp/view.jsp");
    rd.include(request,response);
}
```

Listing 3.3: Retrieving the selected date

The code retrieves the current selected date from the session and sets it in a bean so the view JSP can retrieve the date. Then the view JSP is included via the request dispatcher call.

Having achieved the data sharing, let's take a close look at how we can create the JSPs by using JSTL tags in the next section.

Applying JSTL to Portlet JSPs

When writing JSPs, you often come to a point where you need some Java scriptlet code — for example, to loop through all preferences. Scriptlet code is normally something you should avoid because it makes JSPs hard to read and mixes the concepts of user interface design and programming in Java. To avoid scriptlet code in the JSPs, we'll use the Java Standard Tag Library in the Calendar example.

As you'll see later, you can't use the JSTL expression language (EL) inside the Java Portlet Specification tag library. This is because the Java Portlet Specification taglib is based on J2EE 1.3 and thus isn't compliant with the JSP EL leveraged by JSTL. This restriction will disappear as soon as the follow-on version of the Java Portlet Specification is final.

Creating the Calendar with JSTL

Listing 3.4 shows the JSP view of the Calendar portlet, which uses JSTL tags to create the calendar.

```
<%@ taglib uri='http://java.sun.com/portlet' prefix='portlet'%>
<%@ taglib uri='http://java.sun.com/jstl/core' prefix='c'%>
<jsp:useBean id="bean" class="
com.ibm.samples.portlets.calendar.CalendarBean" scope="request" />

<table><tr>
<td>Sun</td><td>Mon</td><td>Tue</td><td>Wed</td><td>Thu</td><td>Fri</td>
<td>Sat</td>
</tr><tr>
<c:forEach var="link" varStatus="status" items="${bean.dateLinks}">
    <td><c:out value="${link}" escapeXml="false"/></td>
<c:if test="${ (status.count % 7) == 0}">
</tr><tr>
</c:if>
</c:forEach>
</tr></table>
```

Listing 3.4: JSP view of the Calendar portlet

We start this JSP by creating a table with one column for each day of the week and output the names of the weekdays. The CalendarBean contains all links for the current month, and via the forEach tag we loop through all links stored in the bean. We've stored the complete link, which we prefabricated in the Calendar portlet, in the bean to highlight that all JSTL tags produce XML escaped output by default.

> **Note:** For normal markup, you must take this approach to comply with XML-based markups such as XHTML. However, there are a few cases where this isn't true, and one of them is outputting URLs that the user should be able to select. For these cases, you can specify the escapeXml=false attribute and JSTL won't escape the output of this tag.

The last step is to test in the loop to see whether we need to close the current table row and start a new one, having already put seven days in one row.

Now that we've produced a calendar for a single month, let's see how we can leverage render parameters to allow switching between different months in the calendar.

Using Render Parameters

As we mentioned, a portlet can store its view state in render parameters. These parameters are provided with each subsequent render request. New render parameters can be set either in the performAction method or via render URLs. The big advantages of render URLs are that they require less server computing power and they enable "crawlability" because search engines can follow the render URLs without fear of triggering an action that changes some back-end state.

In our Calendar portlet, we use render URLs to switch to either the previous or the next month. The render parameter therefore contains the current selected month. If no render parameter is set, we use the month of the current date.

Setting Render Parameters in the Calendar Portlet

The following listings show the Calendar portlet and the JSP snippets that implement render parameter handling.

As you can see in Listing 3.5, in the doView method we try to get the current selected month from the request as a render parameter. If we don't succeed and no render parameter is available, we take the current month as default. To be able to create the render URLs to the previous and next month, we set these two values in the bean that is attached to the request and can be accessed in the JSP.

```java
protected void doView (RenderRequest request,
                       RenderResponse response)
 throws PortletException, IOException
{
...
    Calendar today = Calendar.getInstance();
    CalendarBean bean = new CalendarBean();

    int month = today.get(Calendar.MONTH);
    int year  = today.get(Calendar.YEAR);

    if ( request.getParameter(MONTH) != null )
    {
        month = Integer.parseInt(request.getParameter(MONTH));
        today.set(Calendar.MONTH, month);
    }
    int prevMonth = (month > 0 ? month - 1 : 0);
    int nextMonth = (month < 11 ? month +1 : 11);
    ...
    bean.setNextMonth(Integer.toString(nextMonth));
    bean.setPreviousMonth(Integer.toString(prevMonth));
    ....
}
```

Listing 3.5: Obtaining the current month

In the next listing (Listing 3.6), you can see how we create the render URLs using these bean values and set the render parameters through render URLs.

```html
...
<table><tr>
<td>Sun</td><td>Mon</td><td>Tue</td><td>Wed</td><td>Thu</td><td>Fri</td>
<td>Sat</td>
...

<portlet:renderURL var="myPrev">
    <portlet:param name="month" value="<%=bean.getPreviousMonth()%>"/>
</portlet:renderURL>
<portlet:renderURL var="myNext">
```

Listing 3.6: Creating and setting the render URLs (part 1 of 2)

```
        <portlet:param name="month" value="<%=bean.getNextMonth()%>"/>
</portlet:renderURL>

<table>
<tr>
<td>
<form action="<%=myPrev%>" method="GET">
        <input name="prev"  type="submit" value="Previous month">
</form>
</td>
<td>
<form action="<%=myNext%>" method="GET">
        <input name="next"  type="submit" value="Next month">
</form>
</td>
</tr></table>
```

Listing 3.6: Creating and setting the render URLs (part 2 of 2)

Via the portlet tags for render URLs, we generate the render URLs and set the render parameter month with the values we've put into the bean in the portlet. Next, we create a table with two forms that only have one button.

> **Note**: We use the HTTP GET method here to permit search engines to follow this link and enable caching systems to cache the content.

Now that we've covered the major functions of the Calendar portlet application, it's time to take a look at the complete portlet code.

The Complete Portlet Code

As we noted before, this portlet application consists of two parts:

- the Calendar portlet, which displays a calendar with links to select a specific date

- the ToDo portlet, which displays the ToDo's for the selected date

Writing the Calendar Portlet Code

Let's first look at the Calendar portlet code in Listing 3.7. The main task of this portlet is to fill the Calendar bean with the links for the days of the currently selected month.

```
package com.ibm.samples.portlets.calendar;

import java.io.IOException;
import java.util.ArrayList;
import java.util.Calendar;

import javax.portlet.ActionRequest;
import javax.portlet.ActionResponse;
import javax.portlet.GenericPortlet;
import javax.portlet.PortletException;
import javax.portlet.PortletRequestDispatcher;
import javax.portlet.PortletSession;
import javax.portlet.PortletURL;
import javax.portlet.RenderRequest;
import javax.portlet.RenderResponse;

public class CalendarPortlet extends GenericPortlet
{
    // key under which to store the shared data in the session
    public final static String DATE = "date";
    public final static String MONTH = "month";

    private final static String CALENDAR_BEAN = "bean";

    public void processAction(ActionRequest request,
                              ActionResponse actionResponse)
    throws PortletException
    {
        // get the selected date
        String date = request.getParameter(DATE);
        String month = request.getParameter(MONTH);
        if (date != null)
        {
            // store the new date in the application session scope
            request.getPortletSession().setAttribute(DATE, date,
                                    PortletSession.APPLICATION_SCOPE);
            // set new render parameter
            actionResponse.setRenderParameter(MONTH, month);
        }
}
```

Listing 3.7: Calendar portlet (part 1 of 3)

```
    }

    protected void doView (RenderRequest request,
                           RenderResponse response)
    throws PortletException, IOException
    {
        response.setContentType("text/html");

        try
        {
            ArrayList links = new ArrayList();

            Calendar today = Calendar.getInstance();
            CalendarBean bean = new CalendarBean();

            int month = today.get(Calendar.MONTH);
            int year  = today.get(Calendar.YEAR);

            if ( request.getParameter(MONTH) != null )
            {
                month = Integer.parseInt(request.getParameter(MONTH));
                today.set(Calendar.MONTH, month);
            }
            int prevMonth = (month > 0 ? month - 1 : 0);
            int nextMonth = (month < 11 ? month +1 : 11);
            int maxDays = today.getActualMaximum(Calendar.DAY_OF_MONTH);
            today.set(Calendar.DAY_OF_MONTH, 0);

            for (int i=0; i<today.get(Calendar.DAY_OF_WEEK); i++)
                links.add("");

            for (int i = 1; i <= maxDays; i++)
            {
                String dateString = getDateString(year,month+1,i);
                PortletURL portletURI = response.createActionURL();
                portletURI.setParameter(DATE, dateString);
                portletURI.setParameter(MONTH, Integer.toString(month));

                links.add("<a href=\"" + portletURI.toString() + "\">" +
                            dateString.substring(0,2) + "/" +
                            dateString.substring(3,5) + "</a>");
            }

            bean.setDateLinks(links);
```

Listing 3.7: Calendar portlet (part 2 of 3)

```
            bean.setNextMonth(Integer.toString(nextMonth));
            bean.setPreviousMonth(Integer.toString(prevMonth));

            request.setAttribute(CALENDAR_BEAN, bean);

            PortletRequestDispatcher rd = getPortletContext().
                        getRequestDispatcher("/jsp/viewDate.jsp");
            rd.include(request, response);

        } catch (Exception exc) {
            this.getPortletContext().
                log("CalendarPortlet: An error occurred ", exc);
            throw new PortletException("CalendarPortlet: An error
                occurred");
        }
    }

    private String getDateString (int year, int month, int day)
    {
        StringBuffer date = new StringBuffer();

        if (month < 10) date.append(0);
        date.append(month);
        date.append("/");

        if (day < 10) date.append(0);
        date.append(day);
        date.append("/");

        date.append(year);

        return date.toString();
    }
}
```

Listing 3.7: Calendar portlet (part 3 of 3)

In the doView method, we have two for loops. In the first, we add empty links so we have the correct offset for the day of the week of the current month for the calendar table when we loop through the links in the JSP. In the second, we create an action link for each day of the month, with the date and month as action parameters. We store the complete HTML markup in the link entry because we want to include the day and month as text for the HTML anchor tag. Last, we store the bean with all the links in the request and include the calendar view JSP.

We now have the date links for our calendar ready and can receive actions on selected dates and store the date into the portlet session. Next, we need to create a ToDo list portlet that will let us store ToDo's for the selected date.

Writing the ToDo Portlet Code

The ToDo portlet displays the ToDo list for the selected date in the View mode and lets the user add and remove items for the selected date in the Edit mode. Listing 3.8 shows the complete ToDo portlet.

```
package com.ibm.samples.portlets.calendar;

import java.io.IOException;

import javax.portlet.ActionRequest;
import javax.portlet.ActionResponse;
import javax.portlet.GenericPortlet;
import javax.portlet.PortletException;
import javax.portlet.PortletPreferences;
import javax.portlet.PortletRequestDispatcher;
import javax.portlet.PortletSession;
import javax.portlet.RenderRequest;
import javax.portlet.RenderResponse;


public class ToDoPortlet extends GenericPortlet
{
    private final static String TODO_BEAN = "bean";

    public void processAction(ActionRequest request,
                                ActionResponse actionResponse)
    throws PortletException, IOException
    {
        if (request.getParameter("remove") != null) // remove
        {
            PortletPreferences prefs = request.getPreferences();
            String date = (String) request.getPortletSession().
                        getAttribute(CalendarPortlet.DATE,

PortletSession.APPLICATION_SCOPE);
            String[] currentValues = prefs.getValues(date, new String[0]);
            String[] newValues = new String[currentValues.length-1];
            for (int i=0, j=0; i < currentValues.length; ++i, ++j)
            {
                if (currentValues[i].equalsIgnoreCase(request.
```

Listing 3.8: ToDo portlet (Page of 1 of 3)

```
                                getParameter("ToDo")))
                    i++;     // remove this item
                if (i >= currentValues.length)
                    break;
                newValues[j] = currentValues[i];
            }

            prefs.setValues(date, newValues);
            prefs.store();
        }

        if (request.getParameter("add") !=null ) // add
        {
            PortletPreferences prefs = request.getPreferences();
            String date = (String) request.getPortletSession().
                                getAttribute(CalendarPortlet.DATE,
                                        PortletSession.APPLICA-
TION_SCOPE);
            String[] currentValues = prefs.getValues(date, new
String[0]);
            String[] newValues = new String[currentValues.length+1];
            for (int i=0; i < currentValues.length; ++i)
                newValues[i] = currentValues[i];
            newValues[currentValues.length] = request.getParameter("ToDo");
            prefs.setValues(date, newValues);
            prefs.store();
        }
    }

    protected void doView (RenderRequest request,
                            RenderResponse response)
    throws PortletException, IOException
    {
        response.setContentType("text/html");

        ToDoBean bean = new ToDoBean();
        bean.setDate((String) request.getPortletSession().getAttribute(
                                        CalendarPortlet.DATE,
                                        PortletSession.APPLICA-
TION_SCOPE));
        request.setAttribute(TODO_BEAN, bean);

        PortletRequestDispatcher rd = getPortletContext().
getRequestDispatcher("/jsp/view.jsp");
```

Listing 3.8: ToDo portlet (Page of 2 of 3)

```
        rd.include(request,response);

    }

    protected void doEdit(RenderRequest request,
                          RenderResponse response)
    throws PortletException, IOException
    {
        response.setContentType("text/html");

        ToDoBean bean = new ToDoBean();
        bean.setDate((String) request.getPortletSession().getAttribute(
                                      CalendarPortlet.DATE,
                                      PortletSession.APPLICA-
TION_SCOPE));
        request.setAttribute(TODO_BEAN, bean);

        PortletRequestDispatcher rd = getPortletContext().

getRequestDispatcher("/jsp/edit.jsp");
        rd.include(request,response);
    }
}
```

Listing 3.8: ToDo portlet (Page of 3 of 3)

The only thing worth noting in this portlet is that we've chosen to store the ToDo's with the date as key and store all ToDo's for a specific date as an array of Strings. Therefore, we need to get all existing ToDo's in the processAction method and either scan for the ToDo we want to remove or add the new ToDo at the end of the list.

Writing the Calendar JavaBean Code

We also have the two beans that the Calendar and the ToDo portlets use. For completeness, we show these beans below. They are plain Java beans without any portlet-specific functionality. We'll start with the Calendar bean (Listing 3.9). This bean stores the links of each day of the current month and the previous and next months. The Calendar portlet fills this bean, and the viewDate JSP accesses it.

```
package com.ibm.samples.portlets.calendar;

import java.util.Collection;

public class CalendarBean {
    private Collection dateLinks  = null;
    private String nextMonth = null;
    private String previousMonth = null;


    /**
     * @return Returns the dateLinks.
     */
    public Collection getDateLinks() {
        return dateLinks;
    }
    /**
     * @param dateLinks The dateLinks to set.
     */
    public void setDateLinks(Collection dateLinks) {
        this.dateLinks = dateLinks;
    }
    /**
     * @return Returns the nextMonth.
     */
    public String getNextMonth() {
        return nextMonth;
    }
    /**
     * @param nextMonth The nextMonth to set.
     */
    public void setNextMonth(String nextMonth) {
        this.nextMonth = nextMonth;
    }
    /**
     * @return Returns the previousMonth.
     */
    public String getPreviousMonth() {
        return previousMonth;
    }
    /**
     * @param previousMonth The previousMonth to set.
     */
    public void setPreviousMonth(String previousMonth) {
        this.previousMonth = previousMonth;
    }
}
```

Listing 3.9: Calendar bean

Writing the ToDo JavaBean Code

The ToDo bean (Listing 3.10) stores the current selected date and is filled by the ToDo portlet and accessed by the view and edit JSPs.

```
package com.ibm.samples.portlets.calendar;

public class ToDoBean {
    private String Date = null;
    /**
     * @return Returns the date.
     */
    public String getDate() {
        return Date;
    }
    /**
     * @param date The date to set.
     */
    public void setDate(String date) {
        Date = date;
    }
}
```

Listing 3.10: ToDo bean

As our next step, let's examine the complete JSP code.

The Complete JSP Code

Our Calendar portlet application consists of three JSPs: one viewDate JSP for the Calendar portlet and one view and one edit JSP for the ToDo portlet.

Writing the viewDate JSP Code for the Calendar Portlet

Listing 3.11 shows the viewDate JSP.

```
<%@ taglib uri='http://java.sun.com/portlet' prefix='portlet'%>
<%@ taglib uri='http://java.sun.com/jstl/core' prefix='c'%>
<jsp:useBean id="bean" class="
com.ibm.samples.portlets.calendar.CalendarBean" scope="request" />

<table><tr>
<td>Sun</td><td>Mon</td><td>Tue</td><td>Wed</td><td>Thu</td>
<td>Fri</td><td>Sat</td>
</tr><tr>
<c:forEach var="link" varStatus="status" items="${bean.dateLinks}">
    <td><c:out value="${link}" escapeXml="false"/></td>
    <c:if test="${ (status.count % 7) == 0}">
            </tr><tr>
        </c:if>
</c:forEach>
</tr></table>

<p></p>

<portlet:renderURL var="myPrev">
    <portlet:param name="month" value="<%=bean.getPreviousMonth()%>"/>
</portlet:renderURL>
<portlet:renderURL var="myNext">
    <portlet:param name="month" value="<%=bean.getNextMonth()%>"/>
</portlet:renderURL>

<table><tr>
<td>
<form action="<%=myPrev%>" method="GET">
    <input name="prev"  type="submit" value="Previous month">
</form>
</td>
<td>
<form action="<%=myNext%>" method="GET">
    <input name="next"  type="submit" value="Next month">
</form>
 </td>
</tr></table>
```

Listing 3.11: viewDate JSP

We already explained the JSTL tag and the render URLs in the previous
sections. One thing worth noting here is that we need to create the render URLs
accessing the bean via the <%= %> scriptlet code and not via the JSTL EL code
${bean.nextMonth}. As we mentioned, this is because the current JSP version
on which the Java Portlet tag library is based doesn't support the expression

language. In the JSP, we first create a table for the calendar and then loop through all the links in the bean and render them in the table. At the end, we create two render URLs for moving to the previous or next month.

Writing the View JSP Code for the ToDo Portlet

Listing 3.12 shows the view JSP of the ToDo portlet.

```
<%@ taglib uri='http://java.sun.com/portlet' prefix='portlet'%>
<%@ taglib uri='http://java.sun.com/jstl/core' prefix='c'%>
<%@ page import="javax.portlet.*"%>
<jsp:useBean id="bean" class="
com.ibm.samples.portlets.calendar.ToDoBean" scope="request" />

<portlet:defineObjects/>

<P>
Current selected date: <c:out value="${bean.date}"/>
</P>
<P>
<P>
<B>ToDo's for the current date:</B><br>
</P>
<c:set var="prefsMap" value="${renderRequest.preferences.map}"/>
<c:if test="${empty prefsMap[bean.date]}">
        No ToDo currently defined for this date.<br>
        To add a ToDo please press "Edit ToDo's".
</c:if>
<c:if test="${not empty prefsMap[bean.date]}">
    <c:forEach var="ToDo" items="${prefsMap[bean.date]}">
            <c:out value="${ToDo}" /><BR>
    </c:forEach>
</c:if>
</p>

<form action="<portlet:renderURL portletMode="edit"/>" method="GET">
        <input type="submit" name="action" value="Edit ToDo's">
</form>
```

Listing 3.12: View mode JSP of the ToDo portlet

Here, we've tried to use JSTL tags wherever possible. First, we retrieve the preferences map from the request and then get the array of ToDo's for the current selected date. We check whether the array is empty, which would mean no ToDo's are defined for the selected date. If the array isn't empty, we output all ToDo's. Last, we provide a convenience link to the Edit mode, where the user can add or remove ToDo's.

Writing the Edit JSP Code for the ToDo Portlet

Having created the view mode JSP, we next need to create the Edit mode JSP of the ToDo portlet, which shows the current ToDo's in a table and lets the user add a new ToDo or remove an existing ToDo. Listing 3.13 shows the edit mode JSP.

```
<%@ taglib uri='http://java.sun.com/portlet' prefix='portlet'%>
<%@ taglib uri='http://java.sun.com/jstl/core' prefix='c'%>
<jsp:useBean id="bean" class="
com.ibm.samples.portlets.calendar.ToDoBean" scope="request" />

<portlet:defineObjects/>

<P><B>Defined ToDo's</B></P>
<P>For date:   <c:out value="${bean.date}"/> </P>

<c:set var="prefsMap" value="${renderRequest.preferences.map}"/>

<form action="<portlet:actionURL portletMode="view"/>"  method= "post">
<table>
      <tr>
      <td>
          <B>Current ToDo's</B>
      </td>
      </tr>
      <c:set var="prefsMap" value="${renderRequest.preferences.map}"/>
      <c:if test="${not empty prefsMap[bean.date]}">
      <c:forEach var="ToDo" items="${prefsMap[bean.date]}">
          <tr><td><c:out value="${ToDo}" /></td>
              </tr>
      </c:forEach>
      </c:if>
</table>
<p></p>
<table>
  <tr>
    <td>
      <input name="ToDo" type="text">
    </td>
    <td>
```

Listing 3.13: Edit mode JSP of the ToDo portlet (Page of 1 of 2)

```
       <input name="add" type="submit" value="Add ToDo">
    </td>
    <td>
       <input name="remove" type="submit" value="Remove ToDo">
    </td>
  </tr>
</table>
</form>
<form action="<portlet:renderURL portletMode="view"/>"  method="GET">
  <input name="cancel"  type="submit" VALUE="Cancel">
</form>
```

Listing 3.13: Edit mode JSP of the ToDo portlet (Page of 2 of 2)

First, we create a table and loop through all currently defined ToDo's for the given date. Next, we create a table letting the user add or remove an item, and we provide the add and remove buttons. Note that we need a separate input field for removing a ToDo and can't add a link behind each ToDo in the table because we want to avoid using scriptlet code. Our approach is also rooted in the fact that the JSTL variable defined in the forEach loop can't be used to create portlet links, and thus there is no way currently to encode the ToDo stored in the ${ToDo} variable in a portlet remove link. Last, we have a cancel button that brings us back into the View mode without any changes. Because we don't perform any changes, we can implement this link as a render URL and use HTTP GET.

Now that you've seen all the code, let's bundle everything together into a portlet application in the next section.

Packaging the Portlet Application

To enable the Calendar and ToDo portlets to access the shared data in the session, we need to package both portlets into one portlet application because each portlet application, like every Web application, has its own session.

Creating the Deployment Descriptor for the Calendar Portlet

First, we create the portlet deployment descriptor (Listing 3.14). To make this descriptor as short as possible, we've added only the bare minimum. First, we define the Calendar portlet and specify that it supports only View mode. Second, we define the ToDo portlet and specify that it supports View and Edit mode.

83

```xml
<?xml version="1.0" encoding="UTF-8"?>
<portlet-app xmlns="http://java.sun.com/xml/ns/portlet/portlet-app_1_0.xsd"
version="1.0" xmlns:xsi="http://www.w3.org/2001/XMLSchema-instance"
xsi:schemaLocation="http://java.sun.com/xml/ns/portlet/portlet-
app_1_0.xsd http://java.sun.com/xml/ns/portlet/portlet-app_1_0.xsd">
        <portlet>
            <portlet-name>CalendarPortlet</portlet-name>
                <display-name>Calendar Portlet</display-name>
                <portlet-class>
                    com.ibm.samples.portlets.calendar.CalendarPortlet
                </portlet-class>
            <expiration-cache>-1</expiration-cache>
                <supports>
                        <mime-type>text/html</mime-type>
                <portlet-mode>VIEW</portlet-mode>
                </supports>

            <supported-locale>en</supported-locale>

        <portlet-info>
                <title>CalendarPortlet</title>
                <short-title>Calendar</short-title>
                <keywords>Calendar</keywords>
        </portlet-info>
    </portlet>

    <portlet>
        <portlet-name>ToDoPortlet</portlet-name>
                <display-name>ToDo Portlet</display-name>
                <portlet-class>
                    com.ibm.samples.portlets.calendar.ToDoPortlet
                </portlet-class>
            <expiration-cache>-1</expiration-cache>
                <supports>
                        <mime-type>text/html</mime-type>
                <portlet-mode>VIEW</portlet-mode>
                <portlet-mode>EDIT</portlet-mode>
                </supports>

            <supported-locale>en</supported-locale>

                <portlet-info>
                <title>ToDoPortlet</title>
                <short-title>ToDo</short-title>
                <keywords>ToDo</keywords>
                </portlet-info>
    </portlet>
</portlet-app>
```

Listing 3.14: Portlet deployment descriptor

Deploying and Running the Calendar Portlet Example

Before being able to run the example, we need to deploy it on WebSphere Portal (Chapter 2 describes how to perform this task). After deploying the Calendar portlet application and putting the Calendar and ToDo portlets on a page, we receive the result displayed in Figure 3.4.

Figure 3.4: The Calendar portlet application view

As you can see in the ToDo portlet, we selected the 10th of July 2006 as the date in the Calendar portlet. You can also see the two buttons with the render URLs in the Calendar portlet that set the month to the previous or next month. In the ToDo portlet, the current ToDo's for the 10th of July are displayed.

Adding a ToDo Item

To add a new ToDo for this day, we click the **Edit ToDo's** button shown in the figure. The ToDo portlet now renders the edit screen. Let's enter the new ToDo "Call Ron" in the input field, as shown in Figure 3.5.

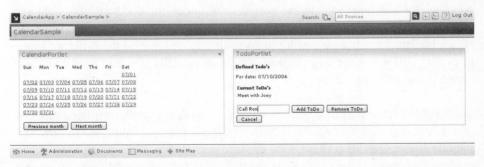

Figure 3.5: Adding a new ToDo in the ToDo portlet

85

The final step is to click the **Add ToDo** button. Figure 3.6 shows that the ToDo portlet now displays the new ToDo item at the end of the ToDo list.

Figure 3.6: View of the Calendar portlet application with a new ToDo item

SUMMARY

In this chapter, we covered the details of the portlet programming model. First, we explained the basic portlet life cycle with the two-phase action processing and rendering. Next, we looked at the different portlet modes and window states that tell the portlet what kind of content to render and how much real estate the portlet has to render that content.

After that, we covered the flyweight pattern, chosen to make portlets scale for large user numbers. This pattern results in different customization levels of the portlet data that can be changed in different end-user roles, such as in the Config, Edit_defaults, and Edit modes.

Next, we took a closer look at the portlet data model, the different persistent and transient states available to portlets, and which kind of data you should store in which bucket. Last, before getting to an example, we covered the different types of portlet URLs — the action, render, and resource URLs — and how you can create these different URLs.

We spent the latter part of the chapter creating an example that explains most of the Java Portlet API concepts we covered in the beginning. You learned how to include JSPs to render content, how to store portlet data in the portlet preferences, how to share data between two portlets via the application session scope, and how to leverage render parameters.

Now that we've laid down all the groundwork, let's get real in the next chapter by developing more complex, real-world portlets with database access.

REFERENCES

1. Abdelnur, A., and S. Hepper. JSR 168: The Java Portlet Specification. *http://jcp.org/en/jsr/detail?id=168.*

2. Gamma, E., R. Helm, R. Johnson, and J. Vlissides. *Design Patterns: Elements of Reusable Object-Oriented Software. Addison-Wesley*, 1995.

Chapter Four

Java Portlet API Code Patterns and Best Practices

After learning about the portlet programming model and creating a few examples showing how to leverage different parts of the model, you're now experienced enough to take a look at portlet patterns and best practices.

First, we'll walk you through patterns useful for portlets, beginning with the basic Model-View-Controller (MVC) pattern. Next, we'll look at different Web frameworks that can help you implement the MVC pattern, such as JavaServer Faces (JSF) and Struts. In the last part of the patterns section, we'll examine asynchronous and distributed patterns that permit better response times — for example, for portlets doing many computations or receiving data from slow back-end systems.

The second part of the chapter goes into the details of best practices for portlets. We'll start with how to best code your portlets and then look at best practices for JavaServer Pages (JSPs), which are included by the portlet. After dealing with these code artifacts, we'll give some more thought to how to store the different state information your portlet may have and how to internationalize your portlet. Last, we'll talk about how to best package your portlets, JSPs, and other elements into a portlet application.

JAVA PORTLET API CODE PATTERNS

In this section, we take a closer look at code patterns that are useful and proven for developing portlets. We start with the Model-View-Controller pattern, which is the basis of the portlet programming model. Next we explore some popular Web frameworks that can make your portlet development a lot easier. Last, we look at patterns for asynchronous and distributed operation of your portlets.

The MVC Pattern Applied to Portlets

You now know what portlets look like. They have different phases for processing actions and rendering content, and they have portlet modes and window states and a quite complex data model for storing and retrieving data. What are the programming patterns for portlets so we can start using them?

Implementing Application Logic and Presentation Markup Together

The simplest way to implement portlets that generate dynamic content is by generating content completely inside the portlet, a scenario depicted in Figure 4.1. How would the client request be processed in this pattern implementation?

First, in step 1, the client sends a page request to the portal server. The portal server identifies the portlets on the page and sends a request for each portlet to the portlet container (2). Now the portlet container sends a request to each targeted portlet (3). The portlet executes the controller logic and responds back to the portlet container (4). The portlet container then generates a response to the portal based on the portlet response (5), and finally the portal creates and returns to the client (6) a response consisting of the whole portal page with the content of all aggregated portlets.

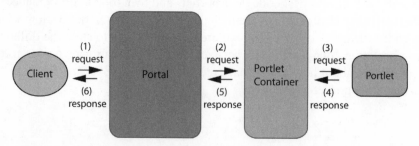

Figure 4.1: Simple portlet generating the markup in the portal

In this implementation, the portlet uses the data model to respond to the client's request, providing a consistent interface through the portal. This concept of implementing application logic and markup generation in one piece of code is appropriate only for very simple applications. It is too inflexible for real-life applications and doesn't appropriately separate responsibilities between Java programmers and content designers.

Separating Logic and Markup

Fortunately, there's a pattern that is still quite simple and resolves many of the shortcomings of the simplest solution: the Model-View-Controller pattern. This pattern, depicted in Figure 4.2, offers much more flexibility and provides a clear separation of responsibilities. In the illustration, the portlet controls the process in which a Java bean holds the data model and a JSP generates the markup.

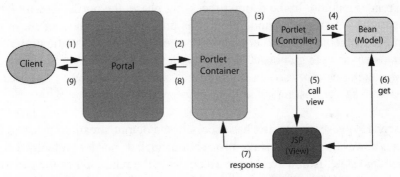

Figure 4.2:Portlet generating markup using the Model-View-Controller pattern

Here is how the request is processed with this pattern. The portlet now acts as controller, receiving all incoming requests (3) and controlling their execution. The new state that results in this business logic execution is stored in the model (4). The model, normally a Java bean, is responsible for storing the application data needed to produce the view. The controller then calls the appropriate view to create the response (5). The view, in most cases a JSP, is therefore responsible for generating the markup and uses the state stored in the model to create state-dependent output (6) and return it to the portlet container (7). The portlet container then gives back the portlet markup to the portal (8), which generates the complete portal page out of the different portlet fragments and returns the page to the client (9).

This separation of responsibilities allows programming and maintaining the controller code and the view code independently and by different persons (e.g., the portlet programmer and the content designer).

The MVC pattern has proven its usefulness for quite some time now in the servlet world, and the authors of the Java Portlet Specification have decided to design this pattern directly into the portlet programming model. Portlets support the MVC pattern in various ways — for instance, in the distinction made between action processing and rendering, in the fact that state changes are allowed only in action, and in the ability to include JSPs and a JSP tag library for using the basic portlet functionality in the JSP without the need for Java code.

The separation between action processing and rendering allows encapsulating state changes in the action processing while performing only the view selection in the render method. In the action processing phase, the portlet doesn't have access to the output stream and therefore is unable to generate content. In the action phase, the portlet can set a new persistent state (e.g., via the preferences), new transient state (e.g., portlet mode), window state, render parameter, or session state or can forward the action processing to another Web resource (e.g., a Web server hosting some legacy system).

In the render phase, the portlet has access to the output stream to produce the markup; however, access to state information, such as portlet preferences or the navigational state, is now read-only. To delegate the rendering of the content to JSPs, the portlet API provides a request dispatcher, letting the portlet include servlets and JSPs.

JSPs can access the portlet-specific objects and data via the portlet tag library that the Java Portlet Specification defines. These tags give access to the render request and response and the portlet context, and they allow creation of action and render URLs via tags.

Beginning with the calendar portlet application in Chapter 3, we've used either the MVC pattern for all our portlets or a Web framework based on the MVC pattern, such as the ones we talk about in the next section.

Web Frameworks

Web frameworks can make your life a lot easier. They give you all the boiler-plate code needed for many more advanced scenarios. The support that such Web frameworks offer ranges from controller frameworks to user interface (UI) widgets. In this section, we introduce some of the popular Web frameworks — JavaServer Faces, Struts, Spring and WebWorks — and explain how they relate to portlets.

JSF

JavaServer Faces is a framework for Web UI components and thus very impor-tant for portlet development. You can use JSF to build function-rich UIs for your portlets. JSR 252 (Reference 1) defines JSF V1.2, and Version 2.0, which will include Asynchronous JavaScript and XML (Ajax) support, was about to start at the writing of this book. JSF V1.2 is now also part of J2EE 5.0 and thus will be widely available, becoming the standard for Web UI components in the Java space. We cover JSF and its use in portlets in great detail in Chapter 6.

Struts

Struts is a popular servlet-based MVC framework that's been around for quite some time. This framework enables different groups of people to handle the design and implementation of large Web applications. Struts supports internationalization, a UI tag library, and form validation. It also supports a variety of view frameworks, including JSF, JSP, Velocity, and XML/XSLT (XSLT stands for Extensible Stylesheet Language Transformations), as well as a variety of model layers, including JavaBeans and Enterprise JavaBeans (EJBs).

Struts was created in 2000, long before portlets were invented, and thus is purely servlet-based and doesn't support portlets. To use Struts with portlets, you there-fore you need a special adapted version of Struts. Several different portlet Struts versions are available, but all are specific to portal products. For WebSphere Portal development, the following two are of interest:

- *WebSphere Portal Struts Portlet Framework:* This framework is shipped with WebSphere Portal and supports Struts V1.1. It also goes beyond the pure Struts functionality and lets your Struts application leverage WebSphere Portal extensions such as inter-portlet communication using the WebSphere Portal property broker.

- *Apache Struts Bridges Framework:* The Struts Bridges Framework is part of the Jetspeed 2 project, the Apache portal. It provides a bridge between portlets and Struts V1.2. This framework has moved all portal-specific dependencies into one file, so adapting this framework to a specific portal is easy.

The Apache Struts project recently changed and now contains two distinct frameworks: the Struts Action Framework and the Struts Shale Framework. Struts Action is the original request-based framework. Struts Shale, on the other hand, is a component-based controller framework that works with JavaServer Faces and reuses the JSF widgets, tag libraries, and Spring for providing beans to the model. Both frameworks are first-class citizens of the Apache Struts project.

Struts is hosted at Apache, and you can learn more about it by referring to Reference 2.

Spring

Spring is a lightweight framework for the model. It lets you use simple Java objects as the model and add persistence via injection. The framework is based on the Inversion of Control (IoC) principle, where the container takes care of code dependencies and injects the required code pieces. Reference 3 provides more information about Spring and the IoC principle.

As a framework for models, Spring can be used together with other MVC frameworks, such as JSF or Struts. There is also a Spring MVC framework (see Reference 3) that builds on top of the basic Spring framework and provides a full MVC framework. Version 2.0 of the Spring MVC framework added support for JSR 168 portlet development.

WebWork

WebWork is another MVC framework that is more lightweight than Struts. It lets you use the Spring framework for the model part and offers many additional features, such as validation, type conversion, internationalization, tag libraries, and Ajax-enabled widgets. For more information about WebWork, consult Reference 4

Version 2.2 of WebWork doesn't directly support JSR 168 portlets, but there are frameworks available, such as MVCPortlet (Reference 5) and WWPortlet (Reference 6), that provide bridges between portlets and WebWork.

The Struts Action Framework and WebWork are merging, so the Struts Action Framework 2.0 will be WebWork 2.3.

Which Framework to Choose?

As you may have expected, there is no silver bullet here, and the answer to the question of which framework to choose depends on your project and the environment in your company. Here some guidelines that may help you in your decision:

- Use JSF and Rational Application Developer if you start from scratch and aren't bound by any restrictions. JSF has very good support in the IBM tools and the WebSphere Portal runtime.

- Use Struts if you already have Struts applications and your developers know Struts inside out, or if you want to migrate a non-portlet–based Struts application to Portal.

- Use Spring for smaller projects if you want to have a simple and light-weight framework or as basis for your own framework.

- Take a look at WebWork if you liked Struts but want to move to a more modern framework and for some reason dislike JSF or have developers familiar with Struts.

Now that we've covered the different Web frameworks you can leverage for portlet development, let's look more closely at various patterns that let you distribute the processing of your portlets and even make it asynchronous.

Asynchronous and Distributed Patterns

The default portlet model has a request/response-based life cycle and runs inside one portlet container as explained in the previous chapters. This pattern is useful for many applications, but not for all. Some applications need to either be distributed or have asynchronous requests to provide a faster UI experience.

Figure 4.3 depicts the different architectures for distributing the content generation. The first one uses Web services within your portlets. With this approach, you can distribute the business logic, but you still need some logic in a local portlet that generates the markup out of the data returned by the Web service. The second pattern uses Web Services for Remote Portlets (WSRP), which lets you render the complete markup remotely and embed it in the portal page. The next two patterns move one step further and do the markup embedding on the client. The first one is Asynchronous JavaScript and HTML (AJAH), which retrieves markup fragments from another server asynchronously and embeds the markup into the current page. The second one is Asynchronous JavaScript and XML, or Ajax, which retrieves the data from a remote server, renders the markup directly on the client, and embeds it into the current page.

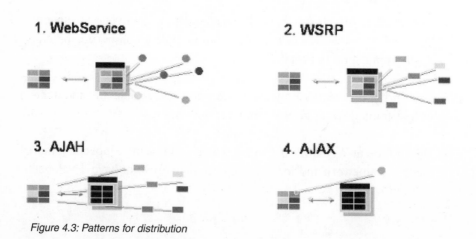

Figure 4.3: Patterns for distribution

Web Services

A Web service is any piece of code that communicates with other pieces of code over the Internet. Using Web services, software can be truly modularized even across networks. Application developers can concentrate on solutions relative to their business rather than thinking about the technical details of how to communicate and exchange data with various business partners. But Web services aren't a single masterpiece. Indeed, Web services are an amalgamation of several standard technologies.

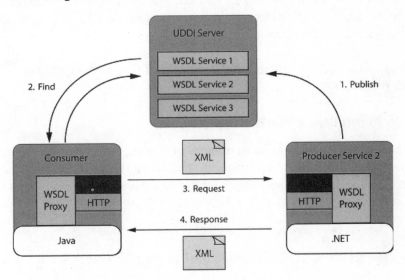

Figure 4..4: Web service scenario

First, a producer of a service — say, a stock quote service — registers its service in a global registry. In our example, this registry is a Universal Description, Discovery, and Integration (UDDI) directory. The producer registers the service interface description — the Web Services Description Language (WSDL) definition — and maybe additional business information about the service. An example would be a stock quote portlet that receives its stock quotes via a Web service. In this case, the WSDL would define that the service expects a company name as an input parameter and returns the stock quote for that company as an output parameter. Next, the portlet looks for a service that will enable it to render the user's preferred stock quotes. The portlet developer searches in the UDDI directory for such a service and finds the entry of our producer. The corresponding WSDL file is downloaded to the consumer, and a WSDL proxy is generated that translates between the Java and the XML world. When the portlet issues a request to the stock quote service, the WSDL proxy translates the request into a platform-independent XML document and connects via Simple Object Access Protocol (SOAP) over HTTP to the service. The service on the other side receives the XML request, and a WSDL stub translates the request into a .NET request in our example. The same mechanism is used for the response of the service, and our portlet finally gets the stock quote it requested. The portlet itself doesn't notice that it talked to a .NET service on the other side. This is the major benefit of using Web services: Your portlets can use services that don't need to be written in Java!

Now let's take a look at why this Web service stuff is something to know as a portlet programmer.

How Do Portlets Benefit from Web Services?

May be you're a Java programmer and now are asking yourself why a portlet programmer would want to use this additional technology that seems to be quite complex at first glance. There may be different reasons why portlets want to use Web services:

- The service may be written in a non-Java language.

- The service is available via the Internet, such as a stock service or a news service.

- The service must be maintained on a central server other than the one running the portal.

- The service may be of interest to applications other than just this portlet and thus should be programmed as a Web service to permit arbitrary applications to use the service.

All these are good reasons for Java programmers to use a Web service and make a deeper dive into this technology. Another reason: We'll leverage this knowledge for Web Services for Remote Portlets, a topic to which we now turn.

Web Services for Remote Portlets

As we've noted, Web services can be quite useful for portlets. However, this traditional way of including Web services in portlets also has some disadvantages, such as the need for proxy code in the portlet and the distribution of functionality between the service provider and the service consumer. In the stock quote service example, the portlet must understand the data format of the stock quote service and render the result accordingly. For portlets, a more elegant solution to this problem exists: Web Services for Remote Portlets (WSRP). WSRP builds on top of the base Web service technology we've described. (Reference 7 provides details about the WSRP specification.)

Running portlets on remote systems offers many benefits, ranging from distributing the workload to letting departments that contribute content to the overall company portal run and manage their own portal system. What do you need to run your Java portlets on remote machines? WSRP is the answer because WSRP provides the capability to aggregate content produced by portlets running on remote machines using different programming environments, such as J2EE and .NET. WSRP services are presentation-oriented, user-facing Web services that plug and play with portals or other applications. For example, you could have a desktop application, such as OpenOffice, display the content of a WSRP stock quote service.

Let's take a look at the differences between normal Web services (which we covered earlier) and WSRP and see how interactive, user-facing applications can benefit from presentation-oriented Web services. Imagine a service provider that provides data about stock quotes for a period of time to its customers. The customers can choose to obtain stock quote data over the course of a day, month, or year. Figure 4.5 shows the different approaches to this problem.

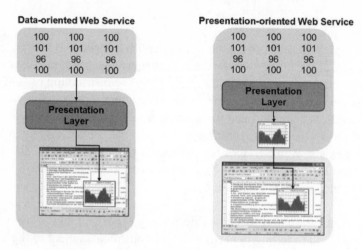

Figure 4.5: Data-oriented vs. presentation-oriented Web services

In the "traditional" Web service scenario, the Web service might provide a Web service operation called getStockQuoteFor(Symbol, Period, Interval), which takes as parameters the symbol of the stock, the period for which data is to be provided, and the interval of the value snapshots. As a result, the Web service delivers an array of float values representing the quotes over the course of time. An interactive application that wants to provide a stock-quote chart to its end users must provide the complete presentation layer that enables the end user to interact with the remote service. For example, it needs to render the chart based on the data obtained from the remote Web service, add navigational elements that let the user select stock symbols and choose between the various periods, and handle failures and present them to the user accordingly.

When using presentation-oriented Web services, a service provider would provide a WSRP service that offers a remote portlet called StockQuoteChart. This remote portlet doesn't just provide plain data that must be interpreted and rendered by the client but instead provides the presentation layer directly. This approach enables the client to integrate the remote service in a straightforward manner into its user interface without the need to develop any user interface parts specific to the remote service. Interaction with the user interface fragments of the Web service are forwarded to the server side and handled there. Results of the interaction are then again provided as user interface fragments back to the client. This also means that you don't need to deploy any specific code on the consumer and that the producer is in full control of the code and can manage and maintain the code at its own pace. This scenario can be very helpful in large companies with central IT departments that don't want to host every portlet; small departments can provide their portlets company-wide as WSRP services.

The close alignment between the JSR 168 specification and the WSRP specification lets JSR portlets act as WSRP services without requiring you to specifically program the portlets for WSRP. This means you get your remote portlets for free once you have a JSR 168 portlet written! It's just an administrative task in the portal to publish a JSR 168 portlet as WSRP service. Due to this alignment, it's also possible to include any WSRP service via a JSR 168 proxy portlet into a JSR 168–compliant portal. The proxy portlet implements a WSRP consumer and proxies the local calls to the WSRP producer. This way, a J2EE portal can easily integrate portlet services from other platforms, such as .NET. Both of these abilities, to integrate WSRP services via a JSR 168 proxy portlet and to publish any JSR 168 portlet as a WSRP service, are supported in WebSphere Portal.

AJAH

Asynchronous JavaScript and HTML gives portlets the ability to update all or parts of their markup asynchronously without a full page refresh. This approach is typically much faster than a full page refresh and thus provides a better user experience. A typical use example for AJAH is retrieving e-mails from a mail server. Figure 4.6 depicts a typical flow of such an AJAH request.

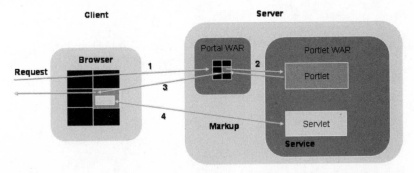

Figure 4.6: AJAH request served by servlet that is referenced from the portlet code

On the first full page refresh, all portlets are rendered, including our AJAH portlet (steps 1–3). The user interacts with the portlet, and, as a result, the portlet wants to update parts of its markup by sending an asynchronous XMLHttpRequest to a servlet serving the markup (step 4). The servlet is necessary because otherwise the portlet has no means in JSR 168 to issue a request that doesn't result in a full page refresh. That markup then gets embedded into the current page via JavaScript that inserts the markup in the browser Document Object Model (DOM) that represents the current page.

As you can see, using AJAH with portlets currently has some limitations due to the fact that the markup must be served via a servlet:

- The markup generation can't leverage portlet context information, such as portlet mode, window state, render parameters, and portlet preferences. All required information would be passed either via the session or as a request parameter.

- The returned markup can't contain any portlet URLs because the portlet response isn't available in the servlet.

- The AJAH request can't change any portlet state beyond the application session scope because the portlet request and response aren't available.

These limitations currently restrict the use of AJAH (and Ajax, which we look at next) in portlets, but the Java Portlet Specification 2.0 (JSR 286) will address these issues. For more information about JSR 286, see Appendix A.

Ajax

Asynchronous JavaScript and XML goes a step beyond AJAH and transmits not HTML markup but data in XML form via asynchronous requests. and the markup is rendered on the client via JavaScript. Figure 4.7 depicts the flow of an Ajax call.

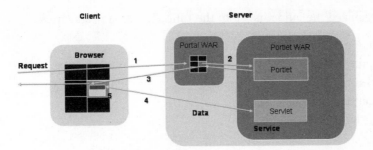

Figure 4.7: Ajax request served by a servlet and rendered on the browser via JavaScript

The flow looks very similar to the AJAH calls but has an additional step at the end to really generate the markup (step 5). As with AJAH, the first request renders the complete page, and subsequent interactions with the portlet generate XMLHttpRequest calls to retrieve XML data from a servlet. Now, the portlet needs to generate markup based on the XML data and insert that markup into the current browser DOM.

The advantage of Ajax compared with AJAH is that the generation of the markup is offloaded from the server to the client. The drawback is that generating that markup is quite complex unless you're using some additional framework, such as Dojo. (For more details about Ajax and Ajax frameworks, see Chapter 14.)

As in the AJAH case, using Ajax with portlets has the some limitations due to the fact that the markup must be served via a servlet. A typical use example for Ajax is paging through lists containing data retrieved from a database.

ADOPTING PORTLET BEST PRACTICES

Now that we've covered the basic patterns for portlet development and you've seen some real portlets coming into life, in this section we provide some best practices that will enable you to write more efficient, more maintainable, and higher-quality portlet code. Remember, though, that guidelines are always for the 90 percent case, and there are always exceptions where one of these rules may not apply. Therefore, use these best practices as rules of thumb rather than as something carved in stone.

We've organized the guidelines into the following broad categories:

- coding portlets
- coding JSPs
- persistent and transient data use
- internationalization
- portlet application packaging

Coding Portlets

Beyond the normal Java-related best practices, such as using Javadoc comments, there are some things specific to portlet development that we'll cover here. You can find the basic definition of the portlet programming model in the Java Portlet Specification (Reference 8).

Use the MVC Pattern and Frameworks

Use the Model-View-Controller pattern, either directly from the portlet by passing data to the view (JSP) as a bean in the request and including the JSP or via additional frameworks, such as Struts or JSF. This approach will yield maintainable and extensible applications and save you lots of time and money later on.

Don't Store Data in Instance Variables

A portlet exists as a singleton instance within the Java Virtual Machine (JVM) of the portlet container. Therefore, a single memory image of the portlet processes all requests and must be thread-safe. Data stored in instance variables will be accessible across requests and across users and can collide with other requests. Pass data to internal methods as parameters. There are other ways to store data across requests, as we've explained, such as using the session or the render parameters.

Include Version Information

To enable portal administrators to differentiate between portlet application versions and provide update support, declare the version of your portlet application in the META-INF/MANIFEST.MF using the Implementation-Version attribute.

Apply the Java Product Versioning Specification's recommendation for the version string by using *major.minor.micro*, where

- major version numbers identify significant functional changes
- minor version numbers identify smaller extensions to the functionality
- micro versions are even finer-grained versions

These version numbers are ordered, with higher numbers specifying newer versions. This way, you can provide portlet updates that are deployed correctly as new versions of your portlet.

Categorize the Portlet State Early in the Design Phase

As we've mentioned, the JSR 168 specification supports different kind of states. The portlet programmer should, very carefully and early on, decide the category of information for each state. The categories are navigational state, session state, and persistent state.

- Use navigational state for all view-related data that will let the user navigate forward and backward using the browser buttons. The scope of navigational state information is the current request. Examples of navigational state information include the current selected article in a news portlet and the current selected stock quote for which the portlet should render more details.

- Use session state for all information that is relevant for the duration of the user session. Don't use session state as a caching store. An example of session state information is the content of a shopping cart.

- Use persistent state for all information that has a lifetime beyond the current user session. Use this state to store customization data and user-specific personalization data. Examples include the server from which to retrieve stock quotes, the default list of stock quotes to display, and the news topics of interest to a specific user.

Avoid Using J2EE Roles

Declare J2EE roles in your portlet application only if absolutely necessary. J2EE roles are separate from the portal roles and need to be managed separately from those roles. Therefore, you should use J2EE roles only to perform access control in portlet applications if the user profile information isn't sufficient.

Always Use P3P User Profile Attributes

The Platform for Privacy Preferences (P3P) defines ways users can control the privacy of personal information on the Internet. One part of this specification defines attribute names for all common user information. Use these P3P user profile attributes whenever possible for accessing user attributes. (For more details about the P3P specification, see Reference 9.) When the portlet needs to access user profile attributes, such as the user name or address, it should always use the keys that P3P defines for these attributes. This practice reduces the administrative effort when deploying the portlet because the P3P attributes are automatically mapped to the attributes in the current user directory, whereas the portal deployer must manually map attribute names not in the P3P list. Appendix D of the Java Portlet Specification lists the P3P attributes.

Use URL Encoding

Use URL encoding for resources inside the portlet application WAR file to permit the portal to proxy resources inside the portlet application WAR file. Thus, you should always encode resource links using the encodeURL method.

Don't Spawn Unmanaged Threads from Portlets

Spawning new threads from portlets results in unpredictable behavior. At present, J2EE doesn't provide an interface for portlets or servlets to spawn new threads. Therefore, managed threads can only be created using the proprietary IBM WebSphere Application Server AsyncBeans bean interface by the portlet or the WorkManager specified and supported by IBM and BEA (see Reference 10 for details).

Optimize for Parallel Portlet Rendering

To allow a portal to render a portlet in parallel with other portlets on the page in the render phase, the portlet should

- expect IOExceptions when writing to the OutputStream or PrintWriter and act accordingly. If a portlet takes too much time to render its content, the portal may cancel the rendering of this portlet, resulting in an IOException when the portlet tries to write to the OutputStream or PrintWriter after the portal has canceled the rendering of the portlet.

- periodically check, in methods expected to take many computation cycles, to see whether the flush method of the OutputStream or PrintWriter throws an IOException. If the flush method throws such an exception, the portal has canceled the rendering of the portlet, and the portlet should terminate its current computation.

Use HTTP GET and POST Correctly

The render phase shouldn't change any state but should provide a replayable generation of the markup. Therefore, you should always handle HTTP POST requests that submit forms in an action by creating an ActionURL, not in render. The only exception to this rule is when the form doesn't consist of any parameters (such as a cancel button) or when the form only updates navigational state. The second case, render URLs being used for Form POSTs with parameters, isn't part of JSR 168 but works in WebSphere Portal V5.1.0.1 and V6. You should always encode Form POSTs that require server state changes as action URLs. For more information about the use of GET and POST, see Reference 11.

Ensure Minimal Portlet Functionality for Unsupported Vendor-Specific Portal Extensions

If your portlet uses extensions specific to a portal vendor, you should also code it to run in a plain JSR 168 environment with no extensions. Degraded functionality is acceptable when running in such an environment. The portlet should check the support extensions of the calling portal at runtime via the PortalContext.getProperty method and act accordingly.

Avoid Naming Confusion Between Portlets and Servlets

Don't name portlets and servlets the same thing in one Web application. Tools and portals may use the portlet name to identify a portlet in a Web application and can get confused if a servlet with the same name also exists in the application.

Coding JSPs

The best practices given here for coding JSPs constitute coding guidelines to consider when writing JSPs that are included from portlets. The emphasis here is on HTML; however, similar rules apply to other markup languages as well.

Honor Portlet-Specific Markup Restrictions

The portal server aggregates the markup of several different portlets into one document that it sends back to the client. Thus, JSPs should only contain markup fragments to allow this aggregation. All markup tags that belong to the document can't be used by the portlet. For more details about tags that the JSP isn't allowed to use, see the Java Portlet Specification.

Use Standard Style Classes

Use the style classes recommended by section PLT.C of the Java Portlet Specification to give the portal page a consistent look and feel across portlet applications provided by different parties. Only if portlets use these predefined styles will whole pages aggregated out of different portlets from different portlet providers be displayed to the portal end user with a consistent interface.

Namespace Portlet-Specific Resources on a Page

Uniform Resource Identifiers (URIs), HTML element name attributes, and JavaScript resources must be namespace-encoded. Because many portlets can exist on a page and it's possible more than one portlet will produce content with like-named elements, there is a risk of namespace collision between elements. To avoid functional problems with the page that might result, use the

<portlet:namespace/> tag to encode such resources with the portlet instance name. For example, to a JavaScript function:

```
<DIV name="javascript:<portlet:namespace/>funct1">
```

Use Tag Libraries

Use tag libraries whenever possible. Encapsulating Java code within taglibs not only lets you reuse common view functions, but it also it keeps the JSPs clean and makes them more like normal HTML pages, letting the page designer concentrate on layout and decoration and reducing the possibility of breaking the embedded Java code. For example, use the Java Standard Tag Library (JSTL) instead of Java code. JSTL defines many commonly needed tags for conditions, iterations, URLs, internationalization, and formatting.

Use IFrames Only as a Last Resort

Use IFrames with caution. IFrames are an easy way to include external content within a portlet, but they undermine the whole portlet principle because the portlet API is just tunneled. Thus, you should use IFrames only for very special cases, such as surfacing legacy applications. Otherwise, you'll end up re-creating a second portal in your IFrames, and all the money you spent on your portal system in the first place will be wasted because the portal integration ends at the IFrames. All links rendered in the IFrames won't contain the navigational state of the other portlets on the page, so clicking on these links will result in losing the state for all other portlets on the page.

Protect Against Cross-Site Scripting

To protect the portal site from malicious code that a user might enter in an input field of your JSP, be sure to encode data entered by the user before writing them to the output stream again. If you don't do this, a user could enter some JavaScript code that is executed when written to the output steam without encoding it. This kind of attack isn't new; it's known for all kinds of Web applications and was reported as *cross-site scripting* by CERT in 2000 (see Reference 12). A simple solution to protect against this attack is to use the Java URLEncode class to encode user input before writing it to the output stream. (For more advanced solutions, see Reference 13.)

Persistent and Transient Data Use

As we mentioned earlier, portlets have access to different kinds of states. The portlet programmer should, very carefully and early on, decide the category of information for each state to most efficiently use these different categories.

SAVE NAVIGATIONAL STATE CONSERVATIVELY

Keep navigational state information to a minimum wherever possible because the portal must aggregate the navigational state of all portlets on the current page and normally stores it in the URL. To keep the URLs small, you should therefore minimize the navigational state that the portlet stores in the render parameters. Keep in mind that most small devices support only a very limited URL length. Of course, storing this information in session isn't an option because that approach is even more expensive. However, if some of the data isn't pure navigational state and the portlet can re-create it, you should store that data in a cache.

Also, program the portlet in such a manner that it takes into account the request nature of the navigational state. This principle means that with the next request to the portlet, all previous navigational state may not be retransmitted to the portlet and the portlet should still produce some meaningful output (e.g., by using a bookmark).

If the navigational state of a portlet gets larger than a specific threshold, the state of that portlet is no longer stored in the URL but instead is moved to the portal session, and only a reference to that state is stored in the URL. This results in a loss of the bookmark capability. You can customize the threshold in WebSphere Portal in the properties via the com.ibm.portal.state.keymanager.renderparameters.threshold constant.

Manage Session State Issues

Limit the use of the portlet session for storing state information. The portlet session is a convenient place to store global data that is user- and portlet-specific and spans portlet requests. However, there is considerable overhead in managing the session, both in CPU cycles and heap consumption. You therefore should store data in the portlet session only if the data is user-specific and can't be re-created by any other means. For example, don't store parsed configuration data (from portlet preferences) in the portlet session, because it can be re-created at any time. Data that can be re-created should be stored using a cache service and not in the session.

Prevent temporary sessions from being generated in the JSP. Add the JSP page directive <%@ page session="false" %> to the JSP to prevent temporary sessions from being created by the JSP compiler, if none already exist. This technique helps guard against attempts to use the session to store global data if the session won't exist past the current request. You'll need to be sure the portlet session exists before trying to use it.

Be aware of session timeouts. Because each portlet application is a separate Web application, each portlet application will have its own session. This results in different timeouts for different portlets on a page because the user may interact with some portlets more frequently than others.

Use attribute prefixing for global session scope. Portlets can write into the Web application session without any prefixing of the portlet container by using the application scope portlet session setting. You can use this setting to share data between a portlet and other portlets or servlets of the same Web application and/or between several entities created out of the same portlet. The portlet must take into account that several entities of it may exist on the same page and that it may need to prefix the global setting to avoid other entities over-writing this setting. One convenient way to do this is provide a read-only portlet preference entry called session-prefix that the administrator can set in the Config mode.

Persistent State

Use portlet initialization parameters to store static information not meant to be changed by administrators or users. You specify this data in the portlet deployment descriptor using the init-param tag, and it is read-only for the portlet. The portlet can access the data via PortletConfig.getInitParameter. An example is declaring the JSP names and directories used for rendering the different modes. This allows changing the JSP names and directory structure without the need to recompile the portlet.

Use read-only portlet preferences to store configuration data. Configuration data (e.g., the name of the news server) is user-independent and should be changed only by administrators in the Config portlet mode. Declare this data in the portlet deployment descriptor using the preference tag together with the read-only tag. The portlet should also provide one or more Config screens to permit the administrator to change this setting. Listing 4.1 shows an example of how to define the support for the Config mode in the portlet.xml deployment descriptor.

```
<portlet-app>
  ...
  <portlet>
  ...
    <supports>
      ...
      <portlet-mode>config</portlet-mode>
    </supports>
  </portlet>
  ...
  <custom-portlet-mode>
    <name>config</name>
  </custom-portlet-mode>
</portlet-app>
```

Listing 4.1: Defining Config mode support in the portlet.xml deployment descriptor

Use writeable portlet preferences to store customization data. Customization data is user-specific data that the user can set to customize the portlet output (e.g., news he or she is interested in) via the Edit mode. You should declare this data in the deployment descriptor with some meaningful default values as writeable portlet preferences. The portlet should provide one or more Edit screens to let the user change these values.

Write persistent data only in the action phase. The portlet must change persistent state information only in the action phase. The render phase must be completely replayable to avoid issues with the browser back button and bookmark ability.

Use String arrays for preference lists because preferences can be either Strings or String arrays. If you have a list of preference values for one key, using String arrays makes things easier to manage.

Internationalization

If you stick to the following recommendations, you'll enable the portal to fully leverage the internationalization provided by your portlet.

Use Resource Bundles

Use a resource bundle per portlet to internationalize the portlet output, and declare this resource bundle in the portlet deployment descriptor. All displayable strings should be stored in resource bundles and fetched using the ResourceBundle Class or in JSPs via the JSTL internationalization tags. The resource bundles should be organized by language under the portlet's WEB-INF/classes directory, and the portlet should always provide a default resource bundle with only the base name to enable the fallback mechanism for locales not supported by the portlet. This approach will make your portlet very robust and easily maintainable in the future.

Instead of using the local system's locale for referencing a resource bundle, always use the locale specified on the render request in order to honor the portal-wide language settings the user has defined.

Reference Preference Data

Define preference names as reference names to the localized name in the resource bundle. The names of the preferences in the portlet deployment descriptor should be references under which the localized name for each preference is stored in the resource bundle. The portlet should use the naming convention defined in the portlet specification for resource bundle entries. This practice will also permit external tools or generic portlets to change the preference data and display the preferences in a localized manner.

Define Supported Locales

Define the locales that the portlet supports in the deployment descriptor. Here, the portlet should define all locales it supports using the <supported-locale> element. This technique enables the portal to show users only portlets for locales they have selected.

Portlet Application Packaging

As we noted earlier, portlets and their resources are packaged together in portlet applications. However, portlet applications should define a meaningful set of portlets to leverage the provided application concept.

Use the Library Pattern

One common pattern that also applies to portlet applications is the library pattern. This pattern suggests that you make common functions available externally to portlets. If the portlet contains common functions that are replicated across several portlets, consider isolating those functions, making them externally accessible by the portlets. The easiest way to do this is to build another JAR file of the common classes and place the file either in each portlet application or in a location that is in each portlet application classpath, such as the shared directory of the application server.

Group Portlets in a Meaningful Way

Another important rule is to group portlets that operate on the same back-end data into one portlet application. In doing so, you permit the sharing of configuration settings — such as the back-end server name, user ID and password, and data such as the current date the user is interested in — between the portlets of the application.

Packaging portlets this way lets you separate portlets that don't relate to each other from each other via the Web application sandbox and enables related portlets to leverage sharing mechanisms, such as the session, that are provided inside the Web application.

SUMMARY

In this chapter, you learned about the most important portlet patterns and best practices. We began with the basic Model-View-Controller pattern that is used in nearly every portlet that goes beyond a simple "hello world." Next, we took a look at different Web frameworks based on the MVC pattern that can make your life easier, along with their portlet support. We'll cover one of these frameworks, JSF, in more detail in Chapter 6. In the last part of the pattern section, you learned how you can leverage distributed patterns with Web services, WSRP, and asynchronous patterns, such as AJAH and Ajax, to make portlets more responsive. Also covered were the current restrictions you'll face with the Java Portlet Specification 1.0. Appendix A of this book provides a preview of what comes next with the Java Portlet Specification 2.0, which also will extend what you can do with AJAH and Ajax in portlets.

In the second part of the chapter, you learned the best practices for developing portlets and the JSPs included by the portlet, how and where to store the persistent and transient data of your portlet, how to internationalize your portlet, and finally how to group your portlets into portlet applications.

Together with what you learned about the portlet programming model in earlier chapters, you have now the basic knowledge for writing portlets. We can therefore move on to more advanced topics in the next chapter, such as supporting different languages and markups in your portlet that go beyond the internationalization best practices covered here.

REFERENCES

1. JSR 252: JavaServer Faces 1.2: *http://jcp.org/en/jsr/detail?id=252*.

2. Struts: *http://struts.apache.org*.

3. Spring Framework: *http://www.springframework.org*.

4. WebWork MVC framework: *http://www.opensymphony.com/webwork*.

5. MVCPortlet WebWork portlet bridge: *http://www.nabh.com/projects/mvcportlet*.

6. WWPortlet WebWork portlet bridge: *http://wwportlet.sourceforge.net*.

7. Web Services for Remote Portlets (WSRP): *http://www.oasis-open.org/committees/tc_home.php?wg_abbrev=wsrp*.

8. JSR 168: Java Portlet Specification 1.0: *http://jcp.org/en/jsr/detail?id=168*.

9. Platform for Privacy Preferences (P3P) specification: *http://www.w3.org/P3P*.

10. CommonJ WorkManager specification: *http://www-128.ibm.com/developerworks/library/specification/j-commonj-sdowmt/index.html*.

11. Use of HTTP GET and POST: *http://www.w3.org/2001/tag/doc/whenToUseGet.html*.

12. Cross-site scripting advisory at CERT: *http://www.cert.org/advisories/CA-2000-02.html*.

13. Sharma, A. "Prevent a Cross-Site Scripting Attack." IBM DeveloperWorks, February 3, 2004. *http://www-128.ibm.com/developerworks/web/library/wa-secxss/?ca=dnt-55*.

Chapter Five

Languages and Markups

Portal developers frequently face a requirement to support multiple languages. For Internet applications, the global reach of the Web makes it possible for users of many different languages to access your Web site. Even within a given geographic context, you might determine a need to support multiple languages to reach a population that doesn't speak the native tongue.

When confronted with multiple language requirements, some Web site designers decide to establish a different Web site or application for each language or geographic area. This approach can be a good one if broad differences exist in the structure of the site or application. Of course, the tradeoff comes in the duplicate development and maintenance efforts. More typically, the preferred choice is to translate the existing content into other languages. In this chapter, we discuss how WebSphere Portal helps support multiple languages in terms of runtime execution, and we examine the tooling support and utilities available to assist with development tasks.

Internationalization (sometimes abbreviated as "i18n," where the number 18 signifies the number of letters the abbreviation omits from the word "internationalization") refers to the design and development of software so that it can adapt to different *locales* — in other words, to the various conventions associated with the language and other preferences of a geographic region. Locales, for example, determine representations such as the language and date and currency formats. The task of modifying software to implement the conventions of a locale is known as *localization* (sometimes referred to as "L10n").

As internationalization has become a bigger issue and Web site and portal development more sophisticated, better standards have developed around the topic, giving developers a consistent approach with which to implement language support.

INTERNATIONALIZATION AND LOCALIZATION

Those in the development community sometimes use the terms internationalization and localization interchangeably. However, a distinction exists between preparing for differences in locale preferences and implementing those changes. To clarify the concepts, let's define these two terms in a bit more detail.

In a broad sense, internationalization means to design and build an application in such a way that you can adapt it to different languages. You build the system so that new language or localization information can be added to it and the application can run with no changes. Text information such as field labels and button names is external to the program so that this information can be read from a source at runtime. Technically, this source is called to retrieve externalized strings from within a program at runtime. In addition to externalizing text within the application, you can externalize the information used to format date, time, and currencies to provide for localization.

Localization builds on internationalization by actually adapting an application for a specific region or locale. In this step, you perform tasks such as translating text to a different language or dialect and providing the specific information required to format numbers and currency within a locale. Localization is more culturally sensitive than straight internationalization, whose focus is broader. Localization is also more comprehensive than simple language translation. Taking into account the nuances of a specific locale may well determine a company's success in that area.

WEBSPHERE PORTAL'S LANGUAGE SUPPORT

WebSphere Portal provides built-in language support that enables users to view a portal in their preferred language. We'll examine some of this functionality as we go, but you can also access much of the information available about portal language in IBM's WebSphere Portal Information Center, which is installed on your portal server and also available at *http://publib.boulder.ibm.com/-infocenter/wpdoc/v6r0/index.jsp*.

WebsSphere Portal itself is enabled for internationalization and is translated into 30 different languages. For a complete list of supported languages, see the InfoCenter. Similarly, portlets can support one or more languages, with a defined default. Later in this chapter, we'll discuss how to enable a portlet for multiple languages.

To set the default language for WebSphere Portal, you use the Global Settings administrative portlet. Naturally, the language displayed to a user will be based on the locale identified for the user. If you use the Portal enrollment process to register users, you can specify the default language selection for the user there. Last, you define the language selection for a user's interaction with Portal using the following selection criteria:

1. the preferred language for the current request, which you can get and set via the LocaleAccessor of the portal state Service Programming Interface (SPI)

2. the preferred language registered for the user

3. the language specified in the user's browser (the first if multiple languages are defined), if supported

4. the Portal default language

5. if the portlet doesn't support the selected language, the portlet's default language

Portal uses the ISO 639 Codes for the Representation of Names of Languages to represent localized resources. The names for directories containing language-dependent resources follow the ISO 639 naming convention.

PORTLET LANGUAGE SUPPORT DEFINITION

You can define portlets to support several different locales or languages, and each portlet must have its own default language. You can specify this information directly within the portlet deployment descriptor file (portlet.xml) that's deployed as part of the portlet WAR file. A better solution is to have the deployment descriptor point to a resource bundle, within which you define the language-specific text strings the portlet uses.

In WebSphere Portal 6.0, the portlet deployment descriptor for the Banner Ad portlet is an example of putting the text strings directly in the .xml file. Listing 5.1 shows a section of that descriptor.

```
<concrete-portlet-app uid="com.ibm.wps.banner.1">
  <portlet-app-name>Banner Ad</portlet-app-name>
  <concrete-portlet href="Portlet_com.ibm.wps.banner">
   <portlet-name>Banner Ad</portlet-name>
   <default-locale>en</default-locale>
...
   <language locale="en">
    <title>Banner Ad</title>
    <title-short>Banner Ad</title-short>
    <description>Create and display a banner ad</description>
    <keywords>Banner, ad, advertisement, display, WPS</keywords>
   </language>
   <language locale="es">
    <title>Anuncio de mensaje de cabecera</title>
    <title-short>Anuncio de mensaje de cabecera</title-short>
    <description>Crear y visualizar un anuncio de mensaje de
    cabecera</description>
    <keywords>Cabecera, mensaje, anuncio, visualizar, WPS</keywords>
   </language>
...
  </concrete-portlet>
</concrete-portlet-app>
```

Listing 5.1: Portlet deployment descriptor containing translated language strings

This example shows just two of the supported languages (English and Spanish). As you can see, the portlet.xml file can become quite large and unwieldy with all the translated language strings for the portlet title, short title, description, and keywords.

With JSR 168, the deployment descriptor supports the use of resource bundles to remove the translated strings from the portlet.xml file. The example in Listing 5.2, from WebSphere Portal's Document Manager portlet, shows the references to the resource bundle and definition of the supported locales.

```
<supported-locale>en</supported-locale>
<supported-locale>ar</supported-locale>
<supported-locale>ca</supported-locale>
<supported-locale>cs</supported-locale>
...

<supported-locale>zh_TW</supported-locale>
<resource-bundle>nls.pdmwar</resource-bundle>
```

Listing 5.2: Portlet deployment descriptor pointing to resource bundle

Here, the translated strings for the portlet title, short title, and keywords are contained in the respective language resource bundle. Not shown in this example is the portlet description, which, if specified, remains in the descriptor file as translated strings.

Portlet Internationalization

Specifying which languages a portlet will support is only the first step in the process of internationalizing your portlet. You also need to enable the portlet to support multiple languages and provide the translated text for each language. To demonstrate how you can apply these techniques to content rendered directly from a portlet, let's consider a portlet that uses JavaServer Pages (JSPs) to render its content.

Two basic approaches exist to enabling translation of content rendered from a JSP. You can translate the entire JSP file into the supported languages (with a specific JSP for each language), or you can retrieve text strings rendered by the JSP from a language-specific resource bundle. In the latter approach, you extract the text string from the JSP, replacing it with a reference to the text string that you add to a resource bundle. Then you translate the resource bundles, and as long as your JSP knows which resource bundle to reference, the portlet application will render the appropriate language content.

Why might you want to translate an entire JSP? If the JSP contains mostly text — one that supports the portlet help function, for example — it makes sense to translate those files completely.

LOCALIZED JSPS

The IBM portlet container supports translated JSPs in the implementation of its implicit search order for JSP files. With this support, you need make no changes to the invocation of the JSP in the portlet controller. Translated files are stored in appropriate directories, and the portlet container searches them in a predefined order that makes distinctions for languages, locales, and browser versions. Using this search-order capability, the portlet container can locate translated JSPs in the appropriate directories (named for their supported language) and select the correct JSP file based on the current locale settings.

With JSR 168 (i.e., standard API) portlets, this JSP search mechanism doesn't exist. For portlets that use this API, you can implement a similar effect in your portlet controller code by checking the current locale and explicitly using that result to generate the path definition of the JSP file before executing the request dispatcher include.

RESOURCE BUNDLES

The second approach to translating JSP content is to use a single JSP and simply externalize the string and formatting information contained in it. This technique greatly simplifies the controller behavior and lets the JSP do all the work of determining which language it will display and how it will format information.

When you externalize strings to a separate file, you group them by language. You can create resource bundles for all the different languages you may support and call the appropriate one at runtime based on the preferred language or locale.

The naming convention for resource bundles is

```
[bundle]_[language]_[country]_[variant].properties
```

The ISO 639 standard dictates the language codes of most languages.

Using this approach simplifies the maintenance effort for a portlet. Editing text strings is much easier than editing a JSP and is a task that can be delegated to individuals other than developers.

The resource bundle must be referenced in the portlet deployment descriptor (as in the snippet of the file you saw in Listing 5.2), and the portlet can access it at runtime by using the PortletConfig.getResourceBundle method.

JAVA STANDARD TAG LIBRARY

Beginning with Version 5, WebSphere Portal started making the migration toward a common JSP tag library for development of portal applications. The JSP Standard Tag Library (JSTL) is a comprehensive set of tags available to standardize and simplify the way we create JSP pages by providing support for conditionals and iterators, accessing URL resources, XML processing, database access (SQL), and internationalization and text formatting. JSTL is a standard from the Java Community Process (JCP). The specification is available from JCP at *http://jcp.org/aboutJava/communityprocess/final/jsr052*.

Using the fmt tag from this tag library, you can easily retrieve text strings from language-specific resource bundles. We'll look at the invocation of this tag more closely as we work through an example.

INTERNATIONALIZATION AND LOCALIZATION FOR THE CALENDAR PORTLET

Let's see how the techniques we've talked about work in the context of the calendar portlet we created in Chapter 3. The source code for that portlet is available, and for this discussion we'll work through the internationalization and localization changes within Rational Application Developer (RAD).

First, we need to specify that the portlet will support multiple languages and identify which languages it will support. To get started, edit the portlet deployment descriptor in the calendar portlet project, and select CalendarPortlet. In the **Supported Locales** section, click **Add**, and then select the two-character code of the language you want to support in addition to English (Figure 5.1). For this example, we'll choose to add Spanish, but you could select a different language. The two-character code defined by the ISO 639 naming standard for Spanish is "es".

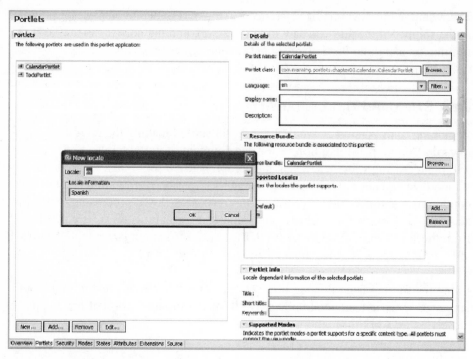

Figure 5.1: Adding a locale

After making your selection, you'll see the language name for the selected locale code. When you save the deployment descriptor, the supported language change is made to the portlet.xml file. Assuming you've already defined a resource bundle for this portlet, when you add the new language to the deployment descriptor, a corresponding resource bundle file is created in the project for the new language (Figure 5.2).

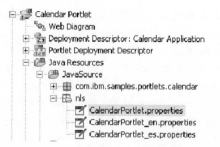

Figure 5.2: Calendar portlet resource bundles

Note that these resource bundles are initially not empty. The portlet title, short title, and any portlet keywords are specified here. Because Portal is enabled for internationalization, those text strings should also be rendered in the appropriate language. To support this functionality, that text is held in properties files, with a different properties file for each supported language. Portal selects the properties file that matches the language preference and renders the text in the correct language. We'll use this technique of language-specific properties files (actually managed as resource bundles, as you'll see later) for translatable text in our Java code and JSP files.

JSP Modifications

Next, let's look at the changes needed for the JSP files to use text strings from the resource bundles. We'll use tags from the JSTL to retrieve translated text from resource bundles. An IBM-provided custom tag named "text" from the portal tag library provides this same function, but it is deprecated in favor of the JSTL tags. To learn more about the use of JSTL tags in JSPs, see the InfoCenter.

Let's start with the viewDate.jsp in the calendar portlet. First, we declare a reference to the fmt JSTL tag library and set the resource bundle name to the base name of our fully qualified properties file by adding the following lines to the JSP.

```
<%@ taglib uri="http://java.sun.com/jstl/fmt" prefix="fmt" %>
<fmt:setBundle basename="nls.CalendarPortlet"/>
```

The text strings that should be enabled for translation on this view are the days of the week (abbreviated) and the labels on the buttons used to select the next or previous month. Adding these strings to the default resource bundle yields the content shown in Listing 5.3.

125

```
# Portlet title strings
javax.portlet.title=Calendar Portlet
javax.portlet.short-title=
javax.portlet.keywords=

# JSP text strings
mon=Mon
tue=Tue
wed=Wed
thu=Thu
fri=Fri
sat=Sat
sun=Sun
prev.month=Previous month
next.month=Next month
```

Listing 5.3: Resource bundle

Next, we need to modify the JSP to use these text strings. Make the changes shown in Listings 5.4 and 5.5 to reference the day-of-week text and button labels, respectively, using the "message" tag from the fmt JSTL library.

```
<table><tr>
<td><fmt:message key="sun"/></td>
<td><fmt:message key="mon"/></td>
<td><fmt:message key="tue"/></td>
<td><fmt:message key="wed"/></td>
<td><fmt:message key="thu"/></td>
<td><fmt:message key="fri"/></td>
<td><fmt:message key="sat"/></td>
</tr>
</table>
```

Listing 5.4: JSP snippet for day-of-week text

```
<table><tr>
<td>
<form action="<%=myPrev%>" method="GET">
  <input name="prev" type="submit" value='<fmt:message
key="prev.month"/>'>
</form>
</td>
<td>
<form action="<%=myNext%>" method="GET">
  <input name="next" type="submit" value='<fmt:message
key="next.month"/>'>
</form>
</td>
</tr></table>
```

Listing 5.5: JSP snippet for button labels

With that, the changes needed to enable one of our portlet views for internationalization are complete. Let's make similar changes to the view.jsp and the edit.jsp files. When we're finished, the view.jsp file will look as shown in Listing 5.6.

```
<%@ taglib uri='http://java.sun.com/portlet' prefix='portlet'%>
<%@ taglib uri='http://java.sun.com/jstl/core' prefix='c'%>
<%@ taglib uri="http://java.sun.com/jstl/fmt" prefix="fmt" %>
<fmt:setBundle basename="nls.CalendarPortlet"/>

<%@ page import="javax.portlet.*"%>
<jsp:useBean id="bean"
class="com.ibm.samples.portlets.calendar.TodoBean" scope="request" />

<portlet:defineObjects/>

<P>
<fmt:message key="current.date"/>: <c:out value="${bean.date}"/>
</P>
<P>
<P>
<B><fmt:message key="todo"/>:</B><br>
</P>
<c:set var="prefsMap" value="${renderRequest.preferences.map}"/>
<c:if test="${empty prefsMap[bean.date]}">
```

Listing 5.6: View JSP enabled for internationalization (part 1 of 2)

```
        <fmt:message key="no.todo"/>.<br>
        <fmt:message key="add.todo"/>.
</c:if>
<c:if test="${not empty prefsMap[bean.date]}">
    <c:forEach var="todo" items="${prefsMap[bean.date]}">
            <c:out value="${todo}" /><BR>
    </c:forEach>
</c:if>
</p>

<form action="<portlet:renderURL portletMode="edit"/>" method="GET">
        <input type="submit" name="action" value="<fmt:message
key="edit.todo"/>">
</form>
```

Listing 5.6: View JSP enabled for internationalization (part 2 of 2)

Similar changes in edit.jsp will look as shown in Listing 5.7.

```
<%@ taglib uri='http://java.sun.com/portlet' prefix='portlet'%>
<%@ taglib uri='http://java.sun.com/jstl/core' prefix='c'%>
<%@ taglib uri="http://java.sun.com/jstl/fmt" prefix="fmt" %>
<fmt:setBundle basename="nls.CalendarPortlet"/>
<jsp:useBean id="bean"
class="com.ibm.samples.portlets.calendar.TodoBean" scope="request" />


<portlet:defineObjects/>

<P><B><fmt:message key="defined.todo"/></B></P>
<P><fmt:message key="date"/>:  <c:out value="${bean.date}"/> </P>

<c:set var="prefsMap" value="${renderRequest.preferences.map}"/>

<form action="<portlet:actionURL portletMode="view"/>" method="post">
<table>
        <tr>
        <td>
                <B><fmt:message key="current.todo"/></B>
        </td>
        </tr>
        <c:set var="prefsMap"
value="${renderRequest.preferences.map}"/>
```

Listing 5.7: Edit JSP enabled for internationalization (Page 1 of 2)

```
            <c:if test="${not empty prefsMap[bean.date]}">
            <c:forEach var="todo" items="${prefsMap[bean.date]}">
                <tr><td><c:out value="${todo}" /></td>
                    </tr>
            </c:forEach>
            </c:if>
</table>
<p></p>
<table>
   <TR>
     <TD>
       <INPUT NAME="todo" TYPE="text">
     </TD>
     <TD>
       <INPUT NAME="add" TYPE="submit" value="<fmt:message key="add.but-
ton"/>">
     </TD>
     <TD>

       <INPUT NAME="remove" TYPE="submit" value="<fmt:message
key="remove.button"/>">
     </TD>
   </TR>
</TABLE>
</FORM>
<FORM ACTION="<portlet:renderURL portletMode="view"/>" METHOD="GET">
   <INPUT NAME="cancel"  TYPE="submit" VALUE="<fmt:message
key="cancel.button"/>">
</FORM>
```

Listing 5.7: Edit JSP enabled for internationalization (Page 2 of 2)

Last, our default resource bundle with the extracted text strings looks as shown in Listing 5.8.

```
javax.portlet.title=Calendar Portlet
javax.portlet.short-title=
javax.portlet.keywords=

# JSP text strings
mon=Mon
tue=Tue
wed=Wed
```

Listing 5.8: Complete resource bundle (Page 1 of 2)

```
thu=Thu
fri=Fri
sat=Sat
sun=Sun
prev.month=Previous month
next.month=Next month
current.date=Current selected date
todo=ToDo's for the current date
no.todo=No ToDo currently defined for this date
add.todo=To add a ToDo please press "Edit ToDo's"
edit.todo=Edit ToDo's
defined.todo=Defined Todo's
current.todo=Current ToDo's
date=For date
add.button=Add ToDo
remove.button=Remove ToDo
cancel.button=Cancel
```

Listing 5.8: Complete resource bundle (Page 2 of 2)

This completes the internationalization for the calendar portlet. As a last step, we copy the text strings into the English (en) and Spanish (sp) resource bundles and translate the text into Spanish in that file. As a final test, change the language preference in your browser to Spanish, and make sure the portlet renders in that language.

Sharing Property Files Across Multiple Portlets

In some portal architectures, it may be important to derive a single set of resource bundles for use within the entire portal. This requirement is often the case when an administrator needs to maintain or edit a single set of language strings without redeploying any portlets. In this situation, you can use an approach similar to the one just discussed but change the path of the resource file.

If you view the directory <WebSphere>\PortalServer\shared\app\nls, you'll find there are dozens of resource files used in various locations within WebSphere Portal. Taking advantage of this centralized resource repository can be a big win for some development efforts. In addition to using the information already available within the portal, teams can add their own set of bundles for sharing across multiple portlets.

130

One drawback you should note when using this approach is that it breaks the "selfcontainedness" of portlet applications and thus requires additional steps by the portal administrator to install or update the portlet applications.

CHANGING A LANGUAGE DYNAMICALLY

As we've noted, you can specify your language preference though the browser setting or in the user profile information supplied when you register as a Portal user. Although specifying a language preference may have some initial benefit, many projects have a requirement to change a language more dynamically, without having the user go through a set of complicated steps to make the change.

WebSphere Portal supports this capability in two mechanisms. The first uses a custom JSP tag to generate a Portal command URL that immediately changes the user locale preference. The second is an SPI that lets you programmatically create a URL that changes the locale.

A relatively common Web design provides a set of buttons on the page that immediately change the page language preference. For example, a page may have a button to show the existing page in English or in French, with the scope of the change being the life of the session. Portal lets you easily implement this functionality by defining a JSP tag (portal-navigation tag) that generates a command URL that Portal interprets as an immediate change in the user locale preference. A parameter on that tag determines the target language (Listing 5.9). This tag is intended to be used in the portal themes (not directly in portlets).

```
<portal-navigation:url command="ChangeLanguage">
    <wps:urlParam name="locale" value="language"/>
</portal-navigation:url>
```

Listing 5.9: Tag to let the user change the language preference

For syntax information and a usage example for this tag, see the WebSphere Portal InfoCenter.

As an alternative, you can use the Navigational State SPI to create a Portal URL that changes the locale. IBM has extended this SPI in WebSphere Portal 6.0 to create a Portlet State Manager Service that you can use from JSR 168 portlets. The Navigational State provides several interfaces, such as the StateHolderController interface, which lets you change state information, and EngineURL, which represents a URL that contains navigational state.

The Navigational State SPI also provides several Accessor factories. One of these is the LocaleAccessor factory, which provides accessors to read and write locale information. You can use the LocaleAccessorController to create URLs that change the locale. Let's look at this technique more closely in a code sample that creates a URL that changes the locale (Listing 5.10).

```
public EngineURL createLocaleURL(final StateManagerService service,
final Locale locale) throws StateException {
    // get the needed factories
    final URLFactory urlFactory = service.getURLFactory();
    final LocaleAccessorFactory locFct = (LocaleAccessorFactory) serv-
ice.getAccessorFactory(LocaleAccessorFactory.class);
    try {
        // get a new URL from the URL factory
        final EngineURL url = urlFactory.newURL(null);
        // get a locale controller which operates on the URL-specific state
        final LocaleAccessorController locCtrl =
locFct.getLocaleAccessorController(url.getState());
        try {
            // change the locale
            locCtrl.setLocale(locale);
            // return the URL
            return url;
        } finally {
            locCtrl.dispose();
        }
    } finally {
        urlFactory.dispose();
    }
}
```

Listing 5.10: Using the Navigational State SPI to change the locale

For more information about the Navigational State SPI, check the Javadoc that comes with WebSphere Portal 6.0.

A Word About Bidirectional Languages

Most of our discussion about languages so far has focused on western languages that are read from left to right. WebSphere Portal also provides built-in support for bidirectional languages, which are read from right to left. More than half the population of the world reads and writes using a bidirectional language, so this type of support is important for truly international portals.

To support languages that should be displayed right to left, Portal provides the <wps:bidi> tag. The tag's dir attribute takes one of two values: "rtl" causes the tag text to be written if the user's language setting is a bidirectional language, and "ltr" causes the tag text to be written if the user does *not* belong to a bidirectional language.

Before WebSphere Portal 6.0, languages defined to be bidirectional were identified in the LocalizerService.properties file. In this file (which resides in the wp_root/shared/app/config/ directory), you specified which languages were to be interpreted as bidirectional languages using the locales.bidi property. You could specify multiple languages, separated by commas. If the user's rendering language was listed here, the content would be shown from right to left.

With Version 6.0, this property in the LocalizerService file is no longer defined. you identify the bidirectional languages using the WebSphere Application Server (WAS) administrative console. For more information about this function, refer to the WAS InfoCenter.

Building a Portlet for Multiple Devices

In addition to languages, WebSphere Portal provides built-in support for multiple devices, clients, and markup types. A significant advantage of using a framework such as Portal is the ability to provide a consistent user interface between portlet applications. Portal supports this goal by providing common functional support for themes and skins as well as supporting a common tag library and cascading style sheets.

Within Portal's themes and skins infrastructure is support for multiple markup languages based on the user client type. Portal supports HTML, Wireless

Markup Language (WML), and Compact HTML (cHTML) markup. The content that individual portlets render must support these same markup types. With the IBM portlet API, support was provided to identify specific JSP files based on the client device type. Support similar to this is not part of the current JSR 168 portlet specification, but, as with the standard API and language support, you can add control logic to your portlet to determine the markup type to render based on the client request.

WebSphere Portal also enables providing device-specific responses to render requests by supporting Composite Capabilities/Preference Profiles (CC/PP) in portlets. CC/PP is a standards specification that provides a description of device capabilities and user preferences you can use to structure the content replied to a request.

For each incoming request, the JSR 168 portlet container determines profile information for the client that issued the request. The portal database contains a repository of client profiles that provides relevant information about the supported clients. JSR 168 portlets can access the profile through a request attribute. The CC/PP specification defines the profile attributes, including the markup name, the markup version, and the list of content types the device supports. With this capability and that provided by Portal themes and skins, the portal site and the deployed portlets can support and respond to multiple device types.

SUMMARY

Our examples here just begin to scratch the surface of language and device integration in a portlet. Handling these topics within an enterprise application requires you to put a lot of thought and effort into the overall architecture and design of the portal. But for beginners, at whom this book is aimed, the information in this chapter is more than enough to get you on the way toward introducing your portal in any number of languages.

We didn't go into great detail about building portlets for multiple devices. We consider that subject an advanced topic, and, unfortunately, we're unable to go deeply into WML and other types of display languages here. For more information about this aspect of portlets, consult the WebSphere Portal InfoCenter as well as any of the numerous books available on various multidevice topics.

Chapter Six

Using JavaServer Faces in Your Portlets

JavaServer Faces (JSF) technology is a user interface framework for J2EE applications. It is particularly suited, by design, for use with applications based on the Model-View-Controller (MVC) architecture and manages the user interface model on the server. JSF began as Java Community Process (JSR 127) and was finalized in March 2004. You can download a reference implementation of JSF at the JavaServer Faces Technology Download page (*http://java.sun.com/javaee/javaserverfaces/download.html*). An open-source implementation called MyFaces is also available from Apache (at *http://myfaces.apache.org*). JSF is now a standard part of J2EE 5.0, and all major platform vendors already support it.

Several features of JSF make it attractive for development:

- validation and conversion

- navigation rules

- prebuilt components

- an event-driven Web programming model

- rapid application development using tools such as Rational Application Developer (RAD)

- preservation of application state across requests

- Pluggable render kits to support multiple client types and markups

Covering the complete set of JSF features is beyond of scope of this book. In this chapter, we introduce you to JSF in the context of Rational Application Developer and WebSphere Portal.

REQUEST LIFE CYCLE

One of the main concepts of JSF is the life cycle and its associated event-based system, which together are pretty much the foundation of JSF. The life cycle of a JSF request is processed in six phases, as Figure 6.1 depicts (the phases are the elements in circles). Built within these phases, an eventing system lets the developer send and receive events. The system's purpose is to permit JSF components to exchange messages between each other.

Table 6.1 gives a more detailed description of the different life-cycle phases.

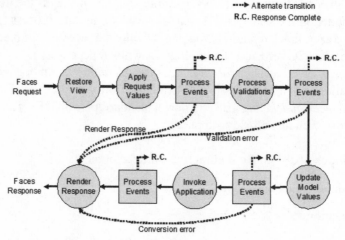

Figure 6.1: Portlet windows on a portal page

Table 6.1: Phases of the JSF life cycle

Phase	Description
Restore View	A JSP in a JSF application is represented by a component tree. The Restore View phase starts the life-cycle request processing by constructing this tree. The controller examines the request and extracts the view ID, which is determined by the path information portion of the request URI. The JSF framework controller uses the view ID to look up the components for the current view. If the view doesn't already exist, the JSF controller creates it. If the view already exists, the JSF controller uses it. This information is then saved and passed on to following request-processing phases.
Apply Request Values	In this phase, the local value of each component in the component tree is updated from the current incoming request. A value can come from a request parameter, a header, or another source. During this phase, a component may queue events, which will then be processed during the process event steps. In the case of an error, the request phase is interrupted and proceeds directly to the Render Response phase.
Process Validations	After the local value of each component is updated, those values are validated, if necessary, in the Process Validations phase. A component that requires validation must provide an implementation of the validation logic. If any value fails the validation, the request phase is interrupted and proceeds directly to the Render Response phase.
Update Model Values	In this phase, the life-cycle object updates the application's model data. During this phase, a component may again queue events, such as conversion errors.
Invoke Application	During this phase, the JSF implementation handles any application-level events, such as submitting a form or linking to another page.
Render Response	In this phase, the JSF implementation renders the response to the client.

The table discusses each life-cycle phase of a JSF request. The life cycle is the most important concept in JSF because it defines the whole idea within which all other JSF techniques work. All other artifacts of JSF are based on JSF components that are called by each phase and therefore can react on each with a different logic.

By now, you know that the Java Portlet Specification introduced two phases: action and render. These two phases are less sophisticated but nevertheless map onto the JSF phases quite well. The Java Portlet Specification dictates that model and state changes must occur during the action phase and that the render phase should be used only to render the view of the underlying model. Therefore, a faces controller for portlets executes all phases besides the Render Response phase inside the portlet action phase. And in the portlet render phase, it executes the Render Response phase only.

JSF WIDGET LIBRARY

The IBM JSF Widget Library (JWL) is a JSF- and JavaScript-based widget library that augments JSP and HTML pages with a rich set of input, output, and navigation components. JWL also includes support for Ajax-based page interactions so that pages can not only include more complex components but also interact with the Web server without requiring a full redraw of the page with each interaction. Examples of widgets in JWL include a section component, a menu bar component, a tree component, a calendar component, a time-picker component, character-by-character input assist, and context-menu management.

JWL consists of three pieces:

- The JSF tag library and runtime, which incorporates the standard JSF tags as well as IBM's extended JSF tags. When using these tags and RAD or the forthcoming release of Workplace Designer, you can place UI widgets on a page simply by dragging and dropping them from a palette.

- A standalone JavaScript runtime that implements the JWL components in an HTML page.

- The Odyssey Browser Framework (OBF) tags and runtime, which support coordinating a client-side data model with HTML tags.

DEVELOPING A PORTLET

Let's create a portlet using JavaServer Faces so you can see how easy it is to develop one. Our sample portlet will retrieve the salesrepid attribute from the user profile and then obtain the customers for the currently logged-in sales representative. For simplicity, we'll assume the salesrepid is stored in the givenName attribute of the user profile. After displaying the customer list, the portlet will let the sales rep edit the customer information and save it back to the database.

Create a Portlet Project

In RAD, select **File > New > Project** (Figure 6.2) to create a new portlet project.

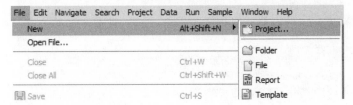

Figure 6.2: Creating a new project

In the **New Project** dialog (Figure 6.3), select **Portal > Portlet Project**.

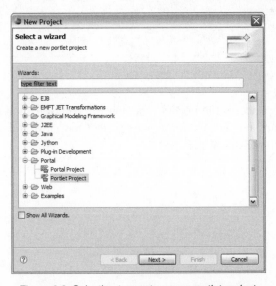

Figure 6.3: Selecting to create a new portlet project

Specify a name for the new project (Figure 6.4). For this example, we'll use the name CustomerMaintenance.

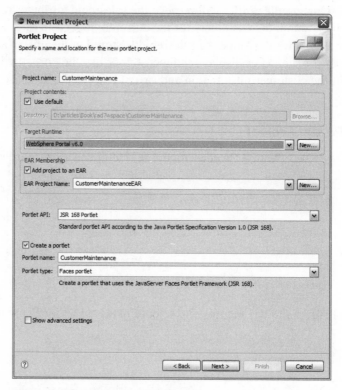

Figure 6.4: Specifying the project name

Next (Figure 6.5), specify the portlet type and information such as the modes the portlet will support. For this example, we'll select the **view** and **edit** modes. Click **Finish** to create the portlet.

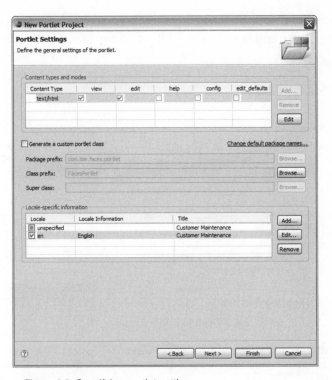

Figure 6.5: Specifying portlet settings

Create Managed Beans

Data for JSF applications are often extracted from data sources that are encapsulated in Java Beans. Although JavaBeans are easy to use, JSF provides a further simplification with *Managed Beans*. Put simply, a Managed Bean is a bean whose instantiation JSF manages whenever your JSP references the bean. This feature lets you access any Managed Bean properties from any JSP in your application, without having to explicitly mention the bean in your JSP source file. Of course, you can still use traditional JSP bean access mechanisms, but the ease of use of the Managed Bean makes it the obvious choice for JSF development. In addition, Backing Beans provide a way to store the components on the form into a bean. Let's create a managed bean using RAD.

141

Select the **Navigator** view in RAD, right-click the **src/com/ibmpress/customer-maintenance** folder, and select **New > Other** to create a class (Figure 6.6).

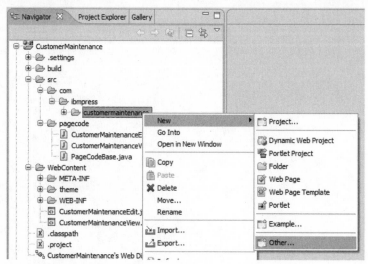

Figure 6.6: Select New > Other to create a class

On the resulting dialog (Figure 6.7), select **Java > Class**.

Figure 6.7: Select Java > Class to create a new class

On the **New Java Class** dialog (Figure 6.8), enter a name for the new class. For this example, we'll use the name CustomerMaintenanceBean.

Figure 6.8: Enter a class name

Next (Figure 6.9), add the required libraries to the class path.

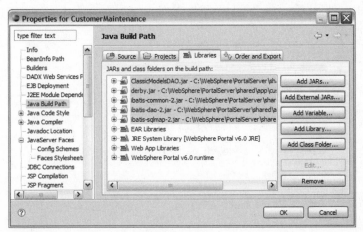

Figure 6.9: Select the dependent libraries

Next, add a method to the bean that returns all the customers for the sales rep who is logged in to portal. Listing 6.1 shows the code for this method, getCustomers.

```
public List getCustomers() {
    int salesrepid = getSalesRepID();
    return
getClassicModelsService().findCustomersbySalesRepId(salesrepid);
}
```

Listing 6.1: Java method getCustomers

The getSalesRepID method (Listing 6.2) shows how to get a hold of the PortetRequest and obtain the user profile information from the portal.

```
public int getSalesRepID() {
    int l_salesrepid = -1;
    String salesRepStr = null;
    String attrName = "givenName";
    PumaProfile pp = null;

    if (pumaHome == null) {
        initPumaHome();
    }

    PortletRequest request =
        (PortletRequest) FacesContext
            .getCurrentInstance().getExternalContext().getRequest();

    pp = pumaHome.getProfile(request);

    try {
        User user = pp.getCurrentUser();
        ArrayList aList = new ArrayList();
        aList.add(attrName);

        ArrayList attrArray = (ArrayList)
                    pp.getAttributes(user, aList).get(attrName);
        if (attrArray != null) {
            salesRepStr = (String) attrArray.get(0);
        }
        l_salesrepid = Integer.parseInt(salesRepStr);
    } catch (PumaException e) {
        e.printStackTrace();
    }
    return l_salesrepid;
}
```

Listing 6.2: Java method getSalesRepID

You can also use the code shown in Listing 6.3 to retrieve the attribute from the USER_INFO map object that JSR 168 portlets provide.

```
public int getSalesRepID() {

    PortletRequest request = (PortletRequest)
FacesContext.getCurrentInstance().getExternalContext().getRequest();

    Map userMap = (Map) request.getAttribute(PortletRequest.USER_INFO);
    String salesRepStr = (String) userMap.get("user.name.given");
    int l_salesrepid = Integer.parseInt(salesRepStr);
    return l_salesrepid;
}
```

Listing 6.3: Obtaining the user profile information from the USER_INFO object

With this approach, though, you'll first need to expose the attribute through the portlet from the portlet.xml deployment descriptor using the XML snippet shown in Listing 6.4; then you can access the attribute from the portlet.

```
<user-attribute>
        <description>Given name attribute</description>
        <name>user.name.given</name>
</user-attribute>
```

Listing 6.4: XML snippet to expose the given name attribute

The JSR 168 standard defines certain standard attribute names, and if you want to access any arbitrary attributes, simply specify the attribute you want to expose within the portlet.xml.

Listing 6.5 shows how to look up and access the Puma Service using JNDI lookup. The getSalesRepID method calls the initPumaHome method so that the service object is available to get the profile information.

```
private static void initPumaHome() {
  try {
    javax.naming.Context ctx = new javax.naming.InitialContext();
    PortletServiceHome psh = (PortletServiceHome) ctx.lookup

("portletservice/com.ibm.portal.um.portletservice.PumaHome");
    if (psh != null) {
        pumaHome = (PumaHome) psh.getPortletService(PumaHome.class);
    }
  } catch (NamingException e) {
        e.printStackTrace();
  } catch (PortletServiceUnavailableException e) {
        e.printStackTrace();
  }
}
```

Listing 6.5: Looking up and initializing the PumaHome object

Add the Bean to the Faces Managed Beans

You saw in the previous section what a Managed Bean is. It is a bean whose instantiation JSF manages whenever your JSP references it. Next, we use the following steps to make our bean a Managed Bean. By doing so, we can access the customer maintenance bean from all the JSPs.

Open the CustomerMaintenanceView.jsp, and go to the Page Data. Right-click **Faces Managed Beans**, and select **New > Faces Managed Bean** (Figure 6.10).

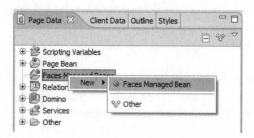

Figure 6.10: Create new Faces Managed Bean

On the next dialog (Figure 6.11), select the option to **Make this JavaBean reusable**. This choice makes the JavaBean available to other pages. When you choose this option, you can enter a description for the JavaBean and select one of the following scopes.

- **none**: The JavaBean's life span is shorter than a request (example: an object created on the fly that is not accessible as a scope variable, such as an instance variable).
- **application**: The JavaBean's scope is the life span of the application running on the server session (example: a database connection).
- **session**: The scope is the life span of the browser accessing the application (example: an end-user's shopping cart).
- **request**: The scope is the life span of a Web page request from a browser (example: a set of detailed data based on a record in a list).

If you don't make the JavaBean reusable, the JavaBean you create is only represented by the getter and setter methods in the page code file for the JavaBean you've added.

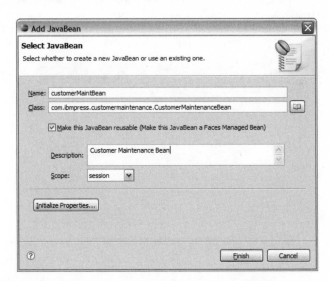

Figure 6.11: Assign a name and select the class for the managed bean

The CustomerMaintenanceBean contains the getCustomers method, which returns a List object. When a List (or Collection) is returned, we need to tell

RAD what the underlying type of the returned object is in the List so it can automatically introspect the contained type and generate the appropriate code when the List property is dropped on a page. Figure 6.12 shows the option to select for this step.

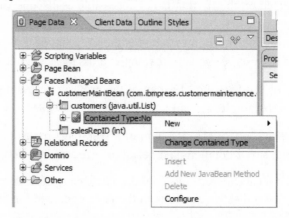

Figure 6.12: Change the contained type for the customers list

In the **Object Type** dialog (Figure 6.13), set the right object type for the customer list.

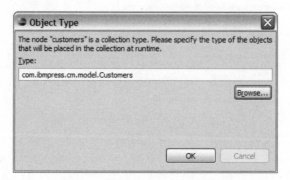

Figure 6.13: Change the contained type for the customer list

Edit JSPs

Next, we'll edit the view JSP to display the customers for the currently logged-in sales rep. We've already written a method in the bean that will pull all the customers from the database based on the salesrepid user attribute. We've also made that bean a managed bean. We'll use the managed bean's "customers" property to display the data in a table format.

Open CustomerMaintenanceView.jsp, and drag and drop the customers property from the Page Data into the JSP (Figure 6.14).

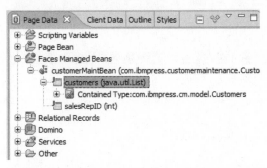

Figure 6.14: Drag and crop customers property into CustomerMaintenanceView JSP

Customize the data table to display the desired fields, as shown in Figure 6.15.

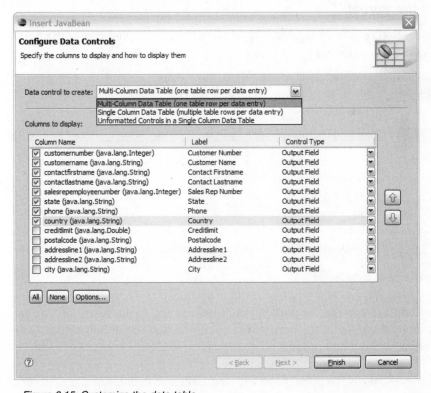

Figure 6.15: Customize the data table

Figure 6.16 shows the design view of the customer data table.

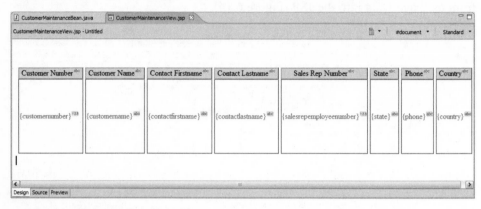

Figure 6.16: Data table in design view

Run the Portlet

Now, in RAD's Project Explorer, right-click the portlet, and choose **Run As > Run on Server** (Figure 6.17).

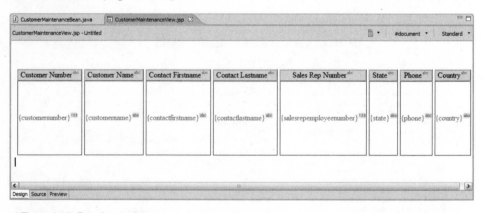

Figure 6.17: Run the portlet

The first time you run the portlet, you'll have to set up the server. If you make that server the default, the portlet will be run on that server automatically the next time without any prompt.

Figure 6.18 shows the portal page with our customer maintenance portlet running!

Customer Number	Customer Name	Contact Firstname	Contact Lastname	Sales Rep Number	State	Phone	Country
103	Atelier graphique	Carine	Schmitt	1,370		40.32.2555	France
119	La Rochelle Gifts	Janine	Labrune	1,370		40.67.8555	France
141	Euro+ Shopping Channel	Diego	Freyre	1,370		(91) 555 94 44	Spain
171	Daedalus Designs Imports	Martine	Rancé	1,370		20.16.1555	France
209	Mini Caravy	Frédérique	Citeaux	1,370		88.60.1555	France
242	Alpha Cognac	Annette	Roulet	1,370		61.77.6555	France
256	Auto Associés & Cie.	Daniel	Tonini	1,370		30.59.8555	France

Figure 6.18: Output of running the portlet

PAGINATION

One of the most common issues with showing a list of items in a table is the number of items in the table. If you have 100 items in the list, you'll usually want to provide pagination controls so that only 10 items show up per page at a time. The data table component has a pagination component built into it. So, if you have 100 items in the list, you can use the widget to show 10 at a time and provide buttons for moving forward and backward through the list. You typically would either spend a lot of time coding this function or use some vendor-provided tag libraries. Let's enable pagination to our dataTable so that only five customers appear at a time.

To do so, open the CustomerMaintenanceView JSP, and click the **dataTableEx** tag.

```
<hx:dataTableEx id="tableEx1" value="#{customerMaintBean.customers}"
```

Click the **Properties** view, and go to **Display Options**. Figure 6.19 shows the display properties for the data table. Set the **Rows per page** value to 5, and select the **Add a deluxe pager** paging option.

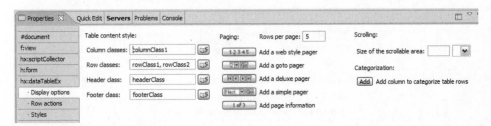

Figure 6.19: Data table properties

Now, we'll run the portlet again. As you can see in Figure 6.20, pagination is now enabled for the table control, and you can use the next and previous arrow buttons to go back and forth without any coding.

Customer Maintenance

Customer Number	Customer Name	Contact Firstname	Contact Lastname	Sales Rep Number	State	Phone	Country
103	Atelier graphique	Carine	Schmitt	1,370		40.32.2555	France
119	La Rochelle Gifts	Janine	Labrune	1,370		40.67.8555	France
141	Euro+ Shopping Channel	Diego	Freyre	1,370		(91) 555 94 44	Spain
171	Daedalus Designs Imports	Martine	Rancé	1,370		20.16.1555	France
209	Mini Caravy	Frédérique	Citeaux	1,370		88.60.1555	France

◁◁ ◁ Page 1 of 2 ▷ ▷▷

Figure 6.20: Output with pagination enabled on data table

ACTION EVENT

You can attach action listeners to components of your portlet such as buttons and links. When the user clicks a button, an action event is called, providing access to the component. Action events usually don't get involved in any of the navigation handling. In our case, we'll use that to get the current customer record and store a reference to it so it's available to the Edit Customer JSP for rendering.

All button and link controls provide an attribute called "action" that controls the navigation. The Controller decides which page to display next based on the outcome the buttons and links return. These outcomes can be static, right from the tag, or they can be dynamic, the result of executing an action.

Let's add a link that lets the sales rep edit the customer. Go to the Properties for the dataTableEx table, and add another column called **Actions** to the table (as shown in Figure 6.21).

Figure 6.21: Add a column for Actions

In the design view, add an action bar to the Actions column by dragging and dropping the action bar from the palette (Figure 6.22).

152

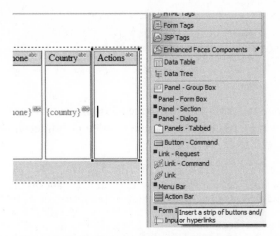

Figure 6.22: Drop an action bar into the column

Next, drag the "Link – Command" item from the palette to the table's action bar (Figure 6.23).

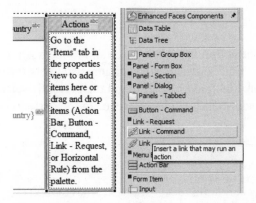

Figure 6.23: Drop a link command into the action bar

Now, we'll add a property called currentCustomer of type Customers to store a reference to the currently selected customer and display when the user clicks the **Edit** button. Listing 6.6 shows the code to create this property.

Tip: Once you create an instance variable, you can right-click the variable and **select Source > Generate Getters and Setters** to quickly generate the getters and setters for that variable.

153

```
public class CustomerMaintenanceBean   {
    private Customers currentCustomer = null;
```

Listing 6.6: currentCustomer property

The snippet of code in Listing 6.7 calls the ActionEvent customerEditListener on customerMaintBean by passing a parameter called customernumber when the user clicks the link.

```
<hx:panelActionbar id="actionbar1" styleClass="panelActionbar">
    <h:commandLink styleClass="commandLink" id="editLink"
        actionListener="#{customerMaintBean.customerEditListener}"
        action="editcustomer">
        <h:outputText id="edit" styleClass="outputText" value="Edit"/>
        <f:param name="customernumber" value="#{varcustomers.customer-
number}"/>
    </h:commandLink>
</hx:panelActionbar>
```

Listing 6.7: Calling the edit action listener from a command link

Listing 6.8 shows the action listener code to add to the bean that's invoked when the sales rep clicks "Edit" customer. The action event gets the parameter attached to the commandLink and makes a call to get the currently selected customer using the classicModelsService. The reference to the currently selected customer is then stored in the bean.

```
public void customerEditListener(ActionEvent e) {
    ExternalContext externalContext =
FacesContext.getCurrentInstance().getExternalContext();
    String customerNumString =
(String)externalContext.getRequestParameterMap().get("customernumber");
    int customernumber = Integer.parseInt(customerNumString);
    ClassicModelsService classicModelSvc  = getClassicModelsService();
    currentCustomer =   classicModelSvc.findCustomerById(customernumber);
}
```

Listing 6.8: Action listener code for edit customer

Our next task is to create a JSP that displays the customer for editing. Create a JSF JSP called EditCustomer.jsp. Then drag and drop the currentCustomer property from the Page Data onto the Edit Customer JSP (Figure 6.24).

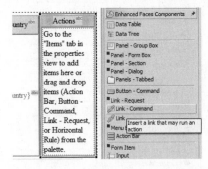

Figure 6.24: Drag and drop the current
customer property into the Edit Customer JSP

When you see the dialog shown in Figure 6.25, click **Finish**.

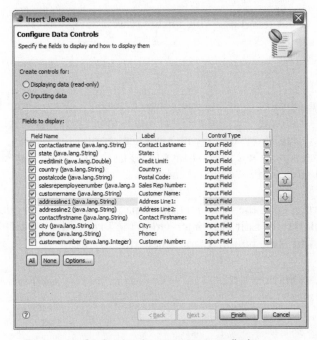

Figure 6.25: Configuring the components to display

Figure 6.26 shows the Edit Customer JSP in the design view.

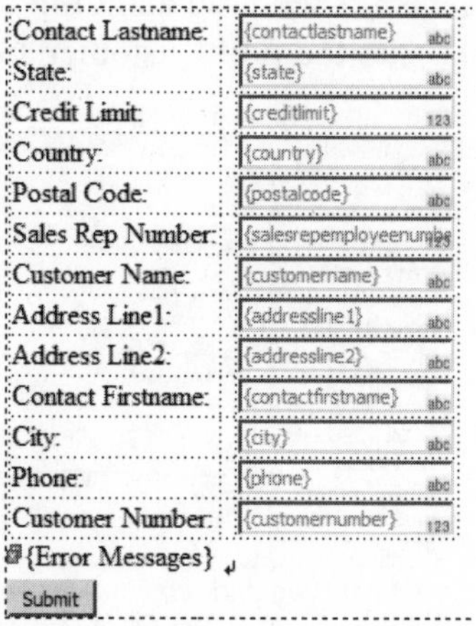

Contact Lastname:	{contactlastname}	abc
State:	{state}	abc
Credit Limit:	{creditlimit}	123
Country:	{country}	abc
Postal Code:	{postalcode}	abc
Sales Rep Number:	{salesrepemployeenumber}	
Customer Name:	{customername}	abc
Address Line1:	{addressline1}	abc
Address Line2:	{addressline2}	abc
Contact Firstname:	{contactfirstname}	abc
City:	{city}	abc
Phone:	{phone}	abc
Customer Number:	{customernumber}	123

{Error Messages} ↲

Submit

Figure 6.26: Edit Customer JSP
in design view

Let's move on to our next task, which is to create a navigation rule.

NAVIGATION

We use navigation rules to create navigation between pages without hard-coding JSP links. We've already created a JSP (EditCustomer.jsp) that displays the customer for editing. Now, let's create a navigation rule for CustomerMaintenanceView.jsp that says to go to EditCustomer.jsp when the outcome from an action is "editcustomer".

To create the rule, open the CustomerMaintenanceView JSP, and click the **commandLink** tag for Edit Customer. Go to the **Properties** view (Figure 6.27), and click the **Add Rule** button to add a new rule.

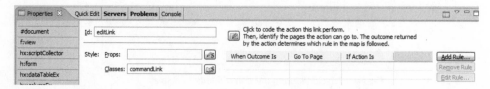

Figure 6.27: Property for commandLink on CustomerMaintenanceView JSP

Complete the resulting dialog as shown in Figure 6.28 to add the navigation rule for the CustomerMaintenanceView JSP.

Add Navigation Rule
Go to the page:
Page: EditCustomer.jsp
When the action returns the outcome:
Any outcome
The outcome named: editcustomer
This rule is used for:
All pages
This page only
This rule is used by:
Any action
This action only: #{customerMaintBean.doEditAction}
When following this rule:
Use request forwarding (parameters work automatically)
Use request redirection (parameters must be coded)
OK
Cancel

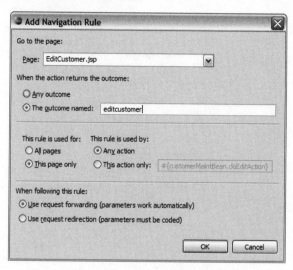

Figure 6.28: Add a navigation rule for CustomerMaintenanceView

We're almost done! Let's run the portlet and see how it looks. Figure 6.29 shows our output.

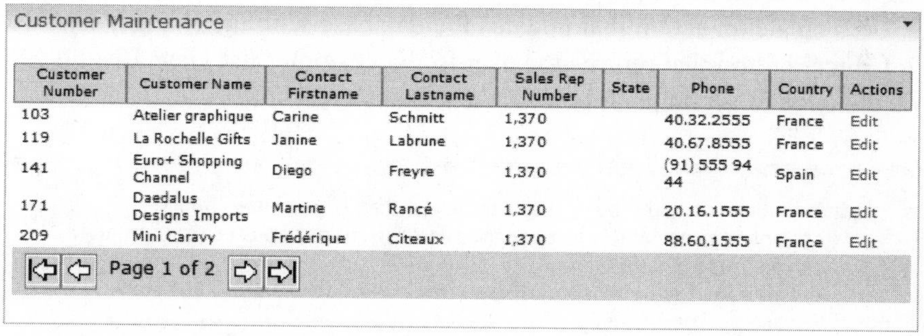

Customer Maintenance
Customer Number
Customer Name
Contact Firstname
Contact Lastname
Sales Rep Number
State
Phone
Country
Actions
103 Atelier graphique Carine Schmitt 1,370 40.32.2555 France Edit
119 La Rochelle Gifts Janine Labrune 1,370 40.67.8555 France Edit
141 Euro+ Shopping Channel Diego Freyre 1,370 (91) 555 94 44 Spain Edit
171 Daedalus Designs Imports Martine Rancé 1,370 20.16.1555 France Edit
209 Mini Caravy Frédérique Citeaux 1,370 88.60.1555 France Edit
Page 1 of 2

Figure 6.29: Default portlet view

Clicking the "Edit" action for one of the customers produces a screen similar to the one shown in Figure 6.30.

Customer Maintenance

Contact Lastname:	Schmitt
State:	
Credit Limit:	21,000
Country:	France
Postal Code:	44000
Sales Rep Number:	1,370
Customer Name:	Atelier graphique
Address Line1:	54, rue Royale
Address Line2:	Address line2
Contact Firstname:	Carine
City:	Nantes
Phone:	40.32.2555
Customer Number:	103

Submit

Figure 6.30: Edit Customer view

So far, so good. However, we don't yet have an action listener tied to the **Submit** button to update the back end with the changes and return the user to the start page. Let's create an action that updates the database with the changes and also add a **Cancel** button that returns the user to the customer list view. Listing 6.9 shows the code to accomplish both of these tasks.

```
<hx:commandExButton id="button1" type="submit" value="Submit"
      actionListener="#{customerMaintBean.updateCustomerListener}"
      action="startpage"
         styleClass="commandExButton"></hx:commandExButton>

<hx:commandExButton type="submit" value="Cancel" id="button2"
      action="startpage"
         styleClass="commandExButton"></hx:commandExButton>
Listing 6.9: Enabling the Submit and Cancel buttons
```

Listing 6.9: Enabling the Submit and Cancel buttons

Now, when the user clicks the **Submit** button, all the changes he or she made will be automatically updated into the currentCustomer property and ready to be saved. We'll just call the service that updates the back-end database (Listing 6.10).

```
public void updateCustomerListener(ActionEvent e) {
    ClassicModelsService classicModelSvc  = getClassicModelsService();
    classicModelSvc.updateCustomer(currentCustomer);
}
```

Listing 6.10: Action Listener code for update customer

Next (Figure 6.31), let's add a navigation rule to the EditCustomer JSP that takes the user to the CustomerMaintenanceView JSP when the outcome from the actions is "startpage".

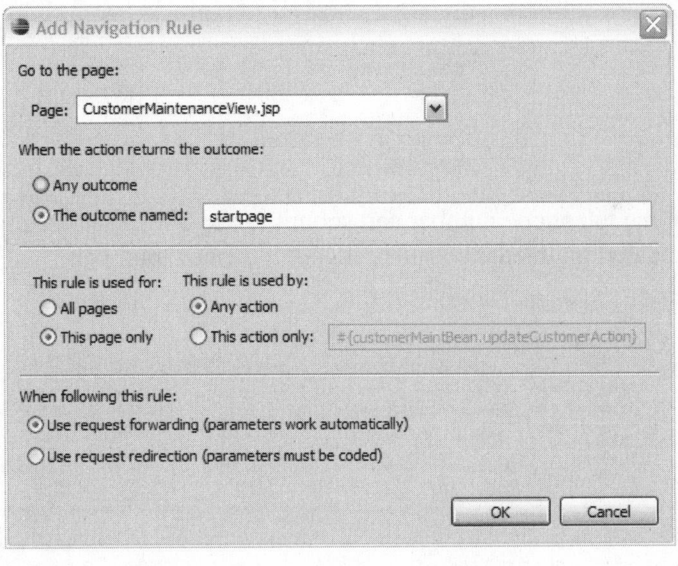

Figure 6.31: Navigation rule for EditCustomer JSP

Now when you run the portlet, you'll see the screen shown in Figure 6.32 when you edit the customer. After you make and submit the changes, the database will be updated with the changes you made.

*Figure 6.32: Edit Customer
JSP rendered*

Let's change the telephone number and submit to see how it works. Figure 6.33 shows the updated maintenance table reflecting the new number.

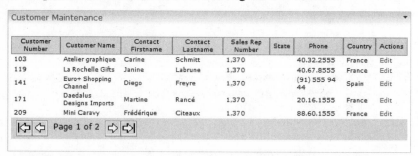

Figure 6.33: Default portlet view with updated telephone number

Using Navigation Handlers

After editing the customer data and calling submit, you may want to display a page that shows that the data has been saved successfully. Once the user views a confirmation page, clicks some other portal page, and returns to the Customer Maintenance portlet, the default behavior is to retain the confirmation page within the same session. But most of the time, the requirement may be to take the user to the customer listing page when he or she returns to the same portlet after that step. To accomplish this, you can add the following snippet at the bottom of the confirmation JSP. This code resets the navigation to show the initial customer listing page when the user returns to the Customer Maintenance portlet.

```
facesContext.getApplication().getNavigationHandler().handle
Navigation(facesContext, null, "startpage");
```

In some cases, you could have your own NavigationHandler for dealing with complicated navigation handling.

Note that we didn't add any validation rules in the example. But you could easily include conversion and validation rules on the input fields from the Properties view in RAD.

INTERNATIONALIZATION

JSF provides tags for using resource bundles. If you externalize your strings into resource bundles for internationalization, you can use the tags to display the results. Here's how you do it.

To initialize the bundles in the JSP, use the following tag.

```
<f:loadBundle var="bundle" basename="com.ibmpress.customer
maintenance.nl.customermsg"/>
```

Then within the JSP, you could use the "value" binding expression to access the messages:

```
<h:outputText styleClass="outputText" value="#{bundle.customer
number}" id="text1" />
```

STRUTS VS. JSF

One common design choice you face when starting a new portlet is whether you should use Struts or JavaServer Faces. Here are a few pointers that can help you make the decision.

> **Note:** You must update the portlet.xml file with the supported locales. To do so, open portlet.xml, go to the **Portlets** tab, and add the desired locales to the **Supported Locales** section. These steps automatically update the faces-config.xml with the updated locales.

- *Navigation:* From the navigation perspective, both Struts and JSF provides flexible navigation schemes and support static and dynamic navigation. With Struts, dynamic navigation is tied to the actions, while with JSF, the actions are tied to pages. This distinction gives JSF more granular and clean control over navigation.

- *User interface:* The wealth and flexibility of UI components available to create sophisticated JSF JSP pages is vastly superior to that of Struts.

- *Standards:* JSF is a standards-based framework for which many vendors have begun providing support. Struts is not a standards-based framework.

- *Maturity:* Struts has been around much longer than JSF, which gives Struts an advantage in terms of maturity, documentation, and stability of code.

- *Rapid application development:* JSF is built with rapid application development in mind. Features such as the ability to drag and drop components make development tasks much easier.

- *Validation:* Both Struts and JSF provide a good validation framework.

- *Bookmarkability:* With JSF, URLs aren't bookmarkable yet because all the requests are submitted as POSTs. With Struts, URLs are bookmarkable. This limitation of JSF is overcome with the IBM versions of the JSF Widget Library, using components such as requestLink, which uses GET.

- *Integration with portlets:* Because Struts was developed before portlets came into being, it doesn't have the two-phase approach of action and render and thus doesn't map to portlets as well as JSF. Therefore, and because the Struts API always deals with server objects, you need to have special Struts Bridges that are portal-specific to bridge from portlets to Struts.

PORTLET CONCEPTS APPLIED TO JSF

This section is a very important, if not the most important, section of this chapter. WebSphere Portal provides a wrapper to the JSF framework that makes the portlet itself transparent to the framework. So, from the developer's perspective, you still deal with the JSF concepts most of the times. But there are occasions when you'll need to use the portlet concepts to get some things done.

In this section, we walk through the portlet concepts and show how you can use them within a JSF application. This capability is particularly interesting because it enables you to use both JSF and portlet features by combining the two technologies. Of course, this brings the best of both worlds together and lets you selectively pick the best capabilities as required. So, for instance, you can reuse nearly all the JSF components that are written for JSF within a portlet and extend them to leverage Portlet API objects, such as PortletPreferences.

PortletWindow Handling

As you learned in Chapter 3, the Java Portlet Specification introduces the term portlet window. A portlet window is defined as a means to include more than one portlet — maybe even the same one — multiple times on a page. *The window is the view into the portlet.*

Technically, the portlet windows let us scope all available data of a portlet and ultimately assign it to one specific window. This lets the user put the same portlet more than once on his or her pages without portlet window A overwriting the state of portlet window B. The data scoped by the portlet window are

- PortletSession
- navigational state

In addition, a portlet can access a request scoping via the PortletResponse.getNamespace method. This method is supposed to be used from a portlet to guarantee that returned markup will be unique on a page. For example, you could access a namespace to prefix a JavaScript method, but if you have the same portlet twice on a page, JavaScript would generate a duplicate method name.

For all cases, you can use the ExternalContext from JSF to get to the respective objects such as PortletSession or PortletResponse, which then in turn automatically scope your data. Listing 6.11 shows how you can achieve this when you have a FacesContext at hand. If you don't have a faces context, you can use the static getCurrentInstance method to get a handle of it.

```
ExternalContext extCtx = facesContext.getExternalContext();
RenderRequest request = (RenderRequest)extCtx.getRequest();
RenderResponse response = (RenderResponse)extCtx.getResponse();

PortletSession session = request.getPortletSession();
String prefix = response.getNamespace();
```

Listing 6.11: Call to get the namespace

Note that there is a slight misalignment between the Java Portlet Specification and JSF in this regard. In many cases, JSF tags write JavaScript methods into the output stream but won't leverage the getNamespace method in the portlet scenario. As a result, you can't display a JSF portlet more than once on a page. However, the IBM JWL components shipped with RAD V7 are portal-friendly by ensuring namespace around the JavaScript. This support enables the same portlet to be placed more than once on a given page.

Action and Render

As we mentioned, the Java Portlet Specification defines two methods, action and render, whereas JSF defines six phases. We also discussed how action and render map into these phases to enable us to use JSF inside a portlet at all. The Render Response phase is mapped to the render phase, and all the other phases are mapped to the action phase.

However, this puts us into another position where we have direct access to neither the ActionRequest/Response nor the RenderRequest/Response. So where do we put all the code that previously has been in the processAction or render method?

For the render method, the answer is easy because programming guides and patterns suggest delegating the rendering to a view such as a JSP. In the portlet case, we also have access to the RenderRequest/Response inside a JSP either programmatically or via tags. In a non-JSP environment, the Java Portlet Specification also gives us a way to access the Request/Response by defining fixed keys for the portlet objects that are available in the ServletRequest.

The action logic is a bit more complicated and requires us to move the logic into a different class. *We recommend moving the logic into a JSF action listener that logically replaces the processAction method in this scenario.*

Validation

In general, we can say that both technologies, JSF and the Java Portlet Specification, define a way to validate settings the user has entered. However, conceptually they are designed in different ways for different purposes. Of course, both have the same purpose of validating settings; the difference is more subtle, and to understand it we need to take a look at the main focus of each specification again.

JSF concentrates mainly on UI aspects and therefore provides a way to generate a rich user experience. The validation concept provided by JSF lets us validate each single UI element individually and return an error message for each single element that does not pass validation.

The Java Portlet Specification, on the other hand, is similar to the Java Servlet Specification and concentrates on a Model/Controller concept and doesn't define anything related to UI. The portlet validation is based on a single validator that checks all preferences at once whenever the preferences are stored. If the validation is unsuccessful, we can return one error message for all invalid references. This can include preferences that have correlations, such as zip code and city, that can be validated only with additional information from some back-end system.

As a result, we are unable to combine these two technologies for validation but rather must decide on a case-by-case basis which validator to use.

PortletPreferences

PortletPreferences are solely a portlet concept that has no overlap with either servlets or JSF. In this and the following sections, we explain how you can work with portlet-only concepts.

The previous sections have already laid an important building block to working with PortletPreferences by explaining how to get hold of the PortletRequest/Response pairs. Doing so enables you to access any portlet object, including PortletPreferences. Looking at Listing 6.12, you can also see how we retrieve and store the preferences f.rom an action event.

```
ActionRequest request = (ActionRequest)_request;
PortletPreferences prefs = request.getPreferences();
String prefValue = prefs.getValue("key", null);
prefs.setValue(key,"XYZ");
prefs.store();
```

Listing 6.12: Accessing the PortletPreference

URL Generation

Another portlet-only concept is the generation of URLs pointing to portlets. Let's look at how to leverage the additional properties that the Java Portlet Specification provides inside URLs, such as PortletModes, WindowStates, and RenderParameters.

Normally, when you create a URL inside a portlet, it looks as shown in Listing 6.13.

```
PortletURL addUrl = response.createActionURL();
addUrl.setPortletMode(PortletMode.VIEW);
addUrl.setWindowState(WindowState.NORMAL);
addUrl.setParameter("add","add");
```

Listing 6.13: URL inside a portlet

As you can see, we have the ability to create a URL that directly points to a specific portlet mode or window state and may contain additional parameters. With the JSF Specification 1.1, we lose all these features, including the ability to create RenderURLs. This means we can use JSF inside portlets, but we can't leverage the render links that allow searchability and performance optimization. To handle these tasks more efficiently, the IBM JWL in RAD V7 provides requestLink and requestRowAction components, which let you create render links with render parameters.

To work around the shortcomings of not being able to specify portlet mode, window state, and render parameters, we developed an action listener that can handle all these portlet-specific properties. The properties are mapped to specific attributes that are retrieved from the action listener and then set on the ActionResponse. In this way, we used another means to set portlet modes, window states, and render parameters — one provided to us by the Java Portlet Specification. Listing 6.14 shows how you can use this action listener with a JSP.

```
<h:commandButton value="#{myText.cancel}" action="cancel"
immediate="true">
    <f:actionListener
        type="com.ibmpress.customermaintenance.PortletActionHandler"/>
    <f:attribute name="PortletMode" value="view" />
    <f:attribute name="WindowState" value="normal" />
    <%- f:attribute name="RenderParameters"
                    value="[name,value],[name2,value2]" / -%>
</h:commandButton>
```

Listing 6.14: Using the action listener to handle portlet-specific properties

State Handling

Every application usually requires some kind of state to work correctly. The state we discuss in this section is responsible for defining the view of an application, sometimes also called *navigational state*. In general, we want any state to be available on the next request, so it must be carried over from request to request in some fashion and not get lost in between.

A normal Web application has multiple ways to carry this state over, the typical and most obvious being cookies, HttpSession, and hidden parameters within a FORM. Every method, of course, has its characteristics. The HttpSession, for instance, is easy to use but has two major disadvantages. First, it is stored on the server side and therefore claims expensive server memory, which you should always keep as low as possible for performance reasons. Second, the session is only a bucket that has no reference to the actual page currently displayed. Especially for view state, it's desirable to bind the session to the browser page; otherwise, you won't get any previous state when you click the back button inside the browser and display the previous browser page or view into the application.

For all these reasons, JSF chooses to use hidden parameters inserted in FORMs to transport its view state. Thus, as soon as the user clicks the back button in the browser, the FORM of the previous browser page is displayed, and any following request issued by any link will contain the previous view state.

Applying this technique to the portal scenario requires a couple of considerations. In the beginning of the book, we explained the concept of a portal. In a nutshell, it means that we have an aggregation of portlets on one page and therefore a couple of players that contribute to the resulting page: the portal application itself as well as all portlets displayed on the current page. As you can see, we now have multiple applications contributing to the page result, in contrast to the Web application scenario, in which only one application returned the page result.

In the end, this means that the view state of the result page comprises the view state of every single application on the page. It also means that one task of a portal consists of aggregating each single view state into one overall state including the portal's state. Looking at the FORMs technique, it seems pretty difficult to solve the problem of nested forms, where we send all data of all forms on one browser page. Actually, there's a solution to this problem using JavaScript and DOM manipulations that we won't describe here because it is beyond the scope of this book.

One elegant way to solve the problem would be to store the view state inside a URL. This technique guarantees that the view state would be bound to the browser page. When you clicked the back button, the previous view state would be resent and the browser page could even be bookmarked. Of course, you also have to deal with the problem that the view state could become very large and therefore not fit inside a URL anymore. Portal vendors may consider this fact and take steps to reduce the size using different compression techniques, as WebSphere Portal does.

Unfortunately, the JSF Specification 1.1 doesn't provide enough flexibility to change the behavior of using URLs instead of FORMs. As a result, a JSF application will lose its model state — which is stored inside a hidden FORM parameter when the user clicks any link outside the portlet itself — unless you implement a complex solution that involves JavaScript and DOM manipulations. The JWL that ships with RAD V7 provides some relief. You can use the requestLink, which uses not FORMs but URLs instead. This way, the link is preserved when the user clicks on any other link in other portlets and then clicks back button after that.

So, basically, with JSF V1.1 you have only limited choices for supporting navigational state and the browser back button. For now, you must count on portal vendor extension and hope that the next JSF version will address this shortcoming.

SUMMARY

By now, you should have an understanding of how the JavaServer Faces framework works within WebSphere Portal. In this chapter, we covered how easy it is to develop a JSR 168 standard JSF portlet using Rational Application Developer. We also examined certain portlet concepts as they apply to JSF. We showed how you can access portlet objects from JSF action events, and we touched on what a JSF widget library is so that you know that a client-side library is available to use with JSF.

This chapter isn't meant to be a complete JSF reference because this topic is a pretty big area. Our intention here is to give you a starting point from which you can explore the possibilities.

Introduction to Part II

BUILDING ON THE JAVA PORTLET API

As of this writing, the Java Portlet API is released with Version 1.0, and the next version of this spec, JSR 286, is in early draft. Because this specification is driven by committee, new functionality is often reviewed and changed by various members before being accepted. This approach tends to slow down the process a bit, but it results in a robust specification that all the vendors and interested parties involved can accept.

Parallel to that process, IBM WebSphere Portal needs to offer advanced functionality that customers require to build their applications. Some of this functionality is carried over from the IBM WebSphere API and needs to be duplicated as customers move to the new API specification. Other functionality consists of new capabilities that IBM feels customers will need as they build more scalable and robust applications. In other cases, there is functionality that is not part of WebSphere Portal but is included in other products available to Portal customers. In all these cases, these extensions are a primary focus of Part II of this book. Building on the Java Portlet API foundation knowledge you gained in Part I, you continue your evolution in creating better portlet applications.

Many of these additional services are made available to your portlets via IBM Portlet Services. Security services, such as the Credential Vault, Content Access Services, Navigation and Model Services, and Portlet Messaging, are available within the WebSphere Portal Framework. We'll look in detail at these services and build one or two in Chapter 11.

BOOK SCENARIOS

This book's goal is to educate but also to provide usable solutions to common business problems — not just portlets in the abstract, but portlets that do things similar to what we need to do. With that goal in mind, we put a lot of thought into how to best deliver content that was relevant to the reader and yet make it possible to download, install, and build the provided samples.

Research has suggested that common use cases such as account setup and account status are among the most frequent scenarios businesses face. Additional use cases include order entry, order status, and payment history. In this book, we won't be able to show you all these use cases. We focus more on different approaches to integrating and demonstrating a breadth of tools rather than building out a portal that illustrates a business scenario. We'll show you some of them and provide general guidelines for building these types of applications.

About the Scenario Data

For our purposes, we've decided to leverage an existing database provided by Eclipse.org. The Business Intelligence and Reporting Tools (BIRT) sample database provides a simple set of tables and data that form the basis for BIRT sample reports. The schema is for Classic Models, a retailer of scale models of classic cars. Figure I.1 shows the Classic Models logo.

Figure I.1: Classic Models logo

The database contains typical business data — customers, orders, order line items, products, and so on. It was designed to illustrate many of the features of the BIRT report designer, but it also happens to be perfect for our portal.

The sample database is open source; you're free to use it for your own use to experiment with other tools, create samples for other tools, and so on. The sample database is provided under the terms of Eclipse.org's Software User Agreement, which you can view at *http://www.eclipse.org/legal/epl/notice.php*. We checked with the Eclipse folks before deciding on this scenario, and they are happy for you to use their sample database.

Scenario Use Cases

The different authors contributing to this book have approached their scenario use cases in different ways. We had some discussion about whether we should have a single set of use cases that followed throughout the book; however, we deemed that approach to be too big of an undertaking. Also, authors wanted the flexibility to illustrate important concepts or examples that might not have not fit well within a given scenario. For these reasons, each author has decided which functionality to provide within different chapters. Many of the examples follow the Classic Models scenario; however, some portlets, especially in Part I, are more standalone examples.

In addition to the Classic Models data, some chapters may use some additional service layers — incorporating outside data sources, for example, or building portlets on top of layers created in earlier chapters. We outline such scenarios in the beginning section of the chapter and help you understand any related dependencies on other chapters or sections of the book.

Database and Schema

Figure I.2 depicts the Classic Models database, which consists of seven tables completely populated with sample data:

1. Offices: Sales offices

2. Employees: All employees, including sales reps who work with customers

3. Customers

4. Orders: Orders placed by customers

5. Order details: Line items within an order

6. Payments: Payments made by customers against their accounts

7. Products: The list of scale model cars

Using this schema with pre-populated data gave us with a large set of sample use cases, from simple lookup tables to complete business transactions.

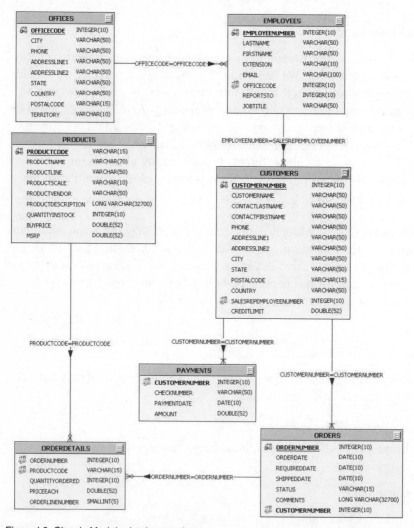

Figure I.2: Classic Models database schema

Using the Data Access Layer

In addition to providing the database, we've built out a set of classes that provide easy access to the data itself. These classes are available as a set of .jar files, which you can include within your portlet or deploy to the portal server itself for use with several different portlets. Most of the functionality within this Data Access Object (DAO) layer will be quite simple and necessary mainly for two purposes:

- to firmly illustrate the separation between the presentation layer and the model that is so necessary in today's applications

- to simplify portlet development and help you focus on core concepts rather than on Java Database Connectivity (JDBC) code or SQL queries

Additional .jar files or Portlet Factory models will also be available, along with installation instructions as necessary to provide integration functionality with Web services or Factory portlets.

Appendix B provides download and setup information for both the database and .jar files. For your convenience, we'll also provide the source code for these jars. By reviewing this code, you'll see how we've built the data access layer; however, we won't discuss the code for the basic data access within this book.

Chapter Seven

Application Architecture and SOA

Building good applications involves a lot more than just using the right API. Sound application architecture requires applications to be robust, scalable, and extensible. Most of this book focuses on the mechanics of building portlets, with some of it looking at how to build a good portlet application. In this chapter, we examine some of those latter issues and take a detailed look at Service Oriented Architecture (SOA) and what it means in the context of WebSphere Portal.

Ask any number of people what SOA is, and you're likely to receive as many different answers. Even if the respondents understand you aren't giving them a test, this variety of responses is simply an aspect of the nature of IT and the way different views and experiences change the way we look at technologies. Up to now, we've focused on the building blocks for creating portal applications, outlining tools and techniques and providing a good understanding of the APIs and technologies available for your development effort. In this chapter, we take another step toward building more complex and, ultimately, more powerful portal applications, letting you learn and leverage the best WebSphere Portal has to offer in terms of applications, tools, and techniques for creating complex and powerful solutions. As you embark on this journey, we must warn you that the complexity grows in direct proportion to your business requirements. However, the return on investment in terms of reuse and the ability to meet the needs of the business more than justifies the effort required.

IBM, as well as nearly every other major technology vendor, is investing heavily in SOA and providing solutions that run the full life-cycle gamut — from methodology and design support, to tooling and development, all the way to monitoring and governance of business services. Let's take a closer look at the meaning behind this important methodology.

WHAT IS SOA?

The term Service Oriented Architecture represents a new approach to a long-term problem: aligning technology with business problems. The "service" part of SOA is really the key: designing and developing reusable services that you can combine and use according to business needs. You can think of the services as the tasks the business requires. Think of the architecture as a design methodology or an approach for putting those services together in a way that reflects the organization's immediate needs.

This idea of using services can provide multiple benefits to IT within the organization. Key among these are flexibility and the ability for different clients to use the services in different ways. This reuse and loose coupling between services also makes it easier to integrate disparate technologies across organizational boundaries.

When people think of services, they usually think in terms of Web services. SOA pundits go to great pains to help people understand that Web services are only one potential way to implement services. In reality, there may be other ways to incorporate this architectural approach into your organization.

In this book, we focus primarily on the technical aspects of building portlets and portal applications, examining the tasks at hand from a purely technical viewpoint. We definitely want to include some of the business needs portals may face and give you examples that make sense in modern-day portals. In general, though, organizations may want to approach their SOA adoption directly from the view of the business. This is commonly the recommended approach, given that one of the major goals behind SOA is to better align technology with the goals of the business. Many resources are available to assist with the task of decomposing the business into a set of services. IBM Global Services offers one way to accomplish this effort with its Service Oriented Modeling and Analysis (SOMA) approach.

There are different ways to look at jumping on the SOA roadmap depending on how SOA is driven within your organization. One possibility is to take a top-down approach — looking at the business first to understand and break down the processes into the required services. When IT drives SOA, however, we often look at services from the bottom up. In other words, of the things I am doing now, how can I break those down into reusable services? Given that SOA's goal is to map IT to be more flexible in supporting the business, this latter approach probably isn't the preferred one; however, it's likely to be the more realistic one for many of today's organizations.

A Logical View of SOA

Now that you know what SOA is, how do you actually do it? One way is to just start building a bunch of Web services. But although we commend a willingness to adopt new approaches, no one is likely to consider this approach a good idea. Because the services in SOA should be based on business-level processes, you need to put some thought into your strategy and consider carefully the needs of the business and how you can adopt, reuse, and integrate services into full business processes.

Figure 7.1, taken from the white paper *IBM's SOA Foundation: An Architectural Introduction and Overview* (Reference 2), provides a logical model of the types of services that may be useful within your strategy. This model can help you break down services into the major types and give you some guidance about the products and technologies used for different logical areas.

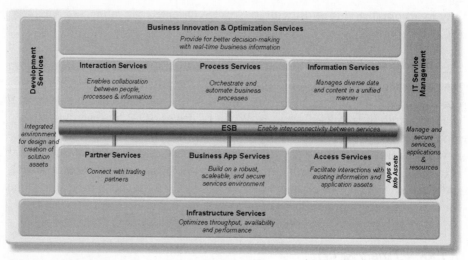

Figure 7.1: *SOA logical model (Source: IBM SOA's Foundation: An Architectural Introduction and Overview, 2002.)*

For this book, our focus is in the Interaction Services segment within the overall SOA logical model. These services play a key role in SOA. In most cases, interaction services provide a window into SOA and enable human interaction with the various processes being performed. Not every service requires a presentation layer, but many of your services (or at least your business processes) will interact with a user at some level. This interface need not be a portal, but portals can furnish some additional capability in this area. Portals provide a single point of entry for many of the different types of users that may interact with various services. Providing a consistent look and feel, similar branding across different applications or functional areas, or perhaps a customized view to different audiences is also valuable functionality that portals easily provide.

Another common question with SOA involves determining the granularity of services within the organization. How fine- or coarse-grained should your services be? This is an extremely tough question that brings with it issues involving performance, reuse, and maintenance. At some point, industry models may become available that provide some guidance about the services required to accomplish common processes within various types of businesses (e.g., healthcare, insurance). This concept is similar to the idea in past years of domain models, in which different industries tried to define industry-standard conventions to facilitate reuse, portability, and adoption.

Another common issue in determining the granularity of services is with performance. We'll dig into this aspect a little later in this chapter.

PORTAL AS AN ONRAMP TO SOA

It's important to understand how a portal may fit into your overall SOA approach. Portals can be so many things to different people that it's easy to be overwhelmed by the capability and functionality you may need to provide. As portals become more and more widespread, developers can apply them to very different segments with a wide variety of targeted users. Different portal scenarios have different requirements, so this variety can make the job confusing for someone who wants to provide applications for portals.

It's generally accepted that "the portal," or in fact the presentation layer, shouldn't drive an SOA strategy; this approach is common, however, because people often think in terms of what they will see and do on the screen. The correct approach is to think of the portal as a way to facilitate the initiation of and human interaction with the business processes that use SOA. You may ask what the difference is, and, admittedly, the line between portal surfacing and process interaction, or the driving process, is sometimes a fine one. One major difference centers on the reusability of services and the interface to those services within the organization. In later chapters, you'll see that portlets can become discrete components that each provide a single function and can be combined in various ways to serve the needs of the business. A common term used to describe this strategy is *composite applications*, and this is the real goal for a process- and SOA-oriented portal.

Unfortunately (or fortunately), you have many options for using portal within your SOA environment. Figure 7.2 portray some of the ways portals can be classified. Drilling down from the logical model to a solid approach and design requires some effort in determining your SOA strategy at the implementation level. Don't worry! We designed this book to give you a lot of information to help you make that decision within the middle layer, or implementation approach.

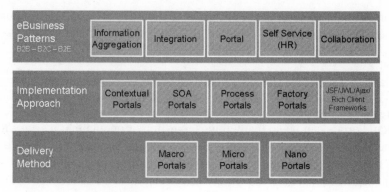

Figure 7.2: Types of portals

IBM Patterns for eBusiness (Reference 2) can serve as a starting point in determining the types of portals that may fit within your business structure. Choosing the correct approach is essential in helping to determine the functionality, applications, and business functions a portal may provide.

In the early days of portal deployment, developers focused portals toward specific tasks and user groups. For this reason, portals traditionally have been classified based on the relation between portal host and portal user. The basic assumption of this classification system is that different users have different needs for the portal. Portals are usually classified into the following categories:

- *Business-to-consumer* (B2C): A portal tailored toward supporting customers of a specific company. The portal's functionality may include product availability, order status, product information, and manuals or customer support. B2C portals often serve as front ends to Customer Relationship Management (CRM) back-end systems.

- *Business-to-business (B2B):* A portal tailored toward companies that deal with the company hosting the portal. B2B portals typically provide a front end for Supply Chain Management (SCM) back-end systems and offer functions such as access to purchase orders, invoices, confirmations, and information about billing and manufacturing processes.

- *Business-to-employee* (B2E): An intranet portal that gives a company's employees unified access to all company IT systems, which may include company news, search engines, travel planning, and collaboration facilities such as discussion groups and team rooms. A B2E portal may also include workflow processes, as in a travel application that requires different steps of approval before booking a travel arrangement.

- *Internet:* A portal accessible by everyone, which thus has a very large user group. Examples of this kind of portal include Excite, Google, and Yahoo, which offer users different services, such as news, search, or e-mail capabilities.

These portal categories are going to fade away because the same user may be an employee one moment and a consumer the next. Users shouldn't have to learn different methods of relating to portals based on their role at a given moment but should expect to do all their work in one place.

As the figure depicts, you can also integrate portals into the IT infrastructure on different levels based on delivery method. Although this book concentrates on what we call the macro level, we see more specialized uses for portals today on a small scale that may become popular in the future. These other types may demand different portlet applications than the macro portals do.

- *Macro portals* are the type of portal covered up to now in the book. Portals of this scale integrate existing back-end applications into one consistent user experience and are accessed by a large number of users. Examples of macro portals include Web portals (e.g., Yahoo) and company portals.

- *Micro portals* are one scale below the macro portals, and only a single user or a small group of users uses them. This kind of portal often functions in online and offline mode because the portal, being very small, is installable in portable devices, such as laptop computers or cars. Examples of this kind of portal include home portals, intermittently connected portals (client portals), and branch portals. Micro portals are often intermittently connected to macro portals to synchronize data held locally on the micro portal with the main macro portal. For example, a sales representative might download company data from an intranet portal to her laptop and work offline at the customer site with this data. As soon as she has access to the intranet again, she can upload the new sales data to the intranet portal.

- *Nano portals* are portals at the smallest level. They are integrated into electronic devices and act as a user interface for devices that may consist of other subcomponents. Examples of this kind of portal are home or telephone controllers, portals integrated into refrigerators or other kitchen appliances (e.g., a slow cooker), or equipment such as computer numerical control (CNC) milling machines.

In between the user-oriented and delivery-oriented classifications lies some of the implementation technology used to deliver the portal. Of course, many different types of portals exist, and any list of discrete types we could provide would have overlap. The following list simply tries to clarify some of the discussion that will arise later in this chapter and within this book.

- *Contextual* portals offer a view to the end user that is directly related to some aspect of what he or she is currently doing within the portal. This view can be task-related or content-related. The portal reacts to different options the user chooses and provides related or directly relevant information based on those options.

- *SOA portals* are portals that interact with services in a direct way. This characteristic isn't a direct contrast to the other types of portals in this list, but it does mean that the portal may not directly involve workflow or process integration. One example might be a portlet that interacts with an existing Web service to provide some type of lookup functionality to the user — for example, a portlet that shows a list of doctors in the user's local area.

- *Process portals* directly offer some type of flow interaction with how an end user interacts with different portlets. Process integration of services is usually managed at a different point within the organization, with the portal surfacing a view where human interaction is required.

- *Factory portals* deserve their own category because the development effort is different from open-standard development. IBM WebSphere Portal Factory is designed to make development easy, especially for non-Java developers moving from a Domino or Microsoft background. Perhaps the factory portal doesn't deserve its own distinction in this list, because it can actually interact with other types of portlets and layers no differently from any other approach. However, approaching implementation this way will change how you tackle some of your integration effort because factory builders are readily available to provide much of the integration capability you may need. With this point in mind, we'll keep factory portals as a separate type of portal.

Over the course of the rest of this book, we'll examine these approaches more closely and look at the issues you may face in designing and developing portals that act as the face of SOA.

Evolution of Portals

It's interesting to understand how portals have evolved over the past few years. This evolution is indicative of how your own organization may need to undergo change and growth over time as portals and portal solutions continue to grow and provide increased functionality. Figure 7.3 illustrates the different stages in the evolution of portals.

- Aggregate portals are really the basis of most portals, bringing together people, content, and applications. The ability to move from a soloed set of applications to a single access point or interface increases end-user productivity and the integration of disparate applications. This aspect of portals remains key in most organizations today as they continue to evolve their portal solutions to provide increased capability and functionality.

- Transaction and collaborative portals aren't a huge leap from the initial idea of the aggregation of information; however, this category provides a different look at the function of a portal for some organizations. These portals feature collaboration between users in a world where human capital is key to driving the business forward — as in a heavy transaction system in a finance or call center type of environment. These distinct-purpose types of portals continue to evolve today as capability grows and businesses realize that a portal can serve as a single access point for a variety of uses.

- *Process-driven portals*, the latest type in the portal evolutionary chain, represent the SOA space and illustrate how portals can be the face of

SOA within your organization. "Collaborative business portals" is really a broad term we can use to represent SOA, process, and contextual portals or really anything in the SOA space.

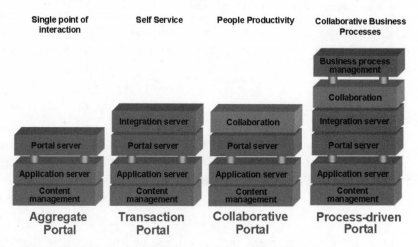

Figure 7.3: Evolution of portals (Source: IBM Portal Evolution, n.d.)

It probably wouldn't be a recommended best practice to try and go from no portal within your organization to a full-blown process and collaborative portal overnight. End users, as well as IT, need to undergo change and evolution a bit more slowly with new technology and functionality. As we indicated earlier, evolution is still the key, although it's possible to jump a few steps in the chain if necessary by leveraging the experience of others who've gone before you. If the technology organization drives the portal, a slower approach that takes the time to see how the business reacts and evolves around the portal is in everyone's best interest. It wouldn't make sense to build a multimillion dollar portal that doesn't fit the needs of the business or one that end users reject as too complicated or too much.

HOW SOA MAY AFFECT A PORTAL

Unsurprisingly enough, provided requirements and the organizational effort around SOA may not always coincide. This is because implementing SOA can sometimes be a time-consuming process, depending on where you are in the roadmap we'll discuss later. Early in the planning, you need to decide whether you're going to release any particular portal functionality early with the goal of updating it to accommodate SOA later or whether some portlets can wait until those services become available. The reality is that many portals will become a mishmash of different types of integration approaches, and this approach is actually okay. The key is to deliver the required functionality to make the business easier or more responsive. You can change the underlying implementation over time, and you probably will several times in the life of many processes.

Figure 7.4 illustrates a sample portal that uses a variety of approaches to provide the necessary functionality. This example derives from a new implementation of a portal that was driven by the business, with IT responsible for providing the required functionality. Although the architecture is fairly clean, it could be cleaner. Specifically, time and cost constraints are key in driving this design, and over time this architecture could evolve to move further down the SOA roadmap.

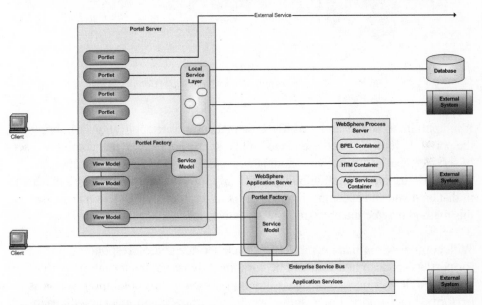

Figure 7.4: Sample SOA portal architecture

PROCESS INTEGRATION AND COMPOSITE APPLICATIONS

Composite applications, depicted in Figure 7.5, can be one of the most powerful uses of a portal but also one of the most difficult to achieve. The idea is that you can compose complete applications by bringing together different services and functionality to serve the user. The focus with this type of approach is on the word *compose*. Administrators or end users compose applications dynamically as they're needed. This composition means taking a set of services and their interfaces (i.e., portlets) and combining or wiring them up together into a single useful application or set of related functions. These functions or services then work toward a single goal that's necessary or useful to the business.

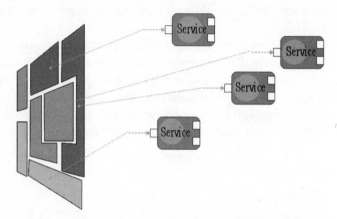

Figure 7.5: Composite applications (Source: IBM Composite
Application Model, n.d.)

It's important to understand the difference that composite applications can bring to the portal. If your goal in design is to build a single application that combines a set of services, that's fine, but you shouldn't consider it a composite application. Rather, it's just an application built specifically for some purpose. There's no shame in that, and you can accomplish much with this approach. In fact, in many cases this method may be the preferred way to deliver functionality to the business.

With composite applications, however, each service and corresponding portlet (or portlets) is designed so it can be combined dynamically at runtime with other portlets to deliver needed business function. Much of this combining action is performed using portlet messaging, whereby portlets communicate with each other using realtime messages to determine which step to take next.

Reusability is a key benefit of composite applications, but you must weigh this potential advantage against the real possibility of reuse. Examine services, or function points, carefully to determine whether reuse is really possible. If not, you might waste your time trying to make something reusable that actually may never be used in another situation. This aspect of design is common in enterprise architecture, especially in the J2EE space. We often add in, or force, the ability to reuse functionality even where no reuse requirement exists. Agile development tends to shy away from this approach, claiming that there's no value in the reuse factor if in fact no reuse ever occurs. Our point here is that although one of SOA's goals is reuse (and reconfiguration in different ways), everything won't fit this model, and spending time, effort, and money on achieving reuse for portlets that won't ever be reused can be wasteful.

For those functions that do lend themselves toward reuse, portlet messaging can be a big step in the evolution of your technical environment. You'll learn more about messaging in Chapter 10. Be aware that using messaging in a single application designed from scratch differs greatly from designing portlets to use messaging that will be determined by an administrator or end user. The need to format the messaging standards so that combinations become almost trivial is a major step in your development evolution and team discipline.

TECHNOLOGY CONSIDERATIONS

Technology considerations aren't SOA-specific but more general to the portal implementation itself, starting with which portal server or platform you're going to use and moving all the way across the spectrum to other applications, integration approaches, and even which programming language you'll use.

The authors of this book are experts in WebSphere Portal and related technologies, so we obviously have a bit of a bias. Because you're reading the book, we make the assumption that you, too, have a bias or at least have chosen WebSphere Portal as your portal platform. However, many decisions remain in terms of how you might implement different functionality within your portal. Our purpose in writing this book is to help with that effort, but many decisions must be made at an organizational level, keeping your best interests in mind.

Often in technology, now even more than before, we're looking for the architectural nirvana — that approach or solution that solves all our problems, provides all required functionality, and is ever-extensible with minimal effort. Unfortunately, the reality is that as functionality expands, so do the requirements. We can never quite get ahead, so it's often all we can do just to make it work. What we are not saying here is to settle, but rather simply to be realistic about what you expect from any solution.

One interesting aspect surrounding SOA is that IT investments should be geared toward the requirements of the business. Although we hope this is usually the case, in the smaller scale reality doesn't always reflect this goal. Individual practitioners and teams often make decisions based on what they think they know to be true, or even based on what they want to learn. Although we all agree that learning is an important aspect of every business, it doesn't always reflect an immediate business need.

One key factor in making technology decisions is the tactical vs. strategic influence within your organization. *Tactical* means something must be done quickly to fill an immediate business need, while *strategic* focuses more on building on reusability across the enterprise.

Portlet Factory vs. JavaServer Faces

Whether to use the Portlet Factory or JavaServer Faces (JSF) is probably one of the biggest technology questions developers or development managers might face in setting up their project. This topic can become even more muddled as you evaluate options such as Struts or the native Java Portlet API. Two key criteria that can help you make this decision are the current skills within your team and your organizational strategy.

- *Current skills*: Does the team currently have Java, portal, or JSF skills? Often, teams coming from a background in Microsoft or Domino technology don't have strong Java skills readily available. Training is probably necessary with any technology you choose if your team lacks the immediate skills to deliver robust, scalable portlets. A technology mentor is also a possibility, although this approach works best when coupled with some amount of training.

- *Organizational strategy*: This decision can often be made at the organizational level to ensure that resources have the same or a similar set of skills and can be used where and when necessary on different projects. To facilitate code reuse as technology evolves within the company, some

190

organizational standards require or ask developers to use open or industry-standard approaches when possible.

The confusing part of choosing between Portlet Factory and JSF is the fact that experts in each of these technologies will tell you that their alternative makes development easy. For the most part, both sides are correct — for those with expertise in these tools. More data points should probably go into your decision, and in some cases you may use a mixture of approaches within your portal based on time, cost, or skills constraints. There is no easy or single right answer for any of the approaches we suggest or compare in this chapter.

Regardless of which type of portlet framework you choose, your team may need training in Java, J2EE, and WebSphere Portal. In any framework, it may be necessary to dig beneath the covers, and the more you know about your developers, the easier this effort will be.

BACK-END CONSIDERATIONS

Later in this chapter and throughout the book, we focus on a separation of concerns within the design of your portal application. In other words, we want to separate the business logic and persistence layer from the actual presentation the portlets will perform. Oftentimes there's some bleeding between the layers, but we've learned over time that the more we can minimize this bleeding effect, the better off we'll be in the long term.

Some of the common questions that arise when integrating services into the portal revolve around which technology approach to use. You saw some of your different options earlier, in Figure 7.4. In the next section, we'll discuss portal service layers, which bring more depth to this topic. For now, it's important to think about the skills and organizational strategy discussion we started above. Are there compelling reasons to accept one approach over another in your situation? Only careful consideration of skills and requirements can guide you in making that decision.

PORTAL SERVICE LAYERS

Remember the mention of loose coupling earlier in this chapter? You knew it would come back to haunt us. Let's look at that concept with a little more detail.

According to Martin Fowler (see Reference 1), the first law of distributed computing is, "Don't distribute your objects!" Yet that is exactly the approach SOA lends itself so nicely toward. Many tradeoffs exist in adopting this style or architecture, but there are techniques you can use to obtain much of the benefit SOA provides while mitigating some of the possible risk.

A *local service layer* is one such approach you can use to wrap incoming enterprise services that are integrated into the portal. This is an important point, and one that developers overlook much too often. Just because you can integrate with an external service, application, database, or whatever doesn't always mean you should. Okay, so maybe this is fine for the first portlet, but what about the second? Duplication of code comes to mind, and what happens when that application interface changes? A second, and maybe more serious, complication could be the performance impact on the external service when multiple portlets on the page are accessing it. Figure 7.6 depicts a simple example of what can happen in this case. As more portlets access the same service and more users start to access those portlets, overload can quickly overcome any service not sized for the required traffic.

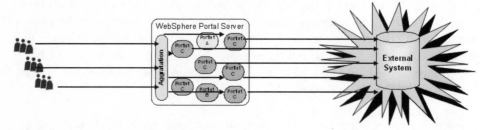

Figure 7.6: Direct connect via portlet

Local service layers can not only abstract business logic from the presentation layer but also solve some of these potential performance issues that may be unique to a portal environment. For now, realize that Figure 7.7 shows how a local service layer not only can provide reuse but also can directly impact performance as necessary.

Remember one of the tenets of using a portal: "It will always be the portal's fault." What this maxim really means is that end users don't know or care about the external system; to them, all that matters is that the portal isn't responding quickly enough to meet their demands. The blame will fall on the portal team

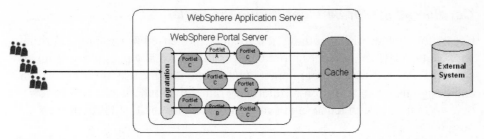

Figure 7.7: Local service layer with caching

every time until it can prove the problem lies elsewhere in the system. Even then, end users will only see the issue as a problem with your portal.

Figure 7.8 illustrates how the portal team can protect itself by providing a local service layer where possible to minimize any back-end problems. (Obviously, service level agreements are necessary to ensure back-end services can perform to the levels required by the portal.)

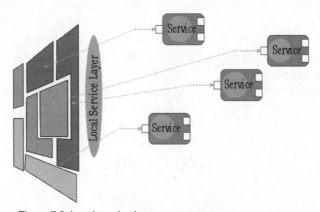

Figure 7.8: Local service layer

Now our composite application strategy looks a little different. Not much, because we can still follow our original ideas — just with the understanding that different layers may be necessary with the final deployment of the application and that we need a greater understanding of how the portlet or service might be used to ensure services aren't overloaded or misused as they become combined in ways we may never have imagined.

Considerations for Services Within the Portal

Separation of concerns is nothing new to any experienced programmer. Writing applications in layers provides more benefits than it's really possible to enumerate here. Object-oriented programmers understand that the use of encapsulation and designing by composition of interfaces rather than inheritance will follow object-oriented best practices and can greatly increase the flexibility of their design.

One key characteristic of building a solid service layer is that it makes building the presentation layer easy. If the right actions are available and there's a well-defined set of business or value objects, creating the layout and binding the different components really can be a trivial exercise. This isn't to say that building a portlet is as simple as all that, but it lets the portlet programmer focus on the user interface, validation, client-side activities, and just making it look good.

Not so long ago, the focus for portlets was to pretty much do everything and design the portlet to act as a complete application. However, learning along with the rest of the J2EE and object-oriented world, we've defined a set of layers that allow the greatest flexibility and still provide the correct result. Figure 7.9 provides an example of what this model may look like. Notice that the presentation layer still includes some helper and utility classes; however, these are mostly used to wrap or namespace encode anything provided to the portlet through the layers below.

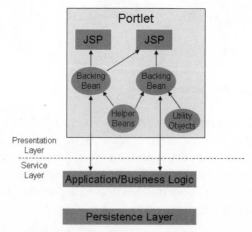

Figure 7.9: Portlet separation of concerns

The persistence layer is another point to discuss. This book doesn't address this layer in any real form other than to note that it's a necessary component of good application design and to discuss in different sections what we've done to handle this layer. Several great reads are available on this subject, along with different frameworks that may help in building the service layer. These layers can not only abstract persistence to the underlying data store but also provide access to remote services via a single set of interfaces.

REUSE OF THE DATA ACCESS SERVICE

Appendix B provides a pretty complete data access service for you to use within some of the chapters of this book. We mainly use this service within the JavaServer Faces and Workplace Forms chapters along with some modifications. Because these are single-use scenarios, the local service works pretty well for use with these sample portlets; however, in a real situation, the service has some major flaws.

Using WebSphere database connection pools is the first issue we should mention. As provided, the service makes a direct connection to the database, which is fine for testing; however, in a heavy load situation, connection pools are the right approach. Ideally, you wouldn't use a database of this type in a real-world production environment but rather a more prominent enterprise database management system (DBMS), such as DB2 or Oracle.

The second issue is concurrent access to the service itself from our portlets. As designed in the appendix, the service provides little protection against different portlets each creating an instance of the service for use within each portlet. This limitation will easily result in multiple instances each trying to access the database in some fashion, which could cause some conflicts.

In this chapter, we discuss the idea of the local service layer and look at some approaches to implementing this layer. Our first thought may be to create a singleton, which ensures that only one instance of the service is created at a time, thus providing better protection against concurrent access of the database by different portlets. Other options for solving this problem exist, such as using a portlet service or employing a lightweight container such as Spring to manage service instantiation.

Creating a singleton maybe the simplest option and requires just a simple change to one class. To create a singleton, you must modify the ClassicModelsService class, which is the API used by the portlet. The sample code in Listing 7.1 shows (in bold) the three main changes that need to be made:

- Add an _instance variable to hold the current instance of the service.

- Change the public constructor to private so other classes can't instantiate an instance of this class.

- Add the getInstance method to the class.

```
public class ClassicModelsService {

private static SqlMapClient sqlMap;
private static ClassicModelsService _instance = null;

/**
 * Set up iBatis SqlMapClient
 */
private ClassicModelsService() {

    try {
        String resource = "sql-map-config.xml";
        Reader reader;
        reader = Resources.getResourceAsReader (resource);

        sqlMap = SqlMapClient
    Builder.buildSqlMapClient(reader);

    } catch (Exception e) {
        System.out.println("ClassicModelsService.constructor - Exception");
            e.printStackTrace();
    }
}

/**
 * Returns an Instance of this class
 * @return ClassicModelsService
 */
public static ClassicModelsService getInstance()
    {
        if (_instance == null)
            _instance = new ClassicModelsService();
        return _instance;
    }
```

Listing 7.1: Converting ClassicModelsService to a singleton

196

The portlets trying to call this class use the getInstance method. Rather than instantiating the class itself, they can use the method as follows:

```
ClassicModelsService myService = ClassicModelsService.getInstance();
```

One note to mention is that JSF tooling doesn't handle singletons very well. The introspection that the tooling does in Rational Application Developer depends on a public constructor to be able to process the services as a Managed Bean. For this reason, you may need to change the service to a singleton after developing your portlet code. It's a simple step to change the instantiation in the JSF portlet to use getInstance after you've tested the portlet. In large development efforts, it would be worth the time to use a different approach as mentioned earlier (e.g., a lightweight JavaBean container) to manage your local services.

Integrating Simple Caching into Your Service

In the section on portal service layers, we mentioned some of the benefits of caching data at this level. There are many reasons to cache data, some of which would take up a whole chapter or book. In this section, we outline a simple case where you can easily integrate caching into your service and where it may provide great benefit to the overall application performance and scalability. If you review Appendix B, you can see that the service provides access to a fair bit of customer and sales data. You'll need to analyze your data and application requirements thoroughly to determine where and how caching should occur. A good knowledge of the caching mechanism and how it may affect the Java Virtual Machine (JVM) is also necessary.

Luckily for us, WebSphere Application Server (WAS) itself provides a robust caching mechanism called the *dynamic cache service*. This service provides several interfaces and can intercept calls at different locations within your application to provide some caching benefit. For example, using this service you can cache servlet and JSP output to store the resulting HTML from a page. This technique results in subsequent calls to the servlet pulling the HTML from the cache and not the servlet itself.

Another set of interfaces into the dynamic cache service are the DistributedMap and the DistributedObjectCache. These simple interfaces can cache and share

Java objects using a reference in the object cache. Access to the cache instance takes place using the Java Naming and Directory Interface (JNDI) namespace.

Before we set up the cache instance in WebSphere, let's make the required changes to our code to use the cache. We've decided there are way too many customer lookups occurring in our code. Being the core object in the application, customers are being accessed by every portlet on every call. Also, it appears that this access occurs in groups, with a small number of customers being used at any given time. This scenario gives us a good reason to go ahead and implement caching on the customer object when it is retrieved from the database. Subsequent lookups can then be retrieved from the cache and won't go back to the database for retrieval.

Fortunately, implementing the caching feature results in us editing the same source file we used to implement our singleton. Listing 7.2 shows the changes needed to set up the dMap for use within our code.

```
public class ClassicModelsService {

private static SqlMapClient sqlMap;
private static ClassicModelsService _instance = null;
private DistributedMap customerDM;

/**
   * Set up iBatis SqlMapClient
*/
private ClassicModelsService() {

   try {
      System.out.println("ClassModelsService init...");
      String resource = "sql-map-config.xml";
      Reader reader;
      reader = Resources.getResourceAsReader (resource);
      sqlMap = SqlMapClientBuilder.buildSqlMapClient(reader);

      InitialContext ic = new InitialContext();
      customerDM =(DistributedMap)ic.lookup("services/cache/customers");

      System.out.println("ClassModelsService init... Finished");
   } catch (Exception e) {
      System.out.println("ClassicModelsService.constructor - Exception");
      e.printStackTrace();
   }
}
}
```

Listing 7.2: Setting up the DistributedMap

Three lines are all it really takes to have access to the dMap for caching our data. We store a handle to the dMap as a private variable within our class for use by the caching method. Listing 7.3 illustrates the actual caching to be done within the findCustomerById method.

```
/**
 * Retrieve a single Customer object by Id.
 * @return Customer
 */
public Customers findCustomerById(int id) {

Customers cust = null;


try {
    String key = Integer.toString(id);
    if ((cust = (Customers) customerDM.get(key)) == null ){
        System.out.println("Customer NOT FOUND in cache");
        CustomersKey custKey = new CustomersKey();
        custKey.setCustomernumber(new Integer(id));
        cust = (Customers)
sqlMap.queryForObject("selectCustomerByPrimaryKey",
                custKey);
        customerDM.put(key,cust);
    }else {
        System.out.println("Customer FOUND in cache");
    }
} catch (SQLException e) {
    System.out.println("ClassicModelsService.findCustomersById -
Exception");
    e.printStackTrace();
}
return cust;
}
```

Listing 7.3: Using the DistributedMap to cache customer lookup

Using the ID of the customer as the cache key, we can convert it to a String for storage. The dMap works only with Strings as the key. This technique also makes it easier for our cache-viewing portlet later on. The additions to the method at that point are really simple; either it finds the customer in the cache or it goes to the database for the customer data. If it does go to the database, it then stores the retrieved customer in the cache.

Setting Up the dMap in WAS

Before you can test your service, you need to set up the cache instance in WebSphere Application Server. You have several options for configuring dynamic cache instances within WebSphere: the administration console, configuration scripts, and resource references in your code. For this example, we'll use the admin console to set up an instance for our service.

Start and open the WAS admin console. Using the left menu, navigate to the **Object cache instances** section (**Resources** > **Cache instances** > **Object cache instances**), as shown in Figure 7.10.

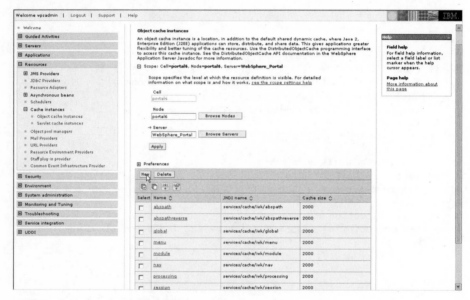

Figure 7.10: Opening the AppServer console

Once on the **Object cache instances** page, click **New** to create a new cache instance. Complete the resulting form (shown in Figure 7.11) as required, using the following sample information to match up with the other changes we've made in the service and the upcoming portlet.

- **Name:** customers

- **JNDI name:** services/cache/customers

- **Description:** <your choice>

Leave everything else at the default, and click **OK**.

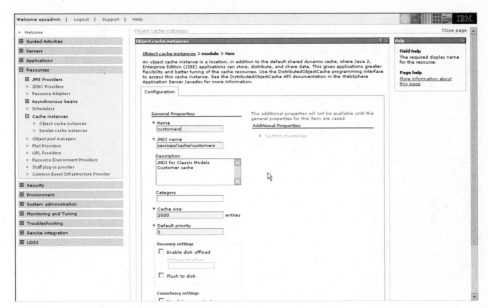

Figure 7.11: Creating a new DMap instance

When prompted as shown in Figure 7.12, click **Save** to apply your changes.

*Figure 7.12: Saving the
new dMap instance*

Before closing the admin console, check to ensure the dynamic cache service
is enabled. This service is enabled by default, so usually this is not an issue.
To verify the setting, navigate to **Servers > Application servers > Dynamic
cache service**. Make sure the **Enable service at server startup** option (shown in
Figure 7.13) is selected. You can now close and stop the admin server and start
the portal.

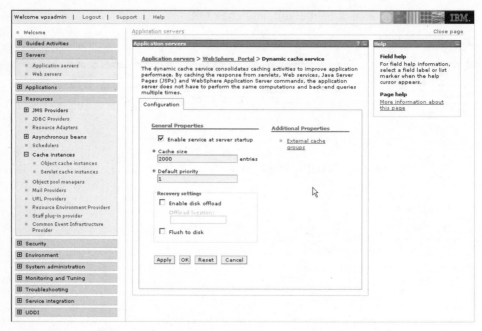

Figure 7.13: Checking the dynamic cache service

During portal startup, you can view the SystemOut.log (Listing 7.4) to ensure your cache instance is configured correctly. Check to verify that the portal is binding the cache instance name and JNDI name as configured.

```
[10/18/06 13:11:01:047 EDT] 0000000a ResourceMgrIm I   WSVR0049I:
Binding abspathreverse as services/cache/iwk/abspathreverse
[10/18/06 13:11:01:062 EDT] 0000000a ResourceMgrIm I   WSVR0049I:
Binding customers as services/cache/customers
[10/18/06 13:11:01:203 EDT] 0000000a TCPChannel    A   TCPC0001I: TCP
Channel SIB_TCP_JFAP is listening on host *   (IPv4) port 10026.
```

Listing 7.4: SystemOut.log

For more information about using the dynamic cache service and distributed map interface, check the WebSphere Application InfoCenter at *http://publib.boulder.ibm.com/infocenter/wasinfo/v6r0/index.jsp.*

DistributedMap Viewer Portlet

Unfortunately, there's no built-in way to view the dMap that is set up in the application server. For this reason, we provide you with a very simple dMap viewer portlet that you can extend and use in your operations. Sometimes you need to view what's in the cache — for example, for debugging purposes, to remove some items from the cache, or to clear the entire cache.

We provide the sample code for this portlet at the code download site. This chapter only points out the highlights of this portlet. If you download the samples, you'll have the complete code.

The doView method, shown in Listing 7.5, does most of the work in obtaining information from the cache for display in the portlet. This method goes through several steps. First, it gets the cache instance. The portlet looks in the portlet preferences to determine the JNDI name for looking up the cache instance. We perform the lookup in the doView method instead of in the init method so that you can create multiple copies and configure them to view different caches.

```
public void doView(RenderRequest request, RenderResponse response)
throws PortletException, IOException {

    // Set the MIME type for the render response
    response.setContentType(request.getResponseContentType());

    //I hate to do it this way, but I wanted to make the cache JNDI name
    //variable but not have to do the lookup every time I passed through
    //the doView. I'll cache the name and if it's null, do the lookup again.
    if (CacheJNDI == null) {
        try {

            //The JNDI value is stored in the portlet preferences.
            //This lets us create new copies of the portlet, each of
which
            // can view a different cache instance.
            CacheJNDI = request.getPreferences().getValue(CONFIG_KEY, null);
            InitialContext ic = new InitialContext();
            dMap =(DistributedMap)ic.lookup(CacheJNDI);
        } catch (Exception e) {
            System.out.println("CacheMonitor.constructor - Exception");
```

Listing 7.5: Dmap viewer portlet doView method (part 1 of 2)

```
            e.printStackTrace();
        }
    }
    //refreshing cached data for display
    //get session bean instance
    ClassicCacheMonitorPortletSessionBean sessionBean =
        getSessionBean(request);
    try {
        if( sessionBean != null ) {
            //set the number of items in the cache for display
            sessionBean.setArraysize(dMap.size());

            //fill in the list of key items in the dmap
            ArrayList result = new ArrayList();
            Set set = dMap.keySet();
            Iterator it = set.iterator();
            while (it.hasNext()) {
                String value = it.next().toString();
                result.add(value);
            }
            //set the bean in the session for use by the JSP
            sessionBean.setArray(result);
            request.getPortletSession().setAttribute(SESSION_BEAN, sessionBean);
        }
    }catch (Exception ex) {
        System.out.println("CMCacheMonitor.refreshCacheData() - Exception");
        ex.printStackTrace();
    }

    // invoke the JSP to render
    PortletRequestDispatcher rd =
getPortletContext().getRequestDispatcher(
    getJspFilePath(request, VIEW_JSP));
    rd.include(request,response);
}
```

Listing 7.5: Dmap viewer portlet doView method (part 2 of 2)

The second part of the method actually looks up the values in the cache and places the key list in the session bean. Method processAction (Listing 7.6) accepts different commands from the portlet to perform different functions.

```
public void processAction(ActionRequest request, ActionResponse
response) throws PortletException, java.io.IOException {

    //clear cache if the CLEAR button is pushed
    if( request.getParameter(CLEAR_CACHE) != null ) {
        dMap.clear();
    }

    //clear an individual key if one is chosen
    if( request.getParameter(CLEAR_KEY) != null ) {
        String tempvalue = request.getParameter("keyvalue");
        dMap.remove(tempvalue);
    }

    //change the JNDI string to let this portlet view another cache instance
    if( request.getParameter(CONFIG_SUBMIT) != null ) {
        PortletPreferences prefs = request.getPreferences();
        try {
            prefs.setValue(CONFIG_KEY,request.getParameter(CONFIG_TEXT));
            prefs.store();
            CacheJNDI = null;
        } catch( ReadOnlyException roe ) {

        } catch( ValidatorException ve ) {
        }
    }
}
```

Listing 7.6: Dmap Viewer Portlet processAction method

Finally, you can install and view the portlet for use with this and other cache instances. Figure 7.14 shows two copies of the portlet. One is in configure mode and can be changed to view another cache instance. The second shows the actual portlet view. This view lists the keys along with the number of keys in the cache and lets you clear an individual key or clear the entire cache.

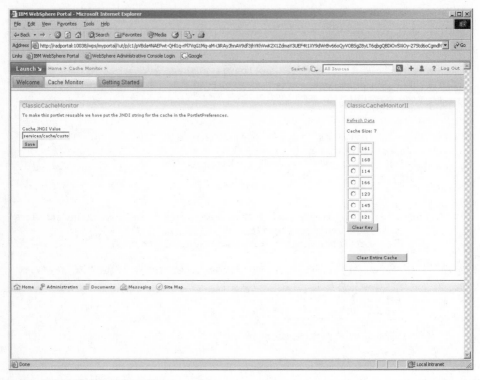

Figure 7.14: DistributedMap Viewer portlet

For your own portlet, you may want to add some functionality that lets the user scroll through the key list by pages; otherwise, you could have several hundred or thousand keys in the list on a single view.

SOA ROADMAP FOR PORTAL

There's no secret for jumping on the SOA bandwagon, nor is there one right way for all our customers. Earlier in this chapter, we mentioned that one approach might be to dissect processes and tasks from a business point of view. Because SOA is really about meeting the needs of the business, this approach makes a lot of sense.

But what if you already have a large portal investment or you want to approach SOA from the technical perspective to help you meet business needs as users request new or modified functionality? In some respects, the business doesn't care, nor should it, how you implement functionality or need to know that it is paying for these changes.

A roadmap is simply a path, or approach, for getting to one place from another. In our case, we want to step into the SOA path at some point along the road and then stay at this location, move slowly ahead, or try to quickly get to the final location. As we've noted, there are many ways to get on the SOA path, so variations of this progression will number larger than any one person can possibly understand.

Figure 7.15 shows the four steps of our SOA roadmap. Our example takes the view that you already have a portal in your environment or are working on a portal engagement.

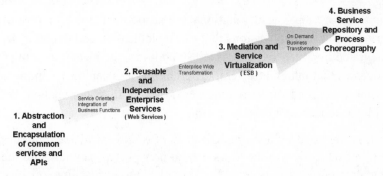

Figure 7.15: SOA roadmap

The steps outlined here are meant to represent an ever-increasing investment in time, infrastructure, and development; however, each step provides a greater return on that investment.

- *Step 1 — Abstraction and encapsulation of common services and APIs:*
  Step 1 is pretty simple and probably something you should be accomplishing in your development already. This book talks a lot about separation of concerns and encapsulation of common layers and services. If you're not at this step, SOA may be a bigger jump than you expect because it requires a lot of discipline to build correctly.

- *Step 2 — Reusable and independent enterprise services:* Consider
  Step 2 an extension of Step 1. The idea is that if you've defined a good set of APIs within your environment, you can redesign these as reusable

207

services that you can combine independently into different applications. The idea of building these processes and tasks using a technology such as Web services lets us bridge the integration gap. That means you can make services developed with different technologies or interacting with different applications available in a common manner to your portal.

- *Step 3 — Mediation and service virtualization:* Step 3 usually involves a major infrastructure investment; however, with that investment comes added benefits. Service mediation and virtualization imply the use of an Enterprise Service Bus (ESB), which you can think of as a design pattern that helps you manage large numbers of services and the interaction between them.

- *Step 4 — Business service repository and process choreography:* You can think of Step 4 as an additional extension in creating a repository of services and service versions that can be looked up and dynamically integrated into business processes. In addition, the idea of creating processes that integrate several different services can be accomplished earlier in the roadmap as requirements dictate. In a later chapter, we'll explore the idea of a process portal.

In this section, we've taken a very small view of what is available, but our goal is simply to introduce you to the ideas behind how portals can play into the SOA space. In reality, portals can become the face of SOA because in many business processes, human interaction is highly integrated.

SUMMARY

In this chapter, we've introduced you to some ideas about how portals and portlets can fit into an overall SOA strategy within your environment. Portals provide a view to the world, and in reality nothing can happen within the business without that view. How you approach that view can make a large difference in whether a portal adds value to your strategy and in how much value versus overhead the portal will add.

This book doesn't cover many of the out-of-the-box features that WebSphere Portal (or any well-designed portal framework) provides — features such as authentication and authorization, navigation, document and content management, collaboration, single sign-on, and integration. These capabilities will provide instant value to your organization because you won't need to build this type of functionality, which is taken for granted in many applications today, into your applications. To learn more about these and other topics discussed in this chapter, visit http://www.portalpatterns.org (Figure 7.16), a site dedicated to sharing information about reusable portal design and navigation patterns.

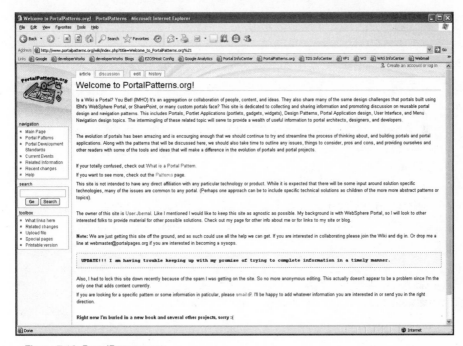

Figure 7.16: PortalPatterns.org

REFERENCES

1. Fowler, Martin. Patterns of Enterprise Application Architecture. Addison-Wesley Professional, 2002.

2. IBM SOA Foundation: An Architectural Introduction and Overview. IBM DeveloperWorks: December 8, 2005. http://www-128.ibm.com/developerworks/webservices/library/ws-soa-whitepaper/index.html?S_TACT=106AJ04W&S_CMP=campaign.

3. IBM Patterns for eBusiness. http://www-128.ibm.com/developerworks/patterns.

Chapter Eight

Fundamentals of Portlet Factory

IBM WebSphere Portlet Factory provides a set of tools for rapidly creating, customizing, maintaining, and deploying portlets. By taking advantage of the Portlet Factory's powerful features, you can greatly streamline the process of developing portlets and take your first steps toward implementing a true Service Oriented Architecture (SOA).

Before we introduce the fundamental concepts of the Portlet Factory, it's important for you to understand some background on the origins of this tool set. This information will help you appreciate the power of the Portlet Factory and why we believe it will change the fundamental way we code.

PORTLET FACTORY BACKGROUND

IBM obtained the Portlet Factory technology in late 2005 as part of its acquisition of Bowstreet, a small New England startup company. Formed in the late 1990s, Bowstreet was focused on software automation and Web services. Andy Roberts, a brilliant engineer and a strategic thinker, conceptualized Bowstreet's flagship product, named Factory. Before joining Bowstreet, Andy was the chief product evangelist at Parametric Technology Corporation (PTC), where he came up with the idea of the Factory. A highly successful provider of mechanical design automation software, PTC is most famous for its computer-aided design (CAD) software packages. Engineers and architects around the world now use

CAD packages to create three-dimensional engineering models and drawings of machines and buildings.

PTC introduced the concept of *parametric feature-based modeling*, in which a designer added a feature to a model, which in turn generated geometry on the object (which is what the designer was really interested in). A feature represented a characteristic portion of an object, such as a pattern of holes, a shelled-out region, or a slot. The designer added a feature to a model and gave it some input parameters (e.g., dimension), and the feature then went off and created the appropriate geometric entities on the object. More important, when the designer changed a parameter on one of the features, a regeneration engine rebuilt the entire object, propagating the change throughout and managing the constraint equations. For instance, if the designer changed a dimension on a circular plate (say, by increasing the diameter of that feature), he wouldn't need to manually adjust any of the other features. The hole pattern feature applied to the plate would automatically react and add more holes, triggering an update by a rounded edge feature, which would alter the edge radius on the holes to accommodate the increasing number of holes. The regeneration engine could rebuild the object because it understood the parametric relationships among features.

You must be thinking, "Why are we talking about CAD packages and parametric modeling? I'm reading this book to learn portlet programming." Well, Andy brought the concept of automatic change propagation to the world of Web applications, and the idea of the Factory was born. Based on this concept of automation and change propagation, the engineering team at Bowstreet, led by chief engineer Jonathan Booth, then invented and designed the Factory. They built the first of its kind: a factory to manufacture Web applications.

CAD software packages and the concept of parametric modeling deeply influenced the vision of the Factory. In the Factory's case, the final object generated by the model is a Web application rather than mechanical objects. Even the Factory's interface looks similar to the CAD software package, as you can see in Figure 8.1.

 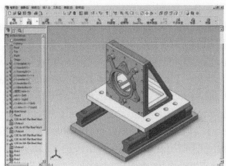

Figure 8.1: Factory vs. CAD package

Despite the fact that you use the Factory to build Web applications rather than mechanical assemblies, the thought process behind using each tool is strikingly similar. Factory users take prebuilt features, or *builders* as they're now called — a form, table, or SQL Call builder, for example — and drop them together in a model to rapidly create or modify entities in the Web application. These builders are parametrically tied to each other: When one input parameter to a builder changes, the Factory's regeneration engine re-creates the Web application, propagating and readjusting the changes throughout the model. A simple example will illustrate this idea more clearly.

Let's say we were to create a simple Web application to display data residing in a relational database or returned by a remote Web service. In the traditional J2EE world, this task would entail writing Java components to invoke an SQL call or a Web service and creating a separate JSP to manage the display (view) of this data. With the Factory, you use an SQL Call builder or a Web Service Call builder to construct code to handle the back-end calls, and you use a Data Page builder to construct the application elements that generate the presentation layer. Behind the scenes, the Factory's regeneration engine writes the same Java and JSP code that developers traditionally would hand-code. Hence the name "Factory" — because it is a factory to produce code!

Is the Factory a code generator? Not exactly, at least not in the traditional sense you may have seen before. Unlike the Factory, traditional code generators aren't designed to handle continuous change. To comprehend this idea better, let's continue with our "display data" use case and develop it further.

The fun begins when you modify the underlying database table or SQL query, or when the interface of the Web service you're invoking changes. In the traditional J2EE world (manual coding), the developer must go back into the code and manually adjust the Java Bean to interface with the changed table structure or Web service. He or she then manages the changes in the JSP file to build the modified view. In the Factory world, though, the SQL Call builder that interfaces with the table automatically detects the changes at regeneration time and adjusts the code (generated Java components) accordingly, the change is propagated to the other builders, and a new view (JSP) is automatically created. So not only does the Portlet Factory rapidly create Web applications; it also manages change with minimal manual intervention by developers as business requirements constantly are updated. It's an intelligent software factory that generates code on the fly.

We can apply this idea of automating software creation to any domain. You can create builders and a regeneration engine for Active Server Pages (ASP) and .NET, PERL, or the language or domain of your choice. In the end, we're creating an assembly line (builders) to produce the final product — in our case, software.

In addition to the regeneration engine (which writes the artifacts), early releases of the Factory had their own execution stack. However, J2EE and .NET players quickly came to dominate the server stacks. The resulting price wars among the major players led to a steep decline in prices, and application servers quickly became an inexpensive commodity. Customers were also nervous about getting locked into proprietary engines. Bowstreet's leadership saw the winds of change and quickly decided to move off their proprietary stack to run on standard J2EE-compliant engines (e.g., BEA, Tomcat, WebSphere). The Factory's fourth release saw a major shift, and the regeneration engine began to produce standard J2EE artifacts (Java, JSP, and XML code). However, by that time it was the year 2002, and the enterprise software market had tanked. Startups were closing at a frivolous pace. Bowstreet had to find a niche, a sweet spot where it could focus and continue its existence. It was then that Jonathan Booth and his team of engineers turned their attention to the Portal market and applied this technology to create portlets, thus inventing the Portlet Factory. The Factory metamorphosed into the WebSphere Portlet Factory, and the rest is history.

Now that you have a high-level understanding of what the Portlet Factory is all about, have learned the interesting history behind its conception and development, and know the origin of the name Factory, let's get down to business and write some code — or, rather, learn how to use the Factory so it can write the code for us. That is the fundamental paradigm shift we all need to get used to. Why manually stitch our clothes when we can use a sewing machine?

BUILDING BLOCKS

As you begin to work with the Portlet Factory, you'll need to commit two new terms to memory: builders and models. Let's examine the concepts behind these two key elements of working with the Factory.

Builders

A builder is a software automation component that captures design intelligence and automates the creation of code. Builders are the fundamental building blocks of the Portlet Factory, and it's worthwhile spending a few minutes to grasp this concept. Similar to customizable robots in an assembly line, builders perform specific software automation tasks based on inputs, or parameters, specified by developers. The WebSphere Portlet Factory software includes more than 120 builders that automate a wide range of tasks, such as creating HTML from a schema or integrating with common back-end systems (e.g., databases, IBM Lotus Domino software, SAP, Siebel). Builders feature easy-to-use, wizard-like user interfaces that make developing portlets both easy and fast. But builders are much more powerful than wizards because you can use them iteratively throughout the entire development process. At any time, you can go back and change a builder's input values and have the entire portlet application updated instantly.

Behind the scenes, a builder consists of a Java class that performs the appropriate automation task (e.g., creating the JSP for a button) and an XML document that defines the builder's characteristics. The screen shown in Figure 8.2, of the SAP View and Form builder, shows the builder generating the Java/JSP artifacts necessary to connect to an SAP R/3 system and pull data to display it on the portlet.

Figure 8.2: SAP View and Form builder writing Java/JSP code

A builder can manage a relatively simple task, such as sorting a list returned from a back-end call, or it can execute something as complex as connecting to an enterprise resource planning (ERP) system (e.g., PeopleSoft, SAP) and managing a transaction, with the result set converted into an XML object. There are builders to build your presentation layer as well. There are simple builders, such as the Button builder, which puts a button on a page, and the Link builder, which puts a link on the page. And there are complex builders, such as the Data Page builder, which builds a complete form, including validation rules, simply by introspecting a schema (one of the input parameters to the builder). When we say a "complex" builder, we don't mean it is complex to use but rather that it manages a complex task that would take a traditional programmer a long time to hand-code. In addition to the base group of builders, products built on top of the base Portlet Factory product, such as the Workplace Dashboard Framework and the SAP Framework, provide sets of additional builders geared toward building particular types of applications (dashboards, employee and manager self-service applications for SAP, and so on). The point is that if you understand how to employ builders and, more important, which builder to use in which scenario, you can master the Portlet Factory.

The coolest aspect of the Portlet Factory is that you can write your own builders as well! If you find yourself writing some code over and over, you should consider building a builder to manage the task. Understanding how to create builders is beyond the scope of this book, but the base Portlet Factory product provides samples and tutorials that illustrate how to write builders. Understanding the artifacts of a builder and how to write them is worthwhile, especially for project architects. In essence, you're writing a component that eventually will write code for you.

Models

Models are the second element at the core of the Portlet Factory. A model is a container of builders that holds the instruction set used by the Factory engine to generate and execute the Web application.

Just as J2EE developers start out by writing JSP files or JavaBeans when they begin to build a Web application, a Portlet Factory developer creates a new model file to build Web applications and portlets. A typical model file consists of several builders that together constitute a Web application. A two-to-one mapping typically exists between a model and a portlet. The first model acts as the data services layer (interacting with your back-end system), and the second model is the presentation layer (containing the front-end builders). Together, these two layers create a single portlet.

Writing Your First Portlet

Let's get down to business now and create our first Portlet Factory portlet. In keeping with the tradition of the programming world, we'll start off by writing a hello world portlet. While doing that, we'll familiarize ourselves with the integrated development environment (IDE) and make sure we've installed and configured our runtime environment and designer correctly. We'll assume you've successfully installed the Portlet Factory and configured it with the Portal Unit Test Environment(UTE) inside your Rational Application Developer (RAD) environment.

The Hello World Portlet

We'll begin by creating a new empty model called HelloWorld. Figure 8.3 depicts the steps to create the new model. Make sure you're in the Factory perspective within RAD, and select **File** > **New** > **WebSphere Portlet Factory Model**.

When prompted to choose the model type (Figure 8.4), select Empty.

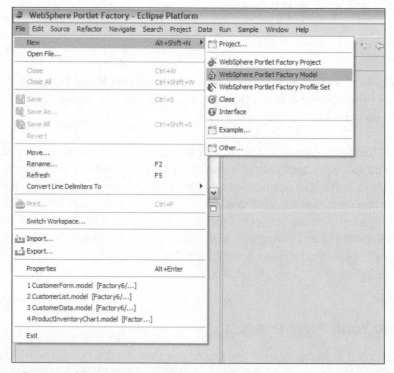

Figure 8.3: Creating a new model

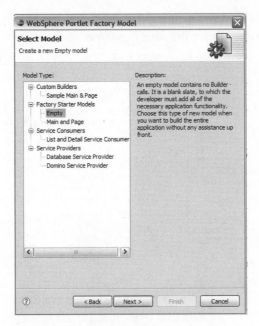

Figure 8.4: Selecting the empty template

Enter the name of the model (Figure 8.5), and click Finish.

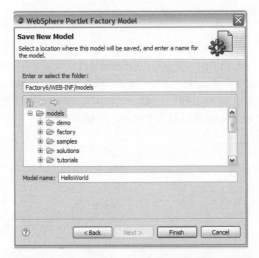

Figure 8.5: Assigning a name to the newly created model

Now, let's take a look at the Factory perspective and the different areas within the IDE. Figure 8.6 highlights the four quadrants of the Factory designer.

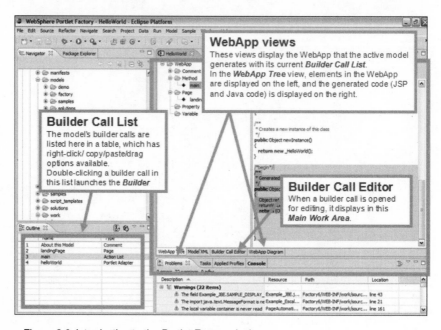

Figure 8.6: Introduction to the Portlet Factory designer

Quadrant I (upper right) contains the Builder Editor (where the builder is loaded) and the WebApp view. In this view, you can watch the application being built by the Factory. The Factory incrementally adds WebApp elements here as you add builders to your model. Quadrant II (upper left) contains the file system. The file structure is similar to a typical J2EE project (Figure 8.7).

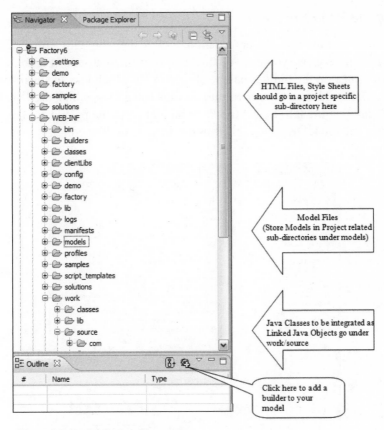

Figure 8.7: Portlet Factory file system

Quadrant III (bottom left) displays the model file currently loaded in the IDE. The model file in turn contains the list of builders, and you can double-click on a builder to load it in the builder editor. Quadrant IV (bottom right) displays any errors or warnings that might occur in your model. If you're using the Portal UTE, this quadrant will contain the portal console as well.

To create the HelloWorld portlet, we need to add a Page builder to display the hello world message in the portlet and an Action List builder to load the page. We'll also add a Portlet Adapter builder, a required step for any model that will be run as a portlet. Let's start by adding the Page builder.

Adding the Page Builder

To add the first builder to our empty model, click the icon with a plus sign at the top of the outline view (you can see this icon near the bottom of Figure 8.7). Doing so brings up the builder palette (Figure 8.8), which lists the available builders. The builders are grouped into various categories, which are listed alphabetically on the left. Select the Page builder from the palette as shown in the figure, and click OK to load the builder in your builder editor.

Figure 8.8: Adding a Page builder

The builder editor opens up the Page builder, showing the builder's entries and HTML content (Figure 8.9). We'll change the text to "Hello World!!" (highlighted). When you click OK, the builder is added to the model.

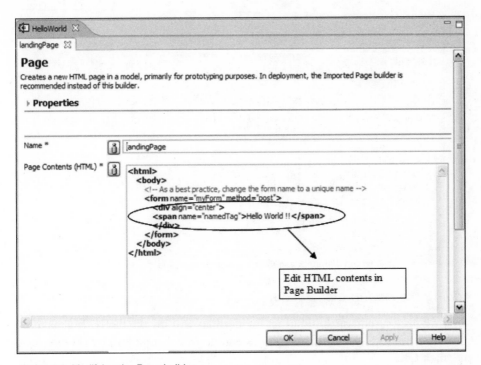

Figure 8.9: Modifying the Page builder

Notice in Figure 8.10 how the WebApp elements are added to the designer as well. We'll discuss the WebApp in more detail later. As you add more builders to your model, it's important to keep an eye on this area and observe the WebApp elements being added.

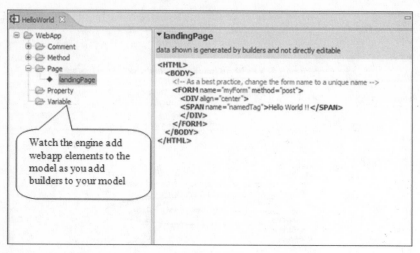

Figure 8.10: WebApp elements added by regeneration engine

Adding the Action List Builder

Next, we need to add an Action List builder that will invoke the HTML page. Click the icon to add a builder again, select the Action List builder (Figure 8.11), and click OK.

Figure 8.11: Selecting the Action List builder

224

As Figure 8.12 shows, we'll name this action **main**. Every directly invoked model needs an Action List builder called main. For Java programmers, the idea of adding a main method is a familiar concept. Next, click the reference chooser icon (three dots), and select **landingPage** as the page to be loaded by this action. At this time, we have only one action in our action list.

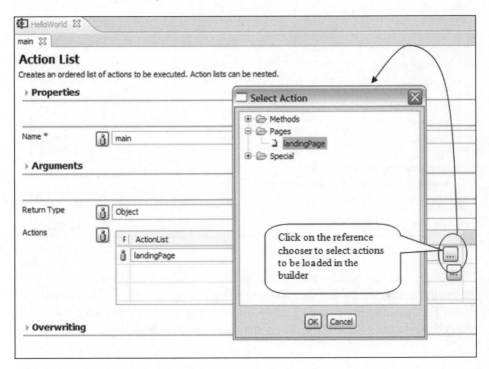

Figure 8.12: Adding the landingPage action

Click **OK**, and you'll see the action being added both to the list in your builder palette and in the designer's WebApp view. The Factory engine generates code as you continue to add builders in the model.

Adding the Portlet Adapter Builder

As our next step, we need to add the Portlet Adapter builder and call it **helloWorld** (Figure 8.13). This builder converts a model into a portlet and is required in every model that needs to be run as a portlet.

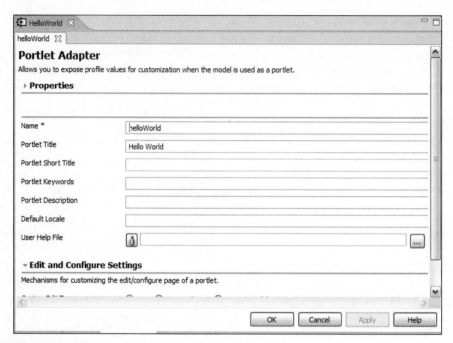

Figure 8.13: Adding a Portlet Adapter builder

The Portlet Adapter builder adds all the artifacts needed to run the portlet inside the portlet container. Notice that the nomenclature best practices for the builder follow the Java naming convention: an initial lowercase letter followed by sentence-style capitalization, with no spaces or special characters.

Running the Model Standalone

Now we're ready to run our model, first standalone and then inside the portal as a portlet. When we click the green arrow icon at the top of the designer window to run the model for the first time, the run model configuration screen, shown in Figure 8.14, appears. (You can launch this screen explicitly by selecting **Run** > **Run**. . . from the designer's menu bar.)

As shown in the figure, highlight the **Run Model** item under **WebSphere Portlet Factory**, and then click **Run**. You'll be prompted to name the configuration. For this example, we'll use the name **Run Model**. The configuration simply contains information about the server on which this model will be run standalone and displays the model's Run URL.

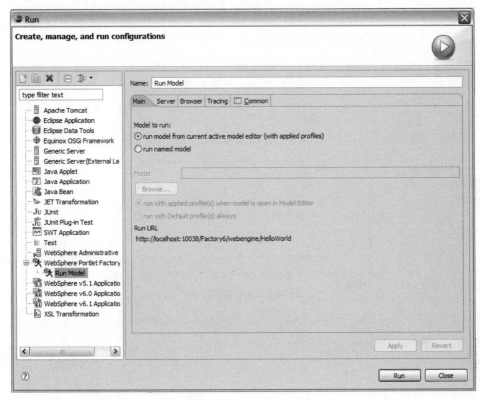

Figure 8.14: Run Model configuration

Make sure your portal server is up and running, and then click the Run button. If all goes well, you should see a new browser window loaded with a "Hello World!!" message on it (Figure 8.15).

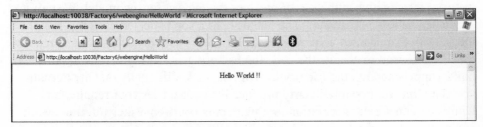

Figure 8.15: Running HelloWorld standalone

Behind the scenes, the Factory engine created the JSP, Java, and XML artifacts required to run the hello world page on the application server. As Factory developers, we provided instructions in the form of builders, and the Factory wrote the software for us. You can view the generated JSP and Java code in the designer's WebApp view (Figure 8.16).

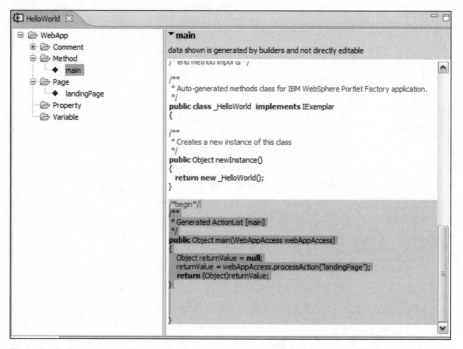

Figure 8.16: Factory-generated code

Many programmers ask us whether they can modify the Java and JSP code generated by the Portlet Factory. The answer to this question is no! The Factory isn't just a regular code generator. It's a software automation tool. The engine spits out the code when the server receives the request for the model. We call it "code generation on demand." The Factory has a sophisticated caching mechanism that ensures no performance hit occurs as it produces code at request time. If you want to change the code the Factory generates, you must modify the builder inputs and tell the Factory to write the code differently. As an alternative, you can write your own builder to produce the code as per your requirement. Unlike a regular code-generation tool that cranks out some skeleton framework and requires the programmer to write the bulk of the code, the Portlet Factory

228

produces a complete final product based on the instruction set (builders). In our case, the final product is a Web application and a portlet.

Running the Model as a Portlet

As a final step for the hello world exercise, we need to run our application inside the portal as a portlet. To do so, right-click the project in the Portlet Factory Navigator view, and select **Rebuild WAR > Rebuild Portlet WARs** as shown in Figure 8.17.

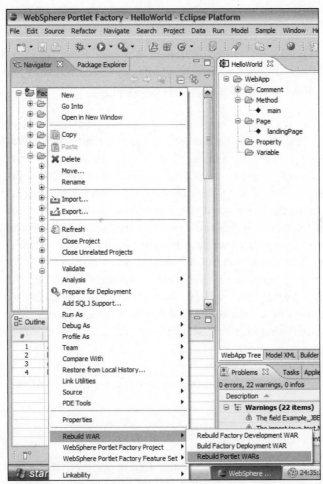

Figure 8.17: Rebuilding the portlet WAR

The Portlet Factory will first generate the portlet.xml file and add the Hello World portlet to the file. Next, it will create a portlet WAR containing all the necessary artifacts for the portlet and deploy the portlet on the portal server. You'll need to sign in as a portal administrator and place the portlet on a page. Figure 8.18 shows the portlet loaded inside the portal.

Figure 8.18: Hello world portlet deployed on the portal

That wasn't so hard, was it? Let's recollect the steps. First, we created a new empty model, then dropped in three builders, and finally rebuilt and deployed a portlet WAR, and we now have a portlet ready to go!

The cool part comes when you want to change the portlet you just built. For instance, say you decide to change the message to read " Hello World! This is my first Factory portlet." All you need to do is go back into the model, open the page builder, change the text, click **OK**, and run the model (by clicking the green arrow icon). You'll see your change in the standalone Web application. Log out and back in to the portal, and you'll see your change in the portlet as well. This is one of the powerful features of the Portlet Factory — letting developers do incremental development without having to rebuild and redeploy the WAR on every change. Developers can build and deploy the portlet WAR (using the menu options) when they introduce a new portlet. Beyond that, the Portlet Factory propagates incremental changes both to the standalone application and inside the portlet. To see this functionality in action, you can make some more minor changes and verify that they're being propagated across environments.

Now that you're familiar with the Portlet Factory designer and have the environment configured correctly, let's move on to write some "real-world" portlets.

CREATING A VIEW PORTLET

The objective of this exercise is to create a view portlet that displays a list of customers. The customer information resides in a customer database. We'll reinforce some of the concepts you've learned as we start building this application. It's important for you to take the time to let some of the underlying fundamental concepts sink in. Once you understand some of the core builders, the others will seem more intuitive, and you'll find them much easier to pick up.

We'll begin by creating a single model for the entire use case to demonstrate the basic process. Later, we'll split this model to create a separate data services layer, which is the recommended best practice for Portlet Factory developers. Building a customer list portlet involves two fundamental tasks:

- fetching the data from the database
- displaying the data in the portlet

We'll use the SQL Call builder to fetch the data and use the Data Page builder and the Page builder to build the view.

Knowing which builder to choose to manage a specific task is the key to mastering the Portlet Factory. The base product provides more than 100 builders, and by no means would most people know the exact details of each one of them. However, at the very least, you should know the names of the builders and have a high-level understanding of what they can accomplish. You'll find it helpful to revisit this list often. You'll also discover that you use a few core builders more often than others. A good Portlet Factory developer looks at a use case, breaks it down into subtasks, and maps a builder for each task. In our case, the two subtasks map to two builders: SQL Call builder to fetch the data and Data Page builder to build the view.

Fetching the Data

We'll start by creating an empty model called CustomerList. We'll add the SQL Call builder from the palette and name the builder getCustomerList. Each builder list has its corresponding help file for reference; you can consult this resource to understand the builder's functionality and parameters. As Portlet Factory developers, we'll provide inputs to the builder (in this case, SQL Call), which will then write all the code to fetch the data. The SQL Call builder leverages the data source set up in the application server. Make sure you've set up the data source (in the application server's admin console) and tested it for connectivity to the customer database (you can download the sample customer database from our download site). It's important to set up the data source correctly first, and you often need to restart your portal server for the data source to be loaded correctly.

After selecting the SQL Call builder, enter the SQL query shown in Figure 8.19; you can leave the other options for this builder at their defaults.

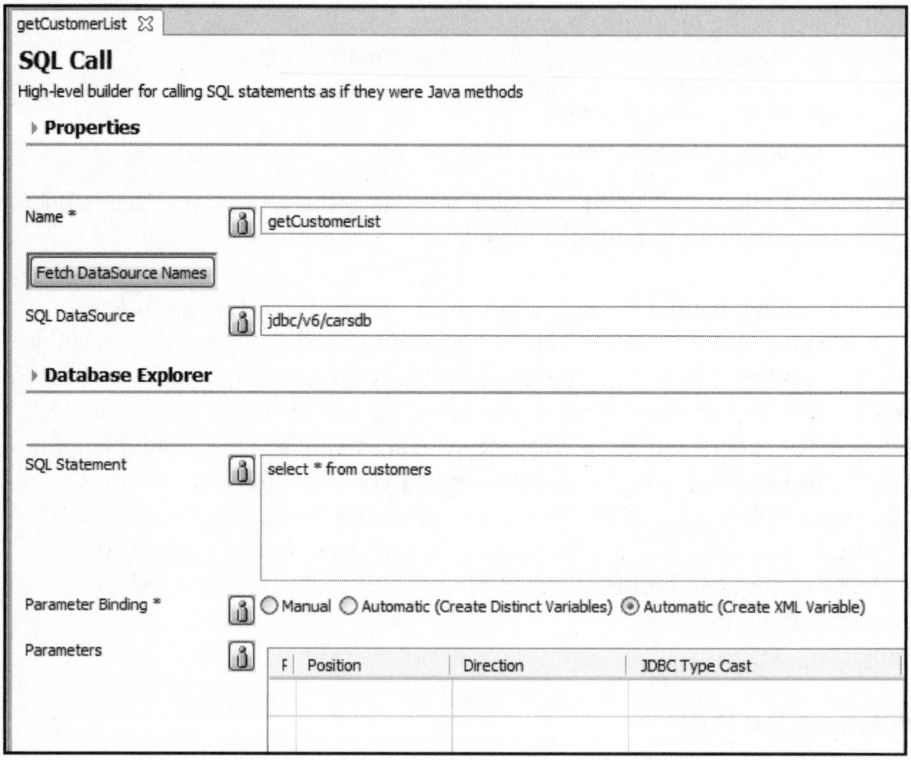

Figure 8.19: Adding an SQL Call builder to fetch data

Click **Apply**. (This button has the same effect as **OK** but leaves the builder editor open.) You'll have to wait a few seconds, depending on your machine and its performance.

Now we come to an extremely important concept of the Factory. When you click **Apply** (or **OK**) after specifying the builder, the regeneration engine (sometimes referred to as "regen") takes the SQL call you entered, actually invokes a call to the database, and receives back a result set. The engine then introspects the result set and creates a series of other artifacts. To see the elements created as a result of the successful execution of this SQL call by the regeneration engine, switch to the WebApp view in the builder editor, and highlight the SQL Call builder. Figure 8.20 shows the artifacts created for the customer list example.

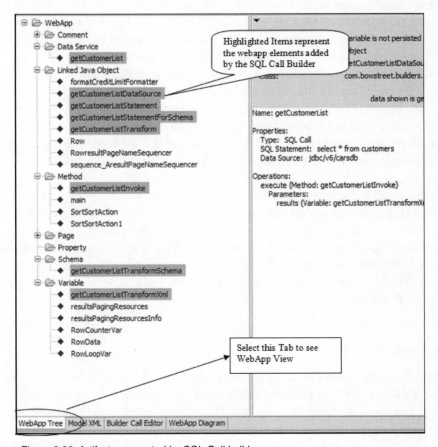

Figure 8.20: Artifacts generated by SQL Call builder

As you can see, the SQL Call builder adds a Data Service that has the same name as our builder. It also adds the Method (WebApp element), giving it the same name as our builder with "Invoke" appended to it (i.e., getCustomerListInvoke). You can select this method to view the code produced by the Factory. The SQL Call builder also creates the Schema and Variable elements, appending

"TransformSchema" and "TransformXml" (respectively) to the builder name. Other Java objects are created as well. In other words, behind the scenes, this builder writes out all the Java code and other artifacts that we otherwise would have to write manually to interact with a database in a J2EE environment. A J2EE programmer would need to do a Java Naming and Directory Interface (JNDI) lookup, initiate a connection, invoke the call, iterate through the result set, and convert the results into an XML variable. The SQL Call builder encapsulates all this functionality and automates the creation of the WebApp elements required for the database interaction. You can select the Schema and see that the getCustomerListTransformSchema holds the schema of the result set of the SQL query. So, at the end of the regen, the model knows what to expect when the query is executed at runtime. This generated schema or variable object will in turn become an input to other builders (e.g., Data Page); the builders are thus "parametrically" tied to each other. Understanding this difference of regeneration and execution is really the key to unraveling the power of the Portlet Factory.

If you don't see the aforementioned WebApp elements at this point and your SQL Call builder reports an error, you'll need to fix the problem before moving on. Double-check the data source, and verify connectivity from the admin console. In addition, check the SQL query to verify syntax, schema names, and so on. If the process still fails, restart your portal server and designer. Successful regeneration and creation of the WebApp elements must take place before you proceed to the next step.

Building the View

In our next step, we'll use the result set of the SQL Call builder and build the view. To do so, we'll employ one of the most powerful builders in the Portlet Factory arsenal, the Data Page builder. This builder is the core to building any user interface, including tables, views, forms, and so on. You may find the Data Page builder a bit overwhelming at first, but if you put an extra effort into under-standing the required inputs, it will quickly become a powerful ally. For the pur-poses of this use case, we'll ask the Data Page builder to look at the returning result set and build a table for viewing the results.

Before we start with the Data Page builder, we need to create the page on which the results will eventually be displayed. To do so, let's add a Page builder to the model. We'll name the builder resultPage and change the name of the HTML span tag to "data" (as highlighted in Figure 8.21).

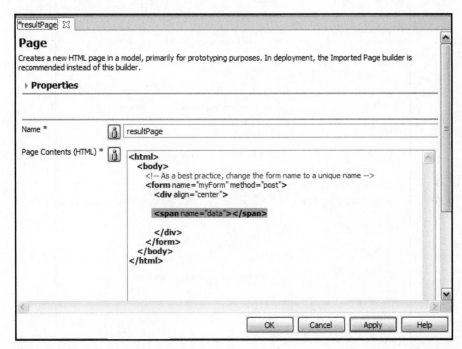

Figure 8.21: Adding a span tag on a page

Now, we can add the Data Page to the model. We'll instruct it to take the result set returned by the SQL Call builder and display it in a table on the result page. Most of the Factory's UI builders need a placeholder on the page to place their code components. We'll use the span tag called data as the placeholder for the result table that the Data Page builder will create. You can use "input" or any "name" elements to place the builders. It's almost like telling the data page to hang the resulting table on the named tag called data. Figure 8.22 shows the input values for the Data Page builder.

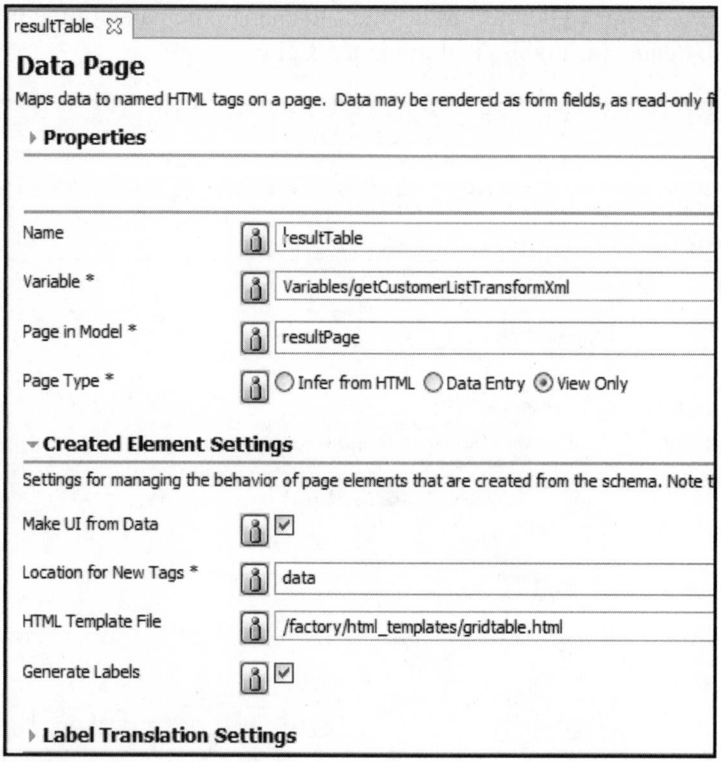

Figure 8.22: Adding the Data Page builder entries

A Data Page builder has four main inputs:

- **Variable**: This value specifies the variable or schema that holds the data structure of the data to be displayed (getCustomerListTransformXml in this case).

- **Page in Model**: This values indicates the page where the data is displayed (resultPage).

- **Page Type**: You use this value to tell the data page whether this page is a view or a form and how to construct the view or form.

- **HTML Template File**: This HTML file tells the data page how we want the data laid out on the page. The file controls the look and feel and the arrangement of the data. (For this example, we'll use the default file, gridtable.html.)

Figure 8.23 depicts these four inputs working on the Data Page builder to produce a view or form portlet.

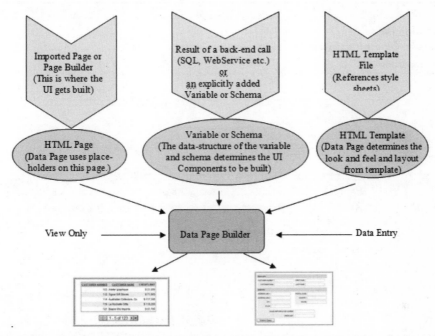

Figure 8.23: Schematic presentation of Data Page builder entries

The help section explains the other inputs to the Data Page builder in detail, but the four listed above are the most important for defining the data page. By selecting the option to **Make UI from Data**, we tell the data page to look at the structure of the results coming from the SQL call (which the Factory knows at regen time) and construct the WebApp elements needed to display the data. When we click **OK**, the Data Page builder creates a few components, including a JSP page to build a table for the result set.

Adding the Action List

At last, we're ready to wire the calls together to fetch and display the data. These calls constitute the "execution time" instruction set. Recall that every invoke portlet/model needs a main action list. So let's add an Action List builder with two actions: invoking the SQL call and displaying the resulting page. Figure 8.24 shows the two actions, which you can select through the reference chooser.

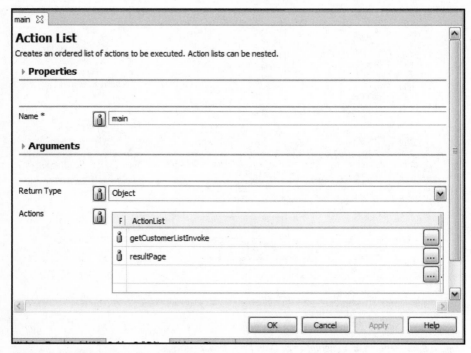

Figure 8.24: Adding the Action List builder

If you now click **OK** and then click the green arrow icon to run the model, you should see a list of customers displayed in a table.

Creating the Portlet

With the standalone Web application working, it's time to convert it into a portlet. To do so, we simply need to add the Portlet Adapter builder to our model. We'll call it the CustomerList portlet. Because this is a new portlet, we must rebuild and deploy the portlet WAR to the portal server. The Portlet Factory updates the portlet.xml file, making a new entry for the CustomerList portlet, and adds the model file to the portlet WAR. Hence, we have a single WAR carrying multiple portlets, which gets updated on subsequent deployments. When you place the portlet on a page, the result should look similar to the screen shown in Figure 8.25.

Welcome	Getting Started	Customer

Customer List

CUSTOMERNUMBER	CUSTOMERNAME	CONTACTLASTNAME	CONTACTFIRSTNAME	PHONE	ADDRESSLINE1	ADDRESSLINE2	CITY	STATE
103	Atelier graphique	Schmitt	Carine	40.32.2555	54, rue Royale		Nantes	
112	Signal Gift Stores	King	Jean	7025551838	8489 Strong St.		Las Vegas	NV
114	Australian Collectors, Co.	Ferguson	Peter	03 9520 4555	636 St Kilda Road	Level 3	Melbourne	Victoria
119	La Rochelle Gifts	Labrune	Janine	40.67.8555	67, rue des Cinquante Otages		Nantes	
121	Baane Mini Import	Bergulfsen	Jonas	07-98 9555	Erling Skakkes gate 78		Stavern	
124	Mini Gifts Distributors Ltd.	Nelson	Susan	4155551450	5677 Strong St.		San Rafael	CA
125	Havel & Zbyszek Co	Piestrzeniewicz	Zbyszek	(26) 642-7555	ul. Filtrowa 68		Warszawa	
128	Blauer See Auto, Co.	Keitel	Roland	+49 69 66 90 2555	Lyonerstr. 34		Frankfurt	
129	Mini Wheels Co.	Murphy	Julie	6505555787	5557 North Pendale Street		San Francisco	CA
131	Land of Toys Inc.	Lee	Kwai	2125557818	897 Long Airport Avenue		NYC	NY
141	Euro+ Shopping Channel	Freyre	Diego	(91) 555 94 44	C/ Moralzarzal, 86		Madrid	
144	Volvo Model	Berglund	Christina	0921-12 3555	Berguvsvägen 8		Luleå	

Figure 8.25: Customer list portlet

Enhancing the Customer List Portlet

We can expand on the existing use case by enhancing the customer list portlet in a variety of ways. To make our portlet more presentable and introduce you to some more interesting builders, we'll now modify the portlet to hide and display certain columns. We'll also add pagination, sorting, and formatting to various columns in the table. As we discussed earlier, the Factory provides a builder for each of these tasks.

The first subtask is to hide certain columns from the result set. We'll use the Data Column Modifier (DCM) builder to manage this task. Figure 8.26 illustrates the relationship between the Data Page, which stands as the foundation builder, and the other Data builders that act on the Data Page artifacts to produce the final required UI.

239

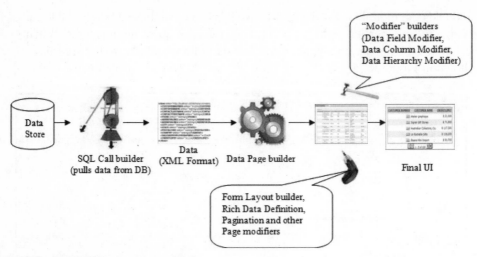

Figure 8.26: Builders in an assembly line

As you drop the DCM builder using the reference chooser, we need to point it to the variable on which Data Page is working (getCustomerListTransformXml). We'll choose to enable paging, as shown in Figure 8.27, causing the Factory to add all the code required to paginate through the result set.

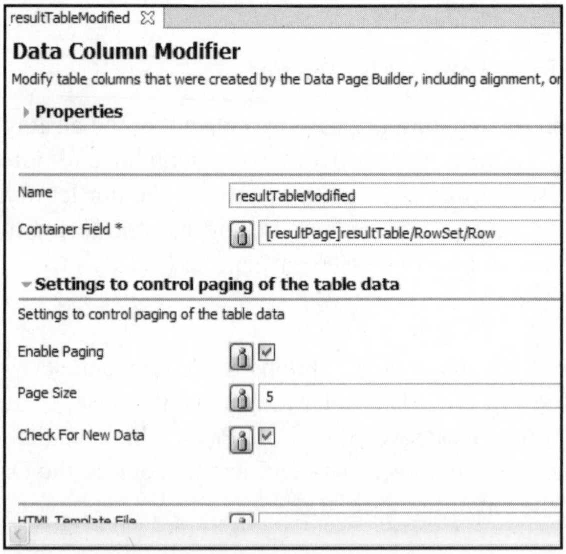

Figure 8.27: Adding a DCM builder

The DCM builder uses the schema generated by the SQL Call builder to pre-populate some of the fields in the builder (scroll down the editor window to see this option), and you can choose to hide or show certain columns. Further, you can choose sorting capabilities provided by the DCM and allow sorting on Customer Number and Name (Figure 8.28).

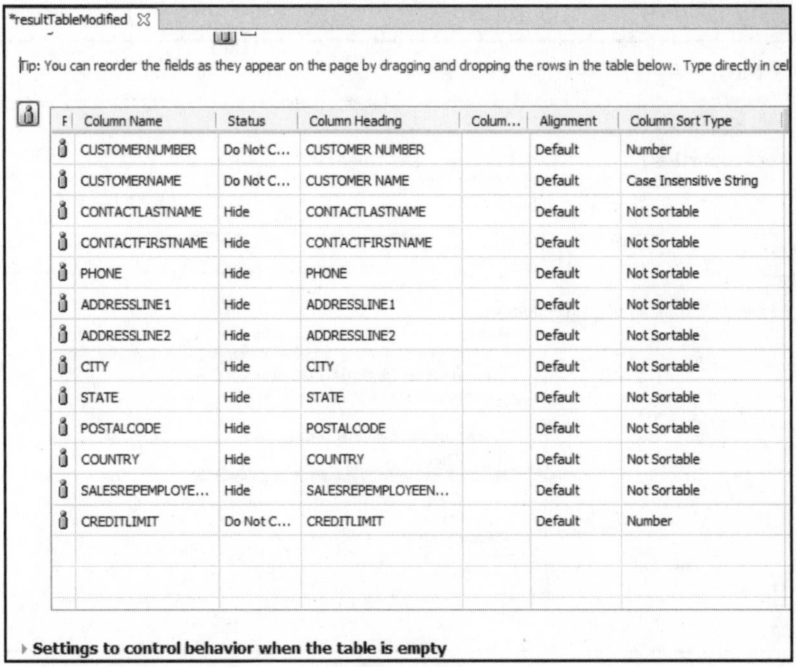

Figure 8.28: Hiding columns in the DCM builder

Once you click **OK**, the Factory engine regenerates the model, and the DCM builder adds code artifacts to hide columns, sort them, and enable paging. The figure indicates which columns have been hidden and sorted. At this point, we should quickly run the model and test it standalone to make sure the new behavior is updated. You may also choose to test the model inside the portlet; simply log out and back in to see the updated changes. No more redeployment. Now that's true rapid application development!

The test run confirms that the pagination capability has been added to the model (displaying five records at a time); however, we don't have any buttons or links to scroll through the next record set. Before we add the paging buttons, we need to add a span tag or a placeholder on the results page. (Recall that every UI component within the Factory needs a span tag or placeholder to place it on the page.) Open up the Page builder (by double-clicking the resultPage builder), add a span tag a shown in Figure 8.29, and click **OK**. Doing so forces a regeneration of the model, and the new span tag is parsed and added to the available placeholder list.

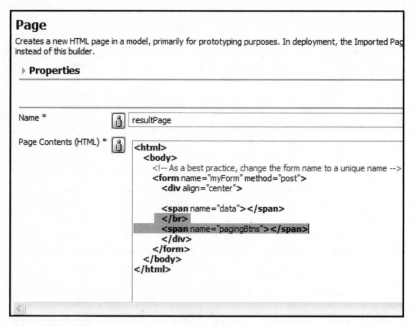

Figure 8.29: Adding span tags for pagination

With the span tag in place, search through the builder palette to add a Paging Buttons builder. We'll place this builder on the result page and on the new span we just added. Point to the Paging Assistant added by the DCM (Figure 8.27). This screen demonstrates how the builders are getting tied to each other and work together to produce the desired behavior. Figure 8.30 shows the Paging Buttons builder and its inputs.

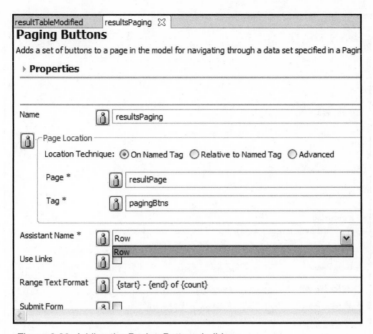

Figure 8.30: Adding the Paging Buttons builder

Click **OK**, and then save and run the model (standalone). Log out and back in to the portal, and verify that the paging buttons have been added. We now have true incremental development and testing with quick turnarounds.

For the final subtask of this use case, we need to format the last column, CREDITLIMIT, as a currency. We'll use the Data Field Modifier (DFM) builder, which can work on individual fields to modify the behavior. DFM is an important part of the Data builder family. We'll point to the CREDITLIMIT field and work in the Formatting section of the builder editor. The Portlet Factory provides the StandardFormatter class, which uses the standard Java expression to format fields. Figure 8.31 shows the entry for the formatting required for our use case.

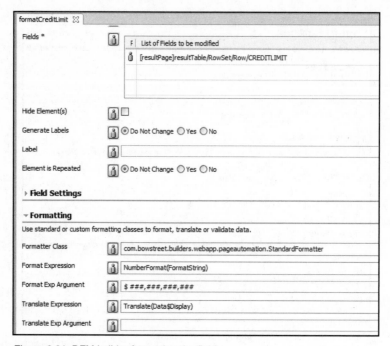

Figure 8.31: DFM builder formatting the field

Click **OK** to regenerate the model and have the DFM produce the appropriate snippets of JSP code on the result page to build the desired effect. To test the formatting, save and run the model. Figure 8.32 shows the modified customer list portlet displaying the paginated, formatted data.

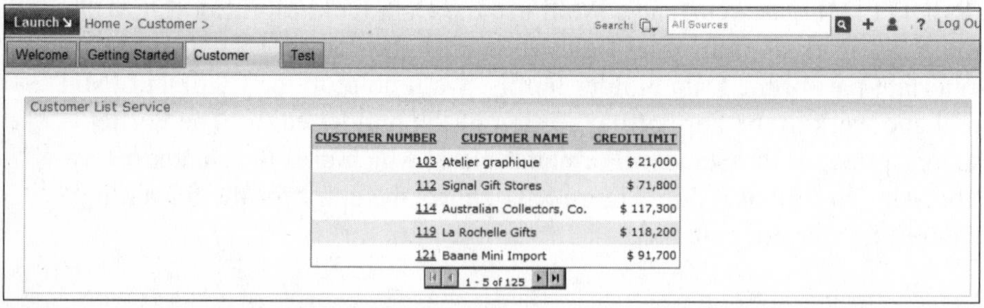

Figure 8.32: Enhanced customer list portlet

We've managed to write a real-world view portlet (with pagination, sorting, and formatting) using eight builders and all without having to write a single line of Java code. Is that cool or what?

Other builders in the base Portlet Factory product, such as the Data View builder and the View and Form builder, could tackle the same use case. Under the covers, these builders use the Data Page, DCM, and other Data family builders in conjunction with SQL Call or other Data Integration builders to accomplish the same work. Hence, if you understand the core builders (e.g., Data Page, SQL Call), getting up-to-speed on the other "high-level" builders will be no issue. As a matter of fact, even Data Page uses atomic builders, such as Link and Text, under the covers to accomplish its work. In the early versions of the Factory (pre–Data Page builder days), we would add Text, Link, Checkbox, Select, and other UI builders to build portlets and Web applications. Then along came the Data Page builder, which captured some of these repeated tasks and gave us the ability to quickly create sophisticated user interfaces.

We found ourselves using Data Page with the SQL Call and Service Call builders to build data integration portlets. The Data View and the View and Form builders were developed to encapsulate these repeated tasks in one high-level builder. Later, many customers wanted to build views with drill-down capability and charting with dashboard features. In response, IBM expanded the product with the Dashboard Framework builder set, which provides the Summary and Drill Down builder, the Summary and Chart builder, and other advanced builders. Behind the scenes, these builders use the same Data Page and Charting builders to manage subtasks. So although it's important to understand the core Data family builders, the key takeaway is that you can always develop more high-level builders by using these granular builders and thus automate creation of more and more Web applications and portlets.

FACTORY AND SOA

We've managed to quickly create a data integration portlet, but the model above is monolithic. The back-end interaction code and the UI components all exist in a single model. Separating the two into different layers, as depicted in Figure 8.33, will not only help us move toward a recommended services approach but also allow a larger development team to focus on different aspects of the layers in a real-world engagement. Further, the separation will enable other portlets or applications (non-portal) to reuse the data integration layer, moving us closer to a true Service Oriented Architecture (SOA).

245

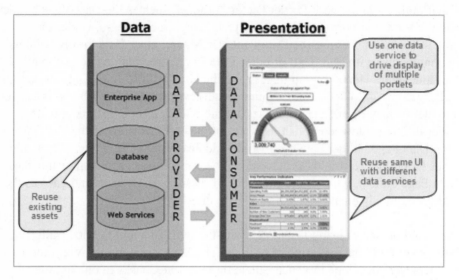

Figure 8.33: Portlet Factory and SOA

We can start by breaking the existing model into two. Better yet, let's create two new models to gain additional practice writing models.

Data Model

We'll start by creating a new empty model (call it CustomerData). We can reuse the same SQL Call builder we wrote for the original model. To do so, just right-click and copy the builder from the original model and paste it into our new model (CustomerData).

Converting this data integration into a service entails simply dropping two builders. The Service Definition builder declares that the model is now "service-enabled" and that any declared public service (which we'll define in a minute) is ready for consumption. Figure 8.34 shows the entries for the Service Definition builder.

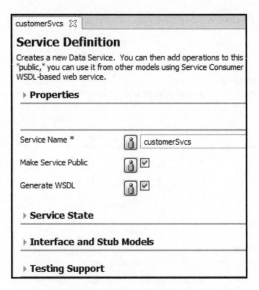

Figure 8.34: Adding a Service Definition builder

The **Generate WSDL** option, used to generate Web Services Description Language (WSDL), is optional, and we don't need it in this use case. In the current scenario, the Service Consumer model, which is our UI model, will reside in the same Java Virtual Machine (JVM) as the data model, and we won't make any HTTP/SOAP calls, as in the case of a classic Web service. However, we'll select this option anyway to understand one of the Factory's most powerful features: the rapid creation of Web services with little or no extra effort. Further, if you explore the Service Definition builder's **Interface and Stub Models** and **Testing Support** options through the help file, you'll begin to appreciate the powerful SOA capabilities provided by the Factory. There could be a completely separate development team that focused on exposing the back ends as services using this tool. This team could test its services standalone before checking its code in for consumption by the UI team.

Moving along in our exercise, we'll next drop the Service Operation builder and declare the getCustomerList/Execute SQL call operation as the one exposed as a service. This service requires no inputs, but it does return results, and the regeneration engine will provide the schema of the returning results to the Service

Operation builder. Figure 8.35 shows the builder inputs for the Service Operation builder.

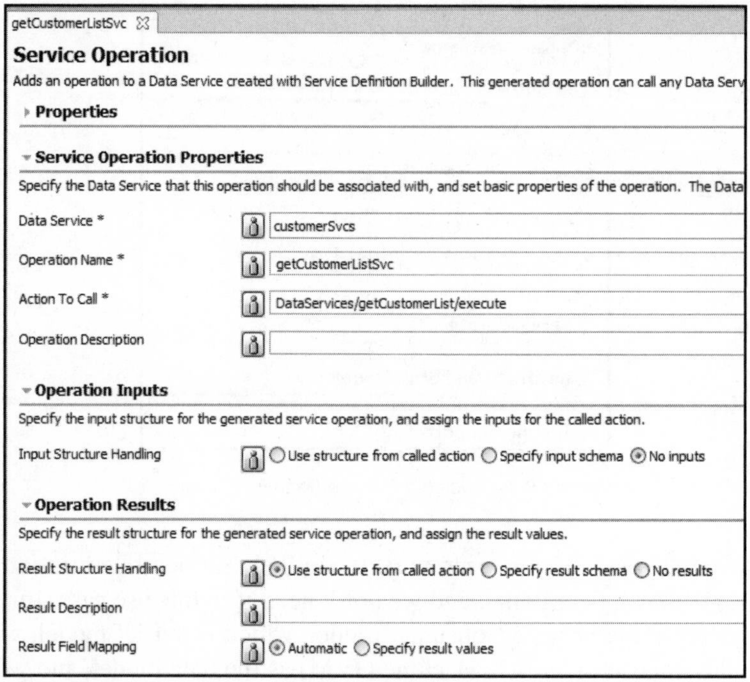

Figure 8.35: Adding a Service Operation builder

The data model needs no main action because it isn't invoked directly. Rather, it's invoked when the consumer model — that is, the UI layer (which we'll define next) — calls the service. We don't need a Portlet Adapter builder either because this model doesn't need to be converted into a portlet.

View Model

To build the view model, we'll start by defining an empty model called CustomerListView and copying the builders from our original model — except the SQL Call builder, of course. The view model needs one additional builder: the Service Consumer builder. As Figure 8.36 shows, the inputs for this builder are straightforward; we simply point to the data model and add all provider (public) operations as available to this model.

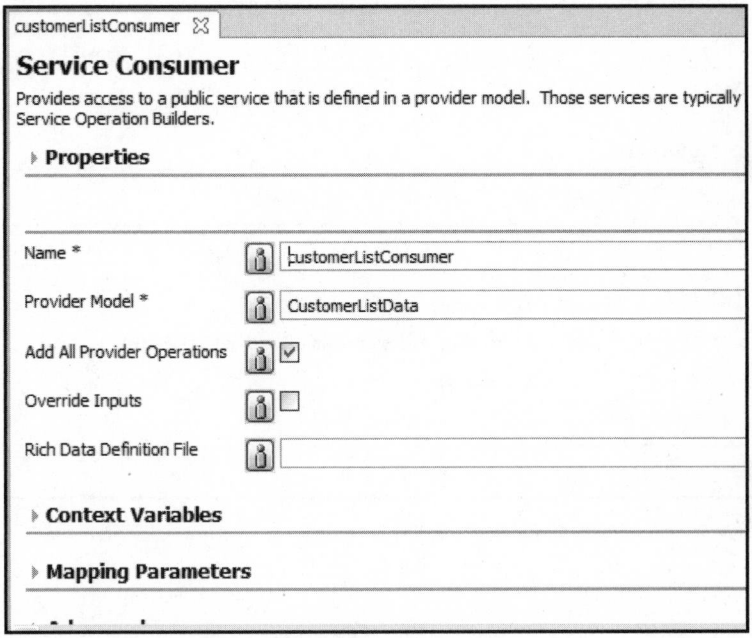

Figure 8.36: Adding a Service Consumer builder

Three more minor changes will happen in the original builders. The first change is in main (the Action List builder). Where we originally invoked the SQL call directly, we'll now invoke the service call (Figure 8.37).

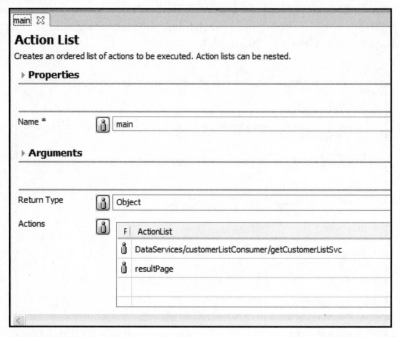

Figure 8.37: Making changes in the main

The second change occurs in the Data Page builder. We simply point to the variable created by the Service Consumer builder (rather than the transformXml variable) because we've moved the SQL Call builder to a different model (Figure 8.38).

Figure 8.38: Making changes in the Data Page

The other Data Page entries remain as they were before. The Service Consumer builder created a variable by taking the name of the Service Consumer builder and appending the name of the Service Operation builder and the "Results" string. The model regeneration ensures that the schema of the return result set is visible to all necessary builders, and they will all regenerate themselves in response to that.

The final change occurs in the Portlet Adapter builder, which we should rename to avoid conflict with our original monolithic portlet. As an alternative, you can delete the original model; in that case, you can leave the portlet adapter as is.

It's time to save the model and run it standalone to make sure it works. If you've renamed the Portlet Adapter builder, you'll need to redeploy the portlet WAR (you can do so right from the designer). Recall that you must redeploy the portlet WAR every time you write a new portlet to generate the new portlet.xml file and redeploy it on the portal server. Although most of the tasks are automated from the designer, it's important to remember this extra step when you need to deploy a new portlet. The Factory manages any subsequent changes automatically; you simply need to log out and back in to your portal to see your changes.

BUILDING THE COMPLETE SERVICES LAYER

Now that we've laid out our SOA, we can expand on the data services layer and put in more services, which other models that will address other use cases in subsequent chapters can consume. Figure 8.39 provides a high-level overview, showing the Service Oriented Architecture and the different roles each builder plays.

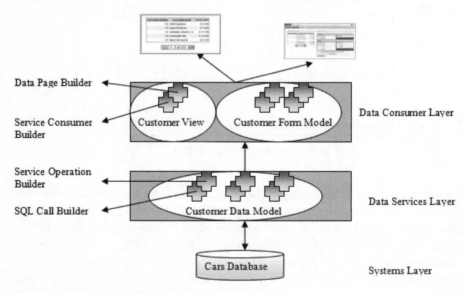

Figure 8.39: Model and builder interaction in a SOA

Right now, we have a single operation exposed as a service (getCustomerList). While in the services layer (CustomerData model), we can go ahead and add more operations (e.g., addCustomer, updateCustomer, getCustomer).

In a Factory world, doing so means adding SQL Call builders to manage each operation and then adding a Service Operation builder to expose each operation as a service, with input and output schema definitions as well. Before adding new SQL Call builders, however, we'll add an SQL DataSource builder that will then be visible to all other SQL Call builders. This step is similar to the idea of capturing global variables and defining them at a model level. Figure 8.40 shows the SQL DataSource and its reference in the SQL Call builder.

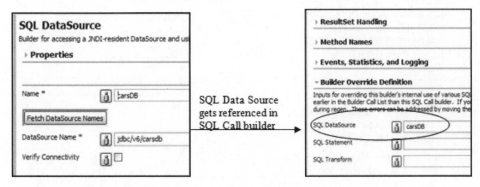

Figure 8.40: SQL data source referenced in SQL Call builder

Next, we'll add the SQL Call builders for each operation. Figure 8.41 shows the SQL Call entries for each operation and a corresponding image of the Service Operation builder. Pay special attention to the Operations Input and Output entries made in the Service Operation builder. Making the wrong selection or specifying the incorrect schema will result in incorrect results being passed to the service consumption layer.

We encourage you to look at the Service Stub and Service Test builders that let you test these back-end calls standalone. Also, you if you selected the **Generate WSDL** option in the Service Definition builder, you should be able to view the WSDL for each of the service calls. Simply invoke the URL **http://localhost:10038/Factory6ssata/Action!getWSDL** to view the WSDL of the generated Web services for each SQL call. In IT organizations, we typically have data application developers exposing their data and back-end systems as services and then making these models available to UI and portlet developers, who use the Service Consumption builder to integrate with these services. In later chapters, we'll build on the existing use cases and consume some of these services.

SQL Call entry	Service Operation builder

Add customer operation:

INSERT INTO.CUSTOMERS
(CUSTOMERNAME, CON-
TACTLASTNAME, CONTACT-
FIRSTNAME, PHONE,
ADDRESSLINE1,
ADDRESSLINE2, CITY, STATE,
POSTALCODE, COUNTRY,
SALESREPEMPLOYEENUM-
BER, CREDITLIMIT)
values
  (?, ?, ?, ?, ?, ?, ?, ?, ?, ?, ?, ?)

- Set the **Parameter Binding**
  option to **Automatic**
  (Create XML Variable).

addCustomerSvc
Data Service *	customerSvcs
Operation Name *	addCustomerSvc
Action To Call *	DataServices/addCustomer/execute
Operation Description	Adds New Customer

▾ **Operation Inputs**
Specify the input structure for the generated service operation, and assign the inputs for the called action.

Input Structure Handling	⦿ Use structure from called action ○ Specify input schema ○ No inputs
Input Description	
Input Field Mapping	⦿ Automatic ○ Specify input values

▾ **Operation Results**
Specify the result structure for the generated service operation, and assign the result values.

| Result Structure Handling | ○ Use structure from called action ○ Specify result schema ⦿ No results |

Update customer operation:

UPDATE CUSTOMERS A
SET   A.CUSTOMERNAME = ?,
A.CONTACTLASTNAME = ?,
A.CONTACTFIRSTNAME = ?,
A.PHONE = ?,
A.ADDRESSLINE1 = ?,
A.ADDRESSLINE2 = ?, A.CITY
= ?, A.STATE = ?, A.POSTAL-
CODE = ?, A.COUNTRY = ?,
A.SALESREPEMPLOYEENUM-
BER = ?, A.CREDITLIMIT = ?
Where A.CUSTOMERNUMBER
= ?

- Set the **Parameter Binding**
  option to **Automatic**
  (Create XML Variable).

updateCustomerSvc
Data Service *	customerSvcs
Operation Name *	updateCustomerSvc
Action To Call *	DataServices/updateCustomer/execute
Operation Description	

▾ **Operation Inputs**
Specify the input structure for the generated service operation, and assign the inputs for the called action.

Input Structure Handling	⦿ Use structure from called action ○ Specify input schema ○ No inputs
Input Description	
Input Field Mapping	⦿ Automatic ○ Specify input values

▾ **Operation Results**
Specify the result structure for the generated service operation, and assign the result values.

| Result Structure Handling | ○ Use structure from called action ○ Specify result schema ⦿ No results |

Figure 8.41: SQL operations and their corresponding services (part 1 of 2)

SQL Call entry	Service Operation builder
Get customer data operation:	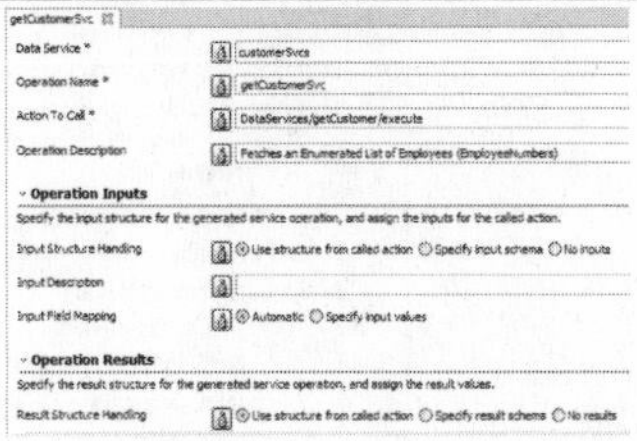

SELECT * from CUSTOMERS where CUSTOMERNUMBER=?

- Set the **Parameter Binding** option to **Automatic (Create XML Variable).**

Get sales rep list operation:

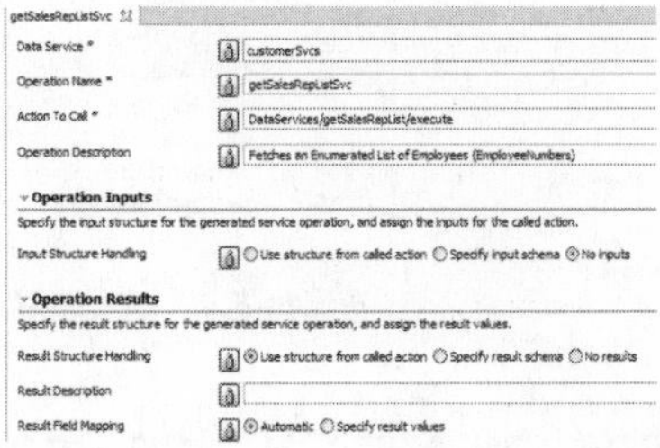

SELECT * from EMPLOYEES where JOBTITLE='Sales Rep'

- Set the **Parameter Binding** option to **Automatic (Create XML Variable).**
- Select **Transform Result as Complete XML Document**.

Get product inventory:

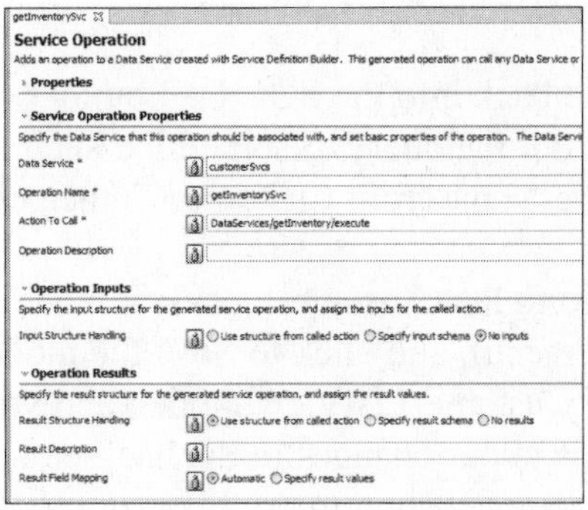

SELECT PRODUCTLINE, SUM (QUANTITYINSTOCK) INVENTORY FROM PRODUCTS GROUP BY PRODUCTLINE

- Set the **Parameter Binding** option to **Automatic (Create XML Variable).**
- Select **Transform Result as Complete XML Document**.

SELECT PRODUCTLINE, SUM (QUANTITYINSTOCK) INVENTORY FROM PRODUCTS GROUP BY PRODUCTLINE

- Set the **Parameter Binding** option to **Automatic (Create XML Variable).**
- Select **Transform Result as Complete XML Document**.

Figure 8.41: SQL operations and their corresponding services (part 2 of 2)

255

Figure 8.42 shows the CustomerData model after we've added all the SQL Call and Service Operation builders listed above.

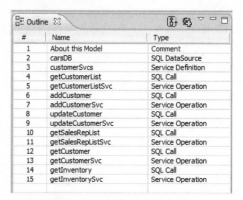

#	Name	Type
1	About this Model	Comment
2	carsDB	SQL DataSource
3	customerSvcs	Service Definition
4	getCustomerList	SQL Call
5	getCustomerListSvc	Service Operation
6	addCustomer	SQL Call
7	addCustomerSvc	Service Operation
8	updateCustomer	SQL Call
9	updateCustomerSvc	Service Operation
10	getSalesRepList	SQL Call
11	getSalesRepListSvc	Service Operation
12	getCustomer	SQL Call
13	getCustomerSvc	Service Operation
14	getInventory	SQL Call
15	getInventorySvc	Service Operation

Figure 8.42: Updated customer data model

REGENERATION AND CHANGE PROPAGATION

To return to our earlier point about the regeneration engine and demonstrate the Portlet Factory's powerful automation capability, let's try making some changes to the service provider model.

First, go back into the SQL Call builder (in the CustomerData model), and change our the query to something such as "Select CustomerNumber, CustomerName from Customers"; then click **OK** and save the model.

Next, go to the CustomerListView model, select **Model > Generate Model** (in the top menu), and click to **Save** the model. Now, click the green arrow icon to run the CustomerListView model, and you'll see the magic! The view model responds to our changes in the back-end model without us having to touch any code. Imagine trying to do this using traditional hand-coding techniques. You'd have to work with the code in at least three places, if not more.

The business world is changing constantly, and IT needs to respond. But our response can't mean going into the code and making changes every time. Rather, we need an automated response. The Portlet Factory, with its parametrically tied builders, gives us powerful automation capabilities that can react to change with ease.

SUMMARY

This chapter's goal was to give you a background on the Portlet Factory and introduce the fundamental concepts of the tool, including the regeneration engine, models, and builders. By now, you should fully appreciate the power of the Factory and not think of it merely as a code generator. Revisit this chapter's sections and exercises (if necessary) until you clearly understand models and builders and can navigate around the new IDE and do rapid incremental development.

Getting used to this new UI will, of course, take some practice. There's a learning curve, and we don't deny that. But once you get over that hump, the possibilities of what you can do with this powerful tool — and, more important, how quickly you can develop —are simply amazing. With the foundation laid, the learning curve is restricted to learning more and more builders and becoming adept at using them. In the following chapters, we'll continue down this path, tackling more use cases, exposing you to more of the core builders, and demonstrating their use.

Chapter Nine

Advanced Concepts in Portlet Factory

As Web application developers, we find ourselves primarily handling two types of use cases. Either we're presenting data/content from some back-end source or we're building forms to capture information from end users to commit to a repository. In other words, we're either presenting or capturing information. The Data Page builder, in conjunction with other Data Family builders introduced in the preceding chapter, operates at the presentation layer and can help us build both views and forms.

Chapter 8 presented the View use case. In this chapter, you'll learn to use the Data Page builder to build forms. Then we'll expand on these use cases and show how to wire the two portlets (the view portlet and the form portlet) together using the portlet event builders. As we move through this discussion, we'll point out some best practices to follow when developing forms using IBM WebSphere Portlet Factory. Next, we'll introduce profiling, a rather important concept of the Portlet Factory. You'll learn how to use profiling to manage personalization and customization in the portal. In the final section, we'll introduce some more advanced builders, such as Charting, Dashboard Framework, and SAP Framework.

This chapter builds on the use cases developed in Chapter 8. If you've skipped certain sections of that chapter, it will be worthwhile for you at least to go to the download site and obtain the necessary code so you can follow the steps as we build on this example.

BUILDING FORMS USING THE PORTLET FACTORY

As you learned in Chapter 8, the Data Page builder is a powerful UI builder that can build both views and forms. The Data Page builder takes as an input an XML structure or a schema and uses its data structure to construct a form. In this section, you'll see how to build forms using the Portlet Factory. We'll build a customer form that users can use to create a new customer or edit an existing customer's data. To demonstrate our point about the services layer and reuse, we'll try to reuse the CustomerData model we created in the earlier chapter to build the form. We'll then extend it as needed to add more features.

As Figure 9.1 shows, we need to provide three entries for the data page: a "schema-typed" variable that will determine the UI components to be built, the page on which the form will be built, and the HTML template that will determine the layout and styles.

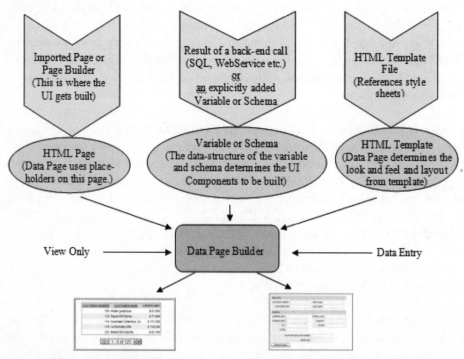

Figure 9.1: Data Page builder inputs

We'll start by adding a Service Consumer builder that is a copy of the consumer builder added in the earlier model. We'll make all operations provided by the service available to this model. As soon as we click **OK**, the regeneration engine kicks in and makes the call to the Service Provider model, and the variable for the various services visible to this model is created in the model. Here, we're trying to create a form to add a customer record to the database. A call to the getCustomerSvc service returns a single record of a customer from the database. We'll reference the corresponding result variable that holds the return value of this service call inside the data page, which should give the data page enough information to intelligently generate a UI (JSP) for us. Hence, we'll reference the customerDataGetCustomerSvcResults variable inside the DataPage.

Next, we'll add a page to the model in which this form will be created.

As Figure 9.2 shows, we'll use a Factory-provided HTML file, view_and_form_inputform.html, for our Imported Page builder.

> Best Practice: Use the Imported Page builder pointing to an external HTML file in lieu of the Page builder. This practice lets you clearly separate the look and feel from the data.

Figure 9.2: Imported Page builder for form

Last, we'll drop a Data Page builder that will create the form for us. The entries for the Data Page builder (for forms) fall broadly into two categories:

- form creation entries
- form submission entries

Form Creation Entries

The Data Page builder's form creation entries determine the basic building blocks for the form. We need to point to the page where the form will be created and to the variable that determines the form's structure, and we must explicitly tell the data page to build a data entry form. Figure 9.3 shows the form creation entries for our use case.

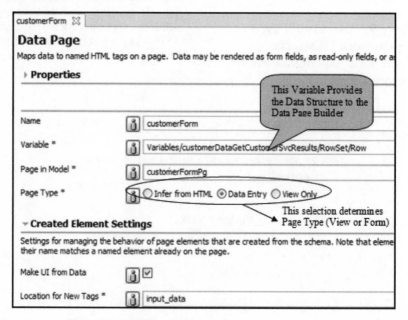

Figure 9.3: Data Page builder entries

The CustomerForm page that we created using the Imported Page builder is referred to here in the Data Page builder, thus tying the two builders together. The new tags and fields created by the data page will be added to the input_data location, which acts as a placeholder. The Factory's HTML template file determines the style, fonts, and layout of the form.

We'll address the second set of entries that govern the form submission behavior and logic. In line with our theory of incremental development with rapid iterations, let's test our model standalone and check the code that the Factory has written thus far based on

> Best Practice: If you need to change any of the Factory template files, it's wise to make a copy first and modify the copy for your specific project.

the instruction set we've provided. Recall that we'll need to add an Action List builder called "main"; at this point, our action builder simply processes the CustomerForm page that in turn loads the Data Page builder. We'll click **OK** and let the main Action List builder and Data Page builder create all the artifacts for the UI. Click the green "run model" arrow icon, and if all goes well a simple form similar to the one shown in Figure 9.4 will been created. The **Submit Query** button that appears at the bottom of the form was present in the original HTML file and has no action associated with it at present.

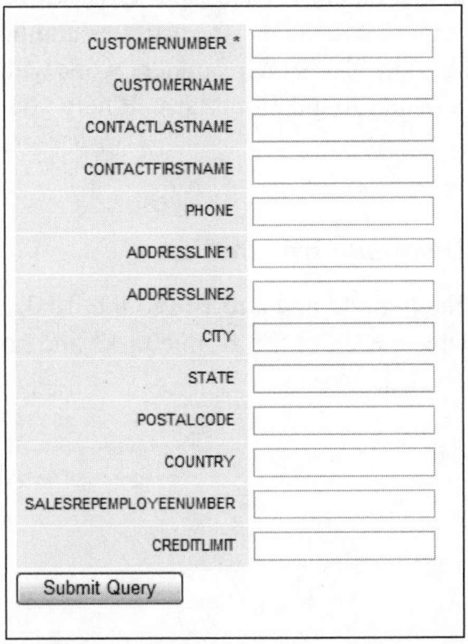

CUSTOMERNUMBER *	
CUSTOMERNAME	
CONTACTLASTNAME	
CONTACTFIRSTNAME	
PHONE	
ADDRESSLINE1	
ADDRESSLINE2	
CITY	
STATE	
POSTALCODE	
COUNTRY	
SALESREPEMPLOYEENUMBER	
CREDITLIMIT	
Submit Query	

Figure 9.4: Basic form generated by data page

Notice how the data page smartly introspected the schema associated with this variable and created data entry fields for the page. The Customer Number column is the Primary Key in the Customer table and has been defined as NOT NULL in the database. The schema generated by the Service Provider builder reflects this constraint.

At this point, we encourage you to do a single-click on the Data Page builder in your designer and check out all the code artifacts generated in the WebApp view. Pay special attention to the CustomerForm page and how the Data Page builder has taken a simple HTML-based page and transformed it into a sophisticated JSP page. Further, the schema CustomerDetailsGetTransformSchema generated by the Factory has the following entry for the CUSTOMERNUMBER Column (notice that nillable="false"):

```
"<xsd:element name="CUSTOMERNUMBER" type="xsd:integer" minOccurs="1"
maxOccurs="1" nillable="false" />"
```

When the Data Page builder generated the form from this schema, it made the CustomerNumber field mandatory (hence the asterisk, which marks the field as required). Taking the time to understand the artifacts and how the SQL Call, Service Provider, and Service Consumer builders work with the Data Page builder will give you a strong foundation that will help you use this tool more effectively.

Submit Form and Database Transaction

We now need to plan the logic to add a record to the database. The flow chart shown in Figure 9.5 depicts each of the atomic tasks and notes the builder that will help us accomplish each one.

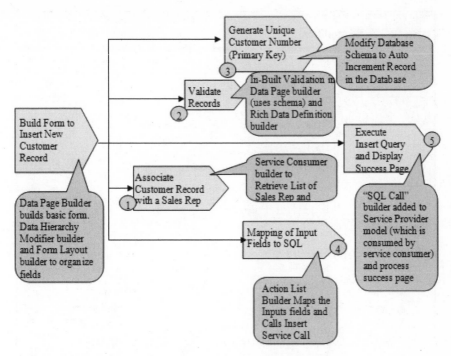

Figure 9.5: Flow logic and builder mapping for customer form portlet

We'll follow the steps in the flow chart and start adding/modifying builders as we progress. The Data Hierarchy Modifier builder (shown in Figure 9.6) groups the various fields in subsections. The Form Layout builder in turn determines the layout of these fields. You can create new groups and drag the various fields in the Data Hierarchy Modifier builder, rearranging them as necessary.

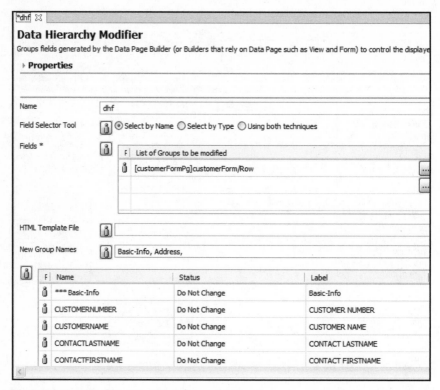

Figure 9.6: Data Hierarchy Modifier builder entries

You can also rename the labels in the Data Hierarchy Modifier builder or the Form Layout builder or select resource bundles in the Data Page builder for the labels.

Best Practice: You should manage labels from resource bundles (tied with the Data Page builder) rather than use the Hierarchy Modifier, Form Layout, or Rich Data Definition builder. Resource bundles also allow easy translation of labels in various locales.

Scroll through the help files to understand the intricacies of each entry. Customer number is the primary key in the database, and we'll need to auto-generate it rather than have the end user enter it. At this point, we'll therefore simply hide it from the form. You can do this using the Data Field Modifier builder. As we explained in Chapter 8, the Data Field Modifier can act on a field or group of fields to modify the components written by Data Page. As an alternative, you can use the Rich Data Definition builder, which lets you modify various fields in one builder. In addition to the reduced number of builders, the Rich Data Definition offers the ability to work from a base definition file (XML file), allowing reuse of common presentation patterns across applications, development teams, and engagements.

We'll add the Rich Data Definition builder, point to the CUSTOMERNUMBER field, and choose to hide this field by selecting the **Hidden** option (Figure 9.7).

Figure 9.7: Rich Data Definition builder entries

Click **OK**, and then save and run the model. Figure 9.8 shows the resulting customer form generated by the modifier builders.

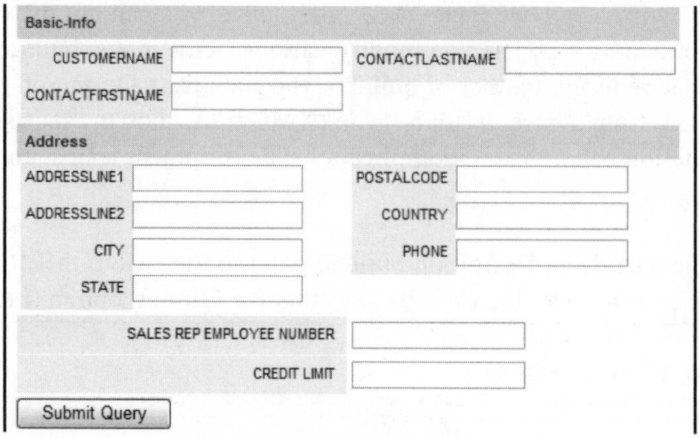

Figure 9.8: Customer form with modified layout

When adding a new customer to the database, the end user must assign a sales rep to manage the customer. To support this function, we need to modify the Sales Rep Employee Number field to change it to a drop-down selection. To populate the drop-down list, we'll first need to obtain a list of sales reps. This is where we leverage the getSalesRepListSvc service call we created in the previous chapter. We invoke this service in the main action list builder by modifying the builder as shown in Figure 9.9.

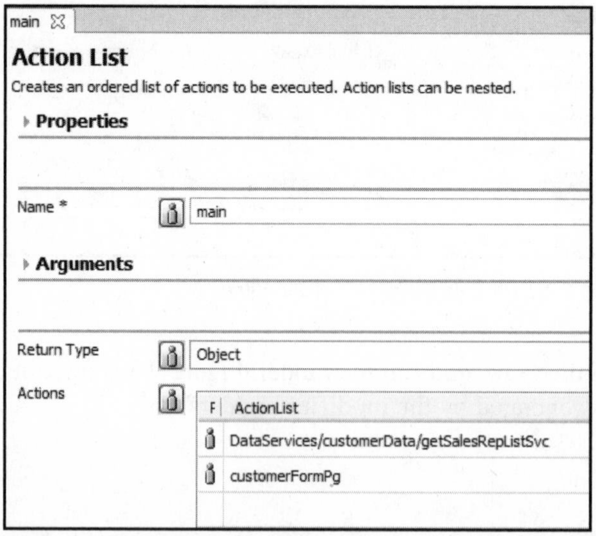

Figure 9.9: Main Action List builder entries

Next, we use the Data Field Modifier builder to build an enumerated list of sales reps. Figure 9.10 shows the necessary entries. Point to the SALESREPEMPLOYEENUMBER field, and reference the customerDataGetSalesRepListSvcResults variable to populate the enumerated list.

Figure 9.10: Data Field Modifier builder entries

269

Click **OK,** and save and run the model; you should see the mapping drop-down list populated with last names of sales reps. The selection will pass the employee number to the submitted form because we selected the EmployeeNumber field as the Value Element in the builder above.

> **Best Practice**: Use server-side validation for portlets written using the Portlet Factory. The Data Page builder has built-in support for server-side validation and provides a better user experience.

We can now move to Step 2 and look at our options for validating the form entries. We can choose either to use the built-in form validation provided by the Data Page builder or to overwrite that field by field (as necessary) using the Rich Data Definition builder. Keep in mind that all this validation happens on the server side. Some organizations choose to include JavaScript and perform client-side validation, which is supported as well. To perform client-side validation, you would follow the standard procedure and include a .js file in your HTML file (Customer Form) with appropriate field names. As a matter of fact, the Factory provides a JavaScript builder to include "inline scripts" or reference an external .js file. Client-side validation, although efficient, isn't user-friendly, and server-side validation is slowly replacing it across organizations. Typically, the scripts are referenced in the header tag of the HTML file. However, the portal tends to strip the header before assembling the various portlets into a single page. A workaround is to include the references and the script inside the body tag.

For this example, we'll leverage the validation provided by the Data Page. The builder in turn references the schema to build validation rules. This harkens back to our earlier discussion about Customer Number being a mandatory field (which is now hidden and subsequently will be generated programmatically). To leverage the Data Page builder's built-in capabilities, we simply need to select the first option, **Both required fields and type information**, in the **Validation from Schema**. You can find this field in the **Input Validation Settings** section in the builder.

Step 3 in our task list is to generate a unique customer number on every insert. We can do this inside our model, by running another query against the Customer table to obtain the highest customer number and programmatically incrementing it by one before calling the insert service. A more efficient way is to modify the database schema to auto-generate the key every time a record is added. The SQL snippet shown in Listing 9.1 alters the Customer table and auto-increments the key on every insert.

```
CONNECT TO CARSDB;
ALTER TABLE CUSTOMERS ALTER COLUMN CUSTOMERNUMBER SET GENERATED AS
IDENTITY (START WITH 1000 INCREMENT BY 1 NO CACHE ) ;
CONNECT RESET;
```

Listing 9.1: SQL Query to alter the CARSDB database

For Steps 4 and 5, we'll invoke the service we wrote in Chapter 8 to insert a new record. Before referencing this service in an action list, we'll add a success page to the model using the Page builder. The success page will simply display a "Database Transaction was successful" message if the insert goes through successfully.

Next, we'll define a new action called addNewRecord, which will control the steps to add a new customer record when the user clicks to submit. This action will map the inputs from the page to the addNewCustomer service call that expects input parameters. The reference chooser displays the various actions available. Under the methods subsection, select the customerDataAddCustomerSvcWithArgs method that is generated by the Service Consumer builder, and map the parameters depending on how they've been laid out in your Data Hierarchy Modifier. The action builder shown in Figure 9.11 shows how this mapping will take place.

Behind the scenes, the Factory generates the Java method to manage the mappings. Also, the action shown above refers to the successPage processing. We'll next add a button builder that will submit the form and insert the record. First, though, we need to complete the form submission entries on the Data Page builder.

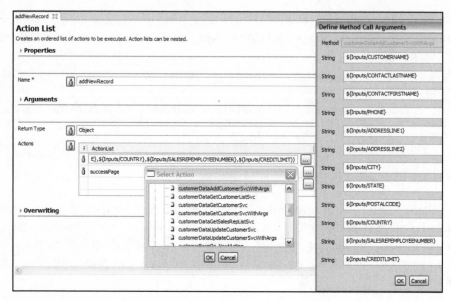

Figure 9.11: Action List that adds a new record

Form Submission Entries

Figure 9.12 shows the form submission entries for the Data Page.

We've discussed the **Validate From Schema** entry previously. You specify the **Post-Save Method** if some processing is needed before inserting the record. For the **Success Action**, we'll invoke the new action builder we added. If the action fails, we'll return the user to the customer form (**Failure Action**). We could log the error and load a generic error page as the failure action.
Click **OK**, and upon regen the Data Page builder introduces a new method called CustomerForm_NextAction. We'll call this method from our button builder. When the user clicks the **Add New Entry** button, the action submits the form and hands control to the Data Page, which validates the entries based on the schema and calls the addNewRecord action, which in turn inserts the record by invoking the addCustomer service call. The success and failure actions are centrally managed by the Data Page.

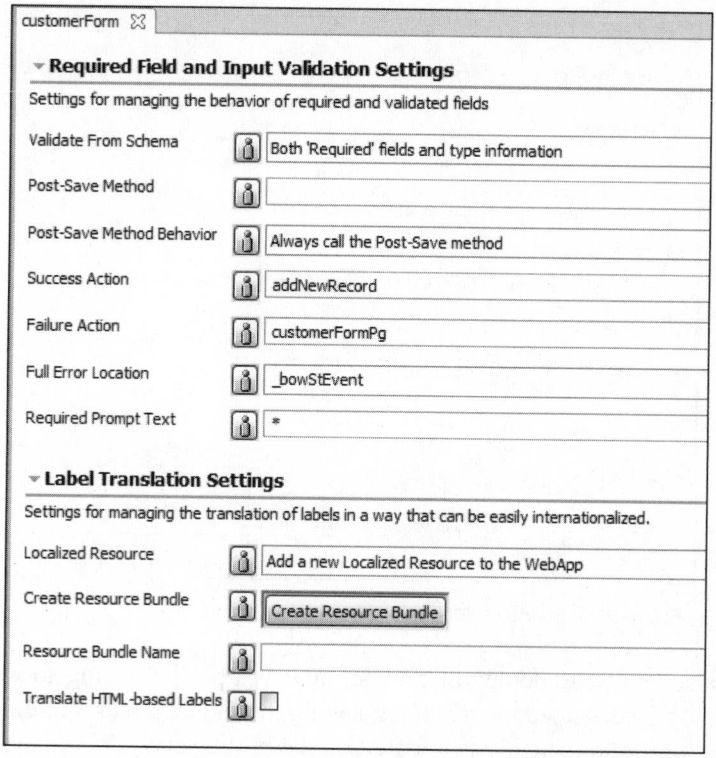

Figure 9.12: Data Page builder calling Add New Record action

You might find all this a bit overwhelming, but going through this exercise again will make things clear, and before long it will become an intuitive part of coding Web applications using Data Page. Figure 9.13 shows the Button builder entries.

Let's do another round of standalone testing. This iteration will ensure that both models are integrated correctly and we are indeed inserting records. In case of errors, the Factory displays the stack trace (on the browser or in the logs). Unfortunately, at this point there is no easy way to step through the generated code. This is one of the drawbacks of the tool that IBM product managers are addressing. We're confident that in due time they will surely improve the debugging capabilities of the Factory.

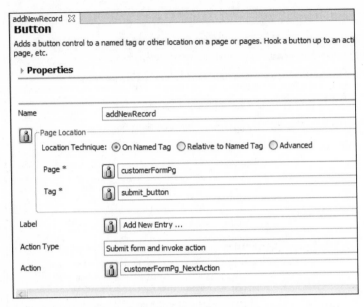

Figure 9.13: Button Builder calling Data Page action

You can also choose to deploy this model now as a portlet. Doing so would entail adding a Portlet Adapter builder, saving the model, and rebuilding the WAR that now automatically is updated on the portal server. We created a page called Customer on our Portal server and placed both portlets side by side. Figure 9.14 shows the portlets as loaded by the portal server thus far.

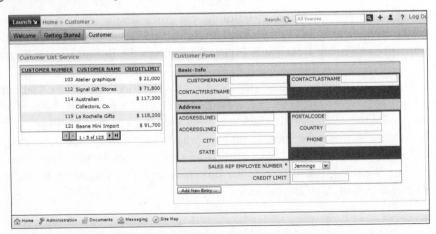

Figure 9.14: Customer view and form portlet deployed on Portal

INTER-PORTLET COMMUNICATION

Having seen how to build views and forms using the Factory, you're ready to learn how to wire the two together. By doing so, you can leverage WebSphere Portal's inter-portlet communication feature to enhance the end user's experience with the portal.

We'll build on our use case further by adding edit capabilities to the customer management application. To accomplish this enhancement, we'll add links on the view portlet to fire the event with the customer data. The customer form portlet in turn will load the customer data in the form, and the user can then update the data. Figure 9.15 shows the two wired portlets and depicts how the data flows

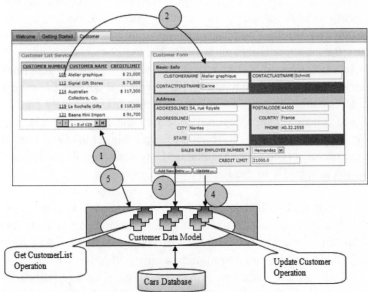

① On portlet load, GetCustomerListSvc is called

② User clicks link, and loadCustomerData event gets fired

③ Form loads data by calling GetCustomerSvc and passes the clicked customer number as a parameter

④ User clicks Update, and updateCustomerSvc gets called - Also RefershPortlet event gets fired

⑤ The event handler in CustomerList portlet then reloads the data and refreshes the screen with the updated data

Figure 9.15: Data flow with inter-portlet communication

across the portlets as well as the interaction of each portlet with the services layer.

We'll follow this transaction step-by-step and add builders to each model as necessary. In keeping with the goal of reuse, we'll leverage the updateCustomerSvc and getCustomerSvc written in our data services layer.

> **Best practice:** Capture multiple Event Declaration builders in a common model, and then use the Imported Model builder to import these builders into your model. This practice ensures all your common 1artifacts are created and managed from a single model file.

The Factory supports two ways to manage inter-portlet communication. You can use the Event Declaration and Event Handling builders to declare and handle events, or you can use the Cooperative Source and Target builders. The latter builders use the Click-To-Action feature of WebSphere Portal. Click-To-Action generates the Web Services Description Language (WSDL) file that defines the events, and you must deploy this file before Click-To-Action works correctly on the portal. Hence, if you choose to add Cooperative Source and Target builders, remember to redeploy the portlet WAR (you'll need to explicitly remove and then add the WAR on the portal server). For this example, we'll use the Event Declaration builder, which is specific to the Factory.

The Event Declaration builder lets the developer pass various data types, including IXML, across portlets and thus makes passing data objects relatively easy. In addition, it requires no redeployment. However, the model using the Event Declaration builder can communicate only with other Factory models. It cannot be wired with non-Factory portlets. In our case, both portlets are Factory-generated, so we'll use Event Declaration and Handling to communicate across these two portlets.

As you can see in the data flow above, we must declare two Event Declaration builders in each model.

Figure 9.16 shows the two events declared.

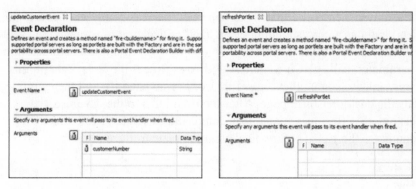

Figure 9.16: Event Declaration builders

Next, we need to make arrangements for the updateCustomerEvent to be fired by the CustomerListView portlet and handled by the CustomerForm portlet. We'll convert the Customer Number column into a link by adding a Link builder to the customerNumber span on the page. This link will then fire the loadCustomerData event and pass the CustomerNumber as the parameter. Figure 9.17 shows Step 2 of our transaction and the passing of the CustomerNumber as a parameter to the target portlet (CustomerForm).

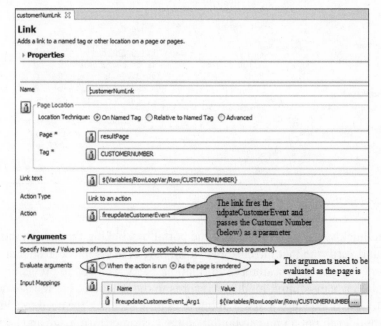

Figure 9.17: Link Builder wired with the Portlet Event Firing

The CustomerForm portlet listens to this event (as it is being broadcast to all portlets) and has a corresponding event handler declared to manage the event. The Event Handler builder, shown in Figure 9.18, takes in the CustomerNumber as a parameter, calls getCustomerSvcWithArgs (to get the latest data on this customer in case some other logged-in user has updated it), and then simply reloads the customer form page. After the round trip to the database, the getCustomerSvcResults variable is updated, and the Data Page builder pre-populates the fields before displaying the page to the end user.

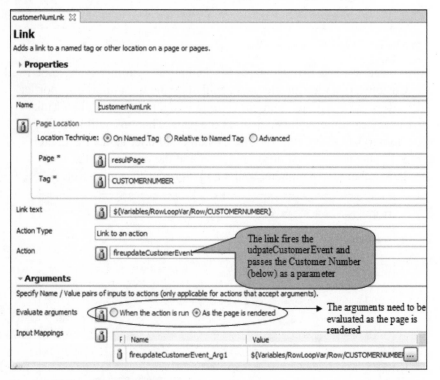

Figure 9.18: Event Handler builder

You can quickly test your portlets on the portal by clicking the link on the view portlet and verifying that the customer form portlet loads the corresponding data. The users can now edit customer information. Next, we need to provision this model so they can commit modified records to the database. For the second part of this transaction (Steps 4 and 5 in our data flow picture), we need to add a Button builder to put an update button on the customer form page and add an updateRecord Action List builder to control the flow logic when a user clicks the update button. Figure 9.19 shows the Action List builder that the Button builder will invoke.

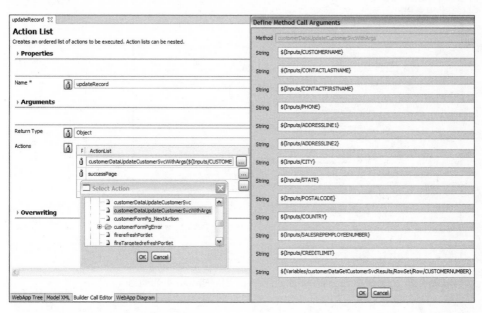

Figure 9.19: Action List to update record

As you can see, the updateRecord action list invokes the UpdateCustomerSvcWithArgs (which we defined in the data services layer in Chapter 8) and passes the page inputs and the CustomerNumber from the getCustomerSvcResults variable. The data service in turn invokes the update SQL Call builder. (You'll need to carefully map the inputs based on how you've arranged the various fields on your form.) A successful update query then returns control to the updateRecord action list, which process the success page.

Figure 9.20 shows the update button. Notice how we've used the relative tag and placed the update button right beside the **Add New Entry** button. Keep in mind that you'll have to choose the **Submit the Form and Invoke an Action** option from the drop-down list for your form to be submitted successfully.

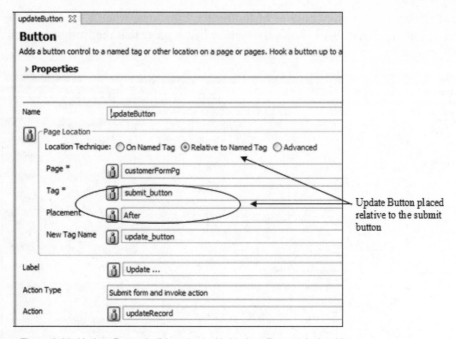

Figure 9.20: Update Button builder wired with Update Record Action List

Save your model, and log back in to the portal to test the event firing and handling. You should be able to click the link and have the customer form model load the data in the portlet. Needless to say, you can't test these changes stand-alone; you need a portal infrastructure as part of the development environment. Change some value on the form, and then click **Update**. A successful update query will load the success page.

We'll add a couple more builders before wrapping up this use case. We need to place a back button on the success page that returns the user to the original customer form, and we need some way to tell the CustomerList view portlet that the data has been updated and it needs to refresh the data in the view. The first enhancement is straightforward; simply define a Button builder with a "Back" label (Figure 9.21) that returns the user to the customer form page.

Figure 9.21: Button builder to return to customer form

The second enhancement entails putting an Event Declaration builder in both models (if you haven't done so already) and adding an Event Handler builder in the CustomerListView portlet to fire the refreshPortlet event when the **Update** button is clicked (this would mean inserting another action in the updateRecord action, as shown in Figure 9.22) and handle the refresh event (Step 5 in the transaction flow diagram).

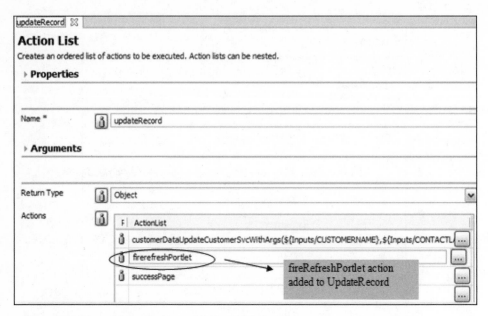

Figure 9.22: Event firing added to updateRecord Action List

Figure 9.23 shows the Event Handler builder, which simply reinitializes the portlet by calling the main action again.

Figure 9.23: Event handler for refresh event

To test the new event handler, save the models and log out and back in to the portlet. A successful update transaction will refresh the customer list view portlet.

Thus far, we've exposed you to several new builders. We hope you're finding the builder and designer interface more familiar and seeing common patterns among various builders. For instance, all UI-related builders have placement tags that determine where these artifacts are placed. Back-end builders, on the other hand, invoke an exposed function or a query, and the regeneration engine writes Java methods to manage those transactions. In the next section, we introduce an important aspect of the Portlet Factory that lets you modify the artifacts generated by the builder, enabling you to rapidly create customized applications for different set of users.

PROFILING

One of the Portlet Factory's most powerful features is its support for *profiling*. Profiling is the secret sauce that clearly sets this product apart, giving Portlet Factory developers the ability to produce customized software on the fly. We as developers simply need to know which aspects of an application the business might want to vary and then profile enable those aspects. Business users or administrators can tweak the profile entries, and the Factory will customize the software and generate an appropriate version.

Again, it's important to understand that the Factory doesn't simply make runtime changes (although in certain use cases it actually does) but rather produces a different set of artifacts when a different profile is applied. Each time a different profile is applied to a model, the Factory produces a different set of JSP/Java or XML code (as necessary). Building customized applications for the end user on the fly (at request time) is a clear differentiator that makes the Factory a powerful machine for building customized software.

As a Portlet Factory developer, you should think about profiling when you encounter a variability requirement in your use cases. For instance, if a requirement dictates a different UI for different roles or requires modified business processes based on certain attributes of the logged-in user, you should immediately think, "Profiling!" Returning to our earlier analogy of the Factory as an assembly line of robots manufacturing a car, in the Portlet Factory world, the builders are the robots and the Web application is the final product (car). By implementing profiling, the same assembly line can now produce multiple variations of the Web application. To achieve this functionality, we need to feed in parameters to the robots to produce a different variation. So, for instance, we feed the "color robot" the color white instead of green to produce a different color variation of the same car. Profiles are sets of parameters fed to individual builders, which then produce different variation of the same application. We've depicted builders as an assembly line before. Figure 9.24 shows a different version of that picture, in which the various profiles applied to the model produce different versions of the same application to cater to different sets of users.

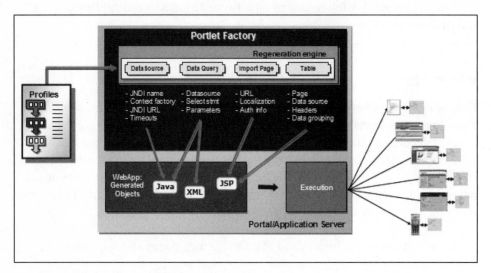

Figure 9.24: Portlet Factory execution with profiles

We'll begin this topic by introducing some basic terminology. Then we'll build on our existing use cases and add some variability to the existing models to reinforce the idea further.

Four terms are key in the profiling world:

- profiles
- profile entries
- profile sets
- selection handler

A *profile* is a set of parameters that feeds into the model and varies the model based on its values. The model typically represents a portlet or an application, and the profiles represent the role of the user or a certain attribute that morphs the application based on the user's profile.

A profile entry is the individual value contained in a profile that feeds into an application and manages its variability. A single profile can contain multiple profile entries.

A profile set is the two-dimensional matrix that contains a set of profiles and its corresponding values. Each profile set can contain single or multiple profiles.

As a Portlet Factory developer, you tie your builder entries to a particular profile entry in a profile set. At this point, you're not responsible for picking the profile — rather, a relationship exists between a builder entry and a profile entry.

The illustration in Figure 9.25 ties these concepts together.

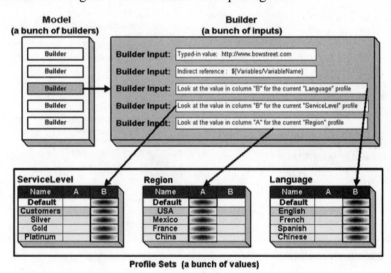

Figure 9.25: Builder wired with entries in profile sets

The image show three profile sets (ServiceLevel, Region, and Language) and depicts how builder entries are wired to various profile values in different profile sets. Profile entries support hierarchy and inheritance. They also support *orthogonal profiling* (applying multiple profiles on the same builder entry). At this point, we're simply telling the builder which profile entry or value will provide it an input. It is the selection handler that determines which profile is applied at runtime. This brings us to the last of the four terms we identified above.

The *selection handler* provides a framework for determining the profile that should be applied to a model so the Factory can produce the corresponding application for the user. The selection handler in turn picks up the correct profile to be applied to the model based on some logic or user attribute. IBM ships multiple "out of the box" selection handlers with the Factory, and they are easily extensible. Figure 9.26 depicts the selection handler making profile selections and the engine then regenerating the model to build the required variation of the application.

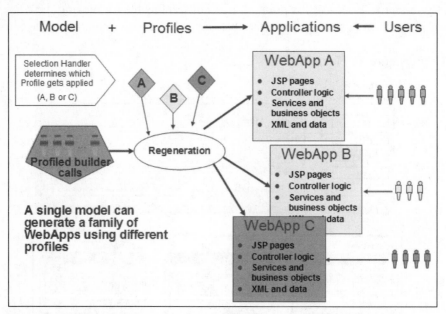

Figure 9.26: Selection handler selecting profiles to be applied to models

This image further demonstrates the idea of a different WebApp being generated for each profile. However, this is only one way to use profiling technology to vary your application. Another technique involves having just one profile and bypassing the selection handler (as the default profile gets applied). This technique involves exposing the default profile and its entries in WebSphere Portal's edit or configure screen. The Portlet Factory thus provides an easy way to expose the profile entries to portal users and administrators by leveraging its personalization and customization screens. Further, the Factory automates the generation of these screens based on your profile entries.

Personalization and Customization Using Profiling

Personalization is the ability of the portal to set different values in the portlet or the portal. For instance, in a weather portlet the end user can enter his or her zip code to receive a personalized weather report. A Portlet Factory developer creates a variable to manage the user's zip code and profile enables it. The profile value can now be exposed as an edit feature. Behind the scenes, the Factory creates a personalization screen for the end user and stores the corresponding zip code in the portal database.

All this is abstracted from the Portlet Factory developer. We simply need to profile enable the variation and expose it as a personalization or customization screen in the Portlet Adapter builder. This brings us to the topic of *customization*, or the ability of the portal to expose certain aspects of the portlet(s) to a group of users for them to customize it. A Factory developer exposes a builder entry in the profile and then ties this entry to customization in the Portlet Adapter builder. The Factory then auto-generates the customization screen. Often, the auto-generated screen won't fully satisfy the requirements as laid out by the business. For this reason, the Factory provides another builder, Portlet Customizer, that permits more control on the screen generated by the Factory. The flow chart shown in Figure 9.27 outlines the logic a portlet developer needs to follow to determine how to best employ profiling.

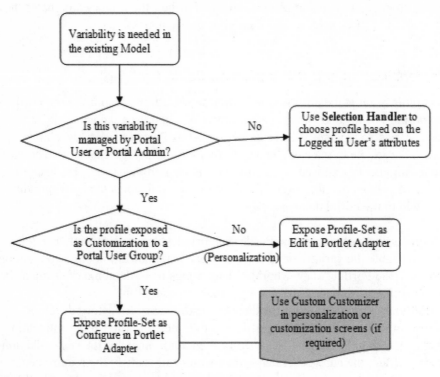

Figure 9.27: Logic to determine profile use in application

Now that you have a broad understanding of the profiling technology and how it is used to vary the application, we'll focus on the use case at hand and add some variability aspects to our application.

Let's enhance the customer view portlet by giving the end user the ability to personalize the number of records he or she wants to see. This change means varying the application for each user. Let's also add the ability for the business administrator to manage the customer view table. These two enhancements will help you understand the most common way to use profiling to expose applications to business users as personalization or customization.

PERSONALIZATION USE CASE

We set the pagination value in the previous chapter, using the Data Column Modifier builder's **Page Size** entry. The current value is set to 5, as shown in Figure 9.28. We need to profile enable the entry so users can personalize the setting. To do so, click the little icon that appears to the left of the builder entry box to bring up the profile editor.

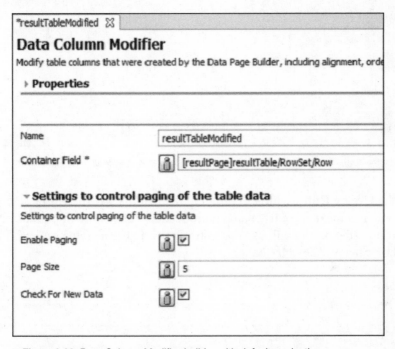

Figure 9.28: Data Column Modifier builder with default pagination

By default, the Factory creates a profile set (if this is the first builder you're profile enabling) and gives it a unique name by appending "ps" to the name of the model. You can rename the profile set if you like. The Factory also creates an entry and a default profile. Figure 9.29 shows the default profile associated with the CustomerListViewps profile set.

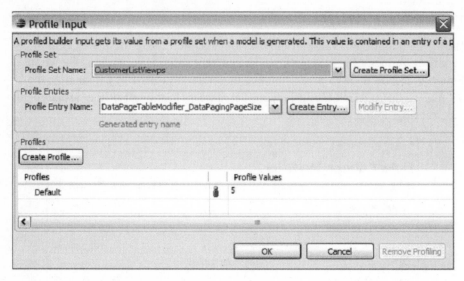

Figure 9.29: Profile enabling the pagination entry in Data Column Modifier builder

Click the **Create Entry** button to bring up the **Modify Profile Entry** screen, where you can make the entry name more readable and, more important, set the user prompt (the portlet will use this entry in the auto-generated screen). Figure 9.30 shows the profile entry editor.

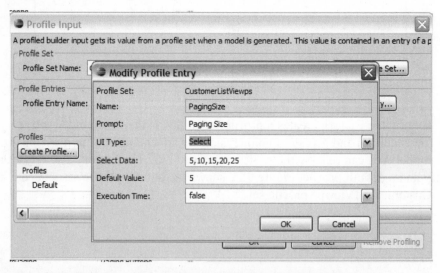

Figure 9.30: Managing paging size entry in the CustomerListView profile

We'll prompt the user for Paging Size and provide a drop-down list of enumerated values. We'll leave the default entry at 5. Click **OK**, and save the model.

The next step, according to the profile logic chart we defined earlier, is to assign this profile set "Edit" access in the Portlet Adapter builder. Figure 9.31 shows this builder with the CustomerListViewps profile set exposed in the user edit screen of the portlet.

customerListService ⌧	

Portlet Adapter

Allows you to expose profile values for customization when the model is used as a portlet.

▸ **Properties**

Name *	customerListService
Portlet Title	Customer List Service
Portlet Short Title	
Portlet Keywords	
Portlet Description	
Default Locale	
User Help File	

Profile Sets

Specify how each Profile Set in this Model should be accessed when it is in a Portal.

CustomerListViewps	Show individual profile values in Edit ▼
	Do not expose in Portal tools
▾ **Edit and Configure Sett**	Show individual profile values in Edit
	Show profile names in Edit
Mechanisms for customizing the ed	Show individual profile values in Configure
	Show profile names in Configure
Custom Edit Type	⦿ None ◯ Imported Page ◯ Custom Model
Custom Configure Type	⦿ None ◯ Imported Page ◯ Custom Model

Figure 9.31: Exposing profiles in the edit screen

Needless to say, we can't test our auto-generated edit screen on the application server because the edit screen is a portal feature. Instead, we must run it as a portlet on the portal server. When you associate a new profile set with a model, you need to rebuild the WAR and redeploy it. A new profile set isn't picked up automatically. However, subsequent changes to the profile set or any of its entries are auto-deployed, and the redeploy needs to happen just once. Before redeploying our portlet, let's tackle the next enhancement for our use case:

customizing the view table and creating the required profile set for the customization screen so we can deploy them both at once.

Customization Use Case

For the customization enhancement, we start in the Data Column Modifier builder because this builder controls the look and feel of the table, including column visibility and labels. Click the profiling icon next to the Column List, as pointed out in Figure 9.32, to reach the default profile entry screen, and open the CustomerListViewps (the profile set we used in the previous enhancement).

Figure 9.32: Profile enabling column management in Data Column Modifier

Given the requirement that this profile set needs to be exposed as configuration, we need to create a separate profile set. To do so, click the **Create Profile Set** button, and rename the profile set to something different. Once you click **OK**, the profile input screen should look as shown in Figure 9.33.

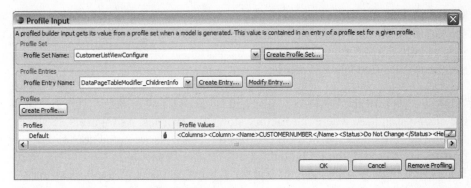

Figure 9.33: Profile input for column management

All the attributes of the table, including the column names and its visibility, reside in an XML variable. Following our profile logic chart leads us to expose this profile set as Configure in the portlet adapter, as Figure 9.34 shows.

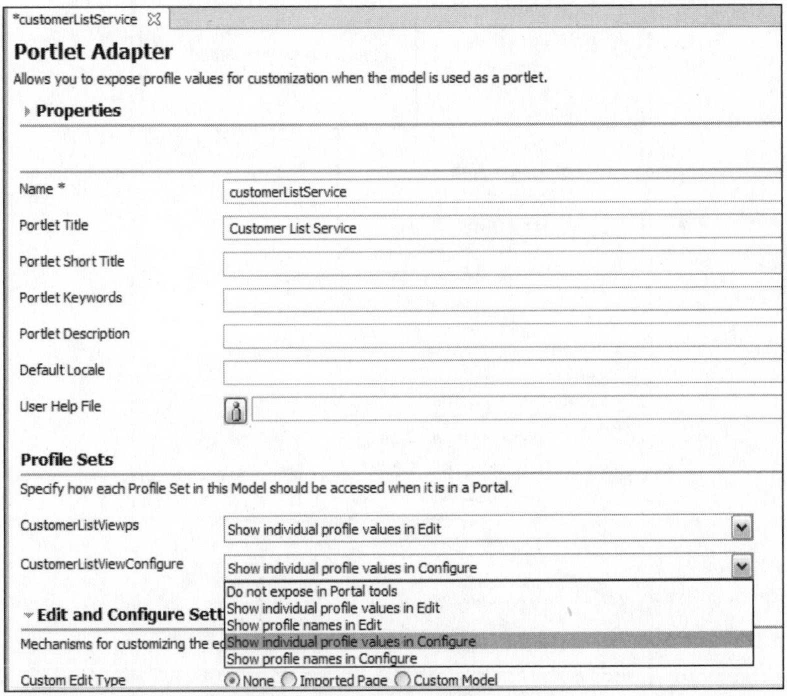

Figure 9.34: Exposing individual profile values in configuration screen

We've now tied the CustomerListViewConfigure profile set to the configure screen in the portlet. When we click **OK**, the model is regenerated. The next step is to rebuild the WAR and update it on the portal server after saving the necessary files (models and profiles).

While we wait for the WAR to be updated (it takes a few minutes), let's revisit the designer and see where the Factory stores the profiles. As Figure 9.35 shows, the profiles are under the web-inf/profiles directory. As we noted above, the profiles are stored in the Portal database if they've been tied to the Configure or Edit screen in the Portlet Adapter builder. Further, notice how the builder has a corresponding profiling icon in the model editor, which tells a developer that the builder has been profile-enabled.

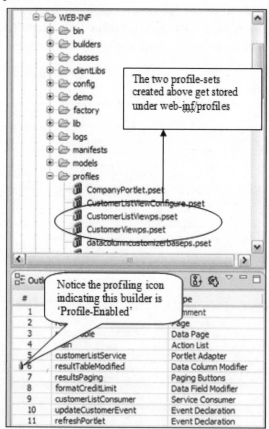

Figure 9.35: Profiles directory structure and profile-enabled model

If you double-click a profile, it will be opened up in the profile editor. Here, you can use the **Entries** tab to manage profile entries and use the **Manage Profiles** tab to manage profiles. The editor also features a selection handler tab, where you can choose the selection handler to be used for the profile set in question. Figure 9.36 shows the profile set loaded in the designer with the **Entries** tab active.

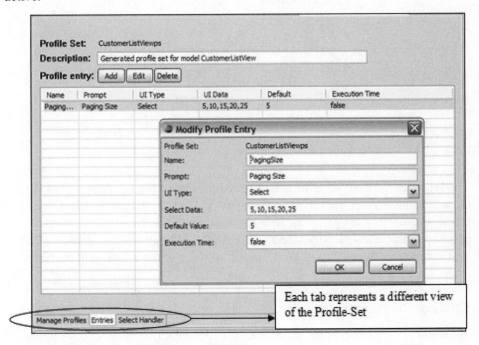

Figure 9.36: Profile set editor within the designer

Once the portlet WAR has been successfully uploaded on the portal server, we'll check whether the configure and edit screens (auto-generated by the Portlet Factory) meet our requirements. Log back in to the portal, and click the arrow icon in the portlet's upper-right corner to load these screens. Figure 9.37 shows the portlet menu and the corresponding screens.

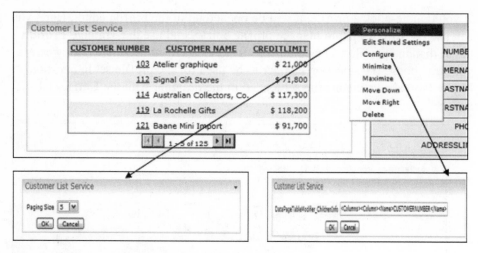

Figure 9.37: Factory-generated edit and configure screens

The screen generated for setting the pagination size seems acceptable, but the customization screen has the table layout as XML data. We can't expect our business users to manage the table layout from an XML variable. We need to provide a more user-friendly screen. This is where the customizer builders kick in. Customizers by definition are UIs built to manage the underlying profile set.

Custom Customizer

We'll start by creating a new model called CustomerCustomizer and dropping a Portlet Customizer builder. PortletCustomizer is a powerful builder that can introspect a profile set and build the entire UI that lets the business user manage the profile. We can further use the Modifier builders (because the Portlet Customizer builder uses the Data Page builder under the covers) and change the screens to fit our requirement. We'll use the Rich Data Definition builder and tweak some of the screen elements generated by the Portlet Customizer builder. Using the Rich Data Definition builder, we'll modify two columns to instead have enumerated options. We'll change the **Status** field (options: **Show, Hide**) and the **Sortable** field (options: **Not Sortable, Case Insensitive String, Number**). Figure 9.38 shows the Portlet Customizer builder.

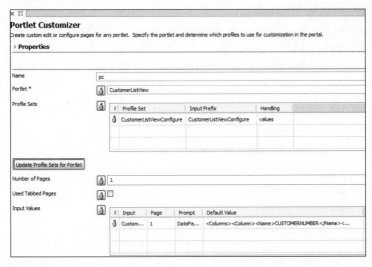

Figure 9.38: Portlet Customizer builder to manage customizer screen

Figure 9.39 shows some important inputs for the Rich Data Definition builder.

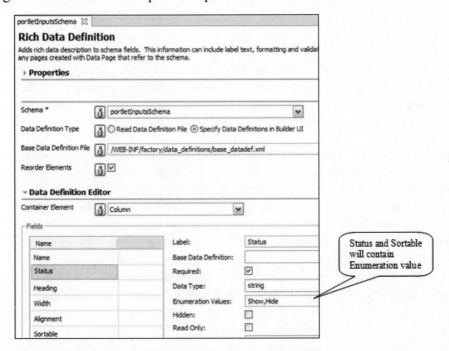

Figure 9.39: Rich Data Definition builder modifying customizer UI

The final step in the customization screen exercise is to inform our Portlet Adapter builder (in the CustomerListView portlet) to use the CustomerCustomizer to generate the UI rather than auto-generate it. Figure 9.40 shows the builder entries we need to change in the Portlet Adapter builder to accomplish the expected behavior.

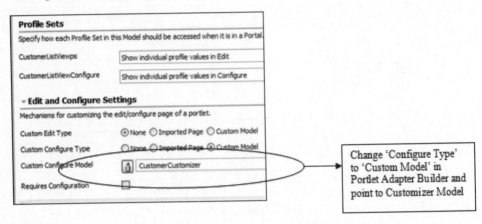

Figure 9.40: Portlet Adapter builder wired with customizer modelscreen

Save the model, and log back in to the portal to check the new configure screen. (You'll see the **Configure** option in the portlet menu in the upper-right corner.) If all goes well, the configure screen will look like the one shown in Figure 9.41. Feel free to change your Data Column Modifier entries from your customizer screen. Click OK to see the portlet respond to the change.

Once again, all the steps might seem overwhelming, but in essence all we've done is create a profile set for the edit screen and the configure screen and expose those profile sets in the portlet adapter. We used the customizer to build a UI that was more user-friendly and acceptable to the business administrator. If necessary, reread the profiling section while trying the exercise on your own. It's important to understand the concepts behind profiling and how to use them effectively. This knowledge will ensure you can not only rapidly create applications but also vary them and create hundreds of variations with a few clicks. Rapid application building that responds to change — sounds exciting!

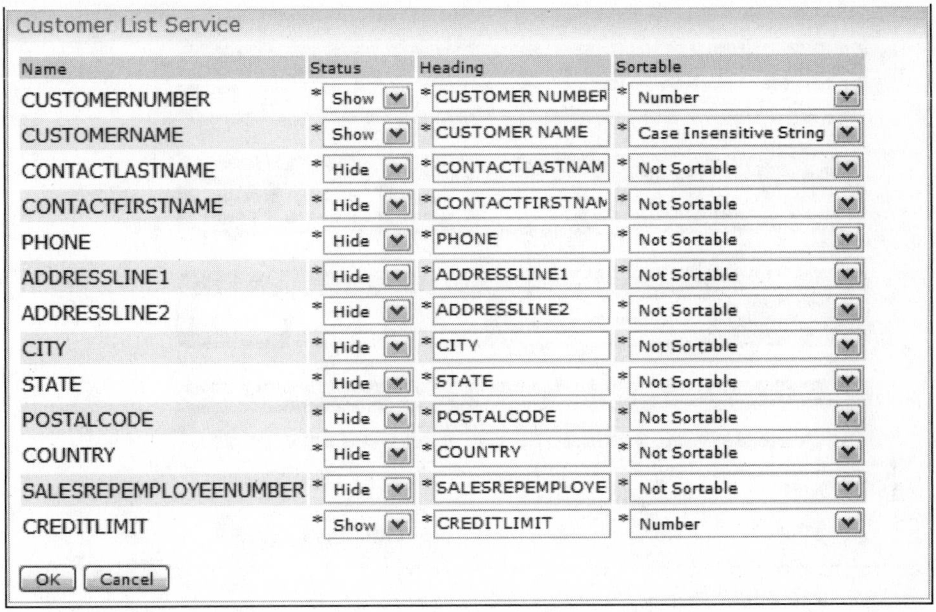

Customer List Service			
Name	Status	Heading	Sortable
CUSTOMERNUMBER	* Show ⌄	* CUSTOMER NUMBER	* Number ⌄
CUSTOMERNAME	* Show ⌄	* CUSTOMER NAME	* Case Insensitive String ⌄
CONTACTLASTNAME	* Hide ⌄	* CONTACTLASTNAM	* Not Sortable ⌄
CONTACTFIRSTNAME	* Hide ⌄	* CONTACTFIRSTNAM	* Not Sortable ⌄
PHONE	* Hide ⌄	* PHONE	* Not Sortable ⌄
ADDRESSLINE1	* Hide ⌄	* ADDRESSLINE1	* Not Sortable ⌄
ADDRESSLINE2	* Hide ⌄	* ADDRESSLINE2	* Not Sortable ⌄
CITY	* Hide ⌄	* CITY	* Not Sortable ⌄
STATE	* Hide ⌄	* STATE	* Not Sortable ⌄
POSTALCODE	* Hide ⌄	* POSTALCODE	* Not Sortable ⌄
COUNTRY	* Hide ⌄	* COUNTRY	* Not Sortable ⌄
SALESREPEMPLOYEENUMBER	* Hide ⌄	* SALESREPEMPLOYE	* Not Sortable ⌄
CREDITLIMIT	* Show ⌄	* CREDITLIMIT	* Number ⌄

OK   Cancel

Figure 9.41: Configuration screen generated by the customizer

SOLUTIONS STRATEGY

More and more customers are buying into IBM's vision in using WebSphere
Portal as an infrastructure component (rather than application) and leveraging
this platform to build and deploy both inward- and outward-facing solutions
across the enterprise. Portlet Factory is a powerful tool that plays very well in the
composite application space. IBM has rolled out multiple solutions built on top
of the Portlet Factory and is gaining enormous traction as customers see a quick
way to rapidly build and deploy customized solutions. Figure 9.42 shows the
Portlet Factory tooling, along with the Framework components that contain commonly occurring architectural patterns captured as builders and the solutions
built on top of these frameworks. The two most widely known frameworks are
the Workplace Dashboard Framework, used to build executive and industry-
specific dashboards, and the SAP Framework, used primarily by SAP customers
to build composite applications surfacing their SAP data with other legacy
systems onto WebSphere Portal.

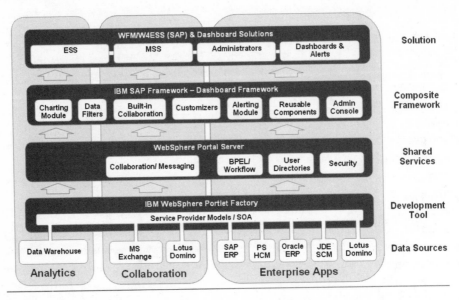

Figure 9.42: Portlet Factory, Framework, and the Solutions Stack

At the time of this book's release, IBM had rolled out the "Employee and Manager Self Service" solution, which surfaces SAP human resources data built on top of the IBM SAP Framework. Other solutions focused on other SAP modules (e.g., Finance, Materials Management) are in the works and will follow soon. The solution framework lets customers surface SAP data and use it in context with data from other legacy applications to build truly sophisticated actionable dashboards. (SAP builders included in the SAP Framework support SAP transactions and workflows.) Rolling out these solutions doesn't require months or years; rather, customers go live in days or weeks, thanks to the powerful automation and variability features of the underlying Portlet Factory on which these solutions are built. The Dashboard Framework lets non-J2EE programmers rapidly create actionable and customizable dashboards that can manage transactions, charting, and alerts. Customers who choose Dashboard or SAP Framework get excited about the idea of surfacing data from multiple back ends onto WebSphere Portal to unlock the value in their powerful platform while continuing to leverage their investments in legacy systems over many years.

Web Charts and Portlet Factory

Before we wrap up the Portlet Factory and associated solutions discussion, let's tackle one more use case by introducing the popular charting builder, which lets Portlet Factory developers write charting portlets with just a few clicks.

IBM ships Portlet Factory with the GreenPoint Web Charting engine. The Web Chart builder provides tight integration with the underlying engine and produces the necessary artifacts (JSP, Java code) at regeneration time that are then executed by the Charting engine. From a Portlet Factory developer perspective, we again are abstracted from these complexities. We simply use the Web Chart builder to roll out a portlet with a chart.

To demonstrate the process, we'll use the last service we wrote in Chapter 8, for the product inventory, and build a bar chart to display the inventories grouped by product category. We'll leave dropping a Page builder with a main action list and a service consumption builder as an exercise to the reader. The important builder in this model is the Web Chart builder, which gets associated with a span tag on the page. Figure 9.43 shows the entries to define the builder.

As you can see, the chart builder simply consumes the results from the service call (make sure you call the "execute" service in your main, or your variable won't contain any values at runtime) and displays the chart with the appropriate settings. Upon regeneration and save, the run model action should display the chart as shown in Figure 9.44. With a few clicks, we were able to produce a chart in a matter of minutes.

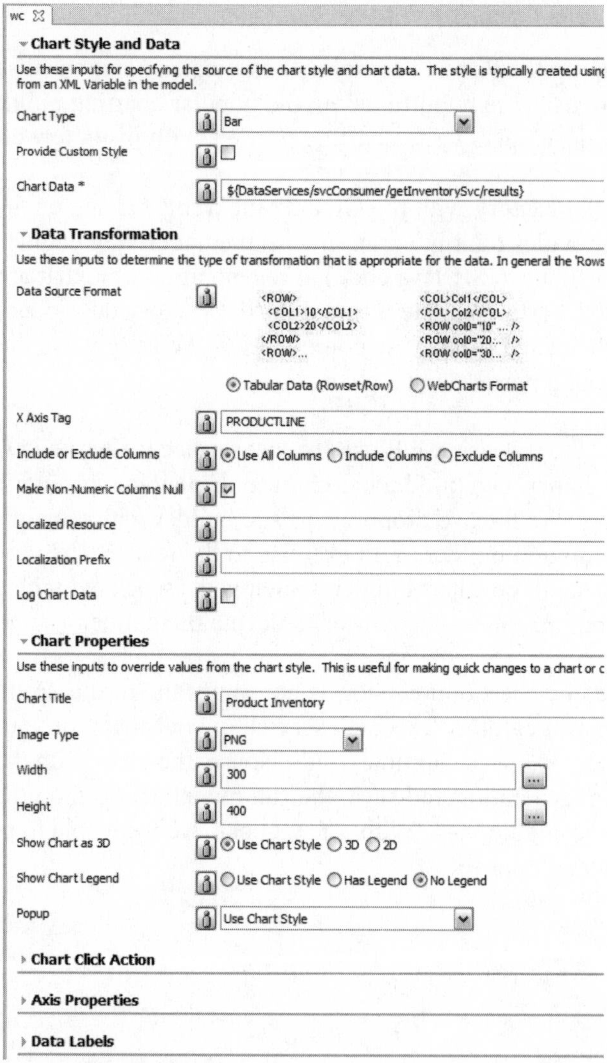

Figure 9.43: Web Chart builder entries

As you become more familiar with the designer, navigating across its sections will become easier and more intuitive. To reiterate our point above, the Factory's software automation capabilities let you fully leverage your investments in the powerful platform of WebSphere Portal.

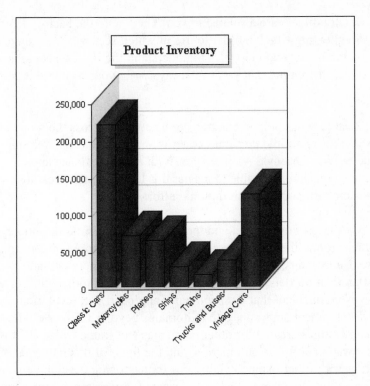

Figure 9.31: Exposing profiles in the edit screen

SUMMARY

In this chapter, we covered the form capabilities of the Portlet Factory's Data Page builder and related builders in the same category, and we wired our portlets together using the Factory's built-in event firing mechanism. We introduced the important concept of profiling, which lets you vary your portlets and expose this variability to your business users. In the final section, we elaborated on IBM's solution strategy and talked about additional products, frameworks, and solutions built on top of the Portlet Factory. We also showed how to use the charting builder and managed to create a bar chart representing the product inventory data in our database.

Although it's impossible within the scope of this book to address each and every builder available in the builder palette, the more important takeaway is to be aware of which builders are available to you. The key to the Factory learning curve lies in knowing which builder to use in which scenario. You can always fall back on the contextual help files to understand the intricacies of each builder. Also bear in mind that you can always write your own builders if required.

The Portlet Factory has helped hundreds of customers across the globe unlock data spread across multiple disparate systems and surface it on WebSphere Portal with a true Service Oriented Architecture. With a little patience and perseverance, you should be able to master this tool and start creating complex JSR 168–compliant portlets with minimal effort.

The vision is that as this product and tool gain traction across developer communities around the world, we'll have hundreds of more builders added to the palette. Consultants, developers, customers, and partners will add builder packs (rather than portlets), enabling business users to automate the software creation. We're confident that the parametric approach will revolutionize software development and propagate to domains beyond J2EE. We'll have builders and engines created for other languages and frameworks. IBM is leading the way in software automation, and the force of this movement will sweep away every other manually laborious tool as rising development costs force organizations to adapt to the future wave of automated software creation.

Chapter Ten

Inter-Portlet Communication

A powerful feature of WebSphere Portal is its support for *cooperative portlets*. Cooperative portlets are portlets that interact and exchange information with each other to improve the end-user experience. In this chapter, you'll learn how portlets can cooperate with each other and how that cooperation benefits the end user.

WebSphere Portal supports two cooperative portlet paradigms:

- wiring
- Click-to-Action (C2A)

Portlets based on the Java portlet API (i.e., the JSR 168 specification) or the legacy portlet API (i.e., the IBM portlet API) can take advantage of wiring. Click-to-Action is currently available only to portlets that use the legacy portlet API in WebSphere Portal. Because this book focuses on the Java portlet API, this chapter concentrates on wiring portlets for exchanging information. For more information about C2A, refer to Reference 1.

IBM introduced Click-to-Action technology in Version 4 of WebSphere Portal. Cooperative portlets, which are an extension of this technology, debuted in WebSphere Portal V5.

COOPERATIVE PORTLET BACKGROUND

WebSphere Portal provides a horizontal portal framework you can use to aggregate processes and information from diverse applications and deliver them in a unified presentation to an end user. When we reflect on the term "integration," we think of integrating back-end applications. When we then put that integration thought in the perspective of a portal running pluggable components (portlets), we realize that integration refers to the integration of back-end applications "at the glass" — that is, at the user interface layer in the application environment. When we examine applications at the glass, we can see that any exchange of information or interaction between applications usually results in extra keystrokes and clicks by the end user.

Cooperative portlets takes this notion of integration and interaction at the glass one step further. Cooperative portlets provide an opportunity to add behavior to portlets collocated on the same page as well as across pages. The term "cooperative" portlets refers to the capability of the portlets to interact with each other and exchange information at the glass. The ability to exchange information or flow a single action or event to other portlets minimizes tedious end-user tasks and improves the user's overall experience and efficiency.

Before diving into details, let's look at the example we'll build in this chapter. It involves a source portlet and a target portlet. The user interacts with the source portlet, which then exchanges information with a target portlet via a *wire*. In our example, the source portlet, CityListPortlet, presents a list of cities to the end user (Figure 10.1). The target portlet, ShowTemperaturePortlet, displays the current temperature for a given city (Figure 10.2).

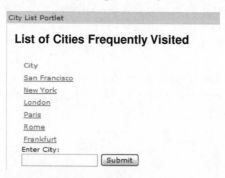

Figure 10.1: CityListPortlet

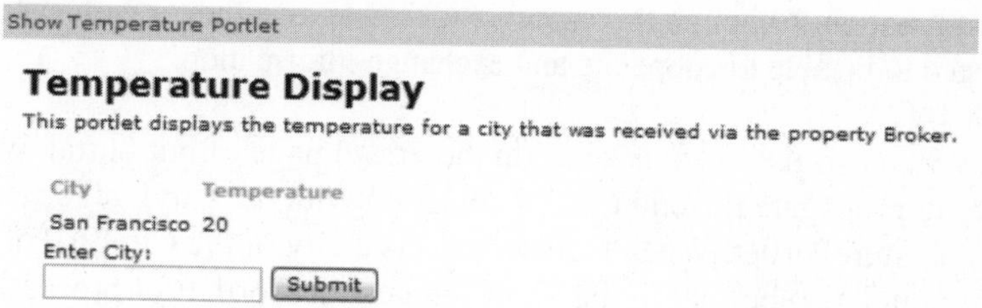

Figure 10.2: ShowTemperaturePortlet

To place a little context around the CityListPortlet, you can think of it as part of a larger travel application running in a portal server and placed on a Travel page. The portlet's purpose is simple: It displays a list of cities — perhaps cities the end user visits often. Interaction with a city in the list might result in the display of additional information in the portlet — local restaurants, airports, or entertainment, for example. Building such functionality goes beyond the purpose of this chapter and would distract us from the details of how portlets exchange information using wires. Therefore, in this example the action of clicking on a city in the list will result simply in the exchange of the city name with a target portlet. Based on this single user action, both the source and the target will be updated.

The target portlet, ShowTemperaturePortlet, does exactly what you'd expect: Given the name of a city, it displays the city's current temperature. (We originally designed the portlet to let the user enter the desired city in an entry field and submit it for processing.) After the user submits the city name to the ShowTemperaturePortlet, the portlet is invoked, the appropriate lookup of the temperature takes place, and the results are aggregated into the page returned to the user.

It's obvious so far that our two portlets are completely independent of each other from a development and end-user perspective. The CityListPortlet and the ShowTemperaturePortlet could have been installed into the portal from the same portlet application, or they could have come from separate portlet applications. An end user or administrator may see some value in configuring a page that contains both the CityListPortlet and the ShowTemperaturePortlet. Ultimately, what the end user wants from either portlet is information about a particular city. The end user could interact with each portlet separately, selecting and entering the city in each place. This interaction would result in two round trips to the portal to obtain the desired information. Although this example is simple in nature, it demonstrates why portlets need to be able to cooperate and exchange information.

To improve the end user's experience on the Travel page of our portal, we need the ability to propagate the end user's interaction with the CityListPortlet to the ShowTemperaturePortlet. When the user selects a city in the CityListPortlet, the selection should also be sent to the ShowTemperaturePortlet for processing.

The ability to discover new applications by placing portlets on a page and wiring them together gives end users and administrators a powerful tool with respect to composing new applications. To enable this type of composition, we must define the exchange capabilities of each portlet without specifying a direct connection between the portlets at development time. This approach lets us preserve the pluggable component nature of a portlet and adhere to a loosely coupled model.

BASIC CONCEPTS

A runtime service called the *Property Broker* facilitates cooperation between portlets in WebSphere Portal. The Property Broker service follows a "publish and subscribe" model. The core concept behind cooperative portlets is that source portlets and target portlets publish their capabilities to the Property Broker service. The service lets portlets declare the "type" of information they can share and consume at runtime. The implication of using a declarative model at runtime means we can develop portlets independently of each other, and an end user or administrator can "discover" their interaction while configuring a page or pages. This approach clearly provides more flexibility than using inter-portlet communication techniques such as portlet messaging, a feature supported by IBM's legacy portlet API that requires portlets to be "hard-wired" together in a development environment.

As we mentioned, the cooperative portlet paradigm for Java API–based portlets requires the definition of a wire. The wire represents a persistent connection in which portlets can communicate. As you'll see, WebSphere Portal provides a "wiring" tool to create and configure wires between portlets. In the example we'll work through, we'll create a wire to enable the exchange of the city name between the CityListPortlet (the source) and the ShowTemperaturePortlet (the target).

A review of the JSR 168 Portlet API specification would reveal that the standard lacks an exchange mechanism. It's important to understand that the Property Broker service is an extension provided by WebSphere Portal that is available to both JSR 168 portlets and legacy portlets. If you're writing JSR 168–compliant portlets that use any of the extensions provided in WebSphere Portal and you plan to use them beyond WebSphere Portal, you should code them to run in any JSR 168–compliant container.

Even without much technical detail so far, you can see that the declarative nature of the cooperative portlet paradigm provides the flexibility for composing loosely coupled applications. To understand how portlets cooperate via the Property Broker service, you really need to understand the role that properties and actions play within the model.

Properties and Actions

A fundamental aspect behind cooperative portlets is the unit of exchange between portlets, which is a typed data item called a *property*. You can think of a property as an exchangeable piece of information that's part of the data model of a given portlet. From a portlet perspective, a property can be either published or consumed:

- *Output properties* are published by source portlets.
- *Input properties* are consumed by target portlets.

Also involved in the exchange of information are portlet *actions*. Portlet actions are the trigger for the exchange of information, which means they can be tied to a control on the screen or produced when an action is executed. When we dig deeper into the details, you'll see that portlet actions provide an opportunity to insert code in a source portlet to produce a property or to insert code in target portlet to process a property. (In addition, portlets based on the legacy API can programmatically trigger an exchange of information.)

The source portlet receives the end-user action (clicking on a city in our case), causing the processAction method of the source portlet to be invoked. This event is an opportunity for the portlet to produce a property that starts the exchange of information. In the same action-processing cycle, the processAction method of the target portlet is also invoked, giving the target portlet an opportunity to consume and process the property.

From what we know so far, we can see that the processAction method of the CityListPortlet must produce a property that contains the name of the city selected by the user. We also have an idea that the output property of the source not only must be mapped to an input property of the target but also must be associated with an appropriate portlet action that is processed by the target portlet. The processAction method of the target portlet, ShowTemperaturePortlet, must receive an action and extract the name of the city. Once it has the city name, it can determine the current temperature.

Let's step back for a moment and think about how the portal renders a page. We refer to the rendering of a page in a portal as the *page aggregation process* or simply *page aggregation*. Page aggregation in a portal involves two phases. The *action phase* handles actions and events, while the *render phase* handles the transformation of data to the appropriate markup of the target end-user device. Therefore, when an end user clicks a link that represents a city in the CityListPortlet, our expectation is that the processAction method of both the source and the target will be invoked in the action-processing phase. One trip is made to the portal server for the page, resulting in the state change and update of both portlets.

At this point, we know that portlets publish their capabilities (actions and properties) to the Property Broker service and that an end-user action triggers the exchange of information. We know that the end user's action of clicking a link or button generates a portlet action, which is processed by the source portlet in its processAction method. This is where the property for the exchange is produced and emitted. What's missing is how the property is sent from the source portlet to the target portlet. Ultimately, the property from the source portlet is mapped to an action and input property of the target portlet. This mapping is defined by a wire and performed by the Property Broker service. Note that an administrator typically performs the wire definition, and the runtime uses this definition to control the transfer of properties and execute actions.

Before we discuss how a property is exchanged, we need to understand its relationship to an action. Figure 10.3 depicts the relationship among a property, an action, and a parameter.

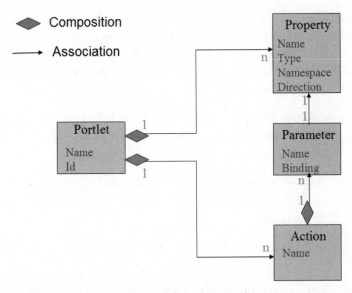

Figure 10.3: Property, action, and parameter relationship

Looking at this illustration, you can see that a portlet "has" both properties and actions. Note that an action can have multiple parameters; however, a parameter is associated with one, and only one, property. An important aspect of the relationship is that parameters serve as a mapping between properties and actions. This means that a source portlet can emit a property as a parameter and the parameter can be mapped to an action and parameter in the target portlet.

As you'll see, a parameter contains not only a value but also specific implementation information that both the developer and the Property Broker service use. The parameter's information tells the developer where to insert the value for a source portlet and where to extract the parameter for a target portlet. It also tells the Property Broker where to "watch" for output parameters and how to map them to input parameters. We call this information, as you might expect, the *binding* information. The binding information defines the parameter's scope — in other words, where the source portlet will insert the source parameter and where the target portlet will expect the parameter.

To maintain a loosely coupled model, cooperative portlets must register their capabilities with the Property Broker service. This registration involves describing the properties, parameters, and actions that the portlet can publish and consume.

A Web Services Description Language (WSDL) file defines the capabilities of the portlet. In addition, the WSDL file contains meta-information about each property, including type, namespace, and direction. The Property Broker service uses this meta-information to match outbound properties of source portlets to inbound properties of target portlets.

- The type is used to represent the semantics of the property — for example, the property being defined could represent various abstractions, such as Address, Order ID, or perhaps City Name.

- The namespace lets us guarantee the uniqueness of property types, thereby avoiding any collision with similarly named properties from other portlet applications.

- The direction indicates whether the property is outbound or inbound.

The main task of the Property Broker service is to match outbound properties to inbound properties based on type. To be able to create a wire so that a source and target portlet can exchange information, the portlets must define the same property type, and the types must be in the same namespace. We'll reinforce this concept throughout the chapter.

Before we jump into the architecture behind cooperative portlets, let's take a closer look now at wires.

Wires

You can see that the cooperative portlet wiring paradigm truly provides a loosely coupled solution for inter-portlet communications:

- Exchange capabilities are defined during portlet development.

- Exchange capabilities are registered with the Property Broker service when the portlet is installed into the portal.

- Exchange capabilities are discovered and mapped from source to target portlets via the definition of wires.

The first bullet is the responsibility of the developer; the second is the responsibility of an administrator; and the third clearly lies in the domain of an administrator or end user. The *Portlet Wiring Tool* is a portlet that provides the ability to define wires in WebSphere Portal. It's used to create persistent channels, also known as *connections*, between portlet instances, where an instance is represented by a portlet window (see the JSR 168 specification for a description of a portlet window) and not the actual object instances in memory. The wires are used to communicate changes in a property defined in the source portlet by invoking an action on the target portlet. To stress the point, the invocation of an action on the target portlet refers to the invocation of the processAction method. The invocation of the processAction method of the target portlet gives the portlet an opportunity to interact with a business model, change the state of the portlet application, and update its view based on the user's interaction with the source portlet. You can think of the definition of a wire as discovering new behaviors between components based on the interaction of source and target portlets. Ultimately, the result can be considered the creation of a new application constructed at the glass by an administrator or end user.

It's important to understand that properties, actions, and parameters are associated with a portlet instance (the single object in memory), while wires are associated with the pairing of a portlet window and a portlet entity. If we compare portlets with servlets, we see that both are represented in memory as a single object instance. No matter how many World Clock portlets we place on a page or across multiple pages, only one instance of the World Clock portlet exists in memory. The portlet instance is one code base and one set of configuration parameters that include the definition of properties, actions, and parameters. The abstraction that represents a portlet on a page is the portlet window associated with a portlet entity. From an end user or administrator perspective, a wire is a communications channel that is established between the portlet window-entity pair of the source portlet and the portlet window-entity pair of the target portlet.

Figure 10.4 depicts the relationship a wire has with a source portlet and a target portlet with respect to page. This relationship is constrained by the requirement that the source and target must have matching property type information to exchange information. This means we can't create arbitrary wires. For example, it wouldn't make sense to create a wire where the source portlet produces a property of type "Order_Id" and the target portlet consumes a property of type "City_Name". Fortunately, the Portlet Wiring Tool enforces this constraint, minimizing the risk of creating a wire with mismatched types.

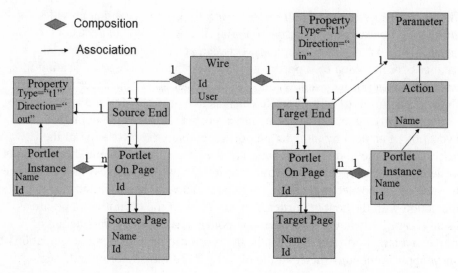

Figure 10.4: Wire relationships

You access the Portlet Wiring Tool by navigating to the desired page and selecting the **Edit Page Layout** option from the drop-down menu list to display the page customizer. From the page customizer, select the **Wires** tab. The Portlet Wiring Tool will be displayed on the page. The tool presents drop-down boxes that display the following information.

- **Source Portlet:** A list of available source portlets on the page.

- **Sending:** A list of available outbound properties for a selected source portlet.

- **Target Page:** A list of available pages. The default selection is the current page.

- **Target Portlet:** A list of available target portlets on the target page.

- **Receiving:** A list of inbound properties.

- **WireType:** The options Public and Personal. Public means the wire is on a shared page and available to all end users who have access to the page. Personal indicates the wire is private.

To create a wire, a user performs the following tasks:

1. Select a source portlet from the drop-down list. Only the source portlets on the current page are displayed.

2. Select an outbound property published by the source portlet.

3. Select the target page. The target page is typically the current page. However, the exchange of properties across pages is supported. Therefore, any accessible page can be selected.

4. Select a target portlet. Once the target page is selected, the wiring tool displays a list of cooperative portlets that can consume the matching property.

> **Note** From a source page, you can select only one target page. For example, if you create a wire between a source portlet on target page A and a target portlet on page B, all targets must be on page B for source portlets on page A.

5. Select the inbound property of the target portlet that will be mapped to the outbound property. The Property Broker will set the inbound parameter with the value of the outbound parameter.

6. Select a wire type of **Personal** if the wire is to be private to a given user. If the wire is to be available to all users who have access to the page, select **Public**.

7. Click the + icon to add the wire.

8. Click **Done** to commit the creation of the wire.

The Property Broker stores the information about the wire in the portal database, enabling the wire to persist beyond the user's session and be exported and imported to another instance of WebSphere Portal. However, if the portal is running in the test environment of Rational Application Developer (RAD) and a test page is automatically generated, the wires are not persisted.

COOPERATIVE PORTLET ARCHITECTURE

We've gone through some of the basic concepts behind the cooperative portlet paradigm for Java-based portlets. With this base level of understanding, let's examine the details of inter-portlet communication with cooperative portlets by delving into the architecture. First, we'll look at some of the benefits that the architecture for cooperative portlets provides.

As cited in Reference 2, the loose coupling between source and target cooperative portlets provides some key advantages:

- A cooperative portlet can stand alone and be reused in multiple scenarios. This means that a source or target portlet has no operational dependencies on the presence of a property-exchange mechanism. If a cooperative portlet is placed in a runtime that doesn't have access to a Property Broker, the portlet will function normally.

- The loose coupling provides the flexibility for independently developed cooperative portlets to form new user-facing applications. End users and administrators can discover new behaviors and interactions can that lead to the composition of new applications at the glass. For example, assume that different parties developed the CityListPortlet and the ShowTemperaturePortlet. An end user or administrator could place both portlets on a page and discover that these portlets can interact or cooperate with each other. In essence, the user or administrator would have composed a new user-facing application.

Let's look at the pieces that make cooperation between portlets possible by examining the high-level architecture shown in Figure 10.5.

Even though we've discussed many of the pieces already, let's bring the story together in one place. (For the moment, you can ignore the numbering you see in the diagram; we'll review the flow depicted by these numbered steps shortly.)

In the center of the figure, we see the *WebSphere Portal Core*. The WebSphere Portal Core is the runtime engine responsible for assembling the page based on an end user's selection. The engine first builds the theme and then constructs the appropriate navigation for the page. Next, the engine aggregates the markup rendered by portlets and inserts it into the page to complete the assembly process. It's important to realize that the runtime environment for the portlets is the portlet container as defined by the JSR 168 specification. The portlet container receives requests from the core portal engine and then dispatches

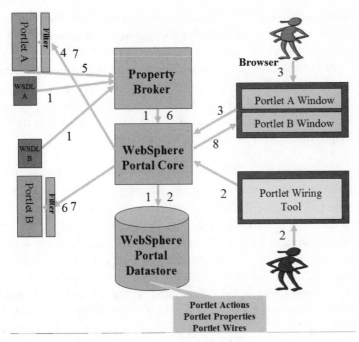

Figure 10.5: Cooperative portlets architecture

the requests to the targeted portlets. A fundamental aspect of the container is that it provides the necessary life-cycle management and the persistence for portlet preferences (see the JSR 168 specification, available online at *http://jcp.org/aboutJava/communityprocess/final/jsr168*).

The next component to discuss is the WebSphere Portal Datastore, commonly referred to as the portal database or the portal repository. The WebSphere Portal Datastore is a repository that contains model information about the portal. For example, the database contains all the pages, their layout, end-user customizations, access control settings, and, as you'd expect, wire information. Also stored in the WebSphere Portal Datastore is the information from the WSDL file associated with a cooperative portlet. When you install a cooperative portlet into the portal, it registers its capabilities with the Property Broker service. Specifically, the information about property types, actions, and parameters is stored in the repository. If the WSDL file for a given portlet is updated, the associated Web module in the portal must be refreshed via the administration portlets for the new settings to be stored in the repository.

317

It's important to realize that the schema of the WebSphere Portal Datastore isn't directly available to developers and administrators. It is exposed via an internal API and externally via a command-line tool known as XMLAccess. XMLAccess provides the ability to query and manipulate the data stored in the WebSphere Portal Datastore. You can use this tool to export a configuration that you want to modify and reimport into the repository. In the situation where a page contains several portlets that are wired together, the wire configuration information is exported along with the rest of the page information.

Continuing with our analysis of the diagram, let's look at the Property Broker. This runtime subsystem contains a generic filter as one of its components. The filter's purpose is to intercept requests to the portlet from the portal core, letting the Property Broker inspect each request to determine whether an action associated with a wire was fired. If the action is associated with a wire, the Property Broker looks for the corresponding outbound property in the scope defined in the binding of the WSDL file for the source portlet. If the Property Broker finds an outbound property associated with the action, it dispatches a request to the portlet container for the purpose of invoking the processAction method of the target portlet. However, before the invocation of the processAction method, the filter for the target portlet intercepts the call. The filter's job is to take the value of the outbound property emitted from the source portlet and insert it into the parameter defined in the binding for the target portlet. Once this mapping occurs, the processAction method of the target portlet is invoked, and the execution of the processAction method continues.

To gain a better understanding of how all the parts fit together, let's walk through a typical flow (indicated by the step numbering in Figure 10.5) that starts with installing the cooperative portlets into the portal.

- A development team hands off a WAR file to an administrator. The WAR file contains two cooperative portlets: a source portlet and a target portlet. The administrator installs the portlets into the portal. The WSDL file of the source and target portlet is processed and stored in the WebSphere Portal Datastore.

- The administrator creates a page upon which he places the source and target portlets. He examines the properties and actions of the portlets and then configures their interaction by creating a public wire. The information about the wire is committed to the WebSphere Portal Datastore.

- An end user logs into the portal and navigates to the page configured with the cooperative portlets by the administrator. The user clicks an action link in the source portlet.

- The WebSphere Portal Core receives the end user's request and dispatches it to the portlet container. As the container invokes the processAction method on the source portlet, the Property Broker Filter intercepts and examines the request. Seeing that an action associated with a wire has been fired, the Property Broker prepares to later look for outbound properties set by the source portlet.

- The source portlet performs its necessary processing by interacting with back-end systems and perhaps changing the state of the portlet. Before execution in the processAction method is completed, the source portlet must insert the outbound property value as an attribute or parameter in the ActionRequest object or as an attribute in the PortletSession object. If there is an outbound property from the source portlet and an active wire exists between the source and the target portlets, the Property Broker triggers an action for the target portlet.

- The portlet container dispatches the action to the target portlet by invoking its processAction method. The Property Broker filter intercepts the call to the target portlet and inserts the appropriate parameters based on the definition specified in the binding information in the WSDL file of the target portlet. Processing continues with the execution of the processAction method of the target portlet. The target portlet has an opportunity to interact with a back-end application and update the state of the portlet.

- After action processing is completed, the render method of each portlet on the page is invoked.

- The markup from each portlet is returned to the portal engine, where it is assembled and returned to the end user. For example, if the request comes from a browser, the portal engine inserts the markup from the portlets into a page and returns the complete page to the user.

In the scenario we've just described, what would happen if portlet B inserted an outbound property for portlet C and there was a wire between B and C? The action-processing phase would continue. The insertion of an outbound property value (a parameter) by portlet B would signal the Property Broker to continue processing with respect to Steps 5 and 6 until all the wires have fired.

You can see that there are three core phases with respect to processing cooperative portlet actions:

- The source portlet sets outbound property values and completes execution of the processAction method.

- The Property Broker listens for outbound property values.

- The Property Broker triggers the action to the target portlet via a wire. The property value and action are delivered to the target portlet. The processAction method of the target continues execution.

The architecture of cooperative portlets provides the opportunity to take any portlet that handles actions and parameter values and make it a target portlet by supplying the necessary definitions in a WSDL file. We use the WSDL file to express the capabilities of the target with respect to the actions and properties it can consume. As for taking any portlet and making it a source of actions and properties, minimal coding is required. The details for creating or modifying a portlet to participate in the exchange of information as a property source will become apparent as we build the sample.

BUILDING THE PORTLETS

To build the portlets, you can use Version 7 of Rational Application Developer, which provides wizards that facilitate the construction of all the parts of a source and target portlet:

- JSPs
- portlets
- WSDL files
- portlet descriptor

However, it's important to realize that RAD isn't required. We'll build the CityListPortlet and ShowTemperaturePortlet introduced earlier in the chapter. A good starting point for developing cooperative portlets is the WSDL files for the source and target portlets, where we'll declare the exchange capabilities.

WSDL Files

The design goal for the service responsible for describing the exchange capabilities between portlets was based on two fundamental principles. It had to rely on existing standards, and it had to be able to leverage existing tool support. WSDL meets the requirement of both principles. First, WSDL is a well-established specification for defining how to describe services as a set of interfaces, or endpoints, that can operate on a message. Because strong tooling support also exists for WSDL, it was the obvious choice for describing the capabilities of portlets. What also made WSDL attractive was the fact that it was designed to support the definition of abstract operations that produce and consume typed data items. This meant it would lend itself well to describing the properties and actions involved in the exchange of information between portlets. However, some custom schema extension work was required to provide a way to describe how portlets implement actions that produce outbound properties and actions that receive inbound properties. As you'll see, the custom extensions were limited to the binding elements of the WSDL file.

Listing 10.1 shows the basic structure of a WSDL file, which consists of six core elements:

- definitions
- types
- message
- portType
- binding
- service

Notice that the first four elements — definitions, types, message, and portType — represent the abstract description of a Web service interface, while the last two — binding and service — describe the implementation details of how the message maps to an implementation (Reference 3). We'll discuss these elements in detail with regard to how we use them to describe cooperative portlet capabilities.

```
<!- WSDL definition structure ->
<definitions
name="CityListPortlet_Service"
targetNamespace="http://jsr.pb.sample"
xmlns="http://schemas.xmlsoap.org/wsdl/"
>
    <!- abstract definitions ->
    <types> ...
    <message> ...
    <portType> ...

    <!- concrete definitions ->
    <binding> ...
    <service> ...
</definition>
```

Listing 10.1: WSDL file outline

Because a WSDL file, also referred to as a WSDL document, simply contains a set of definitions, it makes sense to require a definitions element as the root element in the file. We use the definitions element to specify the name of the service and declare multiple namespaces. The ability to specify multiple namespaces is important because it provides a way to differentiate element declarations and type definitions of one schema from another. It also provides a means of referencing external specifications, such as WSDL, XMLSchema, and, when appropriate, Simple Object Access Protocol (SOAP). Fundamentally, the definitions element contains all the elements that tell us everything we need to know about the service. In our case, it tells the Property Broker service everything it needs to know about a cooperative portlet that is a consumer, a producer, or both. The first element to define within the definitions "container" is type.

We use the types element to define the data types required by the messages in the WSDL file. By default, the types are based on the W3C XML Schema specification; however, WSDL isn't exclusively tied to any specific typing system. Let us emphasize the point that the type specified in the WSDL files for the source and target portlets that cooperate together must match exactly! The first element we define for a source and target portlet that will interact via the Property Broker service must have a matching type defined.

We use the message element to describe the payload. When we think of the payload, we think about parameters that need to be sent to an operation or the return value that results from the invocation of an operation. Message elements are the practical choice for describing the parameters involved with a request as well as a response. A message element contains the name of the message, which can have zero to many part elements. The part elements can refer to the parameters of a request and the return value of the response. Each part element contains a name as well as an associated type, with the type specified as an XML Schema data type. If the operation expects multiple parameters or returns multiple values, you must provide multiple part elements in the message.

From a cooperative portlet perspective, we can consider the exchange of information a one-way operation in which the payload to be exchanged is inferred from the message elements. This means we needn't concern ourselves with describing responses that may result from invoking an operation. Think of messages as being inbound and outbound messages rather than request and response messages. This means a WSDL file for a cooperative portlet could have two message elements, each having multiple parts. Let's look at a section of the WSDL file (slightly modified for this discussion) for the Order portlet that is packaged in the Shipping Sample WSDL file (pbshipexample.war) with WebSphere Portal (Listing 10.2).

```
<types>
  <xsd:schema
targetNamespace="http://www.ibm.com/wps/c2a/examples/shipping">
    <xsd:simpleType name="Month">
      <xsd:restriction base="xsd:string">
      </xsd:restriction>
    </xsd:simpleType>

    <xsd:simpleType name="OrderID">
      <xsd:restriction base="xsd:string">
      </xsd:restriction>
    </xsd:simpleType>

    <xsd:simpleType name="CustomerID">
      <xsd:restriction base="xsd:string">
      </xsd:restriction>
    </xsd:simpleType>
  </xsd:schema>
```

Listing 10.2: Message elements in the Shipping Sample WSDL file (part 1 of 2)

```
</types>

<message name="OrderMonthInput">
  <part name="order_month" type="tns:Month"/>
</message>

<message name="OrderMonthOutput">
  <part name="order_Id" type="tns:OrderID"/>
  <part name="customer_Id" type="tns:CustomerID"/>
</message>
```

Listing 10.2: Message elements in the Shipping Sample WSDL file (part 2 of 2)

We first see that there are three data types defined and two message elements. The messages are OrderMonthInput and OrderMonthOutput. The parts of each message provide insights as to what the portlet can consume and produce. We see that the Order portlet can consume the month and can output an order ID and a customer ID. This doesn't mean there's a relationship between input and output messages. It simply means that the portlet can be a target and consume an action with an input parameter that contains the name of the month. It also means that the portlet can be a source portlet that produces outbound messages containing either the order ID or the customer ID.

> **Note:** A target portlet can consume only a single part of a message, implemented as either a simple type or a complex type.

In a traditional Web service scenario, the portType element, which contains operation child elements, describes the interface and available methods provided by the Web service. Listing 10.3 shows the portType element in the Shipping Sample WSDL file.

```
<portType name="OrdersPortlet_Service">
  <operation name="order_Month">
    <input message="tns:OrderMonthInput"/>
    <output message="tns:OrderMonthOutput"/>
  </operation>
</portType>
```

Listing 10.3: portType element in the Shipping Sample WSDL file

If you're new to Web services, the portType can be difficult to understand. If the Web service is implemented in Java, the portType is represented as a Java interface, and the operations are represented as methods defined on that interface. Looking more closely at the operations, we can see they use message definitions to define their input parameters and return values (outputs). The input message represents the payload sent to the service, and the output message represents the payload returned by the operation. Remember, we're not dealing with a traditional Web service. We're simply leveraging the structure of WSDL as a way to supply information to the Property Broker about cooperative portlets. Looking at the WSDL for the Orders portlet, we see that the value of the name attribute for portType is OrdersPortlet_Service.

Because there really isn't a remote interface that needs to be exposed from a cooperative portlet perspective, it's simply enough to provide a unique name for the portType. Treatment of the operation is similar to that of the portType in that the name simply needs to be unique. The actual interface is the portlet, and the operation is the processAction method. What we need to do next is provide information about how the portType operations map to a "protocol" recognized by the Property Broker service.

Again, as we consider WSDL from a traditional Web service perspective, the means of describing the mapping of operations on interface to a transport protocol is provided by the binding element and its subelements. These elements let us supply the necessary implementation details about how the operations are transmitted between the requester and the service provider. It's important to realize that the transport protocol isn't restricted or limited to just SOAP. The protocols can be based on a wide variety of messaging and encoding styles. What makes this flexibility possible is the extensibility built into the WSDL specification. The cooperative portlet implementation fully embraces the extensibility aspect of WSDL. The extensions provided by WebSphere Portal that are used in the binding element and its subelements permit us to define the protocol that portlets use to communicate via the Property Broker. (We're using the term "protocol" very loosely with regard to cooperative portlets and the WSDL definition.)

The last element we need to mention is the service element. Directly stated, it is not required. Returning to the traditional Web service thought, we use the service element to specify the location of the "service," which is also referred to as the endpoint. Because the portlet itself is the ultimate endpoint or representation of the service, there's no need to provide a definition of this element in the WSDL file.

Let's take a look at the trail we've just laid out, which links the binding element back to the original type we defined. The operation elements in the binding element must have names that match the operations in the portType section. You can have multiple bindings and portTypes, but this is rarely the case. However, if this is the case, the portType that corresponds to a particular binding is matched based on the type attribute of the binding element. Similarly, the output/input element in the binding operation maps to the output/input in the portType operation. The output/input in the portType operation is tied to the specific message. The type attribute of the message links us back to the type from the types section. All the elements are necessary and linked together:

binding -> portType -> message -> type

Now let's take a closer look at the details by building an example.

SOURCE PORTLET WSDL

Before we get into the specifics of the WSDL files, it's important to understand where the WSDL files for cooperative portlets are located. We define the name and location as a portlet preference within the portlet.xml file. By convention, we'll use the name of the portlet as the prefix of the WSDL file name. We'll also create a directory called "wsdl" off the document root of the portlet application, as shown in Listing 10.4.

```
<preference>

        <name>com.ibm.portal.propertybroker.wsdllocation</name>
        <value>/wsdl/CityListPortlet.wsdl</value>
        <read-only>true</read-only>

</preference>
```

Listing 10.4: Portlet preferences in the portlet.xml file

The first order of business is to specify the target namespace and the data type (Listing 10.5). The target namespace we'll use is http://jsr.pb.sample, and the data type is CityType, which is a simpleType.

```xml
<?xml version="1.0" encoding="UTF-8"?>
<definitions name="CityListPortlet_Service"
        targetNamespace="http://jsr.pb.sample"
        xmlns="http://schemas.xmlsoap.org/wsdl/"
        xmlns:portlet="http://www.ibm.com/wps/c2a"
        xmlns:tns="http://jsr.pb.sample"
        xmlns:xsd="http://www.w3.org/2001/XMLSchema">

        <types>

                <xsd:schema targetNamespace="http://jsr.pb.sample">

                        <xsd:simpleType name="CityType">

                          <xsd:restriction base="xsd:string"></xsd:restriction>

                        </xsd:simpleType>

                </xsd:schema>

        </types>
...
...
</definitions>
```

Listing 10.5: First part of the source portlet WSDL file

Next, we provide the necessary information for the message element (Listing 10.6).

```xml
<message name="CityType_Response">

        <part name="CityType_Output" type="tns:CityType" />

</message>
```

Listing 10.6: Message definition for source portlet

327

The message name we'll use is CityType_Response, and the name attribute of the part element is CityType_Output. Notice that the message we're defining is for a response in which the defined part element can be thought of as the return of an operation. The fact that it is a response implies that the implementation will need to define an "outbound" message for the portlet. Remember that we're defining the capabilities of a source portlet that has an outbound property. The type of the name attribute of the part element is CityType, which is the same type we want to exchange between the portlets.

We know that the portType element defines the name of the interface and the operations it supports with regard to traditional Web services. In terms of cooperative portlets, the interface is the portlet interface. Let's step back for a moment and consider what this means. It's saying we can loosely think of a portlet as a service. That said, we'll name the portType CityListPortlet_Service and view the CityListPortlet instance as a service that can publish the name of a city (Listing 10.7).

```
<portType name="CityListPortlet_Service">

          <operation name="CityListPortlet">
                    <output message="tns:CityType_Response" />
          </operation>

</portType>
```

Listing 10.7: portType definition for source portlet

In contrast to traditional Web services that are described using WSDL, the Property Broker hides most of the implementation details by mediating the exchange of information. This means that the portType and operations are used to infer the structure of the exchange rather than the details of the specific interface and methods. Note that we still need to define an input or output element that specifies the message that ties back to the type originally defined.

We now come to the section of the WSDL file that defines the binding information. Harking back to the traditional Web service scenario, this is where we provide the information necessary to map the portType and operations to a specific protocol. For cooperative portlets, the Property Broker service uses the elements in the binding section to identify and match actions and parameters from a source portlet to target portlets. When you see the completed binding section later, you'll immediately notice that there are two namespaces: the default name-space (no prefix) and the namespace identified by the prefix "portlet". The elements with the portlet prefix (i.e., portlet:binding, portlet:action, and portlet:param) are specific to the "protocol" for the Property Broker and are extensions provided by WebSphere Portal. They are responsible for providing specific details with respect to interacting with the Property Broker. The elements without a prefix (e.g., binding, output, input, and operation) are members of the WSDL 1.1 namespace and can be thought of as "generic" WSDL elements.

Now, let's look at the details of what we specify in the binding element. For the binding element itself, we must provide values for the name and type attributes; we'll use the values CityListPortlet_Binding and City_ListPortlet_Service, respectively, as shown in Listing 10.8. Notice that the value of the type attribute matches the value of the name attribute of the portType, thereby establishing a link between the binding element and the portType element.

```
<binding name="CityListPortlet_Binding"

        type="tns:CityListPortlet_Service">
        ...
        ...
        ...

</binding>
```

Listing 10.8: Binding element

Looking at the child elements in the binding section (Listing 10.9), we see that the first one is <portlet:binding/>. It's important to realize that the first child element must be <portlet:binding/>. The purpose of <portlet:binding/> is to identify the section as containing binding extensions for cooperative portlets. The next child element in the binding section is the operation element, which also is a required element. The name attribute of the operation element matches the name attribute of the operation element defined in the portType.

```
<binding name="CityListPortlet_Binding"

        type="tns:CityListPortlet_Service">

        <portlet:binding/>
        <operation name="CityListPortlet">
        ...
        ...
        </operation>
</binding>
```

Listing 10.9: portlet:binding and operation elements

Let's dig into the details of the operation element. The first child element specified within this element must be portlet:action. As you'd expect, the portlet:action element, describes the details about the action. Specifically, it provides information about how the portlet processes actions and parameters. The portlet:action element has the following attributes:

- name
- type
- actionNameParameter
- caption
- activeOn-15p.753StartUp
- description

The name attribute holds the name of the action. If you provide no value for this attribute, the name of the associated operation element is used as the portlet action name. The default is something you won't likely use; it's best always to provide an appropriate name for the action.

After furnishing a name, we need to specify the type attribute, which indicates how the portlet handles the action. If the portlet is based on JSR 168, the type value is Standard. This means the action must be represented as a parameter on the ActionRequest object that is dispatched to the portlet via the processAction method. The values that can be associated with the type attribute are as follows:

- **default:** A DefaultPortletAction object is used and deprecated (legacy portlet API).

- **simple:** A simple portlet action String is used (legacy portlet API).

- **struts:** A Struts action is used (legacy portlet API).

- **standard**: A JSR 168–based (standard) portlet action is used.

- **standard-struts**: A Struts action is used with JSR 168–based (standard) portlet.

Because we pass the action as a request parameter, we need a way to tell the Property Broker service the name of the parameter holding the action. We specify the name of the request parameter as the value of the actionNameParameter attribute of the portlet:action element. The Property Broker uses the actionNameParameter in two fundamental ways:

- When the user invokes an action by clicking an action link in the source portlet, the Property Broker examines the request by searching for the value specified by the actionNameParameter. If the value is found, the Property Broker examines the value of the parameter and searches the associated information defined in the WSDL for a matching portlet:action name. A successful match of the portlet:action name causes the Property Broker to then look for output actions and properties from the source portlet. If the Property Broker finds any outbound properties, it triggers the associated wires (Reference 2).

- When an action is invoked as the result of the Property Broker triggering a wire, the Property Broker sets a request parameter name that matches the value of the actionNameParameter. The associated value of the request parameter will be the value of the attribute name of the portlet:action.

If the WSDL file doesn't provide the actionNameParameter, the following default value is used for the request attribute.

```
com.ibm.portal.propertybroker.action
```

The use of the actionNameParameter by the Property Broker may seem a bit confusing, but it's absolutely necessary. Because JSR 168 portlet actions don't provide a name for an action, we must use a request parameter to store the name for identification purposes. In our example, the value associated with the actionNameParameter is ActionName, as you can see in Listing 10.10. The parameter with the name ActionName has an associated value that is the name of the portlet:action. The name of the action we'll use for this example is Send_City. Send_City will be stored as the value of a request parameter that has the name ActionName. This can be a little confusing, so stop and think about the purpose of the actionNameParameter attribute for a moment and study the code in the listing.

```
<binding name="CityListPortlet_Binding"

        type="tns:CityListPortlet_Service">
        <portlet:binding />
        <operation name="CityListPortlet">

        <portlet:action name="Send_City" type="standard"
actionNameParameter="ActionName" caption="citylist.send.city.action"/>
        ...

        ...
        </operation>
</binding>
```

Listing 10.10: portlet:action in the operation element of the source portlet

Another portlet:action attribute we need to provide a value for is the caption attribute. The caption attribute is a short string used to describe the action. The string is displayed in the wiring tool and facilitates the matching of the outbound properties of the source portlet to the inbound properties of a target portlet. A common practice is to define the string in a resource bundle along with the description.

The portlet:action element's activeOnStartUp attribute can either be "true" or "false". The default value of true means the wire is active as soon as the portlet is initialized. (Note that we don't define this attribute in our example.)

In addition to portlet:action, another child element we must define in the operation section is the input and/or output element. An input element describes a parameter consumed by a target portlet; an output element describes the parameters produced by a source portlet. An important aspect of cooperative portlets is that a portlet can produce *n* number of parameters but can consume only one parameter for a given portlet action. The child element of the output/input element is the portlet:param element. The portlet:param element has the following attributes, as described in the WebSphere Portal InfoCenter (*http://publib.boulder.ibm.com/infocenter/wpdoc/v6r0/index.jsp*):

- **name:** The name of the parameter that stores the value to be exchanged. If you provide no name attribute for the portlet:param element, the value of the partname attribute (described next) is used.

- **partname**: The name that refers to the part element of the operation. You can omit this attribute when the input or output parameter has a single part. The partname attribute establishes a mapping between the implementation in the binding and the actual part of the message.

- **boundTo**: The scope in which the parameter is bound. The parameter can be bound to a PortletRequest parameter, a PortletRequest attribute, a PortletSession attribute, or a Render Parameter.

- **caption**: A string used to provide a description of the parameter to the end user. You typically define this value in a resource bundle.

The code snippet in Listing 10.11 shows the completed binding section with a focus on the output element. Note that the parameter's name is cityId and it is bound to a request attribute. This tells us that the source portlet must set a request parameter in the processAction method that has the name cityId.

```
<binding name="CityListPortlet_Binding"

    type="tns:CityListPortlet_Service">
    <portlet:binding/>
    <operation name="CityListPortlet">

        <portlet:action name="Send_City" type="standard"
actionNameParameter="ActionName" caption="citylist.send.city.action"/>

        <output>
                    <portlet:param name="cityId"
partname="CityType_Output" boundTo="request-attribute"
caption="citylist.city.to.send"/>

        </output>

    </operation>
</binding>
```

Listing 10.11: Complete binding element of the source portlet

Now that you have a solid grasp of what to define in a WSDL file for a source portlet, creating the WSDL for the target portlet will be a straightforward exercise. In general, you must provide a WSDL file for each portlet that exchanges information via portlet cooperation.

Target Portlet WSDL

We'll construct the target portlet introduced at the beginning of the chapter, ShowTemperaturePortlet, which, you'll recall, displays the current temperature for a given city. In the same manner as the source portlet, the target portlet defines its capabilities in a WSDL file. The structure and content of the WSDL file for the target portlet are the same as for the source, except that the target portlet defines an input element rather than an output element in the binding section. Listing 10.12 shows the WSDL file for our target portlet.

```xml
<?xml version="1.0" encoding="UTF-8"?>
<definitions name="ShowTemperaturePortlet_Service"
        targetNamespace="http://jsr.pb.sample"
        xmlns="http://schemas.xmlsoap.org/wsdl/"
        xmlns:portlet="http://www.ibm.com/wps/c2a"
        xmlns:tns="http://jsr.pb.sample"
        xmlns:xsd="http://www.w3.org/2001/XMLSchema">
        <types>
                <xsd:schema targetNamespace="http://jsr.pb.sample">
                        <xsd:simpleType name="CityType">
                                <xsd:restriction
base="xsd:string"></xsd:restriction>
                        </xsd:simpleType>
                </xsd:schema>
        </types>
        <message name="CityType_Request">
                <part name="CityType_Input" type="tns:CityType" />
        </message>
        <portType name="ShowTemperaturePortlet_Service">
                <operation name="ShowTemperaturePortlet">
                        <input message="tns:CityType_Request" />
                </operation>
        </portType>
        <binding name="ShowTemperaturePortlet_Binding"
                type="tns:ShowTemperaturePortlet_Service">
                <portlet:binding />
```

Listing 10.12: Target portlet WSDL files (part 1 of 2)

```
                    <operation name="ShowTemperaturePortlet">
                        <portlet:action name="Update_City_Temp"
                                actionNameParameter="ActionName"
type="standard"
                            caption="Show Temperature of Target City"
                            description="Update temperature for a
                            given city" />
                        <input>
                                <portlet:param name="targetCity"
                                    partname="CityType_Input"
                                    boundTo="request-attribute"
                                        caption="Target City" />
                        </input>
                    </operation>
            </binding>
</definitions>
```

Listing 10.12: Target portlet WSDL files (part 2 of 2)

Let's take a closer look at the binding section of the file. First, you can see that the value of the actionNameParameter is ActionName, the same name we used for the source portlet. This is simply a good programming practice and we do it for consistency. This parameter's value is actually arbitrary; it can be any value appropriate for the portlet. The name of the action we'll use in the target portlet is Update_City_Temp. As we discussed with the source WSDL file, the value of the ActionName request parameter is Update_City_Temp.

Taking a closer look at the input element of the ShowTemperaturePortlet, we see that the specified parameter name is targetCity and the parameter is bound to a request attribute. The Property Broker service needs to map the outbound action and property of the source portlet to the inbound action and property of the target portlets. Ultimately, the Send_City action and the cityId parameter of the source portlet are mapped to the Update_City_Temp action and the targetCity parameter of the target portlet.

Next, let's look at the code required for the source and target portlets.

Source Portlet Code

Before delving into the method body, let's define a few members of the CityListPortlet class that we'll leverage in the example (Listing 10.13).

```
public static final String CITY_ID                = "cityId";
public static final String ACTION_NAME_PARAM      = "ActionName";
public static final String SEND_CITY_ACTION       = "Send_City";
public static final String PBSERVICE              = "pbService";

private boolean pbServiceAvailable                = false;
PropertyBrokerService pbService          = null;

public static final String VIEW_JSP      = "CityListPortletView";
```

Listing 10.13: Source portlet attributes

We also need to include the import statements shown in Listing 10.14.

```
import javax.naming.Context;
import javax.naming.InitialContext;
import com.ibm.portal.portlet.service.PortletServiceHome;
import com.ibm.portal.propertybroker.service.PropertyBrokerService;
```

Listing 10.14: Imports

To facilitate the construction of the CityListPortlet, we need the JavaBean shown in Listing 10.15.

```
package com.pb.sample;

/**
 *
 * A sample Java bean that stores portlet instance data in portlet ses-
sion
 *
 */
public class CityListPortletSessionBean {
        private String[] cities;
        /**
```

Listing 10.15: JavaBean that supports source portlet (part of 1 of 2)

```
      * Last text for the text form
      */
     private String formText = "";

     /**
      * Set last text for the text form.
      *
      * @param formText last text for the text form.
      */
     public void setFormText(String formText) {
             this.formText = formText;
     }

     /**
      * Get last text for the text form.
      *
      * @return last text for the text form
      */
     public String getFormText() {
             return this.formText;
     }

     public String[] getCities() {
             return cities;
     }
     /**
      * @param cities The cities to set.
      */
     public void setCities(String[] cities) {
             this.cities = cities;
     }

}
```

Listing 10.15: JavaBean that supports source portlet (part of 2 of 2)

SOURCE PORTLET INIT METHOD

The first method we need to address is the init method (Listing 10.16). This method is invoked when the portlet is first loaded into memory. It is invoked once and only once over the life cycle of the portlet. Therefore, the init is the ideal place to obtain references to portal services that the portlet requires. Because the source portlet needs to use the Property Broker service throughout its life, we'll retrieve a reference to it in the init method and store the reference in a *guard variable* (Reference 2). We obtain the reference by performing a Java Naming and Directory Interface (JNDI) lookup, which is a standard J2EE technique for locating resources that are available in the environment.

```
public void init(PortletConfig config) throws PortletException{

    super.init(config);

    try{
        Context ctx = new InitialContext();

        PortletServiceHome serviceHome = (PortletServiceHome)
ctx.lookup("portletservice/com.ibm.portal.propertybroker.service.Propert
yBrokerService");

        pbService =
(PropertyBrokerService)serviceHome.getPortletService(com.ibm.portal.prop
ertybroker.service.PropertyBrokerService.class);

        pbServiceAvailable = true;

    }catch(Throwable t) {

        getPortletContext().log("CityListPortlet could not find
property broker service!");

    }

}
```

Listing 10.16: Source portlet's init method

You'll see later how the guard variable is used to determine whether the service is available. Basically, a guard variable is used to protect access to a service. In our case, it protects access to the Property Broker service provided by WebSphere Portal. This function is of special importance when we consider the case in which the portlet is running in a non-IBM portlet container. If a cooperative portlet is running in a portlet container other than the one provided by WebSphere Portal, we can use the guard variable to make sure the portlet behaves appropriately by preventing access to the Property Broker service. We'll use pbServiceAvailable as the name of the guard variable. If the variable's value is true, the portlet can access the Property Broker service.

SOURCE PORTLET DOVIEW METHOD

The doView method (Listing 10.17) performs a few fundamental tasks for the source portlet. First, it "fills" a string array with the names of the cities that will be displayed to the end user. For the purposes of this simple example, we'll hard-code the city names. We'll store the array containing the city names and the guard variable protecting the Property Broker service in a sessionbean accessible to the JSP. The doView method will then include the JSP that will be rendered for display by the portlet.

```java
public void doView(RenderRequest request, RenderResponse response)
throws PortletException, IOException {

    // Set the MIME type for the render response

    response.setContentType(request.getResponseContentType());

    // Check if portlet session exists
    CityListPortletSessionBean sessionBean = getSessionBean(request);

    if( sessionBean==null ) {

        response.getWriter().println("<b>NO PORTLET SESSION YET</b>");
        return;
    }

    // Set the MIME type for the render response
    response.setContentType(request.getResponseContentType());

    String[] cities = new String[6];
    cities[0] = new String("San Francisco");
    cities[1] = new String("New York");
    cities[2] = new String("London");
    cities[3] = new String("Paris");
    cities[4] = new String("Rome");
    cities[5] = new String("Frankfurt");

    sessionBean.setCities( cities );

    if(pbServiceAvailable){
        request.setAttribute(PBSERVICE, pbService);
    }else{
        getPortletContext().log("CityListPortlet...doView...The Property
Broker Service is not available");
    }

    // Invoke the JSP to render
    PortletRequestDispatcher rd =
getPortletContext().getRequestDispatcher(getJspFilePath(request, VIEW_JSP));
        rd.include(request,response);
    }
```

Listing 10.17: doView method of source portlet

SOURCE PORTLET PROCESSACTION METHOD

In our example, the main task of the source portlet's processAction method (Listing 10.18) is to determine whether the ActionName parameter is present in the current ActionRequest object. If the parameter is present and has an associated value of Send_City, we can conclude that a user clicked the hypertext reference (HREF) that displays the city name in the portlet view. The next step is to extract the name of the city associated with the request parameter cityId. Then, the important step: — we must insert the name of the city in the request parameter cityId:

```
request.setAttribute("cityId", city);
```

```
public void processAction(ActionRequest request, ActionResponse
response) throws PortletException, java.io.IOException {

...
...

    String actionName = request.getParameter("ActionName");

    if(actionName == null)
       actionName = "";

    getPortletContext().log("CityListPortlet.processAction....actionName
= " + actionName);

    if(actionName.equals("Send_City")) {

       String city = request.getParameter("cityId");

       getPortletContext().log("CityListPortlet...processAction, city
from the action = " + city);

       if (city == null) {
           getPortletContext().log("There is a problem extracting the
city from the request.");
       }else{
             //Let's inform the Property Broker
             if(city.equals("London")){
                 // if the city is London, do not send it
```

Listing 10.18: processAction method of source portlet (part 1 of 2)

340

```
            getPortletContext().log("CityListPortlet.processAction, The
City is London. Do Not Fire the Wire!");

                }else{
                  //Send all other cities
                  request.setAttribute("cityId", city);
                getPortletContext().log("CityListPortlet.processAction,
Set the City on the request attribute");
                }
             }
      }

} //end of method
```

Listing 10.18: processAction method of source portlet (part 2 of 2)

Based on the information in the WSDL file of the CityListPortlet, the Property Broker service is watching for the request attribute with the name cityId. Note the check in the code for the city of London. If the end user selects London as the city, the design requirement is to not fire the wire. We satisfy this requirement by not inserting the name and value into the request. You can see where we could put application logic that might interact with a business model to help refine the interaction between portlets. Not sending London to the target portlet is just a simple example of filtering wire actions that may result in firing a wire.

Source Portlet JSP

The JSP for the source portlet (Listing 10.19) displays the array cities in an HTML table.

```
<%@ page session="false" contentType="text/html"

import="java.text.*;
import java.util.*;
import javax.portlet.*;
import javax.naming.Context;
import javax.naming.InitialContext;
import com.ibm.portal.propertybroker.service.PropertyBrokerService;
import com.pb.sample.src.*" %>
<%@taglib uri="http://java.sun.com/portlet" prefix="portlet" %>
```

Listing 10.18: processAction method of source portlet (part 1 of 3)

```
<portlet:defineObjects/>

<%

CityListPortletSessionBean sessionBean =
(CityListPortletSessionBean)renderRequest.getPortletSession().getAttribu
te(CityListPortlet.SESSION_BEAN);

PropertyBrokerService pbService = (PropertyBrokerService)
renderRequest.getAttribute(CityListPortlet.PBSERVICE);

%>

<DIV style="margin: 6px">
<H3 style="margin-bottom: 3px">List of Cties Frequenlt Visited</H3>
<DIV style="margin: 12px; margin-bottom: 36px">
<FORM method="POST" action="<portlet:actionURL/>">

      <table border="0" cellspacing="0" cellpadding="3">
      <tr class="wpsTableHead">
        <td>
        City
        </td>
      </tr>
      <%
        boolean areCityIdWiresActive = false;

        if(pbService != true) {

          areCityIdWiresActive =
pbService.areWiresActive(renderRequest, CityListPortlet.CITY_ID);

        }

        String[] cities = sessionBean.getCities();
        for (int i = 0; i < cities.length; i++) {
      %>
          <tr><TD>
      <%
        if ( areCityIdWiresActive ) {
          PortletURL actionURL = renderResponse.createActionURL();
          actionURL.setParameter(CityListPortlet.CITY_ID, cities[i]);

actionURL.setParameter(CityListPortlet.ACTION_NAME_PARAM,
CityListPortlet.SEND_CITY_ACTION);
```

Listing 10.18: processAction method of source portlet (part 2 of 3)

342

```
    %>
                        <A href="<%= actionURL%>">
                          <%= cities[i] %>
                          </A>
      <% } else { %>
                        <%= cities[i] %>

      <% } %>

          </TD></TR>
        <%} %>

      </table>


      <LABEL for="<%=CityListPortlet.FORM_TEXT%>">Enter
City:</LABEL><BR>

            <INPUT name="<%=CityListPortlet.FORM_TEXT%>" type="text"/>
            <INPUT name="<%=CityListPortlet.FORM_SUBMIT%>" type="submit"
value="Submit"/>
            </FORM>
<% /******** End of sample code *********/ %>
</DIV>

</DIV>
```

Listing 10.18: processAction method of source portlet (part 2 of 3)

If the Property Broker service is available and a wire is active, the cities are displayed as HREFs. This means we need to create actionURLs that have the two essential request parameters listed in Table 10.1.

Table 10.1: Request parameters for actionURLs

Parameter name	Value
cityId	Name from the array containing the cities
ActionName	Send_City

The JSP must execute the following steps to determine whether to display the links in the portlet for transmitting the name of a city:

- Determine whether the Property Broker service is available. This step leverages the guard variable we set in the portlet's init method.

- Determine whether a wire is active. We accomplish this step by calling the areWiresActive method on the Property Broker service interface.

- Dynamically generate links by invoking the createActionURL method provided by the renderResponse interface.

The JSP simply needs to determine whether the Property Broker service is available. If the service is available, the JSP presents the cities displayed in the view as portlet action links.

Target Portlet Code

By now, you should have some insights as to what is required to construct the target portlet. We need a doView method that renders a view that lets a user enter the name of a city and displays that city's current temperature. The processAction method handles the action of submitting the city. This method needs to extract the city name from the action sent to the portlet and make it available to for rendering. An important aspect of cooperative portlets is that target portlets require no Property Broker–related code. It is a straightforward exercise to take any portlet and define its action and property consumption capabilities in a WSDL file to enable its participation in the exchange of information between portlets.

For convenience, we provide the code for the target portlet's doView and processAction methods in Listing 10.20. Note that Miami is the default city displayed for the portlets. We also provide the JSP for the target portlet, in Listing 10.21.

```
public void doView(RenderRequest request, RenderResponse response)
throws PortletException, IOException {

    // Set the MIME type for the render response
    response.setContentType(request.getResponseContentType());

    // Check if portlet session exists
    ShowTemperaturePortletSessionBean sessionBean =
getSessionBean(request);

    if( sessionBean==null ) {

        response.getWriter().println("<b>NO PORTLET SESSION YET</b>");
        return;
    }

    String city = (String)
request.getPortletSession().getAttribute("cityId");

    getPortletContext().log("ShowTemperaturePortlet…doview.... city = "
+ city);

//Let's set a default city.. let the default be Miami
    if (null == city)
        city = new String("Miami");

//Since we are hard-coding for simplicity, let's set the temperature to
80 degrees Fahrenheit
    sessionBean.setCity(city);
    sessionBean.setTemperature("80");


    // Invoke the JSP to render
    PortletRequestDispatcher rd =
getPortletContext().getRequestDispatcher(getJspFilePath(request,
VIEW_JSP));
    rd.include(request,response);
}


public void processAction(ActionRequest request, ActionResponse
response) throws PortletException, java.io.IOException {

    if( request.getParameter(FORM_SUBMIT) != null ) {
        // Set form text in the session bean
```

Listing 10.20: Target portlet's doView and processAction methods (part 1 of 2)

345

```
        ShowTemperaturePortletSessionBean sessionBean =
getSessionBean(request);
        if( sessionBean != null )
            sessionBean.setFormText(request.getParameter(FORM_TEXT));
    }

    String actionName = request.getParameter("ActionName");
    if (actionName == null) {
        actionName = "";
    }

    getPortletContext().log("ShowTemperaturePortlet processAction,
actionName = " + actionName);

    if(actionName.equals("Update_City_Temp")){

        String theCity = (String) request.getAttribute("targetCity");
        if(theCity != null){
          getPortletContext().log("ShowTemperaturePortlet
processAction, the city's name is = " + theCity);

        //Do not confuse "cityId" with the property registered with the PB.
        //It is simply used to store the name of the city in the port-
let session
        request.getPortletSession().setAttribute("cityId", (Object)
theCity);
        }else{

          getPortletContext().log("ShowTemperaturePortlet processAction,
the city's name is null!!");
            theCity = new String ("Problem City");


request.getPortletSession().setAttribute("cityId",(Object)theCity );
        }

    }
}
```

Listing 10.20: Target portlet's doView and processAction methods (part 2 of 2)

```
<%@ page session="false" contentType="text/html"
import="java.util.*,javax.portlet.*,com.pb.sample.trg.*" %>

<%@taglib uri="http://java.sun.com/portlet" prefix="portlet" %>
<portlet:defineObjects/>
<%
ShowTemperaturePortletSessionBean sessionBean =
(ShowTemperaturePortletSessionBean)renderRequest.getPortletSession().get
Attribute(ShowTemperaturePortlet.SESSION_BEAN);

%>

<DIV style="margin: 6px">

<DIV style="margin: 12px; margin-bottom: 36px">
<FORM method="POST" action="<portlet:actionURL/>">

<FORM method="POST" action="<portlet:actionURL/>">

<table border="0" cellspacing="0" cellpadding="3">
    <tr class="wpsTableHead">
       <td>
       City
       </td>
       <TD>
       Temperature
       </TD>
    </tr>
    <tr>
              <TD>
         <%=sessionBean.getCity() %>
       </TD>
        <TD>
         <%=sessionBean.getTemperature() %>
       </TD>
    </tr>
</table>
 <FORM method="POST" action="<portlet:actionURL/>">
   <LABEL  for="<%=ShowTemperaturePortlet.FORM_TEXT%>">Enter
City:</LABEL><BR>
   <INPUT name="<%=ShowTemperaturePortlet.FORM_TEXT%>" type="text"/>
   <INPUT name="<%=ShowTemperaturePortlet.FORM_SUBMIT%>" type="submit"
value="Submit"/>
   </FORM>
<% /******** End of sample code ********/ %>
</DIV>

</DIV>
```

Listing 10.21: Target portlet JSP

SUMMARY

The cooperative portlet paradigm offers a way to exchange information between portlets that enhances the end user's experience with the portal. It also provides the ability to discover and compose new applications at the glass by wiring together portlets that could uncover and display new behaviors by working together.

The Property Broker service is the central runtime subsystem that enables the exchange of properties between portlets. Portlets that can produce properties and portlets that can consume properties register their capabilities with this service. The Property Broker service coordinates the exchange of information between portlets via a wire defined by an end user. A wire represents a persistent channel, or connection, used to facilitate the exchange of information.

Because we define the exchange capability of each portlet without specifying a direct connection between portlets at development time, the cooperative portlet paradigm adheres to the principles of a loosely coupled system.

REFERENCES

1. Roy-Chowdhury, Amber, Shankar Ramaswamy, and Xinyi Xu. "Using Click-to-Action to Provide User-Controlled Integration of Portlets." IBM DeveloperWorks, December 16, 2002. *http://www-128.ibm.com/developer-works/websphere/library/techarticles/0212_roy/roy.html.*

2. Roy-Chowdhury, Amber, and Yuping Connie Wu. "Developing JSR 168 Compliant Cooperative Portlets." IBM DeveloperWorks, November 2004. *http://www-128.ibm.com/developerworks/websphere/library/techarti-cles/0412_roy/0412_roy.html.*

3. Skonnard, Aaron. "Understanding WSDL." Microsoft Developer Network, October 2003. *http://msdn.microsoft.com/library/default.asp?url=/library/en-us/dnwebsrv/html/understandWSDL.asp.*

4. Monson-Haefel, Richard. *J2EE Web Services.* Addison Wesley, 2004.

5. Cerami, Ethan. *Web Services Essentials.* O'Reilly, 2002.

Chapter Eleven

Security and the Credential Vault

Security encompasses three broad areas with respect to WebSphere Portal Server: authentication, authorization, and single sign-on (SSO). *Authentication* answers the question "Who are you?" and establishes the identity of the end user. *Authorization* answers the question "What can you do?" In other words, what action can the end user perform and on what resources? The key resource provisioned in WebSphere Portal Server by administrators is the portlet. *Single sign-on* is the mechanism of passing some representation of the authenticated end-user identity through the overall system so that the user needs to present an ID and password only once. In WebSphere Portal, this functionality usually means that the portlets need to represent the end-user identity in some way to the back-end system the portlets are talking to.

Portlets are often tasked to integrate with protected enterprise and non-enterprise applications. These applications are protected in the sense that they implement some amount of security control within the application itself and depend on knowing the end-user identity to perform this function. In this chapter, we cover the Credential Vault Service of WebSphere Portal Server and how it facilitates passing the end user's identity to back-end applications.s

SINGLE SIGN-ON OVERVIEW

Large corporations often face the task of maintaining several identities with regard to accessing enterprise/non-enterprise applications for their end users.

The applications can range from Web-based apps to traditional back-end enterprise systems. Many organizations have custom applications that require end users to establish their identity via some authentication mechanism. A common practice of application developers has been to code the authentication function directly into the application instead of relying on the services of the infrastructure to provide an authenticated user context. Although this practice met the application's needs, it compounded management of identities for the end user and was particularly noticeable in the Web application space.

The goal of many organizations is to have their end users log in to the application space of the enterprise once to establish their identity. The intent is to minimize the number of challenges presented to the user and let the established identity satisfy downstream logon requirements — in essence, to provide a "single sign-on" experience for the end user. Many attempts have been made to provide a complete single sign-on solution, ranging from global sign-on servers that use a password vault to solutions that rely on agents to detect logon requests.

As we analyze the single sign-on problem, we see that it can be divided into two distinct tiers: the Web tier and the application/business process tier. Because the Web tier is typically characterized as access to an enterprise via a browser, single sign-on solutions have usually involved setting a token in a browser cookie that a set of servers in a given realm recognize or accept. The tokens embedded in client-side cookies could be used to present the user's identity to any server in the realm, thereby circumventing the need to rechallenge the user for credentials as he or she accessed different servers in the realm.

However, in some situations, the requirements for single sign-on go beyond a given realm, or the authentication mechanisms become varied and stringent. The situations requiring a broader and more robust implementation for authenticating end users typically have turned to *authentication proxy servers* as a solution to the single sign-on problem. Such servers, also known as a *reverse proxy servers*, not only provide single sign-on capabilities but also deliver the ability to apply fine-grained security policies for artifacts within their protected object space. Because we're focused on Web access, the artifacts of interest are typically Uniform Resource Identifiers (URIs), images, and so on. Even though authentication proxy servers can protect back-end resources, in general they protect only resources accessed via HTTP or secure HTTP (HTTPS).

Many applications, whether Web-based or deeper in the layers of the architecture, need to interact with multiple back-end systems. If the Web identity established for the end user isn't the identity required by the back-end systems, the user could be challenged again for the appropriate credentials, or the user Web identity could be mapped to the appropriate values. It becomes the responsibility of the Web-facing application to provide a framework for storing the necessary credentials required to access the back-end applications. The second tier of the single sign-on problem is defined as the space from the Web application layer to the back-end systems/processes that lie deeper in the architecture.

In the depiction of single sign-on tiers shown in Figure 11.1, the two ovals represent the different tiers, or realms, of the single sign-on problem space. The portal server lies in the first tier of this space. Therefore, the user's Web identity is used to establish the user's portal identity. However, the portal identity may not "match" the identity in the back-end applications.

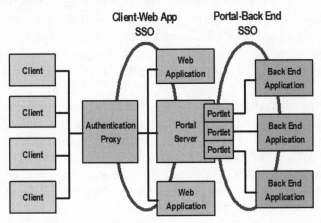

Figure 11.1: Single sign-on tiers

The portal server's core responsibility is to aggregate diverse content that is relevant to the end user. A single sign-on framework to back-end applications must be provided. WebSphere Portal Server includes a Credential Vault Service that facilitates mapping the user's Web identity to the appropriate credential and connecting to the targeted back-end application. The details of the Credential Vault Service are the focus of this chapter.

351

INTRODUCTION TO THE CREDENTIAL VAULT SERVICE

As we stated, the goal of single sign-on is to have the end user log in once and only once. This goal becomes extremely difficult to achieve in the context of a portal that's designed to aggregate content from a diverse set of back-end applications. There are two approaches to retrieving content that is protected in back-end applications and displaying it in a portlet:

- Create portlets that contain embedded logic for applying access control to users and groups.

- Create portlets that pass the appropriate form of the user's identity to the back-end application.

The first approach involves programmatic portlet security, perhaps using a business rules engine, a personalization engine, or an API that integrates the authorization subsystem exposed by the back-end application. With any of the techniques, duplicating the authorization capabilities of the back-end application into a portlet could require significant effort. In addition, a programmatic approach implies that the application will "trust" the portlet front end to properly filter the content, rather than control what content is released in the first place.

The second approach, where the back-end applications are considered part of the downstream authentication process, is the recommended one. With this solution, it remains the responsibility of the back-end application to determine the content and functionality to which the user has access. To facilitate management of the user's identities and enhance the downstream authentication process from a portlet, WebSphere Portal Server provides the Credential Vault Service.

The Credential Vault Service is a service available to portlets running within WebSphere Portal Server. The service provides vaulting capabilities that enable portlets to manage the different user identities required to interact with back-end applications. The Credential Vault Service also provides objects called *credentials*. The credential objects serve two main purposes. First, they provide the interface into the vault for retrieving the user's *secrets* (credentials). Second, they encapsulate the details necessary to establish an authenticated connection to the back-end application.

Because the Credential Vault Service is a service that is registered in WebSphere Portal Server, locating it follows a standard pattern. Listing 11.1 shows how to get the Credential Vault Service from Portal.

```
import
com.ibm.portal.portlet.service.credentialvault.CredentialVaultService;
...
...
public class MyPortlet extends GenericPortlet {
...
private static CredentialVaultService vaultService = null;   // refer-
ence to                                      //the vault service
...
    public static void init(PortletConfig config) throws
PortletException {
        try {
            if ( vaultService == null ) {
                Context ctx = new InitialContext();
                PortletServiceHome cvsHome =
(PortletServiceHome)ctx.lookup("portletservice/com.ibm.portal.portlet.se
rvice.credentialvault.CredentialVaultService");
                if (cvsHome != null) {
                    vaultService =
(CredentialVaultService)cvsHome.getPortletService(CredentialVaultService
.class);
                }
            }
        } catch (Exception e) {
            throw(new PortletException("Error on
MyTestPortletSecretManager.init()", e));
        }
    }
...
```

Listing 11.1: Retrieving the Credential Vault Service in a portlet

Let's not lose sight of the primary purpose of the Credential Vault Service. It is to encapsulate the authentication function, including the ability to abstract "where the data comes from" to establish the back-end connection. A fundamental underpinning of the service is the repository that stores the end users' secrets. Because this repository holds "secrets," it's referred to as a vault.

THE CREDENTIAL VAULT STRUCTURE

The credential vault stores the end-user secrets (typically a password) and identities (user ID) that a portlet needs to access protected applications. As the vault structure shown in Figure 11.2 depicts, the vault can be partitioned into multiple *segments*. These segments can contain multiple *slots*, and the slots can contain one or more secrets. You also see that each segment is configured with a *vault adapter* that maps the logical representation of the vault to an actual implementation. The default, or "out of the box," implementation of the vault is a relational database. Specifically, the default implementation configured for the credential vault is the WebSphere Portal Server database.

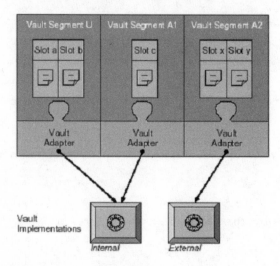

Figure 11.2: Structure of the credential vault

The concept of the vault adapter provides the opportunity to configure existing or new segments to use an implementation other than the portal database. There may be situations that demand a stronger or more secure implementation of the repository. In such situations, a segment could be configured to use the Lock Box of Tivoli Access Manager for eBusiness (TAM). WebSphere Portal Server is shipped with a vault adapter for the TAM Lock Box. This book doesn't discuss constructing vault adapters to integrate other repositories. For information about construction of a vault adapter, see the latest WebSphere Portal Server documentation.

Segments

Two types of segments are available to portlets for storing the end user's secrets. WebSphere Portal Server provides a user-managed segment and an administrator-managed segment that generally meet most portlet requirements. Because an enterprise may have multiple repositories for storing credentials, the portal administrator can define more segments and configure the appropriate adapter for the repository. This point reinforces the thought that a segment is a logical entity inside the vault, with the adapter being the "glue" code that integrates the various repositories.

While looking at the segments shown in the figure, make note of the user-managed segment (U) and the administrator-managed segments (A1 and A2). The intent of the user-managed segment is to give the portlet developer the ability to create slots to store end-user credentials without the intervention of an administrator. In other words, the slots in the user-managed segment are created by portlets and not predefined by administrators. Typically, slots in the user-managed segment contain user IDs and passwords to non-enterprise applications. In contrast, the administrator-managed segment contains slots defined by an administrator. Typically, portlets that access enterprise applications use the slots in this segment. For example, an administrator might create a slot for portlets that access SAP. This single slot could contain all the credentials for the users who access SAP. We'll explain this concept further when we discuss private and shared slots.

Let's look at some important administration rules that pertain to vault segments:

- Administrators can define segments of the type administrator-managed.

- Only administrators can manage (create, delete, edit) slots in an administrator-managed segment by using the credential vault portlet.

- Administrators cannot manage slots created in the user-managed segment. End users manage these slots. The developer must provide for the administration of user-managed slots via the edit mode of the portlet.

- Administrator-managed segments contain only administrative slots and system slots (described next).

- A user-managed segment contains only shared and private slots (described next) that are created by portlets programmatically. In other words, the slots in a user-managed segment are created for an end user by the given portlet. WebSphere Portal Server currently comes with a single user-managed segment. An administrator cannot define more user-managed segments.

Slot Details

We know that the purpose of a vault segment is to serve as a repository for vault slots. We also know that the purpose of a slot is to hold a credential (usually the user ID and password) for an end user. It's important to understand the different types of slots available to portlets. There are four types of vault slots:

- A *system slot* is created by an administrator and resides in the administrator-defined segment. It contains a single user ID and password that can be shared with any portlet. The administrator manages this user ID and password. Enterprises typically use the system slot to store a global or administrative access identity and password that the portlet will use to connect to the back-end application on behalf of any and all users.

- An *administrative* slot is created by an administrator and resides in the administrator-defined segment. It contains many user ID/password pairs, one per end user. The user ID and password in the slot are set by the end user and can be shared among the user's portlets. In other words, an administrative slot can hold one secret per user and isn't bound to a specific portlet. In general, this slot holds an end user's user ID and password for a given application.

- A *shared slot* is created programmatically by a portlet and resides in the user-defined segment. The slot contains a single user ID and password and can be shared among the user's portlets. A shared slot differs from an administrative slot in that it resides in the user-defined segment and contains one secret. It typically is associated with a non-enterprise application.

- A *private slot* is created programmatically by a portlet and resides in the user-defined segment. The slot contains a user ID and password pair specific to an end user and a specific concrete portlet.

A portlet that retrieves and/or stores an end user's credentials can either use an existing slot in the administrator-defined segment or create a slot in the user-managed segment. Let's consider an example in which an administrator defines a slot to hold end users' credentials. To use a predefined slot in the administrator-managed segment, the portlet must be able to obtain the *resource name* of the slot. The resource name is usually supplied via configuration data that is initially set in the portlet.xml file as a configuration parameter. In the portlet.xml snippet shown in Listing 11.2, the resource name is represented by the parameter VaultSlotName. The value of VaultSlotName is MyEnterpriseAppAdminSlot and was specified by a portal administrator when the slot was first defined. The parameter SecretType is used by the SecretManager object to identify the type of slot that holds the secret. It's important to realize that the SecretManager isn't part of the portlet API. It is a helper class generated by Rational Application Developer. The SecretManager facilitates storing secrets and retrieving secrets from the credential vault for use by passive credentials. (We discuss passive credentials in the next section.)

```xml
<?xml version="1.0" encoding="UTF-8"?>
<portlet-app ...>
    <portlet>
        <portlet-name>MyTest</portlet-name>
        <display-name>MyTest portlet</display-name>
        <display-name xml:lang="en">MyTest portlet</display-name>
        <portlet-class>mytest.MyTestPortlet</portlet-class>
        <init-param>
            <name>wps.markup</name>
            <value>html</value>
        </init-param>
        <expiration-cache>0</expiration-cache>
        <supports>
            <mime-type>text/html</mime-type>
            <portlet-mode>view</portlet-mode>
            <portlet-mode>edit</portlet-mode>
        </supports>
        <supported-locale>en</supported-locale>
```

Listing 11.2: Portion of portlet.xml file showing VaultSlotName (part 1 of 2)

```
        <resource-bundle>mytest.nl.MyTestPortletResource</resource-bundle>
        <portlet-info>
            <title>MyTest portlet</title>
        </portlet-info>
        <portlet-preferences>
            <preference>
                <name>.SecretType</name>
                <value>2</value>                        <read-
only>true</read-only>
            </preference>
            <preference>
                <name>.VaultSlotName</name>
                <value>MyEnterpriseAppAdminSlot</value>
                <read-only>true</read-only>
            </preference>
        </portlet-preferences>
    </portlet>
</portlet-app>
```

Listing 11.2: Portion of portlet.xml file showing VaultSlotName (part 2 of 2)

Once the portlet has the resource name of the slot, it's time to retrieve its contents from the Credential Vault Service. Looking at the various methods used to set and get credentials or obtain the description of the slot (shown in Listing 11.3), it becomes apparent that the slotId (String) is the key to identifying the desired slot.

```
public Credential getCredential(java.lang.String slotId,
java.lang.String type, java.util.Map config, PortletRequest request)

public void setCredentialSecretBinary(java.lang.String slotId, byte[]
secret, PortletRequest portletRequest)

public void setCredentialSecretUserPassword(java.lang.String slotId,
java.lang.String userId, char[] password, PortletRequest
portletRequest)

public String getCredentialSlotDescription(java.lang.String slotId,
java.util.Locale locale)
```

Listing 11.3: Methods to set and get credentials and obtain slot description

So, given the resource name, the goal is to find the slotId. The slotId is a String composed of the resource name and an internal identifier. The format is as follows:

```
"ResourceName|Opaque Identifier"
```

The opaque identifier is an internally generated value used by the credential vault framework. The code shown in Listing 11.4 demonstrates how to retrieve the slotId from the Credential Vault Service.

```
Iterator it = vaultService.getAccessibleSlots(portletRequest);
while(it.hasNext()) {

    CredentialSlotConfig config = (CredentialSlotConfig) it.next();

    //search for shared slot name
    if(config.getResourceName().startsWith(slotName)){

        slotID = config.getSlotId();

    }
}
```

Listing 11.4: Retrieving the slotId from the Credential Vault Service

Once the portlet has the slotId, it can retrieve the user ID and password from the administrative slot in the form of a credential.

Before continuing the slot discussion, let's reflect on the role of the resource name. We know that the resource name is part of the slotId, but the name has a more fundamental purpose. The resource name is used to logically partition a segment. This partitioning enables the segment to hold one or more slots that portlets running in the portal server can leverage.

Slots in the administrator-managed segment work well for portlets that access known or managed enterprise applications. However, portlets that access non-enterprise applications (e.g., Hotmail) need a mechanism for creating a slot in the user-managed segment. We create a slot by calling the createCredentialSlot method provided by the CredentialVaultService interface. Listing 11.5 shows the call to this method.

```
public CredentialSlotConfig createCredentialSlot(java.lang.String
resourceName, com.ibm.wps.util.ObjectID segmentId, java.util.Map
descriptions, java.util.Map keywords, int secretType, boolean active,
boolean portletPrivate, PortletRequest portletRequest)}
```

Listing 11.5: createCredentialSlot method

The createCredentialSlot method specifies eight parameters in its signature. The Credential Vault Service uses these parameters to create a slot in the targeted segment. Listing 11.6 shows the values used to create an active private slot that holds a user's secret in the user-managed segment. (We discuss the different types of credentials provided by WebSphere Portal Server in the next section.)

```
String resourceName = new String("BasicAuthTest");
ObjectID segmentID   = vaultService.getDefaultUserCredentialSegmentId();
Map descriptionMap   = new Hashtable();
Map keyWordMap       = new Hashtable();
int secretType       =
vaultService.SECRET_TYPE_USERID_STRING_PASSWORD_STRING;
boolean active       = true;
boolean portletPrivate = true;
```

Listing 11.6: Parameters for creating a user-managed segment

Let's take a closer look at the parameters. First, as you'd expect, we must provide a resource name because it is part of the "key" that makes up the slotId. In the case where access to the portlet is assigned to non-administrators, the segment specified for the location of the slot must be the user-managed segment.

We obtain the ObjectID for the user-managed segment from the getDefaultUserVaultSegmentId method provided by the credential vault interface.

The third and fourth parameters in the createCredentialSlot method are description and keyword maps. These two parameters give the developer and user information used to find and select a slot to use. The description should contain at least the default locale, and the keyword map should contain values that identify the slot appropriately to support searching and browsing a set of available slots. Because a private slot is bound to a specific user and portlet, you probably don't need to set the description or keyword map.

The secret type identifier, which is an integer, represents the type of secret stored in the slot. A slot can store many secrets; however, the secrets must be of the same type. Table 11.1 lists the various slot types available to the developer. Note that the fields in the table are defined on the CredentialVaultService interface

Table 11.1: Slot types	
Data type	**Field**
String	PREDEFINED_SLOT_USER_JAAS_SUBJECT
static int	SECRET_TYPE_BYTEARRAY
static int	SECRET_TYPE_JAAS_SUBJECT
static int	SECRET_TYPE_JAVA_OBJECT
static int	SECRET_TYPE_NO_SECRET_DATA
static int	SECRET_TYPE_UNDEFINED
static int	SECRET_TYPE_USERID_STRING_PASSWORD_STRING

The createCredentialSlot method's sixth parameter is a Boolean value that determines whether a slot is active. If a slot is active, it holds a secret that only an active credential can access.

The next parameter is also a Boolean value. A value of "true" identifies the slot as portlet private. Such a slot is commonly referred to as a private slot. As we noted, a private slot is bound to a specific concrete portlet and a specific user. A value of "false" identifies the slot as a shared slot. As you'll recall, a shared slot can be accessed by any of the end user's portlets.

The method's final required parameter is a reference to the PortletRequest.

Once the slot is created successfully, createCredentialSlot returns a reference to the CredentialSlotConfig object. This object describes the configuration of a given slot. Most notably, it provides the method for retrieving the slotId (method getSlotId). Because a slot in the user-managed segment is unique for each user, the portlet must persist the slotId for future use in subsequent requests or user sessions. After it is created, the slotID is usually placed in the persistent service of the portal server. Because the user supplies the user ID and password when the portlet is in edit mode, the processAction method creates the slot and stores the slotId in the persistent service. Let's take a look at the code for the processAction method.

First, we retrieve a reference to the persistent service from the PortletRequest.

```
public void processAction(ActionRequest request, ActionResponse
response) throws PortletException, java.io.IOException {
...
...
    PortletPreferences prefs = request.getPreferences();
```

Let's assume the name of the resource passed in the createCredentialSlot method is the same name used to store the slotId in the persistent service for the portlet. In the method, we look for the name value pair keyed off the string "BasicAuthTest":

```
String slotID = prefs.getValue("BasicAuthTest", null);
```

If the slotId returned from the persistent service is null, we assume the slot hasn't been created. If this is the first time the end user is configuring the portlet, the slot will be created.

```
if( request.getParameter(USER_SUBMIT)!=null ) {
...
...
    CredentialSlotConfig slot = null;
    if(null == slotID)
      slot = vaultService. createCredentialSlot(resourceName,
                                            segmentId,
                                            descriptionMap,
                                            keyWordMap,
                                            secretType,
                                            active,
                                            portletPrivate,
                                            request);
...
...
```

Once the slot is successfully created, we retrieve the slotId:

```
slotId = slot.getSlotId();
```

Now, we store the slot in the persistence service of the portal server:

```
prefs.setValue(("BasicAuthTest",slotId);
```

Last, we store the end user's user ID and password in the slot. Remember that the slot is active; therefore, an active credential will retrieve the user ID and password from the vault.

```
vaultService.setCredentialSecretUserPassword(slotID, userID,
password.toCharArray(), request);
```

Complete the process of saving the slotId to the persistent store:

```
try{

    prefs.store();

}catch(IOException ioe) {

  ...
  ...
}
```

We now have a slot that contains an end user's secret in the vault and a slotId stored in the persistent service. An important point to stress is that the secret is stored in the vault by calling the *appropriate* method for the type of secret on the CredentialVaultService interface. The next step is to retrieve the secret and use it to access a back-end application in the doView method. We'll discuss this step in the next section when we talk about credentials.

A final note about slots: The portal server doesn't enforce any type of binding rules or policies with regard to a portlet accessing a slot. In other words, there's no access control mechanism in place to prevent a portlet from using a system slot or an administrative slot or from creating slots. However, the credential vault permits only the user who created the credential (secret) to manage or use the credential. The exception is a system slot to which every portlet and user has access, although only an administrator can manage the system slot.

Credentials

The credential is where the rubber meets the road with regard to accessing the secrets stored in the vault. A credential in the WebSphere portlet API is a class that implements the abstract base class.

```
com.ibm.portal.portlet.service.credentialvault.credentials.Credential
```

The credential interface provides the following methods:

- public void init(Map config)
- public int getSecretType()
- public boolean isActive()

At a minimum, the class that implements the credential class must provide an implementation of these methods. Therefore, the secrets are exposed to the portlet by the credential that is passed from the vault service to the portlet. The credential hides, or encapsulates, the details of retrieving the secrets from the vault. Extension of the base credential class enables the development of different credentials that meet the requirements of various authentication mechanisms. In other words, credential objects are able to do much more than simply retrieve secrets from the vault. The WebSphere Portal Server provides several implementations of the base Credential class. The implementations are grouped into two categories: passive and active credentials.

PASSIVE CREDENTIALS

Passive credentials are specifically designed to return the appropriate secret to the portlet. Because the purpose of a passive credential is to return a secret to the portlet, it becomes the responsibility of the developer to supply the necessary code for logging in to the back-end application and establishing an authenticated connection. All passive credentials extend the PassiveCredential class. This class overrides the isActive method, which returns false as expected.

You can think of the UserPasswordPassiveCredential class as a container that holds the user ID and password required by the application targeted by the portlet. It provides the following methods.

```
public UserPasswordPassiveCredential()
public void init(Map Config)
public int getSecretType()
public String getUserId()
public char[] getPassword()
```

Because the secret stored in the vault is a password, the secret type returned by the credential is

```
CredentialVaultService.SECRET_TYPE_USERID_STRING_PASSWORD_STRING
```

Several other passive credential types are shipped with the portal server:

- UserPasswordPassiveCredential (String/char[])
- BinaryPassiveCredential (byte[])
- SimplePassiveCredential (java.lang.Object/BLOB)
- JAASSubjectPassiveCredential (java.security.auth.Subject)

The SimplePassiveCredential is intended for future use. The limitation that prevents use of these credentials is that the vault service doesn't handle these secret types. The JAASSubjectPassiveCredential class can be viewed as providing a convenient and standard pattern for retrieving the Java Authentication and Authorization Service (JAAS) Subject via a credential.

We already know that the user ID and password are set in the slot by calling the setCredentialSecretUserPassword method provided by the credential vault service:

```
vaultService.setCredentialSecretUserPassword(slotId, userID, pass-
word.toCharArray(), request);
```

Let's assume that the portlet user ID and password were previously saved in the slot and that the slotId was persisted via Portlet Preferences. Furthermore, let's assume the doView method of a portlet that requires a specific user ID and password to connect to a back-end application is being invoked. The portlet now has to retrieve the appropriate passive credential from the Credential Vault Service. The portlet calls the getCredential method provided by the CredentialVaultService interface:

```
getCredential(java.lang.String slotId, java.lang.String type,
java.util.Map config, PortletRequest request)
```

The following values are passed into the method.

```
String slotID =
portletRequest.getPreferences().getValue("MyVaultSlotName", null);
String type = new String("UserPasswordPassive");
HashMap map = new HashMap();
```

The HashMap typically contains back-end application-specific configuration information that is required to initialize the credential. The Credential Vault Service may add more information to the configuration from other sources. For example, the vault service may add the user's secret from the actual credential store and any specific parameters from the portal's credential configuration. Because the passive credential requires no extra information, the HashMap simply needs to be created and passed as an argument. The PortletRequest is used to provide information about the user (userID is the ID value assigned to the profile attribute ibm-appuuid required by WebSphere Member Manager) and the portlet (portletId) to the vault service.

Because the getCredential method returns a reference to an object of type Credential, it must be cast to the specific type:

```
UserPasswordPassiveCredential credential =
(UserPasswordPassiveCredential)vaultService.getCredential(slotId,type,m
ap), PortletRequest);
```

We can now use the credential to retrieve the user ID and password:

```
if( credential != null) {
    String userid = credential.getUserId();
    String password = String.valueOf(credential.getPassword());
}
```

The pattern for storing and retrieving secrets with WebSphere Portal Server is to

- create a slot in the user-managed segment or find a slot in the administrator-managed segment

- set the secrets in the slot via methods provided by the CredentialVaultService interface

- retrieve the secrets from the vault with the appropriate credential obtained from the CredentialVaultService interface

It's important to emphasize the fact that secrets cannot be accessed directly from the vault. This architecture becomes extremely valuable when using active credentials. Before we discuss active credentials, it's worth noting that the Credential Vault Service also provides access to the JAAS Subject that is created for each "logged-in" user. As you can see from the following line of code, the only parameter getUserSubject takes is the PortletRequest.

```
java.security.auth.Subject subject =
vaultService.getUserSubject(request);
```

The JAAS Subject holds principal and credential information that can be used by the portlet. However, it's best if the developer first tries to use an active credential.

Active Credentials

Active credential objects provide a similar pattern of interaction to passive credential objects. However, they differ from passive credentials in two fundamental ways:

- Active credential objects hide the secrets from the portlet. Methods to access the secrets are not available.

- Active credential objects provide methods to handle the login process to the back-end application and return an authenticated connection to the portlet.

Active credentials enforce "good programming practice" by denying developers the ability to place the secret in the portlet session. However, there's nothing to prevent a developer from placing the credential itself in the portlet session. To lessen the exposure of placing any credential object in the portlet session, the credentials are not serializable. This restriction prevents the secrets contained in the credential from being placed in a session table that is readily accessible by any application. Therefore, active credential objects are the preferred credential to use when possible.

As we noted, active credentials provide the ability to log users in to the back-end applications. The credential handles all the details of authenticating, caching cookies, IDs, or tokens received from the back-end application. The main purpose of the credential is to use the secret stored in the vault to establish an authenticated connection for the portlet on the user's behalf. The credential delivers the authenticated connection to the portlet, which then proceeds with the conversation with the back-end application.

WebSphere Portal Server provides several active credentials that interact with applications protected by various authentication mechanisms:

- *BinaryCredential*: Stores credentials in binary form.

- *HttpBasicAuth*: Contains the user ID/password. It supports access to applications protected by HTTP Basic Authentication.

- *HttpFormBasedAuth:* Contains the user ID/password. It supports access to applications protected by HTTP Form-Based Authentication.

- *JavaMail:* Contains user ID/password pairs. It supports the authentication functionality of the javax.mail API.

- *LtpaToken or LtpaToken2:* Contains the Lightweight Third-Party Authentication (LTPA) token. It supports authentication within a given Domino and WebSphere domain. LtpaToken2 is available only if attribute propagation is enabled.

- *SiteMinderToken:* Contains the SiteMinder token. It supports authentication with back-end applications protected by SiteMinder.

- *WebSealToken:* Contains a WebSeal token. It supports authentication with back-end applications protected by WebSeal.

- *SSMTokenCredential:* Contains an Openwave token. It supports authentication with back-end applications protected by Openwave SSM.

Now that you know the advantages of using active credentials that encapsulate the "login" process, let's take a closer look at the details. Specifically, let's look at the HttpBasicAuth active credential.

HttpBasicAuth Active Credential Example

The HTTP protocol specifies a simple request/authentication mechanism for identifying end users accessing a server. Servers use this mechanism to present a challenge to end users; clients use it to provide the necessary secrets. The term "basic authentication" is derived from the simplicity of the authentication mechanism. If a request is entered for a resource that is protected by basic authentication, the server returns a 401 status code in the response header. This response informs the client that the user must be challenged to supply his or her credentials (user ID and password) to gain access to the resource. Browsers that support basic authentication present the user with a standard pop-up form for entering the ID and password. Once the credentials are posted to the server, the server authenticates and determines whether the user has access to the resource. If the user has access, the resource is returned and displayed. It's important to realize that a resource configured to use basic authentication requires a user ID and password on each request. Browsers that support basic authentication also provide the necessary implementation details for sending the user ID and password on each request.

Because the portal server aggregates markup on the server side, it's up to the portlet to interact with back-end applications. In the case where a portlet must access a back-end application protected by basic authentication, the portlet bears the responsibility for handling the 401 response code and sending the user ID and password on each request. You can think of the portlet as a client that runs on the server.

Fortunately, the HttpBasicAuth credential provides the necessary functionality for accessing applications that are protected by a basic authentication mechanism. This credential handles the 401 status code in the response header, logs the end user in to the application, and returns an authenticated connection to the portlet. Let's take a closer look at the details.

Let's refine the pattern already established with passive credentials with regard to retrieving and using secrets to connect to back-end applications. For this discussion, assume the slot has already been created and contains a user ID and password. Also, the portlet is being rendered, and the doView(PortletRequest, PortletResponse) method has been called. Figure 11.3 depicts the flow of steps involving the active credential.

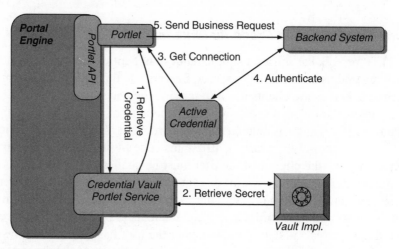

Figure 11.3: Active credential process

The following steps take place:

1. The portlet invokes the getCredential method provided by the CredentialVaultService interface.

2. The Credential Vault Service fetches the user ID and password from the vault and returns them in a credential to the portlet. In this particular case, it's an active credential.

3. The portlet calls getConnection on the active credential.

4. Using the user ID and password retrieved from the vault, the active credential logs the user in to the back-end application and returns an authenticated connection.

5. Using the authenticated connection, the portlet sends a request to the back-end application. Because the example uses an HttpBasicAuthCredential, the getCredential method takes either a java.net.URL or a string that contains the desired URL:

```
http_connection = credential.getAuthenticatedConnection
("http://myhost.com/protectedApp");
```

Creating the slot and storing the secret are handled in the actionPerformed method while the portlet is in edit mode. Listing 11.7 shows the sample code for the processAction method. Note that the URL accessed by the portlet is retrieved from a parameter (theURL) stored in Portlet Preferences. For simplicity, theURL is entered and saved when the user ID and password are supplied via the edit view.

```java
    public void processAction(ActionRequest request, ActionResponse
response) throws PortletException, java.io.IOException {
        if ( request.getParameter(FORM_SUBMIT) != null ) {
            // Set form text in the session bean
            MyTestPortletSessionBean sessionBean =
getSessionBean(request);
            if ( sessionBean != null )

sessionBean.setFormText(request.getParameter(FORM_TEXT));
        }
        if ( request.getParameter(USER_SUBMIT) != null ) {
            // Set userId/password text in the credential vault
            MyTestPortletSessionBean sessionBean =
getSessionBean(request);
            if ( sessionBean!=null ) {
                String userID   = request.getParameter(USERID);
                String password = request.getParameter(PASSWORD);
                String theURL = request.getParameter(TARGET_URL);

                String slotName = "BasicAuthTest";
                // save only if both parameters are set
                if (userID!=null && password!=null &&
!userID.trim().equals("") && !password.trim().equals("")) {
                    try {
                        PortletPreferences prefs =
request.getPreferences();
                        String slotId =
prefs.getValue(slotName,null);
```

Listing 11.7: processAction method (part 1 of 2)

371

```
                          if (slotId == null) {
                              ObjectID segmentID   =
vaultService.getDefaultUserCredentialSegmentId();
                              Map descriptionMap   = new Hashtable();
                              Map keyWordMap   = new Hashtable();
                              int secretType       =
CredentialVaultService.SECRET_TYPE_USERID_STRING_PASSWORD_STRING;
                              boolean active       = true;
                              boolean portletPrivate = true;

                              CredentialSlotConfig slot =
vaultService.createCredentialSlot(slotName, segmentID, descriptionMap,
keyWordMap, secretType,   active, portletPrivate, request);
                              slotId = slot.getSlotId();
                              prefs.setValue(slotName,slotId);
                          } else {

vaultService.setCredentialSecretUserPassword(slotId,userID,password.toCh
arArray(),request);
                          }
                          if (theURL != null) {
                              prefs.setValue(TARGET_URL,theURL);
                          }
                          prefs.store();
                      } catch (Exception e) {
                          e.printStackTrace();
                      }
                  }
              }
          }
      }
```

Listing 11.7: processAction method (part 2 of 2)

At this point, the slotId and the targeted URL are saved in Portlet Preferences, and the action phase has been completed. The doView method is now invoked, with the purpose of returning the appropriate markup to the aggregator. Because a significant effort is associated with handling an input stream of HTML, we've isolated from the doView method the code for retrieving an authenticated connection from the credential. It's in a method implemented for the specific portlet called getConnection, which returns an HttpURLConnection. Listing 11.8 shows the code for this method.

```
public HttpURLConnection getConnection(String theURL, PortletRequest
request, PortletResponse response) throws PortletException,
IOException{
    HttpURLConnection connection = null;
    String slotName = "MyEnterpriseAppAdminSlot";
    // retrieve slotId from persistent portlet preferences
    String slotId = (String)
request.getPreferences().getValue(slotName, null);
    if (slotId == null) {
        //Something is wrong and you need to start debugging the problem
        System.out.println("********** the slotID is NULL");
        return null;
    }
    // bundle the credential config data
    HashMap config = new HashMap();
    config.put( HttpBasicAuthCredential.KEY_CREDENTIAL_SECRET,
                "UserPasswordCredential");
    // get the actual credential from the credential vault
    HttpBasicAuthCredential credential = null;

    try {
        credential = (HttpBasicAuthCredential)
                    vaultService.getCredential(slotId,
"HttpBasicAuth",
                                                config, request);
    } catch (CredentialVaultException e) {
        e.printStackTrace();
    }

    try {
        // get an authenticated connection to the back-end server
        connection = credential.getAuthenticatedConnection(theURL);
    } catch (IOException exc) {
        System.out.println("SSO error IOException = " + exc);
        return null;
    }
    return connection;
}
```

Listing 11.8: getConnection method

The Credential Vault Service provides a clean architectural solution for
delegating or mapping the required credentials from a portlet to back-end
applications. The credential vault framework is readily extensible, enabling the
construction of credentials for accessing back-end systems protected by
authentication mechanisms not covered by the credentials shipped with the
portal server. Central to this thought is the fact that credentials are registered in a

Credential Type Registry of the portal server. Any credential that has registered with the Credential Type Registry is available to any and all portlets.

DEFINING ADMINISTRATIVE AND SYSTEM SLOTS

In the "Slot Details" section, we described the various types of slots available to hold credentials. We discussed how portlets can either use preconfigured slots defined in the administrative segment or create new slots in the user-managed segment. If the portlet is designed to use a preconfigured slot, the administrator must define an administrative slot or a system slot to hold the user's secrets. Let's look at how these slots are defined using the Credential Vault portlet provided by the portal server.

After logging in to the portal as an administrator (typically wpsadmin), follow the first level of navigation to portal administration as shown in Figure 11.4.

Figure 11.4: Portal administration link

Once the Administration page is displayed, expand the Access content node, and double-click the Credential Vault portlet (Figure 11.5).

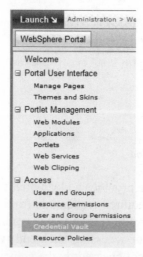

Figure 11.5: Selecting the Credential Vault portlet

In the Credential Vault portlet, click **Add a vault slot** (Figure 11.6).

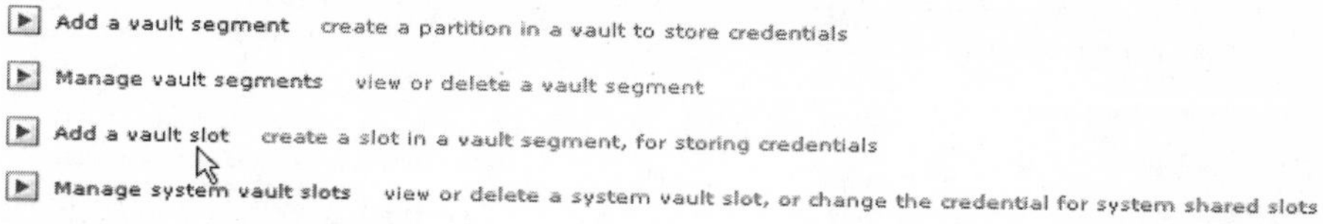

▶ **Add a vault segment**   create a partition in a vault to store credentials

▶ **Manage vault segments**   view or delete a vault segment

▶ **Add a vault slot**   create a slot in a vault segment, for storing credentials

▶ **Manage system vault slots**   view or delete a system vault slot, or change the credential for system shared slots

Figure 11.6: Adding a vault slot

The first slot we'll add is a system slot. As we noted, a system slot stores a single credential that all users and any portlet can share. Figure 11.7 shows a system slot configured to contain a shared user ID and password for accessing a custom back-end application. The following values have been used to configure the slot:

- **Name:** CustAppSlot. The administrator sets the slot name.

- **Vault segment**: DefaultAdminSegment. The default segment is the administrator-managed segment.

- **Vault resource associated with vault slot**: Custom Application. The resource is an arbitrary name used to partition the name space of the vault. It typically represents the application targeted by the credentials.

- **Vault Slot is shared**: A shared vault slot is required.

The administrator also supplies the appropriate user ID, password, and description. For this example, **admin** is the user ID, and **admin** is the password. When you click **OK**, the slot is created.

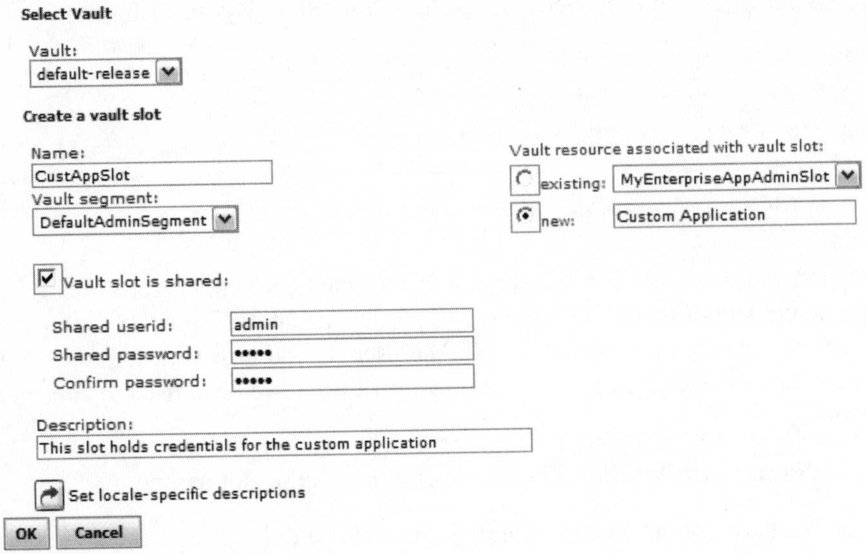

Select Vault

Vault:
default-release ▼

Create a vault slot

Name:
CustAppSlot

Vault segment:
DefaultAdminSegment ▼

Vault resource associated with vault slot:

○ existing: MyEnterpriseAppAdminSlot ▼

◉ new: Custom Application

☑ Vault slot is shared:

Shared userid: admin
Shared password: •••••
Confirm password: •••••

Description:
This slot holds credentials for the custom application

↪ Set locale-specific descriptions

[OK] [Cancel]

Figure 11.7: Creating a system slot

Next, we'll look at configuring an administrative slot. An administrative slot can hold each end-user secret required for authenticating to a given application. In other words, an administrative slot can hold many secrets. Looking at the configuration values in Figure 11.8, note that the **Vault slot is shared** option isn't selected. This doesn't imply that the slot itself isn't shared. On the contrary, a given user's secret stored in the slot can be shared among the user's portlets. When selected, this option identifies the slot as a system slot.

This particular example uses Lotus Notes as the target application. The goal is to create a slot that will hold a credential for each user.

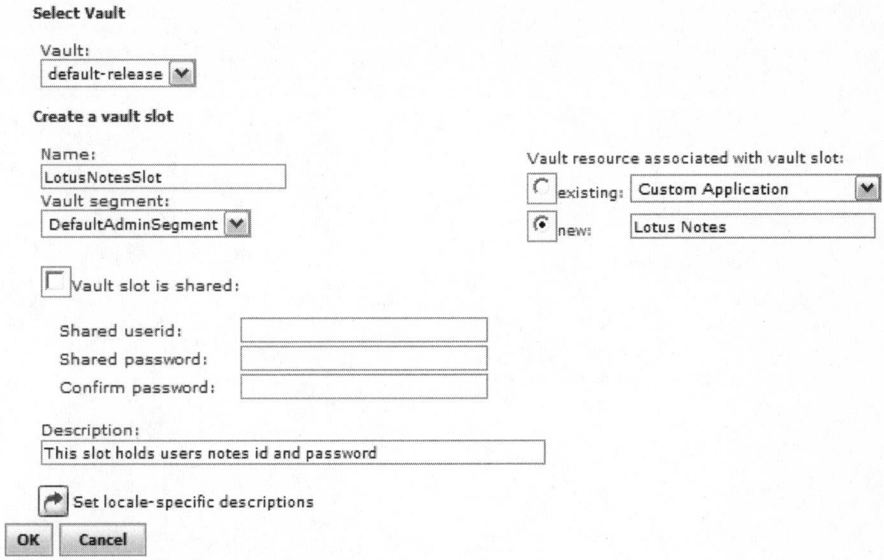

Select Vault

Vault:
default-release ▼

Create a vault slot

Name:
LotusNotesSlot

Vault segment:
DefaultAdminSegment ▼

Vault resource associated with vault slot:

◯ existing: Custom Application ▼

◉ new: Lotus Notes

☐ Vault slot is shared:

Shared userid:
Shared password:
Confirm password:

Description:
This slot holds users notes id and password

↱ Set locale-specific descriptions

[OK] [Cancel]

Figure 11.8: Creating an administrative slot

SUMMARY

WebSphere Portal Server's Credential Vault Service provides capabilities that facilitate implementing a single sign-on solution for mapping end-user credentials to a back-end application. The Credential Vault Service also provides the ability to delegate the end user's portal identity to back-end applications. For example, the service provides active credentials that can pass the LTPA token of the WebSphere Application Server, JAASSubject, and tokens from authentication proxy servers, such as Tivoli Access Manager and Netegrity.

The credential objects in the Credential Vault Service framework are the key abstractions responsible for retrieving secrets from the vault. There are two types of credential objects: active and passive. Passive credentials provide a way to access the user's secret from the vault but require the developer to implement the necessary code to interface with the back-end system. Active credentials hide the secrets held by the credentials from the portlet. Their main purpose is to provide an authenticated connection to the portlet. They are the preferred credentials to use for connecting to back-end applications.

Chapter Twelve

Workplace Forms Fundamentals

In this chapter, we introduce the fundamental concepts of using IBM Workplace Forms in a WebSphere Portal environment. First, we cover product background and essentials, including an introduction to the World Wide Web Consortium's (W3C's) XForms standard and Extensible Forms Definition Language (XFDL). Next, we step through a hello world example in which we create a Workplace Form and deploy it to WebSphere Portal V6. Throughout the chapter, we discuss key considerations and additional resources. Chapter 13 covers more advanced topics involving Workplace Forms.

From the perspective of portal developers, Workplace Forms provides several beneficial capabilities:

- pixel-perfect precision layout for industry-regulated formsthe ability to define a transaction as a single document with business logic

- portable documents across platforms and systems

- offline/disconnected use

- flexible, proven digital signature technology

Conversely, from the perspective of form designers, WebSphere Portal provides

- application context

- a repository to store template forms for access by end users

- the ability to submit and store data and documents

- workflow in validation or approval processes

- the standard benefits of composite application architecture and Service Oriented Architecture (SOA)

IBM WORKPLACE FORMS

IBM Workplace Forms provides a component technology that is 100 percent focused on providing best-of-breed eForm functionality. As of the 2.6 release, the product suite consists of three pieces:

- IBM Workplace Forms Designer
- IBM Workplace Forms Viewer
- IBM Workplace Forms Server

The Workplace Forms Designer is an Eclipse-based visual design environment for eForms. Form designers work in a WYSIWYG environment to perform tasks such as form user interface layout and design, form data modeling, and implementation of digital signatures, input validation rules, and business logic. As with many other Eclipse-based tools, you can customize or extend the Designer by rearranging or installing views and plug-ins.

The Workplace Forms Viewer is a Windows application that presents Workplace Forms to end users so that the users can view, fill, and sign forms. The Viewer supports a rich feature set, including precision layout, broad support for digital signatures, offline use, and extensibility. You can run the Viewer standalone to launch forms from the desktop or run it as a browser plug-in within Internet Explorer or Firefox. The Viewer is designed so that end users shouldn't need training to interact with forms.

IBM Workplace Forms Server is actually an umbrella term that encompasses three discrete components:

- *IBM Workplace Forms Server – Webform Server* provides realtime translation of rich, XML Workplace Form documents into HTML for rendering in standard browsers without requiring the Workplace Forms

Viewer. The Webform Server runs as an application on top of WebSphere Application Server (WAS).

- The *IBM Workplace Forms Server – API* is a code library that provides a range of functions and methods for manipulating Workplace Forms documents. You typically leverage the API from within a Web application (servlet or portlet). Standard uses include inserting or extracting form data, validating form signatures, and a variety of other form-related tasks. The Workplace Forms Server API is tightly coupled to the form document and is not coupled to any external systems. The API is available in C, Component Object Model (COM), and Java versions.

- *IBM Workplace Forms Server – Deployment Server* gives administrators a tool for ensuring that remotely deployed viewers and/or forms are up-to-date.

It's worth noting that although the Workplace Forms API gives developers an extensive set of functions and methods for manipulating Workplace Forms documents, it's not the only way to process Workplace Forms. We need to be careful not to lose sight of the fact that Workplace Forms are 100 percent native XML; you can therefore use the standard range of XML and String-related tools and techniques to insert or extract data and otherwise process a form document. That said, the Workplace Forms API gives application developers a broad range of more complex capabilities that you would certainly *not* want to have to reimplement, including XForms model–related methods, duplication, and digital signature validation. For production-grade form-processing applications, we strongly recommend taking advantage of the Workplace Forms API.

Workplace Forms Background

IBM Workplace Forms technology is based on products initially developed by PureEdge Solutions, Inc., a company IBM acquired in August 2005. PureEdge Solutions had a 12-year track record as an industry leader in providing secure eForm solutions. The company also had extensive involvement in the W3C, contributing to a range of initiatives, including

- XML Canonicalization: *http://www.w3.org/TR/xml-exc-c14n*

- XML Signature: *http://www.w3.org/Signature*

- XForms: *http://www.w3.org/MarkUp/Forms*

- XPath Filter: *http://www.w3.org/TR/xmldsig-filter2*

- XFDL (submitted as UWI): *http://www.w3.org/TR/NOTE-XFDL*

Workplace Forms Terminology

Table 12.1 defines some key terms you'll encounter as you work with Workplace Forms.

Table 12.1: Workplace Forms terminology

Term	Definition
(Form) Template	A form that is "empty" - it does not contain any data.
(XML) Schema	Set of rules defining a valid data structure.
(XML) Instance	A data structure conforming to a schema.
XFDL	Extensible Forms Definition Language. An XML form-definition syntax designed for high-value, business-to-business e-commerce transactions where legal enforcement of records may be required. Unlike many XML derivatives, XFDL is a programming language, providing a rich functionality based on declarative logic and events. Within the context of XForms-based forms, XFDL is considered a "host language" for the abstract UI definition provided in the XForms model.
XForms	The W3C standard for the "next generation" of Web-based forms.
XForms model	In this context, the portion of a form based on the W3C XForms standard. The XForms model standardizes data structure, validation, and business logic, and it provides an abstract definition (not a concrete implementation) of the UI. When using the Workplace Forms Designer, we provide a concrete implementation of this abstract UI by hosting the XForms model within the XFDL presentation layer.

Key Features and Uses of Workplace Forms

Current Workplace Forms technology is based on requirements and input from a broad range of customers, gathered over a dozen years. The following key requirements arise again and again in enterprise eForm solutions.

- Dynamic forms
  - ➢ Form pages can be designed to react dynamically to data and a range of events.

- Support for a range of signature requirements
  - ➢ Workplace Forms supports multi-approval workflows that us incorporate one or more digital signatures — sectional, page, whole-document, out-of-order, and overlapping. In addition, Workplace Forms support digital signing via hardware signature pads and tablet PCs.

- Performance: file sizes
  - ➢ Forms are 100 percent native XML and compress very well, an important factor for ensuring fast upload and download times.

- Performance: server-side processing
  - ➢ Workplace Forms uses a native XML format that does not require extensive server-side processing to serve forms or integrate form data with back-end systems.

- Extensibility
  - ➢ Form designers can create extensions that can run either via the Viewer or on the server side. These extensions can encapsulate business or integration logic.

- Fit with enterprise architecture
  - ➢ Workplace Forms provides a lightweight approach to form processing — "straight-through" data integration, without the need for translation.
  - ➢ Workplace Forms is a highly flexible, component-based technology.
  - ➢ Workplace Forms technology is based on numerous open standards (e.g., JSR 168) easing integration with portals, data-tier, and line-of-business systems.

383

WORKPLACE FORMS DOCUMENT MODEL

Before we proceed, it's important to understand the makeup of Workplace Forms. The key here is that Workplace Forms are based on a *document-centric* approach; each form is represented by a single 100 percent native XML file that defines the eForm. Figure 12.1 summarizes the elements of the Workplace Forms document model.

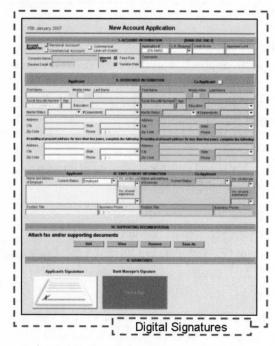

Workplace Forms documents are 100% native, structured XML:

• **User Interface (UI)**
    - Precision Layout Pages
    - Interview-Style Form Pages

• **Business Logic and Validation**
    - Dynamic logic to

• **Data Model**
    - XForms standard based
    - Supports arbitrary XML instances

• **Attachments**
    - All files types supported
    - Can be signed + made tamper evident

• **Signatures**
    - Flexible digital signature technology
    - Support for multiple, sectional, overlapping and out-of-order signing.

Figure 12.1: Workplace Forms document model

Taking a document-centric approach and treating forms as XML objects has several advantages, including giving us the ability to

- use a form when offline or disconnected

- route a form to users using any available routing mechanism

- pass a form along through a workflow

- store a form as a transaction record

- digitally sign the entire representation of a form

- parse the XML data within a form at any time throughout the form's life cycle

Let's examine the XML syntax that makes up Workplace Forms documents.

XFDL

The Extensible Forms Definition Language (XFDL) defines the eForm.

W3C XForms

XForms is the W3C standard for the next generation of forms for the Web. XForms 1.0 became a recommendation in October 2003, and Revision 2 of XForms 1.0 was released in March 2006. The XForms recommendation is available at *http://www.w3.org/MarkUp/Forms*.

The XForms standard is data-centric and defines a standardized structure and processing model for forms. One intention is that form data and the business and validation logic should be abstracted from the UI implementation. This approach makes it possible to reuse the same XForms model in different client environments. To accomplish this reuse, the XForms standard lets you define an abstract user interface, also referred to as an *intent-based* user interface. The intent-based UI definition doesn't describe how controls are presented to users; in fact, it doesn't even contain the concept of "page." XForms gives us more abstract constructs, such as an "input," "textarea," "submit," and "secret." The concrete details of the implementation depend on the target language and/or platform. For example, you might want to use the same form model to capture information from a mobile telephone as well as a browser on a PC. You could "skin" this common XForms model with Wireless Markup Language (WML) for the phone and use XFDL for the PC. This support represents a powerful approach that gives us the ability to reuse an XForms model by hosting it within different presentation layers.

Putting It Together: XFDL + XForms

The Workplace Forms Designer produces either

- 100 percent XFDL eForms
- XFDL + XForms eForms

Recall that XForms on its own is not an eForm without a concrete UI implementation, in this case provided by XFDL.

WORKPLACE FORMS: HELLO WORLD FORM AND PORTLET

Now that we've covered the background material, let's get started creating our first form and displaying it via a portlet.

Hello World Form

Our first task is to create a basic form. To do so, we'll use the Workplace Forms Designer. This exercise will give you a basic familiarity with the Eclipse-based form design environment and illustrate several essential steps involved in creating a Workplace Form you can deploy to a portal.

Step 1: Create a New Form

The first step is to launch the Workplace Forms Designer. At the time of this writing, the current version was 2.6.1. If you have a copy of the Workplace Forms Designer and want to follow along and create, we suggest you use Version 2.6 (or later, if available). For the purposes of this example, we created the project and form shown in Figure 12.2.

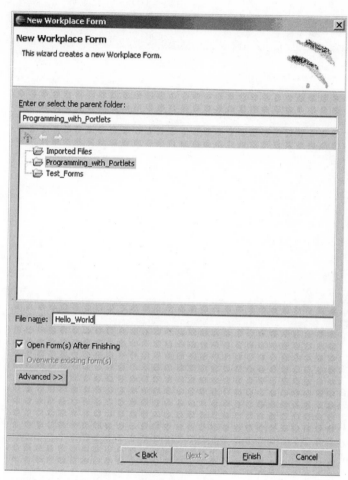

Figure 12.2: Hello World project specifics

Upon completion, you see a blank form canvas similar to the screen shown in Figure 12.3.

Figure 12.3: IBM Workplace Forms Designer 2.6.1 and blank form canvas

Note that if this is the first time you've launched the application, you may see a different screen. Also be aware that, as with many other Eclipse environments, you can rearrange the placement of the views to meet individual preferences.

Step 2: User Interface Layout

Next, we'll begin to lay out our form user interface. As we discussed, within a single IBM Workplace Form document, we have full definition of the user interface, data model, business and validation logic, and any required signatures or extensions. Because this is a hello world style of example, we'll kept the form UI very simple. It consists of an output, called a *label* ("Hello World!"), and, because forms are about capturing data, also an input, called a *field*. In addition, we've used the Properties view (Figure 12.4) to set the dimensions of the form, sometimes referred to as the *form canvas*. Figure 12.5 shows the completed form in Designer.

Figure 12.4: Properties view showing page dimensions in pixels

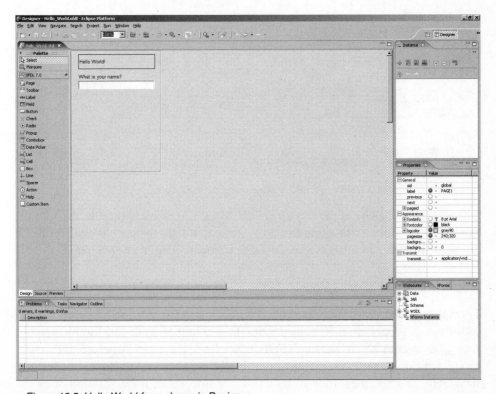

Figure 12.5: Hello World form shown in Designer

If we click on the **Preview** tab near the bottom of the Designer window, the form is presented to us in the Workplace Forms Viewer. In this case, the Viewer runs embedded within Eclipse; however, in production, the Viewer can run standalone or embedded within a Web or Portal page. Figure 12.6 shows how the Form appears when rendered to an end user.

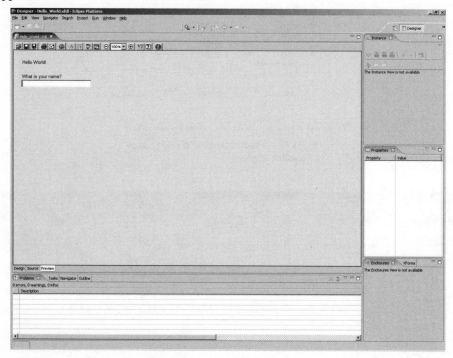

Figure 12.6: Hello World form shown in Workplace Forms Viewer

The actual dimensions of the form page are 240 x 320 pixels. However, the Viewer doesn't display a border around this area, so we don't see the page boundary. We'll consider form size in relation to portlet size in greater depth a little later.

Step 3: Addition of XForms Model

Form data is almost always centralized within a specific portion of a form: in either a data model or an XForms model. Depending on your form implementation (100 percent XFDL versus XFDL + XForms), the exact structure of this model may vary; however, the key point is that we abstract the storage of form data from the implementation of the UI. Let's proceed with the addition of an

XForms model to our form. To do so, we select the **XForms** view (available at the bottom right of the screen by default). Initially, this view looks as shown in Figure 12.7.

Figure 12.7: XForms View – No Model Exists

Right-click the words **No Model Exists,** and select the option to **Add XForms Support.** You'll note that an error condition then appears in the **Problems** view (Figure 12.8).

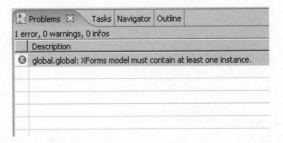

Figure 12.8: Problems View – No Model Exists

This alert is okay and is in fact expected because we took the approach of designing and implementing our UI before creating our data model. In many production implementations, the data model is defined based on one or more XML Schema from an external interface or systems. In that case, we would enclose that Schema into the form and use a model-driven design approach to the creation of our data instance(s). However, in our hello world example, we'll simply create a default model based on the page and widgets we've defined. To do so, click the green plus sign (+) at the top left of the **Instance** view. Doing so results in the creation of an XForms data instance as shown in Figure 12.9.

Figure 12.9: Instance view and
auto-generated instance, based on UI

If you check the **Problems** view now, you'll notice that the error reported earlier has vanished. Let's take a moment to drop into the **Source** view to see what XML has actually been generated. First, let's focus in on the XForms model, which is shown in Listing 12.1.

```
<xformsmodels>
    <xforms:model>
        <xforms:instance id="INSTANCE1" xmlns="">
            <document>
                <PAGE1>
                    <PAGE1></FIELD1>
                </PAGE1>
            </document>
        </xforms:instance>
    </xforms:model>
</xformsmodels>
```

Listing 12.1: XForms model code fragment

As we noted previously, this structure has been created based on the UI. This tends to be the case only for very basic forms or when integration with external systems is not a concern.

At this point, there's one other code fragment worth considering, and that is the expression that defines the relationship between the input (field) in the form UI and our data model element FIELD1. Let's take a look at how this field is defined (Listing 12.2).

```
<field sid="FIELD1">
    <itemlocation>
        <x>20</x>
        <y>60</y>
        <width>208</width>
    </itemlocation>
    <scrollhoriz>wordwrap</scrollhoriz>
    <value></value>
    <label>What is your name?</label>
    <xforms:textarea ref="instance('INSTANCE1')/PAGE1/FIELD1">
        <xforms:label></xforms:label>
    </xforms:textarea>
</field>
```

Listing 12.2: FIELD1 code fragment

You'll note that these 13 lines of XML completely describe the field — its absolute location, its size, and also the label, or message, displayed. The <xforms:textarea> element contains a ref attribute that includes an XPath statement. This statement defines the relationship between this UI element and a target in the data model. Sometimes referred to as a "bind," this statement establishes a bidirectional relationship between the UI and the data model. If, for example, in our portlet we pre-populate the data model based on single sign-on information and then present the form to the user, this statement would be processed at runtime and present the information in the data model (one's name!) via the UI. Conversely, when a user enters information into the UI, the bind conveys that information into the XForms model.

Step 4: Addition of a Submission Button

Our next step is to add a submission button to the form. To do so, simply select a button from the palette — **Button (Non-XForms)** — and place it on the form canvas. Next, double-click the button, and change the displayed text to **Submit Form**. Resize and reposition the button as desired. Figure 12.10 shows our form with the button in place.

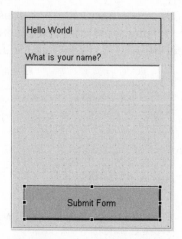

Figure 12.10: Hello World form with button in Designer

Next, we must set the type for the button. To do so, select the button by clicking on it on the form canvas. Then, go into the **Properties** view, select the **type** property, and choose **submit**, as shown in Figure 12.11.

Figure 12.11: Button properties in Workplace Forms Designer

Selecting type **submit** in an XFDL button means that when a user clicks the button, the form (or, in some cases, the form data only) will be submitted via HTTP Post.

Note the **url** property in this view. You use this property to define a target for submission, most often a servlet or portlet (via HTTP Post). For the purposes of this book, we'll focus on how to keep a form within the context of one's portal application; however, we'll postpone discussion of this topic for now because it's beyond the scope of our hello world example. At this time, we'll intentionally leave the **url** button property blank, and the **Submit Form** button won't be functional. We'll examine how to generate and populate the target URL from within a portlet in Chapter 13.

At this point, we're ready to move along and display this form in a portal environment. However, be aware that we've only revealed the tip of the iceberg in terms of form design and creation. Much more extensive training and best-practices materials are available and recommended for professional form designers. For information about how to access additional form design and Workplace Forms materials, see the Workplace Forms documentation at *http://www-128.ibm.com/developerworks/workplace/documentation/forms*.

Displaying the Hello World Form in Portal

We have two main options for displaying a Workplace Form within a portal. We can write a JSR 168 or Portlet API portlet from scratch, or we can extend the Workplace Forms Portlet Framework. Let's compare and contrast the two approaches.

Approach #1: Write the Portlet from Scratch

In this case, we can proceed with writing a standard portlet. We'll focus in on the doView method and JSP because these are all we need for the hello world scenario. Listing 12.3 shows the doView method.

```
public void doView(PortletRequest request, PortletResponse response)
throws PortletException,
IOException(getPortletConfig().getContext().include(VIEW_JSP, request,
response);)
```

Listing 12.3: Hello World doView method

Note that there's nothing here specifically related to IBM Workplace Forms. In this hello world example, we simply return a JSP for rendering. In a production environment, there's typically some more work to do, such as pre-population (passing information into a form); however, we'll leave that to a later example. Let's turn our attention to the JSP.

We need two elements within the JSP to embed the Workplace Forms Viewer:

- the HTML OBJECT element
- the HTML SCRIPT element

JSP Section 1: The OBJECT Element

Listing 12.4 shows an OBJECT section suitable for our Hello World example.

```
<OBJECT id="HELLO_WORLD" classid="CLSID:354913B2-7190-49C0-944B-
1507C9125367" width="450" height="370" ViewAsText>
    <PARAM NAME="XFDLID" VALUE="XFDLForm"/>
</OBJECT>
```

Listing 12.4: Sample OBJECT section

Table 12.2 lists the object attributes, and Table 12.3 describes the object parameter.

Table 12.2: Object attributes

Object attribute	Description
id	Assigns a name to the object; must be unique within the page
width	The width of the object in pixels
height	The height of the object in pixels

Table 12.3: Object parameter

Object attribute	Description
XFDLID	Identifies the SCRIPT element that contains the form

Before we move on, take note of several key points:

- The PARAM element doesn't require an end tag. For more information about the HTML parameter element, refer to the W3C Web site.

- Internet Explorer uses the classid attribute to identify the ActiveX control that activates the Workplace Forms Viewer. To support Firefox or Mozilla, you would instead use the type="application/vnd.xfdl" attribute.

- To provide enough room for the default viewer buttons, we've added size padding beyond the 240 x 320 size of our form canvas. This adjustment will become clearer when you see the portlet deployed and running. In production, we'd likely design the form so that unnecessary buttons weren't displayed.

For detailed information about embedding the Workplace Forms Viewer, including available object attributes and suggested practices for supporting multiple browsers, see Reference 1.

JSP Section 2: The SCRIPT Element

The SCRIPT section of our JSP follows a very simple structure:

1. SCRIPT opening tag and attributes
2. start comment tag: <!--
3. entire Workplace Form body
4. closing comment tag: -->
5. closing SCRIPT tag

Listing 12.5 shows the SCRIPT section corresponding to our hello world form.

```
<SCRIPT language="XFDL" id="XFDLForm" type="application/vnd.xfdl;
wrapped=comment">
<!--
    <?xml version="1.0" encoding="UTF-8"?>
    <XFDL xmlns:custom="http://www.ibm.com/xmlns/prod/XFDL/Custom"
        xmlns:designer="http://www.ibm.com/xmlns/prod/workplace/forms/
            designer/2.6"
        xmlns:ev="http://www.w3.org/2001/xml-events"
xmlns:xfdl="http://www.ibm.com/xmlns/prod/XFDL/7.0"
        xmlns:xforms="http://www.w3.org/2002/xforms"
xmlns="http://www.ibm.com/xmlns/prod/XFDL/7.0"
        xmlns:xsd="http://www.w3.org/2001/XMLSchema"
xmlns:xsi="http://www.w3.org/2001/XMLSchema-instance">
    <globalpage sid="global">
        [~60 more lines of Form XML]
    </XFDL>
-->
</SCRIPT>
```

Listing 12.5: SCRIPT section of JSP

397

The form body is nestled between the start and end comment tags. To obtain this text, we simply entered the **Source** view in the Workplace Forms Designer and selected and copied all the text.

Note that for brevity's sake, we've abbreviated the actual form body in the snippet of code shown. For the complete example, showing the entire JSP (both the OBJECT and SCRIPT elements), consult Reference 1. Several points to be aware of:

- In general, it's a good idea to store the form in compressed format (gzip, base 64 encoded). Storing or submitting forms in compressed format is a native capability of the Workplace Forms Viewer, Designer, and API that form designers can configure.

- If your form contains signed and completed signatures, it must be compressed.

- Character set and encoding considerations are important for those embedding internationalized forms (or any form containing characters outside the ASCII range).

TESTING AND DEPLOYING OUR PORTLET

As a test, you can use the **Preview** option in Rational Application Developer (RAD) to try to render the JSP. If the Workplace Forms Viewer is installed locally and everything is okay in your JSP or HTML page, the preview should look similar to the image shown in Figure 12.12.

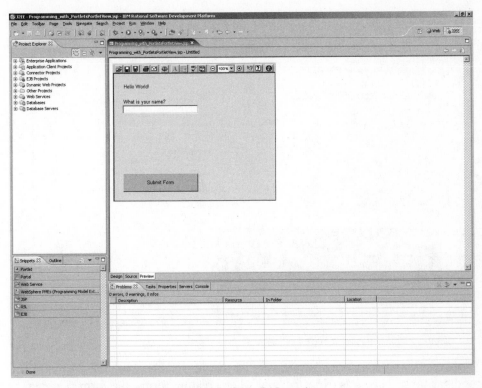

Figure 12.12: Embedded form "Hello World" JSP in RAD preview

This is a good sign and is a suggested step; if you see your form appear in the **Preview** pane, it should be ready for installation.

Time to deploy the form into Portal! To do so, we simply export the project as a .war file and install it into Portal via the Administration interface — nothing nonstandard involved. In Figure 12.13, we've added the Workplace Forms Hello World Portlet to one of the standard Portal 6 Getting Started Pages.

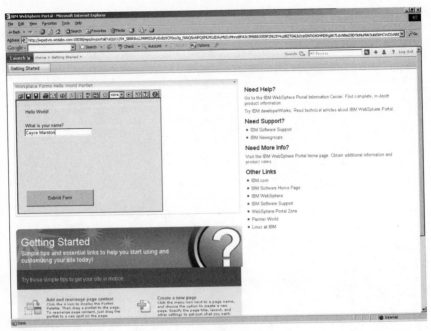

Figure 12.13: Hello World Form Portlet displayed in Portal 6

Note the Workplace Forms Viewer toolbar that appears between the portlet title and our form. This is as expected, and when creating forms, the form designer can control which buttons the users see here. In this case, we accepted the default options, so all the buttons are displayed, and we had to account for their presence when specifying portlet width.

In the figure, we've gone ahead and entered a name into the input field. If we now click the submit button, nothing happens, as expected, because we left the url parameter blank within our form. Submission handling is beyond the scope of a hello world type of example. A little later, we'll look at how we can pass in generated portlet UI that can be used to trigger the processAction method within our portlet.

Some important points to note:

- In production, we almost never declare a form directly inline within our JSP or HTML page. Form templates are often stored in the data tier in an enterprise-grade repository such as DB2 or DB2 Content Manager. You typically would use a bean to pass the form body into the JSP page.

- –Because the form itself is just an XML file, other template storage options include deployment as part of your .war file (store it in the WEB-INF, for example), use of the file system local to the portal server, or retrieval of the template at runtime from an external system.

- To leverage Webform Server and provide zero-footprint form capabilities, a portlet must extend the base class provided by Webform Server. We'll discuss this topic more later.

Approach #2: Extend the Workplace Forms Portlet Framework

The second method of displaying a Workplace Form within a portal is to extend the base class portlet provided with Webform Server. This approach is advantageous for several reasons; most important, it gives us the ability to deploy forms to end users without requiring the installation of the Workplace Forms Viewer on each client desktop (by leveraging the Webform Server, which must be installed to enable zero-footprint).

When installed, Webform Server includes a sample Web application and portal application, located in the <Webform Server Install Directory>\samples directory. If you use the standard installation path on Windows, this path is as follows:

```
C:\Program Files\IBM\Workplace Forms\Server\2.6\Webform Server\samples
```

The sample Webform Server portal application, which you can use for demonstrations or modify to meet your needs, provides two portlets designed to work together: a FormListPortlet that lists the sample forms within a directory and a FormViewPortlet that displays the form selected in the FormListPortlet. Inter-portlet communication is used to update the state of the FormViewPortlet based on interaction with the FormListPortlet. Within the FormListPortlet, there are three ways to display each listed form:

- Click the form name. Webform Server will detect whether you have the Workplace Forms Viewer installed locally. If so, you'll receive the rich, XFDL form, and the viewer will be used to display the form. If not, you'll be presented with the HTML translation of the first form page.

- Click the 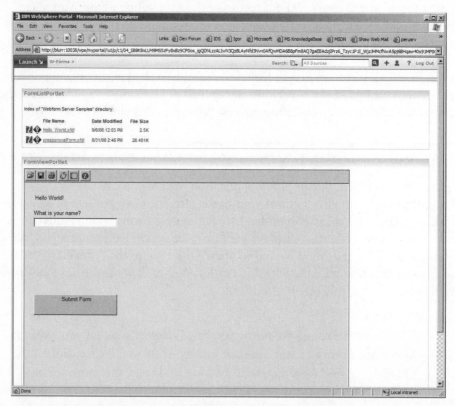 image to force form display via the Viewer.

- Click the ![icon] image to force form display in HTML.

Let's deploy our hello world form to the sample application and see how the form looks in zero-footprint. To do so, we'll copy the Hello_World.xfdl file into the <installed Portal Application> directory. In our case, this directory mapped to the following folder:

```
C:\WebSphere\PortalServer\installedApps\WebformSample
Portlets_PA_fi677bk.ear\PA_fi677bk.war\SampleForms
```

Figure 12.14 shows our form deployed via the Webform Server sample portlets and rendered as HTML by Webform Server.

Figure 12.14: Hello world form rendered Portal using Webform Server

402

Figure 12.15 shows the same form shown in the Viewer (achieved by clicking the 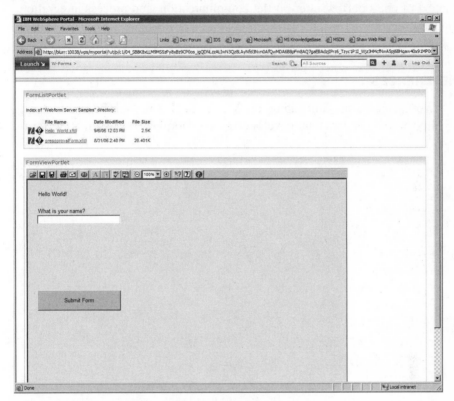 image next to Hello_World.xfdl in the FormListPortlet). Note that the only noticeable visual difference is the buttons provided at the top of the form.

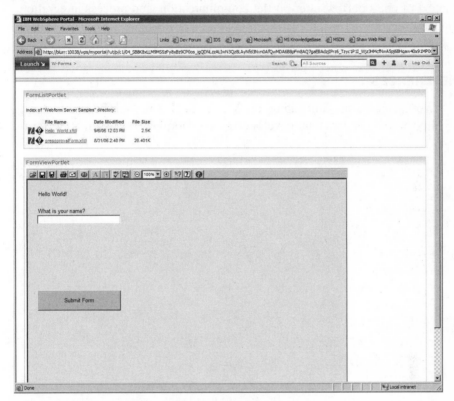

Figure 12.15: Forced display of Hello World with Viewer

If we click the **Submit Form** button, nothing happens. Again, this is the behavior we expect. In Chapter 13, you'll learn how to populate this button with a URL generated within our portlet so that form submissions are kept in context to our application.

SUMMARY

In this chapter, we laid a basic foundation of IBM Workplace Forms knowledge relating to Portal. We used a hello world example to highlight the steps necessary to display Workplace Forms within the context of a portal application. In the next chapter, we'll examine some more technical considerations, such as standard architectures, keeping form submissions in context of one's portlet, inter-portlet communication, and process integration models.

REFERENCES

1. "Workplace Forms Embedding the Viewer in HTML Web Pages." http://www-128.ibm.com/developerworks/workplace/documentation/forms.

Chapter Thirteen

Next Steps with Workplace Forms

In this chapter, we expand on the foundation of IBM Workplace Forms knowledge we laid in Chapter 12 by examining several more technical considerations, including standard architectures, form pre-population, keeping form submissions in context of one's portlet, inter-portlet communication, and process integration models.

WORKPLACE FORMS ARCHITECTURES

You've learned about the components that make up the Workplace Forms product suite: IBM Workplace Forms Designer, IBM Workplace Forms Viewer, and IBM Workplace Forms Server. Let's take a look at how these products overlay onto standard three-tier architecture diagrams. Figure 13.1 shows a standard three-tier deployment of Workplace Forms. The figure depicts a rich-client (Workplace Forms Viewer) deployment.

In the client tier, we have the client PC with the Workplace Forms Viewer installed locally. As you learned in Chapter 12, a single installation lets you run the Workplace Forms Viewer off the desktop and also as a browser plug-in.

In the application tier, we have our portal and application server. Form-based applications are deployed to the server and typically use the Workplace Forms Server API to assist in form processing (pre-population, dynamic assembly, signature validation, notarization, and data extraction — topics we'll go into more

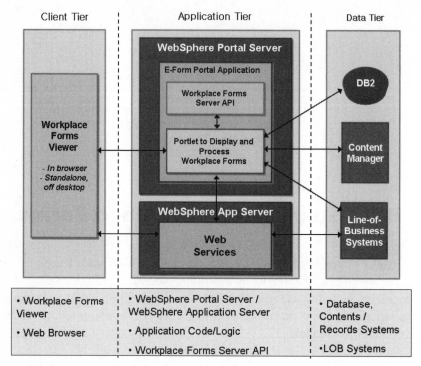

Figure 13.1: Standard three-tier deployment of Workplace Forms

detail about later). Web services are often used as an integration point to line-of-business (LOB) systems or workflow. The Workplace Forms Viewer provides native support for client-side Web services calls (you cam embed Web Services Description Language, or WSDL, directly into the Workplace Forms documents); however, depending on your solution architecture, application-to-service calls may also be used.

In the data tier, we find the standard array of database, workflow, content, and records management systems and LOB systems. It's important to emphasize here that the Workplace Form documents themselves are technology- and platform-agnostic; the fact that they are simply XML files gives us a wide degree of latitude. The document-centric nature of Workplace Forms makes the forms well-suited for transaction records, as well as easy to route and overlay onto enterprise workflow.

Zero-Footprint Support: Webform Server

A common customer scenario is the deployment of forms via both the Workplace Forms Viewer and the Webform Server (zero-footprint). Let's examine the architecture that arises in this case, as depicted in Figure 13.2.

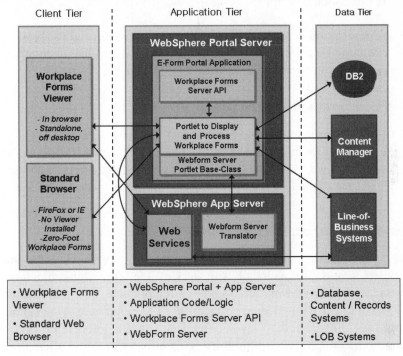

Figure 13.2: "Hybrid" Viewer and zero-footprint deployment of Workplace Forms

In the client tier of this deployment, end users can interact with Workplace Forms using standard browsers, such as Firefox and Internet Explorer, without having to download and install the Workplace Forms Viewer. The use of Webform Server in the application tier makes this possible.

In the application tier, note that our portlet now extends the base class portlet (also known as the Workplace Forms Portlet Framework) provided with Webform Server. This base class handles communications with Webform Server, which runs in a separate instance of WebSphere Application Server. By extending the base class, we gain transparent handling of translation to and from Extensible Forms Definition Language, or XFDL (HTML + JavaScript to/from XFDL/XFDL + XForms).

407

Note that we *do not* access the Webform Server from within our portlets via callouts; this isn't how Webform Server works. Instead, we extend the provided base classes, which handle communications with the Webform Server Translator component when necessary (we can detect whether users have the Workplace Forms Viewer installed or not).

A detailed description of how Webform Server works is beyond the scope of this chapter. For more information, see the Webform Server product documentation and the sample application provided with Workplace Forms Server.

Web Service Support and Webform Server

Note that even when using forms in a zero-footprint model, we still support the use of Web services for integration. The main difference is that without the Viewer, we can't support client-to-service calls; instead, we must use server-to-service calls to update the state of the form and then present the updated form to the user.

Offline or Disconnected Operation

At times, you may want to provide access to forms from within a portal but also let users save the forms locally and work offline. This is possible; however, the Workplace Forms Viewer then becomes a requirement, and your solution architecture must take into account a mechanism to either accept the submission of completed forms from the Viewer (which natively supports HTTP Post) or provide resume or upload handling if using zero-footprint. Most often, this functionality is built into your servlet or portlet.

PRE-POPULATING WORKPLACE FORMS

We typically define form template *pre-population* as loading an empty form with data. This data often is based on a user's role or identity and may include or be based on workflow. Pre-population is an important aspect of application design. In fact, more and more often these days, it is a baseline requirement in eForm solutions.

The definition of *form data* tends to vary greatly depending on context. The following are commonly considered form data and are hosted within the form data model or XForms model.

- information presented to users (e.g., available inventory, account status, personal data — employee number, address, and so on)

- business rule parameters (e.g., maximum expendable dollar amount, type and number of attachments required)

- user role or identity information

- images and branding; look and feel (e.g., color information)

- dynamically generated URI/URL (such as the ones we'll use to submit the form back to our portlet)

In some situations, you might also design forms that consider the following to be data:

- text strings
- Alt labels
- help messages

For simple forms, encapsulating all text strings into the data model provides a clean way to abstract the language from the user interface implementation to deliver multilingual forms. The downside to this approach is that form designers must carefully design the form layout so that it can accommodate strings of varying lengths (what may take five characters in English may require more than 20 in German, or vice versa). This consideration, combined with the fact that large numbers of binds can negatively affect performance, makes this approach realizable only for simple, short forms.

Pre-Population Example: Hello World Revisited

To show a simple example of form pre-population, we'll build on the hello world example we worked with in Chapter 12. We have three standard options for passing information into a form template:

- Use the Workplace Forms API or standard code to programmatically insert data into the form within the portlet.

- If using a JavaServer Page (JSP) and the Workplace Forms Viewer, provide a SCRIPT object containing a data instance. (The Viewer will merge this data into the form upon rendering.)

- Use an Internet Form Extension (IFX) — a Java or C code extension to perform client-side pre-population, typically from a local data source or repository. Note that in some situations, IFX may also be deployed on the server side.

Example: Form Template Pre-Population Using the Workplace Forms API

Starting with the hello world example from Chapter 12, let's implement a basic pre-population example. The first step is to install the Workplace Forms API into our development and runtime environments. For detailed information about this task, see the product documentation (available at *http://www-128.ibm.com/developerworks/workplace/documentation/forms*).

The next steps involve modifying the project and portlet code. First, we must include the Workplace Forms API libraries in our project. To do so, select the project in Rational Application Developer (RAD), and navigate to **Project > Properties > Java Build Path > Order and Export to** access the **Java Build Path Properties Order and Export** screen.

Add these four files from the Workplace Forms API installation:

- uwi_api_native.jar
- pe_api.jar
- pe_api_native.jar
- uwi_api.jar

The location of these files may vary depending on the specifics of your API installation. Figure 13.3 shows an example from our test project.

```
☐ 🗔 uwi_api_native.jar - C:\Program Files\IBM\Workplace Forms\Server\2.6\API\redist\msc32\PureEdge\70\java\classes
☐ 🗔 pe_api.jar - C:\Program Files\IBM\Workplace Forms\Server\2.6\API\redist\msc32\PureEdge\70\java\classes
☐ 🗔 pe_api_native.jar - C:\Program Files\IBM\Workplace Forms\Server\2.6\API\redist\msc32\PureEdge\70\java\classes
☐ 🗔 uwi_api.jar - C:\Program Files\IBM\Workplace Forms\Server\2.6\API\redist\msc32\PureEdge\70\java\classes
```

Figure 13.3: Required Workplace Forms Server API libraries in RAD

410

Next, we import the necessary classes into our portlet. Add the imports shown in Listing 13.1.

```
import com.PureEdge.DTK;
import com.PureEdge.IFSSingleton;
import com.PureEdge.error.UWIException;
import com.PureEdge.xfdl.FormNodeP;
import com.PureEdge.xfdl.XFDL;
```

Listing 13.1: Imports for Workplace Forms API example

At this point, it's a good idea to examine the Workplace Forms Designer's **Problems** view to make sure the classes are being resolved correctly. You should see warnings that the imports aren't currently used; this is to be expected.

Now, we can dig in and start to code. Note that we need to initialize the Workplace Forms API before we can use it. To do so, add the code shown in Listing 13.2 to the portlet's init method. You may want to rethrow or otherwise handle the exceptions. Feel free to do with them as you like based on your company's best practices for coding, logging, and error condition handling.

```
try {
        DTK.initialize("WorkplaceFormsDemo", "1.0.0", "7.0.0");
} catch (UWIException initE) {
        System.out.println("init(): api init exception occured: "+
        initE.toString());
} catch (Exception anE) {
        System.out.println("init(): exception occurred: "+
anE.toString());
}
```

Listing 13.2: Workplace Forms API initialization code snippet

Next, we need to declare some form-object related variables (Listing 13.3) within our portlet's doView method.

```
//Workplace Forms Objects
XFDL theXFDL = null;
FormNodeP theForm = null;
```

Listing 13.3: Form object declarations

Next, we use the Workplace Forms API to pre-populate the hello world form template with a name. In production, you'd likely base this name on login or single sign-on credentials, but for the purposes of this demo we'll simply use a static value. However, before we can use the API to pre-populate the form template, we need to change the structure of the portlet and JSP so that the form body is passed into the JSP page instead of being statically coded. The new approach involves four steps:

1. Load the form template.
2. Pre-populate the form template.
3. Write the updated form into a bean.
4. Set the form into the JSP.

For a complete description of and more information about the API, see the *Workplace Forms Server API Java User's Manual*, available at *http://www-128.ibm.com/developerworks/workplace/documentation/forms*.

Load the Form Template

We'll load the form from the file system using the Workplace Forms API. Recall that form templates are simply XML files and can be stored within a Web project, in a database or content management system, or, as in this case, on the server file system. Listing 13.4 shows a snippet of the readForm code.

```
theXFDL = IFSSingleton.getXFDL();
theForm = theXFDL.readForm("c:\\testform.xfdl", 0);
```

Listing 13.4: readForm code snippet

Pre-Populate the Form Template

We'll pre-populate the name "Cayce Marston" into the form (now resident in memory) using the API. When pre-populating a form, you can either set individual values or set an entire section of the data model. The latter approach is obviously more efficient if you need to pre-populate a lot of data into a form template. In either case, because our hello world example is an XForms-based form, we'll use the replaceXFormsInstance method in the Workplace Forms Server API. Listing 13.5 shows the method's parameters.

```
public void replaceXFormsInstance(
String theModelID,
String theNodeRef,
FormNodeP theNSNode,
java.io.Reader theReader,
boolean replaceRef
) throws UWIException;
```

Listing 13.5: replaceXForms Instance method

To push a data value into our form using the single-value approach, we need to know how to reference the target. Fortunately, the Workplace Forms Designer gives us an easy way to generate the required XPath statement. Launch the Designer, and open the Hello World form. Expand the **Instance** view, right-click **FIELD1**, and select **Copy Reference** from the shortcut menu, as shown in Figure 13.4.

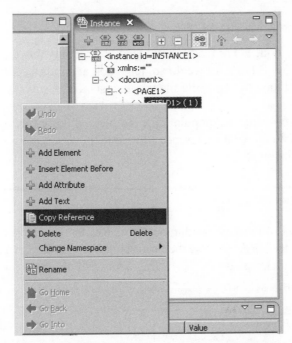

Figure 13.4: Obtaining an XPath reference in Workplace Forms Designer

An XPath reference to the FIELD1 node in the XForms model will be placed into the clipboard:

```
instance('INSTANCE1')/PAGE1/FIELD1
```

Upon inspection, you can see that this reference actually isn't too complex; given some familiarity with XPath, you could easily code such expressions by hand.

Now, we'll complete the pre-population code in RAD (Listing 13.6).

```
theForm.replaceXFormsInstance(
null,
"instance('INSTANCE1')/PAGE1/FIELD1",
        null,
new StringReader("<FIELD1>Cayce Marston</FIELD1>,
true);
```

Listing 13.6: replaceXFormsInstance method call for FIELD1

Okay, so far so good! We're ready to proceed with setting this form into our bean and then JSP. But before we do so, let's look at another code fragment that shows pre-population by replacing the whole instance.

As with the single-value pre-population example, we'll use the Workplace Forms Designer to obtain an XPath reference; this time, however, the reference is to the entire data instance:

```
instance('INSTANCE1')/.
```

Next, we assemble an instance within our StringReader. To understand the required structure of this instance, examine the **Source** view in the Workplace Forms Designer. Listing 13.7 shows the XML fragment we'll construct for pre-population.

```
<document>
            <PAGE1>
                    <FIELD1></FIELD1>
            </PAGE1>
        </document>
```

Listing 13.7: XML fragment used for form pre-population

Listing 13.8 shows the new pre-population code.

```
theForm.replaceXFormsInstance(
null,
        "",
        null,
        new StringReader("<document><PAGE1><FIELD1>"
+ "Cayce Marston" + "</FIELD1>"
+ "</PAGE1></document>"),
true);
```

Listing 13.8: replaceXFormsInstance method call for single value

Examining this code, you'll notice that we're assembling an XML instance inline within our method. Pretty messy. You may wonder why this approach is of value. There are two reasons.

Workplace Form documents can natively host XML data instances based on an external system interface. In enterprise systems, XML is being used more and more often as the language of choice for defining external interfaces. Developers are using XML schemas to define and standardize the interfaces for a broad range of systems, making it easier for systems to interoperate.

In addition, native form support for externally defined XML data enables "straight-through integration" to other systems. As such, if we were creating a form that was pre-populated using an ACORD 111 XML message (an insurance industry standard), we would design the form to host this data instance, and pre-population would become as simple as requesting an ACORD 111 message for a given customer and then merging it into the form template. You can also use the standard range of Document Object Model (DOM) and Simple API for XML (SAX) tools to define, create, and manipulate XML fragments within the portlet.

Write Updated Form into a Bean

We created a bean that contains a HashTable and provides simple accessor and mutator methods. Listing 13.9 shows the code used in the portlet to write the form into this bean. Note that we first obtain the form as a String, then pass it into the bean, and finally store it into the request.

415

```
//Obtain the form as a String
ByteArrayOutputStream baos = new ByteArrayOutputStream();
theForm.writeForm(baos, null, 0);
baos.flush();
String formString = baos.toString();

//Write the form into the bean
ProgrammingPortletsBean bean = new ProgrammingPortletsBean();
bean.setValue("formString", formString);

//Write the bean into the request
request.setAttribute("bean", bean);
```

Listing 13.9: Writing pre-populated form Into a bean

Set the Form into the JSP

Now, we'll access the bean within our JSP to set the form body at runtime. We need to add the first snippet to the JSP and then replace the body of the hello world form with the getValue call to our bean.

1. Include the bean:

```
<jsp:useBean class="programming_with_portlets.ProgrammingPortlets
Bean" id="bean" scope="request" />
```

2. Write the form body into the JSP:

```
<SCRIPT language="XFDL" id="XFDLForm" type="application/vnd.xfdl;
wrapped=comment"> <!--   <%=bean.getValue("formString") %> -->
```

At last, we're ready to deploy and test our code. When we display the portlet, you'll see that the name has been pre-populated, as shown in Figure 13.5. Recall in this case that we used a static value for the name. In production, the name value could be based on authenticated session information or other externally provided data (e.g., from a database, Lightweight Directory Access Protocol server, line-of-business system).

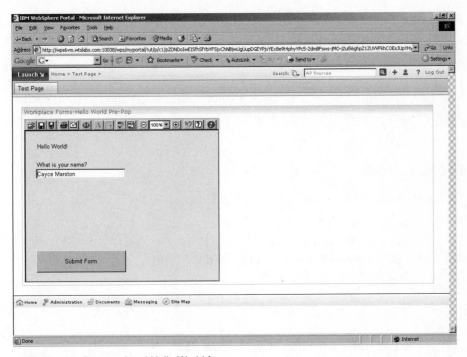

Figure 13.5: Pre-populated Hello World form

KEEPING FORM SUBMISSION WITHIN CONTEXT OF YOUR PORTAL APPLICATION

Our next step is to build on the concept of pre-population to permit us to keep form submission "in context" of our portal applications. When designing a form to be submitted to a servlet, the form designer typically sets the submission target (http://...) directly within a button in the form. When the user clicks the button, the form document (or specified form data) is submitted via HTTP Post to the servlet.

In a portlet, we can take much the same approach; however, given that we don't know the URL in advance, we need to design our forms with this fact in mind. We'll set the URL that defines the submission target dynamically at runtime — another application of form pre-population (recall our discussion about what is considered form data). Let's build on the hello world example to show how you can do this.

417

Example: Setting a Form Submission URL from a Portlet

Because you've already seen an example of using the Workplace Forms API to set a value into the XForms model directly, this time we'll apply the approach of using a script block within our JSP to pre-populate the form template. Let's start by subdividing this task into the coding work within RAD and the form design work within the Workplace Forms Designer.

STEPS IN RAD

We'll perform the following steps in RAD:S

1. Generate the URI.
2. Pass the URI into the JSP.
3. Handle form submission and read in the form.
4. Modify the form view JSP.
5. Create a "Submission Received" results page.

Generate the URI and Pass It into Zthe JSP

The first code modification is to create a URI. There's nothing out of the ordinary here. As we did in the pre-population example, we'll use a simple bean to pass the URI value into the JSP. Recall, though, that instead of using the API to insert the value directly, this time we'll provide a script block that the Viewer will load at runtime. Listing 13.10 shows the code used to generate the URI and provide it to our JSP.

```
//Generate a submission URI, add the "save" action, and write it into
the bean
PortletURL submitURL = response.createActionURL();
submitURL.setPortletMode(PortletMode.VIEW);
submitURL.setParameter("submit","submit");
bean.setValue("submitURI", submitURL.toString());
```

Listing 13.10: Generating the form submission URL and storing in bean

418

Handle Form Submission and Read in the Form

For the first time in our forms examples, we'll modify the processAction method. We'll read in the action and then set the state for the doView method based on the action indicated. For example, if the action is submitForm, we'll set a request attribute that will display the appropriate response within doView. This might be a "submission received" type of response or a request for more information.

Be aware, however, that although it's a general rule to try to validate as much form input as possible before submission, in some cases form data can be validated only upon submission, and thus round-tripping may be required. This is sometimes the case in the banking and insurance industries, where server-side rules engines are used for more complex validation.

Modify the Form View JSP

We add the following line to the OBJECT section of the JSP to trigger runtime pre-population.

```
<PARAM NAME="instance_1" value="PORTLET_DATA_SCRIPT1 xforms;
replace=&quot;instance('SUBMISSIONINFO')/.&quot;"/>
```

Next, we add the script block containing the pre-population instance:

```
<SCRIPT id="PORTLET_DATA_SCRIPT1" type="application/vnd.xfdl;
wrapped=comment">
```

```
<!--<data xmlns:xforms="http://www.w3.org/2002/xforms">
<URI><%= bean.getValue("submitURL")%></URI>          </data>-->
</SCRIPT>
```

The addition to the OBJECT section indicates that we'll pass a data instance to the Viewer at runtime (as specified in the SCRIPT section with id=PORTLET_DATA_SCRIPT1). Note how we use the same bean to pass in our generated submission URL. For more information about embedding the Workplace Forms Viewer information, refer to the documentation.

Create a "Submission Received" Results Page

We've created a new response JSP that displays a simple "submission received" message. In practice, you can return whatever type of response you desire. Listing 13.11 shows the code from the response JSP for our example.

```
<%@ taglib uri="http://java.sun.com/portlet" prefix="portlet"%>
<%@ page language="java" contentType="text/html; charset=ISO-8859-1"
pageEncoding="ISO-8859-1" session="false"%>
<portlet:defineObjects />
<P>
        <H2>IBM Workplace Forms Hello World Example</H2> <BR>
        <H4>Thank-you! Your Form Submission Has Been Received.</H4>
</P>
```

Listing 13.11: "Submission received" JSP markup

Steps in Workplace Forms Designer

We'll use the Workplace Forms Designer to perform the following steps:

1. Modify the XForms model.
2. Modify the submission button.
3. Bind the submission button to the XForms model.

Modify the XForms Model

To store the submission URI, we'll create a data instance within the XForms model. In general, it's considered a best practice to define any data that will be pre-populated within the forms data model or XForms model. In the **Instance** view, the new instance appears as shown in Figure 13.6.

Figure 13.6: New SUBMISSIONINFO XForms instance

This corresponds to the XML shown in Listing 13.12 within the **Source** view.

```
<xforms:instance id="SUBMISSIONINFO" xmlns="">
<data>
                <URI></URI>
        </data>
</xforms:instance>
```

Listing 13.12: SUBMISSIONINFO instance XML

You can see that the generated XML is in fact quite simple. Although the most common way to add a new instance is by using the **Instance** view, more experienced form designers can add or edit the XForms model directly in the **Source** view.

Modify the Submission Button

Next, we'll change the type of our submission button so that when a user clicks the button, the form is submitted to the server. To accomplish this functionality, select the button, and then expand the tree in the **Properties** view. Locate the **type** setting under the **General** heading. Then select the **submit** value as shown in Figure 13.7, and press Enter. (If you want the result to appear in the same window, select type **done** instead.) You can experiment with this setting on your own.

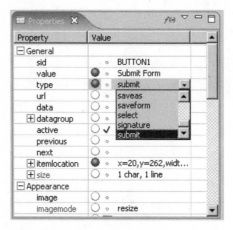

Figure 13.7: Setting the button type in Workplace Forms Designer

Bind the Submission Button to the XForms Model

Now, we need to establish a link between the target for our submission button and the URI element in our XForms model. To do so, we'll write a custom "compute" inside the form button. An in-depth discussion of how this works and why we take this approach is beyond the scope of this chapter; however, the basic principle is that we'll write a "declarative compute" inside the submission button that obtains the desired URL value from the XForms model. To configure the button, take these steps:

1. Select the button on the form canvas.

2. Click the **Source** tab to switch to the **Source** view. Once the form is loaded, you'll see the XML representing the button.

3. Add the XML shown in Listing 13.13 to the compute attribute's url element. If the url element doesn't exist, create it. Your button text should appear as shown. On the URL line, note the addition of the "compute" that contains a reference to our XForms model. We've replaced the quotation marks used in our XPath statement with """ so that the statement can be parsed correctly.

```
<button sid="BUTTON1">
    <itemlocation>
    <x>20</x>
    <y>262</y>
    <width>208</width>
    <height>49</height>
    </itemlocation>
    <value>Submit Form</value>
    <type>submit</type>
    <url compute="get('instance(&quot;SUBMISSIONINFO&quot;)/URI', '',
'xforms')"></url>
</button>
```

Listing 13.13: XML markup for submission button

A final comment is that you can also use a "pull" approach to load parameters specified in the JSP into the form. You do so by using the param function. As is often the case, there are design-time tradeoffs to consider with this approach. The benefit of centralizing the submission URL in a single place in the data model is that you can reference it from multiple submission buttons if, for example, they were provided on multiple pages.

Testing Form Submission

Now that we've made the necessary changes, let's redeploy and test out pre-population example. Figure 13.8 shows the form upon loading.

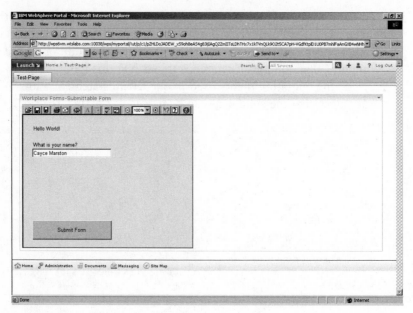

Figure 13.8: Form before submission

When we click the **Submit Form** button, we see the JSP shown in Figure 13.9.

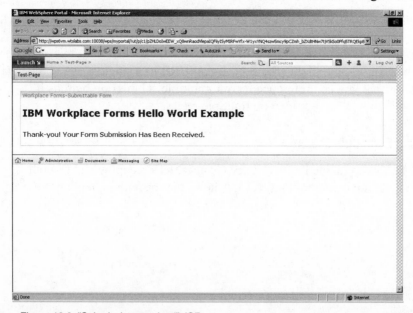

Figure 13.9: "Submission received" JSP

In a real-world application, the form submission would be processed and based on the form and related form business process, and a nontrivial response would be presented to the user.

FORM PROCESSING AND DATA EXTRACTION

The next logical step is to discuss form submission handling and processing in greater depth. Once a user fills out and submits a form, what happens next? How do we process the form and integrate it with other systems? We'll break down this question into four parts:

- processing submitted forms
- signature validation and form notarization
- data extraction
- data integration

Let's drill down into each of these topics.

Processing Submitted Forms

Now that we've received a form submission within our portlet, what we do with it depends on the requirements of our application. Fortunately for us as developers, the Workplace Forms API is a powerful tool for processing form documents. Common activities include

- validating form signatures
- applying a server-side timestamp and/or signature
- extracting form data

You may recall, however, that the API provides methods that are form-centric and don't involve external systems. The Workplace Forms API can help us to extract form data or obtain the form document; however, as developers, we'll rely on standard code, connectors, adapters, and Web services to integrate with external systems.

Signature Validation and Form Notarization

Developers often apply digital signatures in forms to "lock down" either all or part of the document. IBM Workplace Forms provides flexible signature

425

technology, allowing multiple signatures, out-of-order and sectional signing, and whole document signing. If signed form content is tampered with, the signature is invalidated and the tampering can be detected using one of these methods:

- validating signatures with the Workplace Forms API
- launching the form in the Workplace Forms Viewer
- rendering the form with Webform Server

In production environments where data tampering and security are concerns, programmatic validation of form signatures is important. Listing 13.14 shows how we can programmatically validate the signatures on a form within our portlet.

```
//Validate Form Signatures
if(theForm.verifyAllSignatures(false) == FormNodeP.UFL_SIGS_OK){
    System.out.println("Form signatures were valid");
}else{
    System.out.println("Form signatures were invalid");
    throw new Exception("Warning: This form has been tampered with; one
or more form signatures are invalid.");
}
```

Listing 13.14: Code snippet to validate form signatures with the API

The Workplace Forms API makes this task easy for us; we simply call the verifyAllSignatures method on the form object and test the result. If we wanted to at this point, we could take more granular action or initiate exception processing within the application. The getSignatureVerificationStatus method offers another approach; for a complete description of this alternative, see the API documentation.

A brief comment about notarization before we move on: *Server-side form notarization* is a term used to describe the application of a digital signature to a form on the server side. Quite often, this application takes place upon form submission, after validation of user signatures. This technique provides an added layer of security because the signature and timestamp are applied on the server side. Note, though, that the form must be designed to be signed in this fashion.

Data Extraction

Following form submission and signature validation, it's a common practice to extract form data and provide it to one or more additional systems. To extend our example, let's extract the form data instance and obtain the form as a String. The snippets of code presented here will let us do so in several different ways.

Extracting a Data Instance with the Workplace Forms API

We can choose which instance to extract and also where we'd like the data to be stored — in a stream, file, or writer. In this case, we'll extract the instance INSTANCE1, which contains the name entered into our form. Listing 13.15 shows the code to extract the form data.

```
//Write the data instance to the file system
theForm.extractXFormsInstance(null, "instance('INSTANCE1')/.", true,
false, null, "c:\\datainstance.txt");

//Write the data instance to a StringWriter
StringWriter formData = new StringWriter();
theForm.extractXFormsInstance(null, "instance('INSTANCE1')/. ", true,
false, null, formData);
```

Listing 13.15: Code snippets to extract form data

Once again, we can use the Workplace Forms Designer to obtain the XPath reference to the desired instance — a nice feature for those who aren't experts on XPath expressions.

Extracting a Data Element with the Workplace Forms API

Extracting a data element is much the same as extracting an entire instance. We simply provide a different XPath reference. The code in Listing 13.16 extracts the name field.

```
//Write the data instance to a StringWriter
StringWriter formData = new StringWriter();
theForm.extractXFormsInstance(null,
"instance('INSTANCE1')/PAGE1/FIELD1", true, false, null, formData);
```

Listing 13.16: Code snippet to extract an XForms model element

However, if we print out this result, we'll see that it appears as follows:

```
<FIELD1>Cayce Marston</FIELD1>
```

If you want only the actual value and not the start and end tags, it's suggested that you write a utility method to select the substring. Listing 13.17 shows a simple example.

```
private String getElementValue(String XMLElement) throws Exception {
int start = XMLElement.indexOf('>')+1;
        int end = XMLElement.indexOf('<', start);
        return XMLElement.substring(start, end);
}
```

Listing 13.17: Sample method for removing start and end tags

Calling getElementValue on the contents of our StringWriter results in the following:

```
Cayce Marston
```

Extracting Form Data with XML or String Parsing

For simple applications — where you're not interested in signature validation, pre-population, dynamic form assembly, or other more advanced applications of the technology — it's possible to use standard code to manipulate the form as XML (via DOM or SAX) or even as a string without using the Workplace Forms API. Take the getElementValue method shown above as a simple example. Note, however, that for production environments we strongly recommend using the IBM Workplace Forms API.

Data Integration

Now that you've seen several approaches to extracting form data, let's discuss what we can do with that data. The key point here is that we can do pretty much anything! At this point, we have the ability to gather and validate data and extract it from a form. As application developers, we can provide the forms or selected form data to one or more systems, initiate or interact with business processes or workflow, and persist the form document as a record. The implementation details depend on solution needs and the products and systems involved; with 100 percent native XML documents based on a W3C open standard (XForms), we have a high degree of platform independence and freedom.

INTER-PORTLET COMMUNICATION AND WORKPLACE FORMS

Inter-portlet communication can play a variety of roles within Workplace Forms Portal applications. You can use the standard means of passing information between portlets in conjunction with pre-population techniques. One or more of these portlets can be used to display a form; however, some may be used for informational display purposes and may not contain a Workplace Form. Here are some examples where you might use inter-portlet communication:

- client list portlet
- form view portlet
- form workbasket
- marketing/promotions portlet
- help portlet
- form template list portlet

For example, a portlet might display a list of clients. One action provided in this portlet might be to initiate a new purchase order. By doing so, you could

- cause a purchase order template form to be loaded, pre-populated with the selected client's information, and presented in a form view portlet

- cause a purchase order template form to be loaded, pre-populated, and added to a form workbasket

In a self-serve/kiosk environment, you could provide contextual marketing materials based on the data entered into the form — for example, promotions or up-sell campaigns. For instance, if a purchase order exceeded a certain dollar amount, you could provide information about a one-time offer or discounts to become a platinum member. If the value was below the threshold, you might offer only silver-tier membership or benefits.

The concept of a separate help portlet makes sense for complex forms. A **Help** or **Detailed Instructions** button on the form could trigger the presentation of information based on the current page, section, or field within the form.

WORKPLACE FORMS/PROCESS INTEGRATION MODELS

Although an in-depth examination of this topic is beyond the scope of this book, it's important to at least touch on the common models for form and process integration. The standard Workplace Form and process integration models include the following:

- initiation of a process upon form submission
- use of a form for a human task in a long-running process
- use of callouts to claim tasks and update task state

Initiation of a Process Upon Form Submission

The most common approach is to kick off or initiate a new process upon successful form submission. The following steps are typical within the portlet.

1. Read in form submission.

2. Validate form signatures.

3. Extract any form data instance(s) needed and provide as needed.

4. Store entire form into the data tier (database, content/records management system); obtain key/reference to form document.

5. Call out to business process server to initiate new process. Provide required parameters, which may include

   - extracted form data
   - reference to stored form document
   - entire form document (can be heavy-weight)

Use of a Form for a Human Task in a Long-Running Process

Another common scenario is the case where human data entry into a Workplace Form constitutes part of a long-running process. In this case, the following steps are typical within the portlet(s):

1. Present a list of tasks/forms.
2. Upon claiming the task/initiating form filling:
   a. Update the task state.
   b. Present the form to the user.
3. Process the form submission.
4. Store the form and/or form data.
5. Update the task state.

Use of Callouts to Claim Tasks and Update Task State

Yet another approach is to partition functionality and design the form so that there is a higher level of task granularity. For example, instead of having a task such as "Fill Out Application Form," we might want to subdivide the form-filling process into multiple steps:

1. Fill out initial form questions.
2. Access rules engine; get rating information.
3. [Supplemental Form] Fill out aviation questionnaire.
4. [Supplemental Form] Fill out credit-card billing application.
5. [Supplemental Form] Fill out direct debit application.
6. Obtain applicant signature.
7. Obtain approval signature.
8. Store completed form.

It may be desirous to assign states to each of these steps and provide insight into how many processes are in each state. Multiple approaches exist for updating task state:

- Submit the form to the server side/portlet between each step and call out to update the task state.

- Make calls to a Web service façade to the process server either directly from the Viewer (client-to-service calls) or from the server side (Webform Server portlet/standard portlet).

SUMMARY

In this chapter, you've expanded your knowledge of using IBM Workplace Forms with Portal and added several additional tools to your toolbox. This chapter and the previous one are, however, only the tip of the iceberg. Intended to give you a foundation of knowledge about Workplace Forms, they are just a starting point for Portal and Forms application developers. The options and possibilities for using this 100 percent native XML-based component technology within Portal are as broad and varied as our customers' requirements.

Chapter Fourteen

Enhancing the User Experience with Ajax

There's an enormous interest in Ajax in the Web programming community. Ajax warrants its own dedicated-topic conferences, and in other technical meetings it consumes many tracks and sessions. Dozens of books dedicated to Ajax topics are available, and new ones are debuting with amazing frequency. Ajax is clearly the hot topic in Web design and development.

With so much attention already being paid to Ajax, we certainly won't try to condense that body of knowledge into a single chapter here. We will, however, discuss in some detail the intersection of Ajax and WebSphere Portal. We'll begin with a brief introductory discussion of Ajax, including its history and evolution. We'll describe what Ajax is and describe the alternatives to Ajax available to help develop a more interactive portal user experience. With that background, we'll look at how you can use Ajax within a Portal environment, including some potential issues for which we need to be cautious. Last, we'll discuss future enhancements to the Portal environment and the tooling frameworks available to better integrate Ajax.

INTRODUCTION TO AJAX

The name Ajax is attributed to Jesse James Garrett of Adaptive Path, LLC. In his article "Ajax: A New Approach to Web Applications" (*http://adaptivepath.com/publications/essays/archives/000385.php*), Garrett defines Ajax as shorthand for "Asynchronous JavaScript + XML" and describes this approach to creating Web applications that deliver a more interactive user experience. Ajax enhances the user experience by providing the capability to dynamically (and asynchronously) update only portions of a Web page without incurring a full page refresh. This concept is relatively simple, but it allows for dramatic improvements in the user interface.

Ajax isn't a new technology or product but an approach to Web application design that includes client-side function through JavaScript that uses an XMLHttpRequest object to asynchronously retrieve data from a server and then update the Document Object Model (DOM) of the previously rendered page with that data to give a richer user experience. At this point, probably everyone who has been even remotely interested in Ajax has referenced Google Suggest and Google Maps as the standard examples of how a richer user experience can be achieved.

Microsoft initially defined the XMLHttpRequest object as an ActiveX object in Internet Explorer. It is available as a native object in Mozilla 1.0, Safari 1.2, and later versions of several other Web browsers and is currently standardized at W3C (*http://www.w3.org/TR/XMLHttpRequest*). It is through this object that JavaScript makes asynchronous HTTP requests. We'll look at the mechanics of using Ajax later in this chapter.

Predecessor Techniques

Although Ajax has exploded on the scene in recent years, techniques for accomplishing similar results have been around significantly longer. One popular approach used frames, which were introduced some 10 years ago. With frames, developers can segment a Web page into multiple parts and manage each part as a separate document with its own source URL. The component frames are relatively independent, with each executing its own requests to the source server for its content.

Of course, the most popular use for frames was to allow the easy aggregation of content from different servers at the browser. But how and where a frame's content is rendered can be controlled through the initial markup generated for the frame and through JavaScript.

With that capability in hand, a technique for more dynamic user interaction, "the hidden frame technique," was created. With this approach, you define a frame in the page markup such that it itself does not render content to the page (you can do this by setting the frame's width or height to zero pixels). The other frame or frames in the Web page's frame set are responsible for rendering the page content. The hidden frame is used as the communications vehicle to the server defined as its source URL. Then, through the use of JavaScript, user interaction on the Web page could cause the frame to be refreshed, and the content returned from the server request by the hidden frame could be used to dynamically update some portion of the rendered content on the page.

The hidden frame technique produced a user interaction similar to Ajax, with the following characteristics:

- A user action causes a client/server interaction running in what appears to the user to be the background.

- From the client perspective, the server interaction is asynchronous, letting the user continue to interact with the Web page while the process is executed.

- The server response doesn't replace the Web page, nor does the server request update the browser's current address or history. This fact suggests implications to the relationship between the "state" of what the user sees in the browser and the URL address identified as the current page. We'll discuss this point in the context of bookmarks and the back button later in the chapter.

- JavaScript is automatically invoked when the server response is received, and through direct manipulation of objects in the DOM, the Web page is updated in place.

A further refinement of the hidden frame technique used an iframe instead of a frame and frame set. The iframe tag let the hidden frame be more easily (and even dynamically) created.

These developments led the way to what we now know as Ajax.

Using Ajax

Ajax represents the next evolution in these techniques for an enhanced user experience through asynchronous client/server interaction.

The mechanics of enhanced client/server interaction took another step forward with Microsoft's introduction of the XMLHttp object. By using the XMLHttp object through JavaScript, developers no longer needed the hidden frame (or iframe) to act as the client agent. They could use the XMLHttp object to generate the HTTP request to the server, check on return status codes, and retrieve the returned content. Mozilla adopted a similar approach and created an object called XMLHttpRequest to perform the same function.

To keep the discussion simple, we'll refer to the XMLHttpRequest object in the remainder of this chapter, although we in fact mean either depending on the browser. In fact, in the absence of a finalized standard, something similar to the JavaScript code shown in Listing 14.1 is typically used to create a new instance of this object.

```
function createReq() {
    var xmlHttpReq;
    if (window.XMLHttpRequest) {
        xmlHttpReq = new XMLHttpRequest();
    } else if (window.ActiveXObject) {
        xmlHttpReq = new ActiveXObject("Microsoft.XMLHTTP");
    }
    return xmlHttpReq;
}
```

Listing 14.1: Creating an instance of the XMLHttpRequest object

You use the XMLHttpRequest object to make asynchronous calls to a server from the client JavaScript, check the result status, and retrieve the response data.

AJAX PROCESSING FLOW

The sequence diagram shown in Figure 14.1 represents the fundamental execution flow for Ajax processing. From a quick glance, you can see that the execution is fairly straightforward, with a limited number of interactions to consider. However, as with any significant JavaScript processing, we must be extremely careful when considering browser (and browser level) differences. We'll talk about this a little more when we discuss Ajax toolkits later in the chapter.

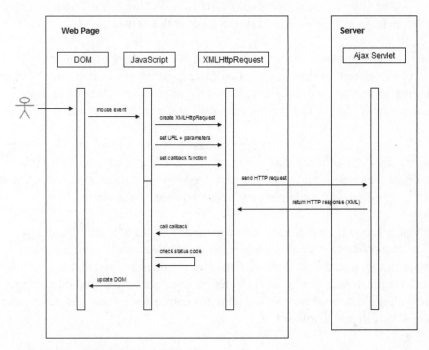

Figure 14.1: AJAX processing flow

Let's walk through the Ajax process flow with an example in mind. Consider the simple case where the user makes a choice through a process of continuously scoping the final selection. For example, say we have a Web site that requires the user to select an investment fund. We might want the user first to select a type of fund — stock fund, mutual fund, or index fund. Then, having made that selection, the user can choose a fund family and finally a specific fund. Given this scenario, without using Ajax we'd either (a) load all possible fund types, families, and funds with the initial page load so that the user can make his or her selection without further server interactions; or (b) load the fund types with the initial page load and then, once the user makes that selection, perform a server request and a page refresh that loads only the fund families for the selected type (and then repeat the process for the funds within the selected family).

Both of these approaches are valid and have their own benefits and shortcomings. For the first method, the benefit is that we don't have intermediate page refreshes, and using data available on the client means we can develop a more interactive user experience. The shortcoming, of course, is that we can have a potentially very large amount of data to download to the client, which adds to the page refresh time as well the load on the network and server.

For the second approach, the opposite is true. We minimize the amount of data that gets transmitted to the client by deferring what data is loaded until filtering selections have been made, but we give up the interactive nature of the user experience by forcing a full page refresh during the selection process.

Ajax blends the best of these two approaches by letting us defer the request to the server for data until the user has made the filtering selections. But those subsequent requests to the server are performed in the background and without a page refresh to let us maintain a very interactive user experience.

With that processing in place, we can choose any user interface behavior we want to obtain the user input and show the results. We can implement this example simply as three drop-down lists whose values are updated via the Ajax calls as the previous list option is selected. It can be a very visual interaction, where rolling the mouse over an image representing a selection updates another selection list already displayed.

As we walk through the Ajax process flow with this example in mind, notice that the selection of the UI representation of the data isn't a critical part of the process flow.

1. A user typically will trigger the Ajax processing to begin by interacting with a UI component.

2. An event handler will have been added to the UI to trigger a JavaScript function call to perform the server call.

3. That JavaScript function first creates an instance of the XMLHttpRequest object.

4. Next, the source URL is set on the XMLHttpRequest object; any required query parameters are also added to the URL. In our example, we'd either add a parameter named "type" with the value of the selected

fund type or add a parameter named "family" with the value of the selected fund family. Our server can then respond with either a list of fund families or funds, depending on the request.

5. Before we send the request to the server, the callback JavaScript function needs to be identified. This is the function that the XMLHttpRequest will call (asynchronously) when the server response is received.

6. The HTTP request to the server is sent.

7. The server handles the request and responds back with, typically, XML data.

8. The XMLHttpRequest object gets the response and calls the JavaScript function that was set as the callback.

9. The callback checks the HTTP status code (a 200 indicates success).

10. Last, the callback retrieves the response data from the XMLHttpRequest and updates the DOM object with the new data.

Ajax: Advantages, Strengths, and Weaknesses

You can see that Ajax offers significant advantages for dramatically improving the user experience. The strength of Ajax revolves around getting the right data to the client. Later, we'll briefly discuss some competing technologies, such as Flex, which places a heavier emphasis on enhancing the user experience through media.

As we've discussed, using an approach such as Ajax provides the capability to deliver data only when needed, thereby reducing the burden on the server and network. Similarly, context-dependent data can be delivered to the Web page and updated in place in a dynamic manner that gives the user a highly interactive experience. With the interest in Ajax at a near fever pitch, there are several development toolkits available and open-source initiatives underway (e.g., Open Ajax) to provide tooling support and Ajax-enabled UI components/

These advantages are hard to argue against. But what are the downsides to the use of Ajax? It's hard to imagine amid all the industry hype associated with Ajax, but there are considerations to take into account.

- Dynamic HTML (DHTML) is an integral part of Ajax, and large JavaScript libraries are a typical part of an organized approach to Ajax, whether through homegrown frameworks or Ajax toolkits.

- Integrated development environments (IDEs) with debugging capability are not generally available for the client-side components of Ajax.

- Separation of the client state and the page URL (and history) disrupts the effective use of the back button or bookmarks.

- Accessibility becomes more difficult as the user experience becomes more visual and more dynamic.

- A focus in good design is the separation of content and presentation. Many believe Ajax promotes the presentation within JavaScript.

- Depending on the server-side function, Ajax may segment the server logic in unnatural ways to allow some coordination between the Ajax processing that resides in specific function services and the Web application navigation state.

- Many security considerations with Ajax applications are the same for non-Ajax Web applications. However, the use of Ajax does require that we assess any added security considerations. There are issues of authorization associated with executing remote services, issues associated with protecting the user data being transmitted between the client and the server, and finally security implications with executing JavaScript function.

- If Ajax applications are designed poorly and create many small requests to the server, they will create additional load on the server, and the network latency will become obvious. Depending on the size of the JavaScript code on the client and the amount of XML processing, performance issues may also arise on the client due to the added memory consumption or processing required.

Later in the chapter, you'll see that using Ajax within Portal introduces some additional considerations. We'll look in more detail at issues of access control, security, portlets as Ajax servers, and client/server state synchronization.

All things considered, Ajax offers enormous benefit, and these potential weaknesses can be managed appropriately. The industry interest in Ajax is all but ensuring that emerging toolkits, frameworks, and tooling will minimize these concerns. Ajax initiatives are busy creating Ajax components that can be incorporated into Web applications with minimal effort.

Alternatives to Ajax

The goal of providing a highly interactive user experience on the Web isn't limited to Ajax. Several alternative technologies provide similar function. Perhaps the best known is Macromedia Flash. Unlike Ajax, which uses technologies that are basic components of Web browsers (Cascading Style Sheets, DOM, JavaScript — i.e., DHTML), Flash relies on a browser plug-in that provides its runtime processing engine. Flash is so prevalent that most browsers are installed with this plug-in already available.

For client-side processing, Flash relies on ActionScripts, which are analogous to JavaScript that executes on Flash-based movie content. Flash also provides the capability for client processing to access server data asynchronously. Flex uses the same browser plug-in runtime as Flash and is geared toward application development (as opposed to media content).

As alternatives, Flex and Ajax both provide great benefit to interactive Web applications. From a runtime perspective, Flex has a bit of an advantage over Ajax in that it is rendered at the client by the Flash Player (browser plug-in) and not by the browser. So, it is (more) platform-independent. From a runtime perspective, Flex also comes with an IDE that features debugging. However, efforts such as Open Ajax (*http://www.zimbra.com/community/open_ajax.html*) and the availability of a number of development toolkits, such as Dojo, are quickly eliminating these differences. Flex has some comparative disadvantages, too. Development is more complicated, requiring skill beyond more mainstream JavaScript skill, and it doesn't allow the popular "mashups" that integrate two different applications via direct manipulation of the DOM to create a new, composite application (for an example of a mashup, see *http://www.housingmaps.com*, which combines Google Maps with houses you can buy from Craigslist).

Although Flex is a popular choice for creating interactive Web applications, several other tools and technologies participate in this space. We'll mention a couple of them here and leave the details of their relative strengths and weaknesses to other sources. Two enhanced markup languages aimed at creating dynamic user interfaces are XML User Interface Language (XUL) and Extensible Application Markup Language (XMAL). XUL is available for Mozilla browsers, and XAML is available in Microsoft's Avalon.

Ajax Server Response Format

As we mentioned previously, the name Ajax itself references XML as the right data format for the server response. However, you can use other format options as long as the server response data format matches the expected format of the JavaScript that will process the results.

XML

XML is clearly the most common format for data transmission and is found often in Ajax implementations. Because of its popularity, many existing servers that support this format are already available. Extending a site to use that server function is made easier because the resulting data format can be readily consumed in an Ajax function.

Let's look at the other options and consider the alternatives.

HTML Fragments

If a server returns an HTML fragment, you may be able to include that markup directly in the DOM by setting an object's (e.g., a div's) innerHTML. The advantage of this approach is that the client-side processing to include the data is simple. The obvious disadvantage is that the markup included in the response HTML fragment, if it is not carefully constructed, can cause serious formatting problems in the rendered page. In Chapter 4, we referred to this technique as Asynchronous JavaScript and HTML, or AJAH.

JSON

JavaScript Object Notation (JSON) is a lightweight data format based on the JavaScript syntax. Like XML, JSON allows for the nesting of data elements. JSON is based on two element structures: an object and an array. The advantage to using JSON is that because the syntax is based on JavaScript, it's easy to incorporate JSON data into the Web page. You can simply use the eval function in JavaScript to parse the JSON text and generate an object.

Another advantage of JSON is that it is less verbose than XML. Representing the same content in JSON requires fewer bytes of data than in XML. Also, several tools are available to assist in the encoding and decoding of JSON data into various server languages. JSON is a bit less readable than XML, and manually creating JSON text can be a somewhat more error-prone process than for XML because the syntax relies on commas, quotes, and brackets.

AJAX IN THE PORTAL ENVIRONMENT

Chapter 4 introduced the topic of Ajax in the context of the Portal environment. Ajax is somewhat complicated in this environment because we want to have server function that provides a specific service and returns, typically, XML data. This idea doesn't fit well into the existing portlet model defined by the Java Portlet Specification V1.0.

Portlets render content fragments that are aggregated with the theme markup, the skin markup, and the other portlets on the page. The Ajax server would optimally respond back with a specific data set in a format that is easily consumed by the client. And, naturally, we'd like this function to run in the context of the Web application and share in its user profile information, session information, and security context.

The best approach for this today is to deploy a servlet in the portlet Web application to act as the Ajax server. We can define it to return responses in the data format of our choice without dealing with complicating issues of aggregation and theme content. By deploying the servlet in the portlet WAR file, we enable the servlet to share session data with the portlets.

However, the servlet won't have access to the portlet context. Portlet objects such as portlet preferences, portlet request, and portlet response aren't available, nor are the render parameters, portlet mode, or window state.

Let's look at the flow of an Ajax-enabled portlet again. We saw this in Chapter 3. Figure 14.2 shows that on the first page request, all portlets are rendered, including our Ajax portlet A (steps 1–3). Now the user interacts with portlet A, and as a result portlet A wants to update parts of its markup by sending an asynchronous XMLHttpRequest call to retrieve XML data from the servlet. The JavaScript may update that response XML data directly into a DOM object, or it may need to first generate specific markup based on the response XML data and insert that markup into the current browser DOM.

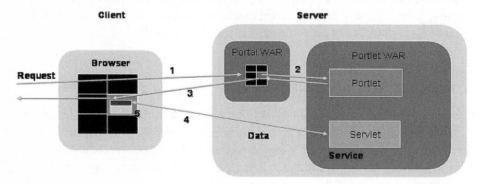

Figure 14.2: AJAX request served by a servlet and rendered on the browser via avaScript

We'll look at toolkit assistance for the generation of the JavaScript processing function as well as the client-side logic for generating the markup.

Ajax in Portal

WebSphere Portal embraces the notion of the Ajax-like function of enhancing the user experience while helping to manage server load. With Portal 6.0, two obvious areas demonstrate this. The first is the context menus that are part of the page navigation in the theme, and the second is the context menus in the portlet title bar.

Okay, we may have misrepresented things a little by calling this section "Ajax in Portal" because neither of the components we've just identified, strictly speaking, use Ajax. But that distinction is a matter of implementation. The key is that both components provide an interactive user experience and defer some workload until the data is really needed, but when it is needed, the data is retrieved dynamically without causing a page refresh.

Let's consider these two components. First, the default portal theme defines the context menu for page navigation. When the user clicks the navigation main menu icon, an asynchronous call is made to the server to retrieve the page navigation data that is used by JavaScript to build a navigation menu displayed over the page. Aside from the user interaction advantages, this approach saves some real estate on the portal page by hiding the navigation links until the user needs them. Also, the navigation links aren't built by default when the page is created, so if they're not needed, we save the cost of the server processing and data handling of that content.

Similarly, the portlet skin has a single icon for the portlet menu. Again, this is an asynchronous call to the server to determine which portlet menu items should be available for the specific portlet; the data is prepared and returned, and JavaScript shows the context menu for the function when requested. This approach saves server processing because the portlet container must determine for each portlet on the page which menu options are applicable. That processing will be performed only when actually needed.

Consider also the portlet palette and people palette introduced in Portal 6.0. Neither of these represents an Ajax-like interaction. They are not asynchronous, nor do they use XML. However, they do perform DOM manipulation and involve a fair amount of JavaScript. We mention them here to help introduce the next topic, which is when to use Ajax.

The palettes provide similar benefits to both the user and the server workload. Let's consider the people palette. When selected, the people palette appears to fly in onto the current page. The palette shows the portlet that is the interface to your instant message contact list and status. Maintaining this portlet on every page would present some complications. First, it would take up a considerable portion of the page. Second, it is relatively expensive in terms of server processing. But users want quick access to the Instant Messenger interface. Having the palette operate in the form of a fly-in, where the people status is updated only when needed, solves these concerns.

Client-Side Page Aggregation

A key development in the Portal architecture for the future is in client-side aggregation. Typically, Portal server function would aggregate the page response to an HTTP request by applying the page theme definition and adding the markup fragments returned by render calls to the portlets on the page. With client-side aggregation, we essentially defer this function to the client.

JavaScript function in a bootstrap HTML document manages the navigation, aggregation, and page manipulation. We use Representational State Transfer (REST) services to retrieve the navigation information, page definitions, portlet settings, and other control information needed to manage the representation and behavior of the page content. REST services also provide access to individual portlet views for aggregation on the client.

Content aggregated on the client can originate from the portal or can be generated from other services, such as ATOM or RSS feeds. This approach greatly extends the potential for highly interactive user interfaces. Portal navigation and aggregation don't refresh the entire HTML page document but only what really has changed. Page manipulation results in direct user experience, showing the changed view immediately while sending the changes to the server asynchronously.

This functionality lets Portal leverage Ajax and REST architectural styles and extend that capability to portlet developers. Thus, portlet developers need to apply Ajax in their portlets only where they really want to update a small part of the portlet content.

Ajax in Portlets

Choosing when to use Ajax is critical not only to good Web design but also to ensuring a well-designed application. We mentioned some of the implications of using Ajax in a Portal environment. Let's look at the considerations that will help us determine when Ajax is the right technical approach. Note that some limitations currently restrict the use of Ajax in portlets, but the Java Portlet Specification 2.0 (JSR 286) will address these issues. For more information about JSR 286, see Appendix A.

- User *interface design:* you can use Ajax to deliver the right data to the Web user in a highly interactive manner. The visual presentation of that data (whether components fly in, pop up, or change in on the page) isn't really part of the Ajax interaction. It is design work that relies on the Ajax-supplied data but isn't really part of Ajax itself. Still, it's important to understand from a UI design perspective when it is valuable to have current server-supplied data so that the result is valuable to the user and not distracting in its presentation.

  To the extent that we can defer specific data requests until the user actually makes them, we can save resources at the server and potentially improve the UI by removing the data but providing a quick method for data access.

- *Servlet execution:* Because portlets aren't directly addressable, the server function used for Ajax calls is typically a servlet running either in the same Web application (if it needs to share session data with the portlet) or in its own Web application

  Because the Ajax server function is running outside the portlet container, it esn't have access to any of the portlet context objects. Portlet objects such as portlet preferences, portlet request, and portlet response aren't available, nor are the render parameters, portlet mode, or window state. Therefore, the function we expect to execute for our Ajax call shouldn't depend on these objects. JSR 286 is addressing this restriction.

- Portlet state: Because the Ajax server is running in a servlet and not in the portlet itself, we can't change portlet state. Therefore, we shouldn't expect to change the portlet's navigation state or any portlet state by the Ajax interaction. JSR 286 is addressing this restriction as well.

- *Portlet URLs in Ajax data:* Portlet URLs can't be generated in the Ajax servlet, nor can they be generated in JavaScript on the client. Therefore, the Ajax function can't generate navigational links to portlet pages. Again, changes planned in the Java Portlet Specification in V2.0 will provide the ability to generate portlet URLs through Ajax communications directly to a portlet.

- *No unique access control or security requirements:* Access to the Ajax servlet is protected by the security policy that WebSphere Application Server provides for the servlet depending on how it is deployed. However, access to the servlet function can't participate in the portal access control mechanism. So, the Ajax function can't be protected by unique portlet access control. Again, with the changes planned for JSR 286, having the portlet provide Ajax server function will alleviate this constraint.

- *Implications to separation of application logic:* Consider the implications of separating the application logic between portlet and servlet carefully when determining what function may be executed through Ajax function. In some cases, this separation may result in good application architecture. In others, the application may be segmented in a way that overly complicates development, deployment, and maintenance.

- *Client/server state:* An implication of Ajax processing is that the client state can become out of sync with the server state. That is, after Ajax execution, the page URL and the portal server state become out of sync with the data being displayed on the Web page. If the page is bookmarked, returning to that bookmark won't result in the same page representation. When considering Ajax uses, ensure that the current page state won't affect the correct execution of the Ajax function and that a bookmarked page doesn't lose context.

- *Performance:* When done right, Ajax applications can provide a better user experience and reduce the load on the server. However, you can also achieve the opposite result with poorly designed Ajax applications. For your Ajax application, keep in mind that a tradeoff exists between many requests that provide only a small amount of data and the load this generates on the server. In cases where your Ajax portlet isn't deployed in an intranet scenario with high-bandwidth connections, network latency may also become an issue and make Ajax applications seem slow to the user when too many requests are issued.

- *Security:* Ajax interactions can complicate the security model of the Web application. We discuss security implications later in this chapter.

- *Accessibility, search, and versioning:* When considering the use of Ajax, you must also take into account the implications to accessibility. Highly interactive user interfaces have great appeal but complicate the task of meeting accessibility standards. Search function may also be impacted because the represented content isn't mapped directly to the Web document URL. When building portlets based on common JavaScript function such as Ajax, you need to manage the potential collision of different versions of that function when deployed with portlets that are aggregated on the same page. Ajax poses potential implications to a wide range of function, and it's important to consider the impact to the entire site.

AJAX EXAMPLE

For an example of Ajax used within a portlet, let's consider the requirement for asking the user to make a selection from a list of items. To reduce the list of items presented, the user is asked to scope the selection in some way. In this example, we'll ask the user to select an office location, perhaps for a store or an office of some international organization. We'll present the user with a list of countries where the offices are located. After selecting a country, the user will be asked for a region and then finally for a location within that region.

We'll demonstrate Ajax here with the data represented in drop-down lists. This technique is a good choice for an asynchronous server call for several reasons:

- It lets us defer handling the data until the user needs it.

- We can transmit only the data needed to meet the user's request.

- We can create some interactive user interface that displays the help content in a more dynamic way.

- There are likely to be no issues of security or portlet state management with this function.

It is especially useful as an Ajax implementation if the selection lists are additionally filtered based on the user, a user attribute, or other parameters that could help focus the selection. These are application-specific criteria.

The portlet we'll create will simply render this selection process. This portlet certainly isn't dramatic in presentation, but it does let us focus on the mechanics of the Ajax implementation. We'll leave the application of a relatively common requirement such as this to a more interesting creative design of your creation.

Ajax Servlet in a Portlet Application

We provide the complete source code for this application on the download site. In the next several sections of this chapter, we discuss some key areas of the code. Our portlet is very simple and essentially just defines a JSP for view mode rendering. The JSP renders the drop-down lists for the office location selection and provides a basis for our Ajax implementation.

Starting from the portlet project in Rational Application Developer (RAD), we'll first add the servlet that will function as our Ajax server. The easiest way to do this is to select the portlet project and use the new servlet creation wizard (**File > New > Other > Servlet**).

After completion of the wizard for a servlet named OfficeLocationsFinder, a servlet class that extends HttpServlet and implements Servlet is created. The wizard also updates our Web deployment descriptor to add a reference to this servlet. Let's look at the web.xml file (Listing 14.2) to see those changes.

```
<servlet>
        <servlet-name>OfficeLocationsFinder</servlet-name>
        <display-name>OfficeLocationsFinder</display-name>
        <description></description>
        <servlet-class>
        com.ibm.sample.OfficeLocationsFinder</servlet-class>
</servlet>
<servlet-mapping>
        <servlet-name>OfficeLocationsFinder</servlet-name>
        <url-pattern>/OfficeLocationsFinder</url-pattern>
</servlet-mapping>
```

Listing 14.2: Changes to web.xml file for OfficeLocationsFinder servlet

The changes reference the OfficeLocationsFinder class with the package name we specified in the wizard. The servlet mapping is also specified here. Keep the url-pattern in mind because we'll need to reference this servlet in our JavaScript code for the Ajax function, and this value will be included in the URL we need to create.

Next, we need to modify the servlet code to provide our Ajax function needs. Let's consider what that XML should look like. In the example, we'll let the user select a country first and then be presented with a set of office regions for that country. After selecting the region, the user will see a set of office locations for that region. In the first step — the country selection — we'll simply provide those selection options as part of the portlet view rendering. Once the user chooses a country, the Ajax server should return a list of regions. The XML for this data collection could look like that shown in Listing 14.3.

```
<regions>
 <region>
  <regID>001</regID>
  <name>Northeastern</name>
 </region>
 <region>
  <regID>002</regID>
  <name>Southern</name>
 </region>
 <region>
  <regID>003</regID>
  <name>Mid-Atlantic</name>
 </region>
</regions>
```

Listing 14.3: XML for region data collection

Our server defines the XML content. In this case, we have a collections of regions that are defined as a regID and a name. In the example, we simply use the region name, but we've shown the regID to demonstrate more complicated XML data.

In the final step of our scenario, the user selects a region and then is presented with a set of locations. Our Ajax server must be able to respond to this request and return the locations. The XML for the locations might look like that shown in Listing 14.4.

```
<locations>
 <locations>
  <locID>101</locID>
  <name>Raleigh</name>
  </locations>
 <locations>
  <locID>102</locID>
  <name>Charleston</name>
  </locations>
 <locations>
  <locID>103</locID>
  <name>Atlanta</name>
  </locations>
 <locations>
  <locID>104</locID>
  <name>Columbia</name>
  </locations>
</locations>
```

Listing 14.4: XML for location data collection

This XML content is similar in format to that returned for regions. Again, we have an ID field and a names field.

To distinguish these requests to our server, we'll require the servlet call to include a query parameter that provides the context for the request as well as the identification of the selected region or location. For the sample data shown here, we received the following servlet requests. The hostname is localhost for our test environment, and the Portal port number is provided. The context is created from the portlet context and the url-pattern of the servlet created. In addition, we've specified the query parameter for the country specification or the region specification. You'll see later how to programmatically determine the portlet reference.

```
http://localhost:9081/wps/PA_1_0_12D/OfficeLocationsFinder?
country=US
http://localhost:9081/wps/PA_1_0_12D/OfficeLocationsFinder?
region=Mid-Atlantic
```

With this information in mind, we can code our OfficeLocationsFinder servlet. The servlet is straightforward because our example simply uses hard-coded data values for a subset of our application data (Listing 14.5).

```
protected final String US_regions[][] = {
                {"001","Northeastern"},
                {"002","Southern"},
                {"003","Mid-Atlantic"},
                {"004","Mid-West"},
                {"005","Northwest"},
                {"006","Western"}};

protected final String NE_locations[][] = {
                {"101","Boston"},
                {"102","Philadelphia"},
                {"103","New York"},
                {"104","Baltimore"}};

protected final String MA_locations[][] = {
                {"101","Raleigh"},
                {"102","Charleston"},
                {"103","Atlanta"},
                {"104","Columbia"}};
```

Listing 14.5: Hard-coded data values

Next, we need to add the logic to query the request parameter and return the appropriate data in the correct XML format. The code snippet shown in Listing 14.6 returns the regions for the selected country.

```
String country = request.getParameter(COUNTRY);
if (!"".equals(country) && country!=null) {
  response.getWriter().write("<regions>");
  if ("US".equals(country)) {
    for (int i=0; i<US_regions.length; i++) {
       response.getWriter().write("<region>");
       response.getWriter().write("
<regID>"+US_regions[i][0]+"</regID>");
       response.getWriter().write("
<name>"+US_regions[i][1]+"</name>");
       response.getWriter().write("</region>");
    }
  }
  response.getWriter().write("</regions>");
}
```

Listing 14.6: Generating the region list as an XML response

Similarly, the code snippet in Listing 14.7 shows how the locations are returned from our servlet. Again, we've hard-coded the data references for the server function here to make the sample implementation easier.

```
String region = request.getParameter(REGION);
if (!"".equals(region) && region!=null) {
  response.getWriter().write("<locations>");
  if ("Northeastern".equals(region)) {
    for (int i=0; i<NE_locations.length; i++) {
      response.getWriter().write("<locations>");
      response.getWriter().write("
<locID>"+NE_locations[i][0]+"</locID>");
      response.getWriter().write("
<name>"+NE_locations[i][1]+"</name>");
      response.getWriter().write("</locations>");
    }
  }
  if ("Mid-Atlantic".equals(region)) {
    for (int i=0; i<MA_locations.length; i++) {
      response.getWriter().write("<locations>");
      response.getWriter().write("
<locID>"+MA_locations[i][0]+"</locID>");
      response.getWriter().write("
<name>"+MA_locations[i][1]+"</name>");
      response.getWriter().write("</locations>");
    }
  }
  response.getWriter().write("</locations>");
}
```

Listing 14.7: Generating the location list as an XML response

With these changes, our Ajax server is completed. We can deploy the portlet Web application to Portal and validate that the servlet function is working successfully by pointing our Web browser to the servlet. However, we'll need to determine the portlet context for that, so let's wait until we complete the client-side portion of our example to validate the servlet.

Creating the Sample Code JSP

Most Ajax-related client-side changes reside in the JavaScript. Some portion exists, of course, in the page markup to invoke the Ajax JavaScript function and provide the DOM objects on which the function operates. In our example, the JSP simply renders three drop-down widgets and associates the Ajax function with them to populate the list options appropriately. Of course, some more interactive user behavior is expected with Ajax, so we'll liven up this simple example by animating the visualization of the lists themselves. Let's look at some interesting sections of the JSP.

In the snippet of code shown in Listing 14.8, we see the creation of our first drop-down list, with two JavaScript function calls associated with the select widget onChange event. When the user selects a new item from the list, the functions OFC_regionSlider and OFC_getRegions are invoked.

```
<div id="country" class='list'>
   <select id="OFC_countrySelect" style='width: 136px;'
       onChange='OFC_slideOut("OFC_regionSlider"); OFC_getRegions()'>
     <option value="" selected>Select a Country
     <option value="US">US
     <option value="Canada">Canada
     <option value="England">England
   </select>
</div>
```

Listing 14.8: Creation of country drop-down list

The regionSlider method is a generic function that expands a collapsed DOM object. In the next snippet, you'll see a div tag named OFC_regionSlider that is created in a collapsed state (width set to 1 in this case). Executing the slideOut function with the object's ID as a parameter causes it to be expanded. As it is expanding (that function is also asynchronous), the OFC_getRegions function is called. This is the invocation of our Ajax call. You'll see shortly how that function works.

First, let's finish looking at the JSP. The next snippet (Listing 14.9) shows the creation of the second drop-down list, the one wrapped in the OFC_regionSlider div.

```
<div id="OFC_regionSlider" class='listcollapsed';">
  <div id="OFC_regions" class='list'>
    <select id="OFC_regionSelect" style='width: 136px;'
        onChange='OFC_slideOut("OFC_locationsSlider");
OFC_getLocations();'>
      <option value="" selected>Select a Region
    </select>
  </div>
</div>
```

Listing 14.9: Creation of region drop-down list

Again, we see the definition of the drop-down list, this time the one associated with the regions. We specify two function calls on the onChange event. The first expands the third drop-down list, and the OFC_getLocations function invokes the Ajax function to get the location options. Listing 14.10 shows the snippet of JSP code for the last list.

```
<div id="OFC_locationSlider" class='listcollapsed';">
  <div id="OFC_locations" class='list'>
    <select id="OFC_locationSelect" style="width: 136px;">
      <option value="" selected>Select a Location
    </select>
  </div>
</div>
```

Listing 14.10: Creation of office location drop-down list

Last, in our JSP we need to include the file that contains the JavaScript for the Ajax functions as well as the slider function. Also, we'll use the portlet request object to create a global JavaScript variable that references the correct URL to our servlet. Listing 14.11 shows this code. We'll append the query strings to this URL as needed before sending the URL request. Note that you need to encode the final URL to make it work in scenarios where session rewriting is enabled or when running the portlet as a Web Services for Remote Portlets (WSRP) remote service.

```
<script type="text/JavaScript">
var OFC_serverURL =
"http://localhost:9081<%=request.getContextPath()%>/OfficeLocationsFinder";
</script>
```

Listing 14.11: Setting the Ajax server URL

A Word About Namespace Encoding

Because portlets are aggregated in the same Web page, there's a possibility of namespace collisions between global variable and function names defined in JavaScript and HTML tag IDs in the page markup. Managing this potential problem is further complicated because the portlets placed on a given page could come from a variety of sources. To protect against these collisions, any globally referenceable client-side objects should be namespace-encoded. Portal provides a namespace tag in the portlet tag library that returns a unique namespace we can use for this purpose. The difficulty is that the diligent use of the tag makes the code cumbersome, and it's difficult to use this function for JavaScript function that is not generated as part of the JSP but resides in a .js file instead.

In the example, we used a prefix on the global variable references to help protect these items. This technique helps for the more obvious cases but does not ensure protection. For the purposes of the sample code, we didn't want the namespace encoding scheme to distract from the Ajax points. In your application, with the growing use of client-side processing, you'll need to give issues such as namespace encoding careful consideration.

The JavaScript Function

Next, let's look at the Ajax JavaScript function to see how this really works. We won't discuss the JavaScript that performs the expand function because it's not critical to our discussion of Ajax. However, it is provided in the sample code and isn't very complicated.

Let's look at the OFC_getRegions function (Listing 14.12). As we mentioned, this function is called when a selection is made in the country select list.

```
function OFC_getRegions()
{
    if (window.XMLHttpRequest) {
        req = new XMLHttpRequest();
    } else if (window.ActiveXObject) {
        req = new ActiveXObject("Microsoft.XMLHTTP");
    }
    var selectedObj = document.getElementById("OFC_countrySelect");
    var newURL =
        response.encodeURL(OFC_serverURL+"?country="+selectedObj.value);
    req.open("GET", newURL, true);
    req.onreadystatechange = OFC_regionsCallback;
    req.send(null);
}
```

Listing 14.12: OFC_getRegions function

You can see the browser-specific code that creates a new instance of either the XMLHttpRequest object or the XMLHttp object. Next, we get the value of the selected country and update the Ajax server URL to include a query string with the value specified for the "country" parameter.

After setting the URL on the XMLHttpRequest object, we specify the callback function. This is the JavaScript function that will be called when the HTTP response is received from the server. Finally, the request is sent.

Next, let's look at the code for the callback (Listing 14.13).

```
function OFC_regionsCallback()
{
    if (req.readyState == 4) {
        if (req.status == 200) {
            OFC_regionsReply();
        }
    }
}
```

Listing 14.13: OFC_regionsCallback function

This code first checks the response ready state and status. A readyState value of 4 on the response indicates that the response is "loaded" — that is, the data transfer has been completed. The other possible ready states from 0 to 3 are uninitialize, open, sent, and receiving. For more information about these values, see the W3C working draft of the XMLHttpRequest Object specification.

After verifying that the response is loaded, we check for a successful HTTP request status code. Given a good ready state and status, we then call our function to process the returned XML (Listing 14.14).

```
// Get the region IDs and names
var IdObjs= req.responseXML.getElementsByTagName("regID");
var nameObjs= req.responseXML.getElementsByTagName("name");

// Update the select tag
var regionSelectDiv = document.getElementById("OFC_regions");
var options="<select id='OFC_regionSelect' style='width: 136px;'
  onChange='OFC_slideOut(\"OFC_locationSlider\");
OFC_getLocations();'>";
options = options + "<option value='' selected>Select a region";

for (var i=0; i<nameObjs.length; i++) {
  var name= nameObjs[i].childNodes[0].nodeValue;
  options = options + "<option value='"+name+"'>"+name;
}

options = options + "</select>";
regionSelectDiv.innerHTML=options;
```

Listing 14.14: Dynamic update of the DOM objects

We have two options for retrieving the response: responseText and responseXML. Depending on the expected format, one or the other of these may be used. ResponseText is used for all non-XML formats, such as plain text and JSON. Because our server returns XML formatted data, we use responseXML. With the XML parsed, we can retrieve the elements we want using the getElementByTagName function on the responseXML We get the region IDs first and then the names. These are each placed in arrays so we can iterate over the collection and generate the DOM updates.

We complete the function by re-creating the HTML markup for the select tag with the new option data. Last, we use that markup to set the innerHTML for the div tag that wraps the select tag in our DOM.

459

That's it! There's not a lot to a basic Ajax invocation. Of course, the complexity comes in the extensive ways in which you can use this technique. We won't review the JavaScript code for the Ajax call to get the locations once the region has been selected because that is essentially the same as we just discussed for the locations. Again, the source code is available, and you can look at the implementation there. For more information about the standardization of the XMLHttpRequest object and its specification, go to *http://www.w3.org/TR/XMLHttpRequest*.

FRAMEWORKS

The nature of Ajax lends itself very well to applying frameworks and development toolkits to aid in the development of Ajax components. JavaScript has inherent complications due to browser differences (as we see with the basic set of creating an XMLHttpRequest object). Ajax-enabled UI components can be made available for reuse in many applications. The ability of IDEs to support JavaScript testing and debugging is critical to improve development efforts. All these needs and the enormous interest in Ajax provide a great opportunity for frameworks to emerge.

Dojo

Dojo is an open-source JavaScript toolkit that helps with Web development by providing a collection of UI widgets and help for creating new UI widgets. It supports an aspect-based event system to support extending UI component function. Dojo libraries provide framework support for Ajax calls, container widgets, trees, menus, slide shows, animation effects, and a growing variety of other widgets.

Dojo assists with the creation of new widgets based on HTML and JavaScript. It provides an extensive JavaScript library, but the Dojo packaging system ensures that the runtime includes only needed files. The package system provides a mechanism to ensure that the correct files are included with the Web page.

The Dojo event system provides a powerful notification mechanism that lets JavaScript functions be notified when other functions are executed. It extends the notion of events to include all JavaScript function.

460

Beyond the available widget library and framework support for creating new widgets and extensions to the JavaScript event model, Dojo is probably most commonly recognized as an Ajax development toolkit. Dojo provides Ajax support by abstracting core client function to provide a simple interface while hiding browser-level differences.

The code snippet in Listing 14.15 shows the dojo invocation method for an asynchronous server call.

```
ar bindArgs = {
    url:        "/DojoJ2EE/MyURI",
    mimetype:   "text/javascript",
    error:      function(type, errObj){
        // handle error here
    },
    load:       function(type, data, evt){
        // handle successful response here
    }
};
// dispatch the request
var requestObj = dojo.io.bind(bindArgs);
```

Listing 14.15: dojo invocation method for an asynchronous server call

For the latest information about dojo, go to *http://www.dojotoolkit.org*.

Kabuki Ajax Toolkit

Kabuki is an object-oriented widget library for JavaScript that hides browser-level differences and enables Ajax development. The library supports new user interface development, both asynchronous and synchronous server communications, XML document utilities for creation and manipulation, and an extended user interface event-handling model. A DHTML widget toolkit with event model extensions (registered listener model) provides the framework for widget creation.

Like Dojo, the Kabuki Ajax Toolkit is an open-source initiative. Zimbra, Inc., is a cofounder and key contributor to the Open Ajax Alliance, with the goal of "making the delivery of rich Ajax user interfaces substantially easier."

Open Ajax supports multiple Ajax runtimes, including both Kabuki and the Dojo Toolkit. For more information and download links for Kabuki, go to *http://www.zimbra.com/community/kabuki_ajax_toolkit_download.html.*

Eclipse Ajax Toolkit Framework Project

According to the Eclipse Web site:

> "AJAX Toolkit Framework (ATF) will provide extensible frameworks and exemplary tools for building IDEs for the many different AJAX runtime offerings (Dojo, Zimbra, etc.) in the market. These frameworks will contain features for developing, deploying, debugging and testing AJAX applications."

Key advantages of extensions to the tooling framework are edit time JavaScript syntax validation and JavaScript debugging and inspecting. ATF will also support a Personality Framework to allow Ajax development with a variety of Ajax runtimes. For details as this proposal develops, refer to the Eclipse project Web site at *http://www.eclipse.org/proposals/atf.*

SECURITY CONSIDERATIONS

As we consider moving application logic between the portlet and servlet (or the portlet and any other server mechanism), we must take into account implications to application and data security. As we discussed briefly earlier in this chapter, for Ajax server function executing as a servlet, access to the servlet is protected by the security policy that WebSphere Application Server provides for the servlet depending on how it is deployed. Because the portal (portlet) and servlet share the same WAS security framework, we can share the user authentication mechanism (Lightweight Third-Party Authentication, or LTPA, token) between the two.

However, because the servlet isn't a portal component, it can't share in the portal access control mechanism. Therefore, we can't use managed access to a portlet based on the Portal Access Control framework to protect the servlet-based function.

Beyond considerations for security access to Ajax services, there are security considerations when moving application function to a browser client: protected JavaScript execution and protecting user data.

JavaScript execution integrity is an ongoing concern of browser vendors and standards organizations. Policies revolve around "server of origin" (JavaScript function cannot establish communication to a domain other than from where it originated) or "cross-site scripting." The browsers largely address these issues, but it pays to be aware that with extended emphasis on client-side execution, JavaScript execution integrity is critical.

Standard security methods for protecting user data communications naturally still apply. For example, using secure socket connections (HTTPS) protects the data between the Ajax client and the server. However, if you want to encrypt text over HTTP, there are JavaScript implementations of secure hash functions (e.g., MD5, SHA-1) that let you encrypt data on the client and decrypt it on the server. As the design for Ajax function develops, it's vital to understand how the user data will be secured, especially if the Ajax server executes under a different security architecture than the rest of the application.

SUMMARY

In this chapter, we've discussed Ajax and how it can be used to create a more interactive user experience for the Web application. We briefly described the history of Ajax and its predecessor technologies.

We covered in some detail the processing flow for Ajax and discussed the many strengths and advantages of using this approach. As with all technologies and approaches, some tradeoffs exist, and we discussed where the Ajax weaknesses are. We also talked about alternatives to Ajax, with the most popular alternative being Flex. We concluded that section of the chapter with a discussion of the format choices for the Ajax server's response data.

Then we looked at Ajax implementations from a Portal perspective. We started by discussing how Portal uses Ajax-like technologies in its most recent version and suggested that more Ajax integration is coming. Next, we took a deep look into a portlet's use of Ajax and the need for the Ajax server to reside outside a portlet (such as a servlet that can be deployed in the portlet's Web application).

To illustrate the points we discussed, we spent most of the rest of the chapter looking at a sample implementation of a relatively common task that can take advantage of asynchronous server calls to enhance the user experience and at the same time save server processing and reduce unnecessary data transmission. We concluded the chapter by discussing emerging frameworks that provide widget libraries and toolkits for Ajax development, and we reviewed the security considerations that apply when considering Ajax deployments.

Appendix A

Looking Toward V2.0 of the Java Portlet Specification

The second version of the Java Portlet Specification began in November 2005 as Java Specification Request (JSR) 286 under the Java Community Process (JCP). Because JSR 168 was the first version of the Portlet Specification, it addressed only the basic portlet programming model, and developers had to use vendor extensions to solve more advanced use cases. JSR 286 therefore covers the most requested features missing in JSR 168, including coordination between portlets, resource serving, Ajax support, portlet filters, and more. JSR 286 will be based on Java 2 Platform Enterprise Edition (J2EE) 1.4, letting portlets use J2EE 1.4 enhancements, such as JavaServer Pages (JSP) 2.0.

Another major goal of JSR 286 is alignment with Web Services for Remote Portlets (WSRP) 2.0, a specification also currently under development. As with the Java Portlet Specification 1.0 and WSRP 1.0, the goal is to be able to publish remote Java portlets and create proxy Java portlets that can proxy WSRP remote portlets into J2EE portals. For example, even if your portlet is running remotely, it will be able to send/receive events to/from local running portlets.

Note that at the time of this writing, the first early public draft of JSR 286 had just been published; therefore, the final version of the specification may differ from the content described here.

COORDINATION

JSR 286 introduces three different coordination concepts to make it easier to create composite applications using portlets from different portlet applications:

- *Events:* for sending and receiving events

- *Shared render parameters:* for sharing render parameters between portlets and thus creating a page context

- *Shared session attributes:* for sharing session data beyond the current Web application

Let's take a look at all three in more detail in the next sections.

Events

JSR 286's event support provides a way to send and receive events between portlets. This capability provides a more integrated end-user view because different portlets from different portlet applications can be wired together to provide a consistent user experience. A calendar portlet may, for example, send out an event containing a date the user is looking at, and a ToDo portlet may take this event as input and display all ToDo's due on this date.

Events also allow structuring the user interface in a more modular way and therefore enable applications such as selection and browser portlets. In a selection portlet, the user can select a topic of interest from a list, such as a news article, and the browser portlet then displays the complete article. The user can place such portlets on the page wherever he or she likes, or even on different pages.

Event Model

The event model that JSR 286 defines is a loosely coupled, brokered event model. In this model, the portlet defines the events it can receive and the ones it may publish in the portlet deployment descriptor. At runtime, the portal administrator or business users can wire together the different portlets. This concept is similar to the model introduced in WebSphere Portal V5.1.0.1 with the property broker extension for JSR 168 portlets.

The portlet receives events via the processEvent method of the EventPortlet interface that the portlet needs to implement:

```
processEvent (EventRequest request, EventResponse response) throws
PortletException, java.io.IOException;
```

The processEvent method provides an event request, letting the portlet access all data from the portlet request, such as current render parameters, portlet session, portlet preferences, and the event sent to the portlet via the getEvent method.

The portlet can publish events at runtime using the setEvent or setEvents method on the action or render response.

Note that the event payload needs to be Java-serializable to be transferred to different Java remote systems and must be Java Architecture for XML Binding (JAXB)–serializable to be transferred via the WSRP protocol to potentially non-Java based portlets as XML data. You only need to do anything special for complex Java types.

Shared Render Parameters

For use cases that don't require server-side state changes but define the view state of a page, JSR 286 introduces shared render parameters. Shared render parameters let you define a page context that is shared between portlets and that can be bookmarked. Examples include a specific customer ID or zip code for which the different portlets display information.

You declare shared render parameters in the portlet.xml file, and the portlet automatically receives these parameters if they are not null. In contrast to non-shared render parameters, the portlet needs to set shared render parameters only if the value should change. From the API point of view, shared render parameters are treated like normal render parameters and thus can be accessed with the render parameter methods.

Shared Session State

In normal J2EE applications, the Web application sessions are private per Web application to protect independent Web applications from each other. This approach is perfectly fine for traditional applications, but in the portlet world, things are a bit different. Here, the different portlet applications, which reside in different Web applications, are aggregated via the portal to larger applications. And these larger applications may want to share a common session. An example is an e-commerce shop that integrates portlets written by different portlet providers into the shop. All portlets should share the user's currently selected items in a common shopping cart that is stored in the session.

To support this scenario, JSR 286 provides shared session attributes that are permitted to be shared across Web applications. In the portlet.xml file, you define the attributes that can be shared declaratively and then use the existing portlet session APIs and the application session scope to share the attributes across Web applications. As for events, the requirement for the payload is that it is Java-serializable and JAXB-serializable.

RESOURCE RENDERING

In JSR 168, the only way for portlets to render resources is via direct links to the resource or serving the resource through a servlet. Although direct links are very efficient for static resources that are the same for all portlet states, they are insufficient for use cases where you'd like to take information from the portlet context into account. Examples include rendering different resources based on the portlet mode, window state, current render parameters, or portlet preferences.

Another benefit of rendering resources directly through the portlet is that in this case the resource is accessed through the portal and thus protected through the portal access control. Of course, this advantage comes with the cost of an additional portal request that puts more load on the portal server.

To support the resource rendering use case through the portlet, JSR 286 introduces a new, optional, life-cycle interface called ResourceServingPortlet with the serveResource method:

```
public void serveResource(ResourceRequest request, ResourceResponse
response)
```

Via the resource request, the portlet has access to the request data, including the input stream to support file upload use cases. The resource request also provides the current render parameters and additional resource parameters, but the serveResource call cannot change any portlet state besides the session data (e.g., portlet mode, window state, render parameters, portlet preferences). As in the render phase, it is not advisable to change session state in serveResource to make resource serving an idempotent operation and honor the Web model that allows reloading and navigating between pages without changing these pages.

You can trigger the serveResource call with a ResourceURL that the portlet can create via the PortletResponse.createResourceURL method. A resource URL contains the current transient state of the portlet (portlet mode, window state, render parameters) but cannot set new values for this state. A resource URL may have additional resource parameters that are set on the resource URL.

AJAX SUPPORT

When we introduced Ajax and how portlets can leverage Ajax in Chapters 4 and 14, we noted some of the limitations you currently have with portlets and Ajax. The JSR 286 specification will provide additional means to overcome these limitations. JSR 286 will introduce

- The serveResource call (mentioned earlier), which lets you render markup fragments asynchronously without coordination with the portal by using the standard XMLHttpRequest. The portlet can leverage all the information in the portlet context, including portlet mode, window state, render parameters, and portlet preferences. The limitation is that you can't change any of the previously mentioned states in such a call.

- Coordinated Ajax, where the portlet doesn't issue the direct XMLHttpRequest, but the portal provides this functionality for the portlet. That way, the portal can hook into the Ajax call and, before returning the new markup fragment to the client-side JavaScript of the portlet, adjust the content of the rest of the page (e.g., update all the links in case the portlet's render parameters have been changed). This coordinated Ajax lets the portlet issue Ajax actions and thus change its state and send events to other portlets. The technical details of how JSR 286 will implement coordinated Ajax were still under discussion at the time of this writing.

BETTER SUPPORT OF EXISTING WEB FRAMEWORKS

More and more Web frameworks now support portlets beside servlets as a programming model. Examples of such Web frameworks include JavaServer Faces (JSF), Spring, Struts, and WebWork. Most of these frameworks started before portlets were born and thus have strong ties into the servlet programming model. To make the adoption of portlets as the controller part in the Model-View-Controller (MVC) pattern easier in these frameworks, JSR 286 introduces the ability to dispatch to servlets and JSPs in all life-cycle methods (e.g., for implementing controller logic in a servlet) and supports portlet filters for presetting values in the request or wrapping objects in the portlet request. (For information about the MVC pattern, see Chapter 4.)

CLIENT-CAPABILITIES ACCESS

Access to client capabilities gives the portlet the ability to take special client capabilities, such as screen size, into account when generating the markup. For client capabilities, the Composite Capabilities/Preferences Profiles (CC/PP) standard from W3C allows defining device capabilities, and the User Agent Profile (UAProf) provides specific attributes definitions for individual devices.

The CC/PP standard is now available as a Java API specified in JSR 188 (for information about the JSR 188 specification, see *http://jcp.org/en/jsr/detail?id=188*). However, because JSR 188 was developed in parallel with the portlet specification, it doesn't take portlets into account, and the factory in CC/PP that lets you get the profile of a client takes only HttpServletRequest, not PortletRequest, as an input parameter. Therefore, either the CC/PP API needs to be extended to also take a PortletRequest as an input parameter or the portlet specification needs to add a method that directly returns a CC/PP client profile.

ADVANCED CACHING

At present, the caching options for portlets are restricted to expiration-based caching. However, this is a very static approach that is too coarse-grained for many applications. Advanced caching capabilities would enable the portlet to provide caching information that goes beyond this simple expiration mechanism of the first version.

One enhancement could be to distinguish between content that is user-specific and needs to be cached per user and content that is shared between users and therefore needs to be cached only once. This support would dramatically reduce the caching storage needed for portlets that users can't personalize, such as a company-wide announcement portlet that displays the same message for all users.

Another area of improvement is providing more fine-grained control to the portlet via validation mechanisms that let the portlet check, based on a validation tag, whether the given content is still valid. This support lets you generate markup only for the views that have expired as a result of the action instead of for all output the portlet has produced.

PORTLET WINDOWS

Portlet windows are only indirectly reflected in the first version of the Java Portlet Specification, as part of the prefix that the container generates for portlet-scoped session entries. Version 2.0 now makes the portlet window ID available to the portlet via the request; the portlet can use this ID to key data it wants to store.

A common use case this support enables is caching of data in the portlet (e.g., data that are retrieved from slow back-end systems and differ for different portlet windows). With the portlet window ID, the portlet now has the means to cache these data in cache systems provided by the application server (e.g., the WebSphere Application Server DynaCache) or any other caching system.

PORTLET FILTERS

Portlet filters can be put in front of any life-cycle method call available in V2.0 (processAction, processEvent, render, serveResource) to provide a wrapped request and response to these life-cycle methods. Similar to servlet filters, portlet filters must be defined in the portlet.xml deployment descriptor.

The filter component must implement the javax.portlet.filter.Filter interface that consists of a generic doFilter method:

```
void doFilter(PortletRequest request, PortletResponse response,
FilterChain chain)
```

Inside the doFilter method, the filter code needs to check via instanceof for the specific requests and responses (Action, Event, Render, Resource), perform its filtering function, and then call the next filter in the chain with either the original request and response or a wrapped version using the wrappers provided in the javax.portlet.filter package.

You can also restrict filters to specific life-cycle methods via the lifecycle element in the portlet.xml file. This practice is recommended if your filter doesn't apply to all life-cycle methods, to reduce the overhead of calling the filter for methods to which it doesn't apply.

FURTHER ITEMS

At the time of the writing of this book, the early public draft 1 of JSR 286 was available and covered only parts of the features planned for the specification. Thus, the final version may include additional features beyond those mentioned here, such as setting of headers or additional tags, and some items mentioned here may have changed in the final version. Therefore, be sure check out the final version of JSR 286 once it is available.

For more information about JSR 286, see *http://jcp.org/en/jsr/detail?id=286*. For details about Web Services for Remote Portlets (WSRP), visit *http://www.oasis-open.org/committees/tc_home.php?wg_abbrev=wsrp*.

Appendix B

Setting Up the Data Components

As we've mentioned several times within this book, there's more to portlet development than just portlets. Portals and portlets are the interface to the world, but a lot of complex function goes on behind the scenes. Layers within your architecture are a good thing, and many of the portlets you've seen in this book follow this approach.

One goal of the book was to give you a simple data layer that could serve as a foundation on which to build your portlets and other portal components. Data access can be a tricky thing, so we certainly didn't want to try and teach you that aspect of programming. There are too many books available that can introduce you to the details of that topic.

USING IBATIS

iBATIS is an open-source data mapper framework that lets you pretty easily and quickly create an object-to-relational data mapping layer. Available at *http://ibatis.apache.org*, iBATIS is a strong contender in the open-source world. Comparable to Hibernate, iBATIS works standalone or with Inversion of Control (IoC) containers such as Spring. As of this writing, there's not a lot of detailed information about the framework available other than a few articles and some FAQs; however, the framework is fairly easy to learn and, even with some ramp-up time, should provide a long-term savings in time and cost.

There are two main ways to use iBATIS: SQL Maps, which provide a quick way to access and update your data, and Data Access Objects (DAO), which offer a more robust framework for larger applications. Because our main goal was to quickly and easily put in place a data layer on which to build the portlets and other components, our approach uses SQL Maps for simplicity and ease. For more complex applications, we might have chosen the DAO approach to build a layered data access architecture.

We actually looked at several different approaches to build this layer, considering Hibernate, iBATIS, straight Java Database Connectivity (JDBC), Spring, and some combination of these approaches. Knowing readers would be viewing the examples even if the samples weren't the focus of the book, we chose one of the simplest approaches possible that added value to the development effort.

DATA ACCESS USING A SINGLETON MODEL

In Chapter 7, this book gives some insight into some of the options surrounding building a local service layer; however, it was important for us to provide a common data layer for many of the examples within this book. For simplicity, we've provided a singleton with a set of methods necessary for accessing many of the tables in our sample database. Some simple Java Doc is available for these classes, along with the Value Objects used to represent Customers, Employees, and Orders within the database. In the introduction to Part II of the book, we provide a detailed overview of the Classic Models sample database and how it can be used.

The singleton provides the following methods:

- Customers findCustomerById(int id)
- java.util.List findCustomersbySalesRepId(int id)
- OrdersWithBLOBs findOrderById(int id)
- java.util.List findOrdersbyCustomerId(int id)
- java.util.List getAllCustomers()
- java.util.List getAllEmployees()
- java.util.List getAllSalesReps()
- void updateCustomer(Customers cust)
- void updateOrder(Orders order)

Check the Appendix B download materials for a zip file containing some simple Java Doc.

QUICK START SETUP

Even though our goal was to make the setup of the data access layer as simple as possible to remove much of the burden from your learning exercises, there's still a bit of setup you need to do. We've boiled this down to a few simple steps. Follow these steps, and your portal will be ready without any other work; however, after this quick start section, you'll find some additional optional steps you may want to follow to learn more about how to set up these types of data sources and data access layers.

To set up your data, take the following steps.

1. Unzip file ClassicModelsDb.zip to some location on your hard drive. By default, the configuration file is pointing to this being at the root of your C drive.

2. Unzip file ClassicModelsLib.zip to your WebSphere Portal, at PortalServer/shared/app directory. Doing so creates a subdirectory called classicmodelslib within that directory and places several files there. These files are the actual data access layer and the supporting iBATIS and data access library files, along with a few configuration files. (Note: If you unzipped the DB somewhere other than the C drive, edit the database.properties file in directory classicmodelslib to point to the right location.)

3. Configure the extended library in the server console. This step is really simple but consists of several tasks to be carried out carefully.

   a. Open and log on to the WebSphere administration console, and navigate to the Shared Libraries area under Environment (Figure B.1). You can leave the scope of the shared library at the node level or go ahead and scope it down to the server level by choosing Browse Servers and then WebSphere Portal. In this case, we left the scope at the node level.

475

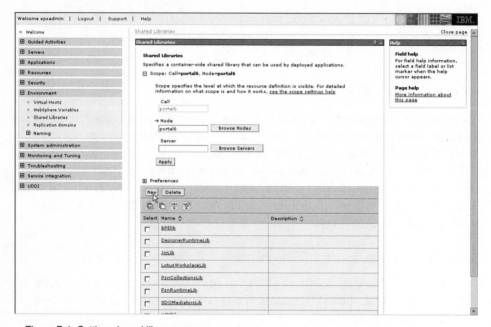

Figure B.1: Setting shared library scope

Once you have the library scope set at the level you want, click New to create a new Shared Library instance. Name the new library, and enter the path to where you extracted the ClassicModelsLib.zip files. The rest of the entries are optional at this point, and you can change the actual name of the shared library without breaking any of the files. For this example, we'll use the values shown in Figure B.2:

- **Name:** cmlib

- **Description:** "This is the classic models data access layer and supporting library files."

- **Classpath:**

  ➤ ${WPS_HOME}/shared/app/cmlib

  ➤ ${WPS_HOME}/shared/app/cmlib/CMDAO.jar

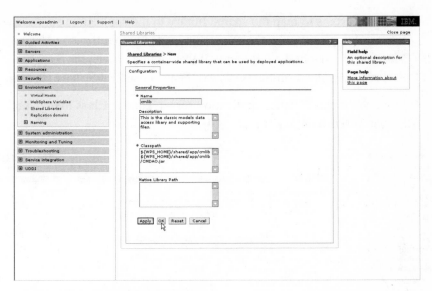

Figure B.2: Creating a new shared library

b. When you've completed the form, click **OK** to continue and save the configuration (Figure B.3). This is the last step in setting up the data access layer.

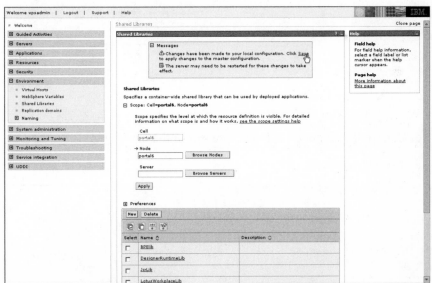

Figure B.3: Saving your configuration

c. The next task is to map the shared library to the application server class loader. Doing so will let the classes be loaded within the Java Virtual Machine (JVM). In the left menu of the admin console, navigate to **Servers > Application Servers**, and then choose **WebSphere_Portal**.

d. In the WebSphere_Portal application server, choose **Class loader** under **Server Infrastructure** (Figure B.4).

Figure B.4: Mapping the shared library

e. Choose the single class loader present in the list (Figure B.5).

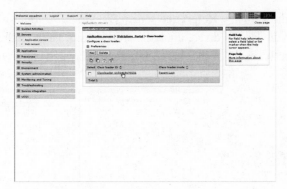

Figure B.5: Choose the class loader

f. From the class loader screen (Figure B.6), select **Libraries** under **Additional Properties**.

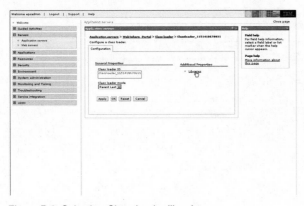

Figure B.6: Selecting Class loader libraries

g. Once in the **Library Reference** screen (Figure B.7), you can add a new library to the list. To do so, click the **Add** button. Then, in the **Library Name** list, select the name of the shared library you created earlier (Figure B.8).

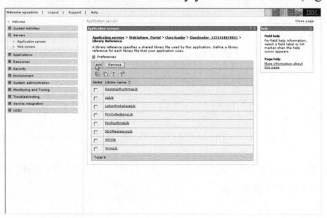

Figure B.7: Choose to add a new library

Figure B.8: Adding library cmlib to the library references

h. When you're finished, click **OK**. Don't forget to save your configuration as shown in Figure B.9 before exiting the admin console.

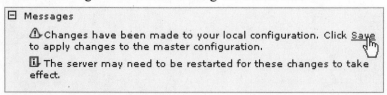

Figure B.9: Saving your configuration

At this point, you can close the admin console and start or restart WebSphere Portal. Your database and access libraries are ready to be used. There's another setup option for using the database in Rational Application Developer (RAD) that we'll show later in this appendix.

Testing Your Setup

Before you get too far in development, you should test your configuration to be sure you put everything in the right place. You can use a test portlet you unzipped along with all the shared library files, TestCMDAOPortlet.war, for this purpose. Figure B.10 shows the test portlet. You can install and run this portlet to ensure the installation and database are set up correctly.

Using the Data Components in RAD

In the quick start section, we focused on getting the libraries set up within WebSphere Portal. This is the most generic option for users who are developing with a test server. To use the libraries within your local portal test environment, the libraries also must be set up correctly. At the time of this writing, Portal Version 5.1 was the only test environment available for illustration.

Figure B.10: Shared library test portlet

To set up the data access components within RAD, follow steps 1 and 2 in the quick start section above. For step 3, however, mapping the libraries is much simpler. It requires only the following:

a. Open the administration console of the test environment, and navigate to the **Environment** tab, shown in Figure B.11.

b. Click the **Add External Folder** button, and then browse for the cmlib folder you unzipped under your local test environment. In a typical installation, this location might be C:\Program Files\IBM\Portal51UTE\PortalServer\shared\app\cmlib.

c. Close the admin console, and restart the test environment to have your changes to take effect.

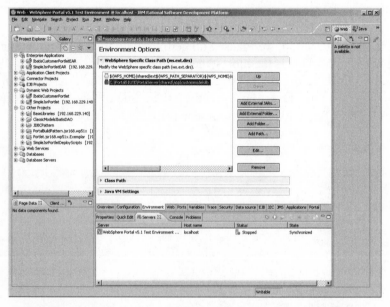

Figure B.11: Setting up a shared library in Rational Application Developer

CUSTOM SETUP OPTIONS

We've made every attempt to keep this aspect of the book as simple as possible so you can focus on the work at hand — portlet programming — and try to ignore some of the underlying work that goes on in many projects. We've found that portal developers often undergo an evolution, and it takes time to absorb and understand all the aspects of a development project.

Knowing this, there may be cases where some readers of this book need to make changes or customize portions of this set of library files. For this reason, we include some information about setting up the database and customizing the library configuration.

Setting Up the DB from Scratch

The provided database uses Apache Derby, an open-source Java-based database engine. You can download Derby online at *http://db.apache.org/derby/derby_downloads.html*, along with complete setup instructions. For your convenience, and to ensure you use the same versions of the code we use in this book, we've included a copy of the download along with the source code used to access the data.

This example sets up Derby and associated files on the Microsoft Windows platform, which is what many developers use on their desktop or laptop for a development environment. For information about setting things up on another operating system, see the Derby documentation on the Web.

Install and Configure Derby

To install Derby and the sample database files on your machine, unzip the include package called db-derby-10.1.2.1-bin.zip to a directory on your local drive. For this example, we used directory C:\derby10.1.

The Apache site provides some instruction on getting Derby to run in your environment at *http://db.apache.org/derby/papers/DerbyTut/install_software.html*. Unfortunately, at this time the information isn't complete, but it should be usable for most folks.

The next step is to set up a Java Development Kit (JDK) on your machine. Because you already have Eclipse or RAD installed, a JDK should already be available. You also need to set up some paths in the environment. You can do this in a couple of ways, most easily at the command line by entering the commands shown in Listing B.1.

```
C:\> set JAVA_HOME=C:\progra~1\ibm\rational\sdp\6.0\eclipse\jre
C:\> set DERBY_INSTALL=C:\derby10.1
C:\> set PATH=%PATH%;C:\derby10.1\frameworks\embedded\bin
C:\> set
CLASSPATH=%DERBY_INSTALL%\lib\derby.jar;%DERBY_INSTALL%\lib\derbytools.jar;
%DERBY_INSTALL%\frameworks\embedded\bin
```

Listing B.1: Environment path setup

We recommend setting up these values in your environment or profile so they're always available. To test your setup, try the following commands from anywhere on the command line:

```
C:\> java -version
C:\> java org.apache.derby.tools.sysinfo
```

You should see a result similar to that shown in Listing B.2. If you see this result, you have Derby successfully installed and configured.

```
C:\WINNT\system32>java org.apache.derby.tools.sysinfo
---------- Java Information ----------
Java Version:    1.4.2
Java Vendor:     IBM Corporation
Java home:       C:\progra~1\ibm\rational\sdp\6.0\eclipse\jre
Java classpath:  C:\derby10.1\lib\derby.jar;C:\derby10.1\lib\derbytools.jar
OS name:         Windows 2000
OS architecture: x86
OS version:      5.0
Java user name:  Administrator
Java user home:  C:\Documents and Settings\Administrator
Java user dir:   C:\WINNT\system32
java.specification.name: Java Platform API Specification
java.specification.version: 1.4
------ Derby Information ------
JRE - JDBC: J2SE 1.4.2 - JDBC 3.0
[C:\derby10.1\lib\derby.jar] 10.1.2.1 - (330608)
[C:\derby10.1\lib\derbytools.jar] 10.1.2.1 - (330608)
----------------------------

---------- Locale Information ----------
----------------------------


C:\WINNT\system32>
```

Listing B.2: Confirmation of successful Derby setup

484

Create the Database

Now to create the sample database. First, create a directory under the Derby root directory called "databases" and copy the SQL files and data directory to this new directory.

Open a command window, and navigate to the directory where you want to set up your databases. In our example, this location is

```
C:\derby10.1\databases
```

Create the database with ij

For much of the interaction with Derby, you can use an interactive Java-based scripting tool called ij. This command-line–based program is generally used with scripts for building and modifying databases. Start ij at the command line by entering the command:

```
C:\derby10.1\databases > ij
C:\derby10.1\databases > rem set DERBY_INSTALL=
C:\derby10.1\databases > java -Dij.protocol=jdbc:derby: org
apache.derby.tools.ij
ij version 10.1
ij >
```

Create the database to use:

```
ij > connect 'jdbc:derby:ClassicModelsDb;create=true';
ij >
```

Now quit out of ij:

```
ij> exit;
```

Use the dir command to list the contents of your directory (Listing B.3), and you'll see the new directory for your database and the derby.log file. The file should be empty, but it could be a place to look if problems occur.

```
C:\derby10.1\databases>dir
 Volume in drive C has no label.
 Volume Serial Number is 481D-156E

 Directory of C:\derby10.1\databases

03/30/2006  01:20p    <DIR>          .
03/30/2006  01:20p    <DIR>          ..
03/30/2006  01:20p    <DIR>          ClassicModelsDb
03/24/2006  11:41a            3,191 create_classicmodels.sql
03/30/2006  01:04p    <DIR>          datafiles
03/30/2006  01:20p              515 derby.log
03/24/2006  11:41a            2,000 load_classicmodels.sql
              3 File(s)          5,706 bytes
              4 Dir(s)   7,524,315,136 bytes free

C:\derby10.1\databases>
```

Listing B.3: Listing the directory with derby.log

Create and Populate the Tables

Start ij again, and reconnect to your database:

```
C:\Derby10.1\databases>ij
C:\ Derby10.1\databases>rem set DERBY_INSTALL=
C:\ Derby10.1\databases>java -Dij.protocol=jdbc:derby:
org.apache.derby.tools.ij
ij version 10.1
ij> connect 'jdbc:derby:ClassicModelsDb';
```

Run the command to create the database:

```
ij> run 'create_classicmodels.sql';
```

You'll see the script go through and create the table structure. Now, run the second command to populate the data:

```
ij> run 'load_classicmodels.sql';
```

You should see some output as the script loads the data. Watch for errors. Do a quick check after the script runs to ensure the data is loaded correctly. Run a query to check:

```
ij> select * from employees;
```

If you see a stream of data from the query, exit ij and close the window. You're ready to use this database.

Using a WAS Data Source

The common best practice is to use a WebSphere Application Server (WAS) data source when accessing any application database. This approach lets the developer take advantage of WebSphere's built-in ability to manage and cache database connections through pooling. If this is a best practice, why haven't we done this by default? The real reason is simplicity, both in setup and use of the data. We realize this isn't going to be a production database (unless you're planning to sell models as your business). Our goal is to give you the tools to learn portlet programming in a realistic manner without making you spend hours trying to configure things.

The good thing about our approach is that iBATIS does allow for the use of a WAS data source to access a database. We've included a configuration file, sql-map-config-datasource.xml, that is deployed with the library files for use with this approach. Simply swap out this file with the original file, sql-map-config.xml, and modify it for the data source name you've configured.

Modifying the Source Code

All the source code has been made readily available in the form of a Rational Application Developer Interchange file. You'll find this file under the Custom Setup folder. This code contains not only the base source files but also some of the examples from chapters in this book that build off this data access layer.

As we mentioned earlier, iBATIS can be challenging to learn initially due to the lack of official documentation. Once you've learned it, however, you'll find it extremely powerful. Feel free to use this code to understand how we've used SQL Maps to perform many of the underlying queries.

487

Index

NOTE: Boldface numbers indicate illustrations or code listing